"Winter reminds us
that rest is not
the absence
of productivity;
it is productivity
in another form"

Teanna x

Dedication

This book is dedicated to those living with chronic illness, especially the hidden, misunderstood, and unseen, whose winters are long, whose pain is real, and whose survival is an act of courage.

And to Jane -
a soul who stood beside me through the darkest hours.

Though we have never met in person, our lives have been woven together across more than twenty years. We first found each other online as young mothers navigating twinhood, and later reconnected through shared experiences of migraine and loss. What began as a conversation slowly became a friendship of confidence, guidance and trust.

We walked side by side - through a difficult birth, through illness, through pain that reshapes a life. We spoke for hours when words were scarce elsewhere, holding space for one another in ways only those who truly understand can.

This dedication honours a quiet truth: support does not always come from proximity.
Sometimes it comes from recognition. From being met.
From someone who can say, without explanation, I know this place.
For that knowing, and for her steady presence across time and distance, this work is dedicated to her - and to all those who endure unseen.

First Edition 2025
ISBN 978-1-917816-11-3
Published by MJT Publishing

www.TeannaTaylor.com

 This book/workbook is created and published for informational purposes only. It is not intended to be a substitute for professional medical advice and should not be relied on as health or personal advice. Always seek the guidance of your doctor or other qualified health professional with any questions you may have regarding your health or a medical condition.

WINTER

A time to slow down, reflect deeply,
and prepare for new beginnings.

A Gentle Note on Readiness for Shadow Work

I am not a doctor or mental health professional. Shadow work can evoke deep feelings or memories, and if anything becomes overwhelming, please seek support from a qualified therapist or counsellor. You do not have to navigate this process alone. Reaching out is an act of strength, not weakness.

Use this workbook as winter moves - slowly, softly, and with compassion. Your only tasks are to stay present, stay curious, and be kind to yourself.

Shadow work invites deep self-reflection and awareness. While this process can be nourishing and transformative, it's important to honour your own readiness, capacity, and timing. If you are currently feeling emotionally overwhelmed, ungrounded, or in a period of intense distress, it may be kinder to pause this work or approach it with additional support.

This is especially true if you are moving through a major life transition such as bereavement, separation, serious illness, or significant loss. During times like these, the nervous system often prioritises stability and care over deep excavation.

You are welcome to engage with this material at a gentler pace, to focus on grounding and regulation, or to step away entirely if that feels supportive. Choosing to slow down or rest is not avoidance - it is wisdom.

This work is reflective in nature and is not a replacement for therapy, medical care, or crisis support. If at any point the practices feel too activating or unsafe, please pause and seek guidance from a qualified health or mental health professional.

Listening to your limits is part of the work. Shadow work unfolds best when the body feels safe, supported, and resourced.

Contents

Key

General Information and Instructions

The Science Behind the Exercise

Exercise Start

Things You Will Need

Meditation Online
www. TeannaTaylor.com

Optional Altar Items

Auditory Learner

Reading / Writing Learner

Kinesthetic / Somatic Learner

Visual / Creative Learner

How To Use This Workbook

This workbook is designed to accompany the book
Unlock Your Cosmic Flow

It follows a Perennial Lunar Framework, which aligns with the natural rhythm of Winter and the sequence of Moon phases: First Quarter → Full Moon → Last Quarter → New Moon → Repeat. The journey begins with the Winter Solstice, which typically occurs around December 21st.

By anchoring each week's practice to the Moon rather than the Gregorian calendar, this workbook remains timeless and usable every winter, along with a journal, regardless of the year. Connecting you directly with the true energy of the season, rather than a man-made calendar.

If you are unsure about the lunar calendar, I have included a copy for the next five years at the back of this workbook, and an up-to-date version is also available on my website. At the beginning of each exercise, you will find space to write the date of the First Quarter, Full Moon, Last Quarter, or New Moon, if you wish.

Progress through the workbook one phase at a time. Each Moon phase has its own emotional tone and distinct layer of inner work. Full Moons feature deeper rituals, while the weekly phases guide you through gentle practices that cultivate safety, awareness, and integration.

Each exercise is designed to go beyond generic self-help books and is offered in four versions to accommodate different learning styles. Additionally, practices are tailored to your specific archetype(s). Which will be discovered on the way. You may choose to complete only the version that resonates with you or explore multiple approaches if you feel drawn to them.

Take your time and move with the Moon. Allow Winter to set the pace. You cannot fall behind; healing follows rhythm, not strict rules.

At each full moon, you will find an index, which lists the exercises for that moon. These can be done in one night or over the course of a few days. There is no rush - flow - I also provide details of any rituals and altar items, along with the recommended meditation, which is available online

Why Altar Work Works

Altar work is effective not because objects hold power on their own, but because humans are wired to respond to symbols, ritual, and intentional space.

Neuroscience shows that the brain processes symbolic action differently from abstract thought. When we physically arrange objects with meaning, we engage multiple systems at once - attention, memory, emotion, and sensory awareness - helping intentions feel real and embodied rather than theoretical. Rituals also create predictability and safety, which calms the nervous system.

Studies in psychology show that simple, repeated actions, such as lighting a candle or arranging space, can reduce stress, increase focus, and support emotional regulation. This is partly because ritual shifts us from the brain's threat-response mode into a more reflective, grounded state. They are mini mindfulness moments.

Altar work further supports values-based behaviour, a concept used in modern therapies such as Acceptance and Commitment Therapy (ACT). By visually anchoring values and intentions in a physical space, we strengthen our ability to remember and act on them in daily life. The altar becomes a quiet reminder, one that works not through belief, but through attention, meaning, and repetition.

In this way, altar work is less about spirituality alone and more about how humans make meaning, create focus, and support inner change. It is a practical tool for reflection, grounding, and alignment; rooted as much in psychology and neuroscience as in tradition.

It does not have to be a big space; mine is a simple, small tray, with the seasonal items. It is a visual daily reminder - to just be - to just flow.

My suggested base, i.e., the core elements, which stay throughout all moon phases, are:

- A dark cloth or tray - representing grounding
- A small bowl or empty space at the centre to allow change and intention

Introduction

Why Winter Supports Deep Inner Work

After the natural release and gentle reflection that accompany the unfolding of autumn, winter arrives as a sanctuary, offering the quiet space you need to integrate your experiences, to stabilise your energy, and to move toward healing in a way that feels unhurried and deeply supportive. It invites you to pause for a while, to soften your focus on the outer world, and to turn inward so that you may listen to the deeper layers of your own being. Winter is a season shaped by stillness and restoration, a time when life retreats beneath the surface in order to gather strength and prepare for the renewed expression that will eventually rise with the coming of spring.

This season is not meant for pushing forward or striving for outcomes, nor is it a time for demanding answers from yourself or from life. Instead, winter encourages a simplicity of spirit and a gentleness of heart, reminding you that the most meaningful transformations often unfold in the quiet moments when you choose to stop forcing clarity and allow understanding to emerge softly from within. During this time, the work before you is not about creating more or accomplishing more, but about nurturing what already lives inside you and giving inner truths the spaciousness they need to breathe.

For countless generations, winter has been regarded as a time for storytelling, contemplation, and spiritual renewal. Communities would gather around the warmth of a fire, sharing wisdom and resting deeply as they embraced a slower rhythm that honoured the natural world around them. Even in the often fast-paced and brightly lit world we now inhabit, this ancient rhythm continues to move quietly within us, following a biological pattern that is known as an 'infradian rhythm'. Unlike the circadian rhythm, which completes its cycle over the span of a single day and shapes our sleep, alertness, and daily functioning, an infradian rhythm moves more slowly and influences our energy, cognitive patterns, emotional processing, and intuition over several weeks or months. While the menstrual cycle is a familiar example of such a rhythm, it is not the only one, as all human beings are subtly guided by seasonal infradian cycles that shift as daylight, temperature, pace, and environmental cues evolve around us.

These seasonal shifts create real and measurable effects on the nervous system and on our emotional well-being. During the winter phase of this longer rhythm, our bodies naturally respond to reduced sunlight with significant biochemical changes. Melatonin levels rise as the darker days send signals to the brain that encourage deeper rest, while serotonin levels, which are responsive to light, shift in ways that can influence mood and emotional sensitivity. This gentle recalibration is not a sign of weakness or decline, but rather an invitation to turn inward and slow down so that we may listen more closely to ourselves.

Because of this natural shift, winter creates an ideal environment for **shadow work.** The darkness and stillness surrounding you mirror the inner landscapes that you are gently invited to explore, and with the nervous system moving into a quieter state, emotions that may feel overwhelming during times of high activity can emerge in ways that are softer and easier to hold. The psychological invitation of the season is clear and compassionate: turn inward and listen.

Symbolically, winter resonates with the deeper layers of the self, the places where truth, longing, fear, unprocessed emotion, and possibility reside. The qualities of the season, including slowness, solitude, honesty, and rest, create the perfect atmosphere in which to meet your shadow with compassion rather than resistance.

In this way, understanding your infradian rhythm allows you to reframe winter not as an empty or stagnant period, but as a biologically supported season of healing, reflection, and meaningful renewal.

As you move through the practices in this workbook, allow the energy of winter to guide you toward deeper self-awareness. Let the slower pace support the settling of your nervous system, let the quiet moments help you hear the voice of your intuition, and let the stillness provide the spaciousness your emotions need to unfold safely and naturally.

Winter is your invitation to rest, to reconnect with your inner truth, and to prepare the soil of your being for the intentions you will plant when spring arrives.

Move slowly. Trust the darkness. Honour your own rhythm.

What is Shadow Work?

Shadow work is an inner journey in which you slowly and tenderly turn toward the parts of yourself that you have learned to avoid, suppress, or feel uneasy acknowledging, and you allow them to be welcomed back into your awareness with patience and care.

These hidden aspects may appear as fears, insecurities, impulses, long-standing habits, or emotions that were once too overwhelming to process. They may also include strengths or talents that were pushed into the background because they did not feel safe to express.

The idea originates from the work of psychologist Carl Jung, who described these concealed layers of the psyche as the shadow, a space within us where unexpressed truths quietly reside beyond the edge of conscious awareness. When you engage in shadow work, you are not forcing yourself to change or evaluate what you discover; instead, you are gently illuminating what has been unseen and offering compassion to the parts of yourself that have waited in silence.

This practice invites you to become more accepting and more connected to your full inner landscape. As you recognise and tend to these deeper layers, you begin to create balance within your emotional world, and the heaviness of tension, shame, and old limiting stories gradually softens. In this softening, a spaciousness begins to open, making room for clarity, healing, and meaningful transformation. As the shadow becomes integrated rather than held at a distance, your energy flows more freely, and that newfound space becomes a fertile ground for positive change, manifestation, creativity, and the unfolding of the dreams you are ready to bring into your life.

Shadow integration is not a process of fixing what is broken, but of reclaiming what has long been forgotten, so you may move forward with a deeper sense of truth, inner power, and ease

Psychological Frameworks Commonly Used

There are several established psychological frameworks that guide or support shadow work. Each brings a different lens, yet all share the goal of making the unconscious conscious.

Jungian Archetypes - Carl Jung's work forms the foundation of modern shadow work. He believed that the psyche contains universal patterns known as archetypes, which influence how we behave, think, and feel. According to Jung, every person has a conscious identity and an unconscious shadow that carries the parts they learned to hide.

Working with archetypes allows you to understand the roles you play in your life and the inner characters you repress. This framework helps you recognise both your dominant traits and your hidden aspects, making it especially effective for emotional and spiritual development.

Internal Family Systems Theory (IFS) - IFS teaches that the psyche is made up of many different internal parts, each with its own emotions, memories, and roles. Some parts protect you, some hold pain, and others drive behaviour. Shadow work within this model involves meeting these parts with compassion so they can be heard and healed rather than ignored or forced away. It is a gentle and deeply validating approach. - *Compassion is used as a week long excercise.*

Cognitive Behavioural Theory (CBT) - CBT focuses on how hidden beliefs and early experiences create automatic thoughts and emotional reactions. In shadow work, CBT techniques help uncover the deeper beliefs that drive unhealthy patterns. It is particularly useful for understanding the mental stories we have internalised. - *I explain what is happening in the brain as we move through the process.*

E**motion Focused Therapy (EFT)** - EFT teaches that emotional awareness and expression are essential for healing. Many shadow aspects are simply emotions we were never taught to process. EFT provides a safe structure to acknowledge, feel, and release these emotions. - *We explore emotions in-depth*

Somatic and Nervous System Approaches - Because the shadow is not only held in the mind but also in the body, somatic work helps uncover subconscious reactions stored as tension, fear, or contraction. This approach ensures that shadow work does not become overwhelming because it teaches you how to regulate your nervous system as deeper material arises. - *This is used in the learning types*

Why I Have Chosen an Archetypal Framework

Although there are many excellent frameworks for shadow work, I have chosen to guide you through an archetypal and seasonal approach for several important reasons.

First, archetypes make the subconscious more accessible. It is easier to understand hidden behaviour or emotional patterns when they are expressed as simple, relatable archetypes rather than abstract psychological concepts. Archetypes are intuitive, symbolic, and universal. They allow you to see your shadow not as a flaw but as an inner character with a story, a purpose, and a message.

Second, archetypes gently reveal patterns without overwhelming you. Instead of directly confronting painful memories, you explore the roles you tend to play, the parts of yourself you hide, and the fears that influence your decisions. This creates a softer, safer entry point for shadow work, especially for those who are new to deep inner exploration.

Third, an archetypal framework aligns beautifully with the rhythm of nature. Just as winter holds the energy of introspection, hidden growth, and quiet transformation, the archetypes reveal the inner patterns that lie beneath the surface of your life. Using this symbolic language helps you flow with the natural cycle of the season as you turn inward and begin the work of healing.

Most importantly, archetypes support both clarity and compassion. They help you understand your shadow without becoming lost in self-judgement. They create enough emotional distance for you to explore difficult truths while still staying connected to kindness and self-respect. This makes the entire experience safer, steadier, and more rooted in self-love.

Using archetypes, seasonal wisdom, and gentle psychological guidance together creates a supportive and meaningful path for shadow work, allowing you to explore your inner landscape at a pace that honours your heart and your wellbeing.

"Shadow work is not the act of
digging for darkness;
it is the art of making space
for the parts of you
that were never allowed to speak."

Teanna x

The Role of Emotion in Shadow Work

Why Your Learning Type Matters

Shadow work is more than understanding your past or analysing your thoughts from a distance. At its heart, it is an emotional and embodied journey, shaped by the feelings you once found overwhelming, unseen, or unsafe to express. These emotions settled beneath the surface of your awareness and quietly shaped the beliefs, patterns, reactions, and behaviours that influence your life today. Because the shadow was formed through emotion, it can only be softened and integrated through emotion.

This means transformation unfolds not through thinking your way into change, but through allowing the parts of you that once felt afraid, silenced, or rejected to be met with new feelings of safety, compassion, acceptance, and empowerment.

*"Emotion becomes
the doorway through which
the shadow learns
that it no longer needs to hide."*

Teanna x

This is where your learning type becomes more important than you may realise. Every person processes emotion differently. Some feel most deeply when hearing words spoken aloud, while others connect most naturally through movement or physical sensation. Some discover clarity when they write, and others access their emotional depth through imagery, colour, or symbolic visual cues. When you work against your natural learning style, shadow work can feel distant, forced, or frustrating. But when you work with your innate way of processing, the emotional pathways open gently, and the work becomes deeper, kinder, and far more aligned with who you are.

There is also a profound neurological reason this matters. The brain cannot distinguish between a real experience and a vividly imagined one. When you intentionally evoke emotions such as gratitude, courage, safety, or self-compassion, even for a brief moment, your nervous system responds as though these feelings are already part of your present reality. Networks such as the Reticular Activating System (RAS) begin to pay attention to anything that matches these emotional states, reinforcing new neural pathways while softening the ones linked to old wounds and outdated stories. In shadow work, this means you are not only recognising hidden parts of yourself, but you are also teaching your mind and body that new emotional experiences are safe and available.

This is the quiet heart of transformation, and why this workbook is unlike the many who advocate 'one shoe fits all'.

You may already know your learning type from previous workbooks; if so, skip to page x. If not, take the simple quiz on the next page and learn your learning type - this is a very important step.

"When you offer your shadow new feelings,
it begins to trust you.
It steps out from its hiding places.
It softens. It integrates. It heals."

Teanna x

Practical Exercise
Personal Learning Style Quiz

Your learning style is not meant to place you in a box. It is meant to give you a compass, a way to understand which tools, rituals, and practices will help you access emotional truth with ease rather than resistance.

Every weekly exercise has been adapted for each learning type so that your shadow work becomes not only effective but also emotionally resonant, embodied, and personally meaningful.

When you work in harmony with your natural way of feeling and processing, you create a direct and compassionate pathway into your inner world.

Just answer each question and keep track of how many times you choose A, B, C, or D.

Your dominant learning style(s) will be revealed at the end!

*There have been many studies over the years on learning styles, each presenting slightly different percentages (the ranges are included in the descriptions).

The majority of people are multi-modal learners, meaning they use more than one learning style. However, some individuals are very rigid in their preferred learning type. For these people, this exercise can be a real eye-opener—not only in understanding how they learn, but also in recognising why certain types of training or manifestation methods may not have worked for them in the past.

For example, if you are a strongly auditory learner, writing affirmations over and over again is unlikely to be effective and may simply feel boring or frustrating.

1. When trying to remember something, you usually...
A) Picture it in your mind
B) Say it out loud or repeat it in your head
C) Write it down or read over your notes
D) Try to act it out or physically do something with it

2. In a class or seminar, you prefer...
A) Diagrams, charts, or slides
B) Lectures, discussions, and podcasts
C) Reading handouts or written guides
D) Hands-on activities or group projects

3. When learning a new skill, what helps most?
A) Watching a video or looking at pictures
B) Hearing someone explain it step-by-step
C) Reading instructions or writing notes
D) Trying it yourself and learning by doing

4. Which of these tools excites you most for manifesting/intentions/resolutions?
A) Vision boards and Pinterest mood boards
B) Guided meditations, affirmations, or music
C) Journalling, scripting, or making a plan
D) Dancing, moving, or physically stepping into your "future self"

5. How do you best express how you feel?
A) Drawing, doodling, or using visuals
B) Talking it out or using voice notes
C) Writing in a journal or texting someone
D) Through body language, gestures, or movement

Tally your answers!

A's	B's	C's	D's

Mostly A = Visual / Creative Learner

50- 70% of the population*

You prefer to see information to understand and remember it. You often use charts, diagrams, mind maps, and colour-coded notes to help organise your thoughts. Watching videos, viewing demonstrations, and using visual aids can significantly enhance your learning experience.

To evoke emotions, you will succeed more with 'sight-based' tools.

- Vision boards with emotionally charged images
- Visualisation practices (imagine scenes in vivid detail)
- Mind maps
- Watching inspiring videos or films that spark emotion
- Colour-coded affirmations or journaling
- Creative visual scripting
- Watching your future self like a movie in your mind

Mostly B = Auditory Learner

25-30% of the population*

You absorb information best through sound, learning most effectively when you listen to instructions, engage in discussions, or hear concepts explained out loud.

To evoke emotions, you will have more success with 'sound-based' tools.

- Spoken or sung affirmations (with emotion)
- Voice notes or audio journaling
- Guided meditations with vivid language
- Binaural beats and solfeggio frequencies (e.g., 528 Hz, 432 Hz)
- Playlists or emotional music
- Talking through visualisations with a coach or friend
- Chanting or mantras

Mostly C = Reading / Writing Learner

2 - 4% stand alone, but are often grouped under visual learners

You thrive through written words, absorbing information by reading textbooks, taking detailed notes, journaling, or rewriting ideas in your own words. You enjoy working with lists, essays, and written exercises, and often prefer quiet, independent study time.

To evoke emotions, you will succeed more with 'text-based' tools.

- Scripting in a journal
- Gratitude journaling with emotional depth
- Reading inspirational books, quotes, or stories
- Writing affirmations and repeating them
- Letter writing

Mostly D = Kinaesthetic /Somatic Learner

5% - 45% of the population*

You learn best through physical activity and hands-on experience.

You will prefer actively participating in the learning process, whether building something, experimenting, or using movement to reinforce concepts. and often benefit from roleplaying, interactive tasks, or even walking around while studying. The more you can involve your body, the better you learn.

To evoke emotions, you will succeed more with 'touch and movement-based' tools.

- Embodiment exercises
- Dance or movement to music that evokes emotion
- Physically writing affirmations or scripting (pen to paper)
- Vision walks (visualising while walking or exercising)
- Creating rituals with physical objects (candles, crystals, symbolic items)
- Roleplaying or acting out future scenarios
- Sensory anchoring (using smell, touch, and movement to lock in emotion)

Multimodal learner

60–70% (overlap with others)*

You combine two or more learning styles and switch between them depending on the task or subject. For example, you might prefer reading to learn new material but find it easier to remember through discussion or drawing diagrams.

Being multimodal allows for flexibility; you often benefit from mixing techniques to keep your learning dynamic and engaging.

To evoke emotions, you will have more success with a blend of styles, so feel free to mix and match the exercises as you work through the workbook.

- Listen to your voice-recorded while journaling
- Create a vision board and describe it aloud
- Meditate while visualising and repeating mantras
- Script by hand, then read it aloud with a feeling
- Dance to a playlist while visualising

"Nature has already given us the perfect timeline for growth. It whispers to us through the seasons"

Teanna x

Beginning Gently

Winter invites a natural turning inward, but reflection in this season is not an invitation to judge your past or to revisit memories with harshness. It is a quiet request to meet your truth with compassion, curiosity, and presence.

Shadow work grows from this soil of gentle honesty. It invites you to explore the emotional patterns and reactions that usually remain tucked beneath the surface of daily life, waiting patiently for your attention. Beginning your journey with reflection, gratitude, and restoration is not a formality; it is essential emotional preparation.

- **Reflection** helps you recognise what has shaped you.
- **Gratitude** softens your nervous system and anchors you in safety.
- **Restoration** replenishes your energy so you can meet your inner world with steadiness rather than depletion.

Reflection creates spaciousness for awareness, activating the parts of the brain that support insight and emotional regulation. Winter naturally supports this process by slowing cognitive rhythms and reducing external stimulation, making it easier to notice patterns and truths that might otherwise be missed.

Gratitude follows as a gentle warmth, balancing the emotional intensity that deeper inquiry can bring.

Restoration completes the foundation by settling the nervous system and allowing deeper layers of the psyche to rise safely.

Together, these practices create the conditions for this growth in a meaningful, transformative way, so instead of entering your inner work with pressure, you approach it with presence.

*"Every strong
emotional reaction
is a doorway
to a story
that has been
waiting
to be heard."*

Teanna x

Winter teaches that growth often begins in quiet places, beneath the surface, long before it becomes visible.

Shadow work begins by setting these foundations in weeks 1 and 2, with the first deep dive starting in week 3 - during which you will discover your archetype and then engage with bespoke exercises for reflection, gratitude and restoration, thus providing you with a solid foundation.

However, winter brings a stillness that can feel both comforting and unsettling. When the world quiets, your inner world becomes clearer, and sometimes louder. Doubt, fatigue, resistance, or emotional heaviness may appear unexpectedly; these are not signs that you are failing, they are reminders that shadow work gently stirs what has been waiting for your attention.

Motivation naturally ebbs and flows during this season. Growth often happens in ways you cannot see, much like seeds gathering strength beneath frozen soil long before they sprout. When your motivation dips, return to the intentions that once guided you. Remember the clarity that rose in spring, the vibrant movement of summer, and the wisdom gathered in autumn. These memories anchor you in your purpose and remind you that you are part of a larger rhythm.

Self-care becomes essential in winter.

Rest is not avoidance; it is integration. When you slow down, your nervous system recalibrates, your emotions settle, and your mind becomes open to insight. The practices within this workbook are designed to support you gently, inviting soft awareness and steady progress. Instead of pushing through challenges, meet them with compassion. Trust that winter prepares you for renewal and that you are not required to feel energised at every moment. You simply need to remain willing to return to yourself again and again.

Your mind and body hold an ancient and instinctive wisdom about the pace that is truly safe for you, and when you learn to trust this quiet inner intelligence, your healing unfolds in a way that feels more organic, sustainable, and deeply aligned with your emotional truth.

You are never meant to face every shadow all at once - if you push yourself too hard or try to rush your transformation, you can unintentionally disrupt the delicate process of integration, which thrives on softness and patience, so it becomes essential to listen closely to the subtle signals within you and allow your unfolding to move at a rhythm that feels spacious, kind, and naturally in harmony with your inner world.

Only the emotions and memories that are ready to rise will come forward, emerging gently in their own time and allowing your healing to progress in a way that honours your capacity and your inner rhythm. So it may take a few winter seasons for them all to balance, but they will become lighter each year. Remember, you are on a journey.

The chapter "Supporting Your Nervous System" contains carefully crafted tools to support the unique needs of each learning and archetype, offering steadiness and compassion during moments that might otherwise feel overwhelming or intense. Refer back to those at any time.

"Let emotion be the language
through which you heal.
Let your learning style
be the pathway
that carries you home
to yourself."

Teanna x

Supporting Your Nervous System

Tools to Stay Grounded, Safe, and Steady

Shadow work is powerful, transformative, and often deeply liberating - but it is also emotional work. As you explore the layers of your inner world, some weeks may feel soft and revealing, while others may bring old memories, tension, or unexpected vulnerability to the surface. This is not because you are doing anything wrong. It is simply the natural movement of your nervous system responding to change, truth, and emotional release.

Before you step into the deeper practices, it is important to understand how your body responds to emotional work and how to support yourself if you ever feel overwhelmed. Shadow work is not about pushing yourself into discomfort; it is about creating the conditions for gentle, safe, sustainable transformation.

The steadier and more supported your nervous system feels, the deeper and more compassionate your inner work becomes.

This chapter offers tools that help you stay grounded, calm, and connected through your winter journey. These practices are simple, supportive and rooted in Polyvagal Theory, a scientific framework that explains why we sometimes feel centred and present, and why at other times we feel anxious, shut down or overstimulated.

By learning how to read your nervous system, you gain the power to guide yourself back to safety whenever you need it.

Understanding Your Nervous System's Response to Shadow Work

Your nervous system is always scanning your inner and outer world for cues of safety or danger. When something triggers a memory, emotion or unresolved experience, the body may shift into old protective patterns even if there is no real threat.

You may recognise these states in yourself:

Fight
Irritation, defensiveness, tension, feeling on edge
Flight
Restlessness, anxiety, the urge to escape or distract
Freeze
Shutting down, feeling numb or foggy, disconnecting
Fawn
People-pleasing, self-abandonment, trying to "fix" everything

These states are not personal failures. They are protective reflexes - strategies your body learned long ago to keep you safe. When a shadow is touched, the nervous system reacts first, long before the mind has time to understand why.

This is why safety, grounding and soothing practices matter so deeply. When your body feels safe, your inner world becomes easier to meet with compassion rather than fear.

How to Know When You Need a Pause

Shadow work should stretch you, not break you. Take a break if you feel:

- emotionally flooded
- numb or dissociated
- physically tense or shaky
- stuck in mental loops
- unable to focus

Rest is part of the healing process, not a detour from it.
Return when your body feels steadier.

Calming Techniques Index

As you move through the early stages of this journey, emotions or bodily responses may arise before you have developed language to express them. These tools are here to support you in those moments, offering grounding, reassurance, and gentle regulation.

Kinesthetic / Somatic Learners
1. Physiological Sigh
3. Hand-to-Heart
4. Humming
5. Butterfly Tapping
6. Grounding
7. Neck Release

Reading / Writing Learners
2. Orienting
8. Compassionate Self-Talk

Auditory Learners
1. Physiological Sigh
8. Compassionate Self-Talk
4. Humming
5. Butterfly Tapping

Visual Learners
2. Orienting
3. Hand-to-Heart
6. Grounding
7. Neck Release

Caretaker:
3. Hand-to-Heart
8.C Self-Talk

Controller:
1. Physiological Sigh
2. Orienting

Outsider:
3. Hand-to-Heart
6. Grounding

Rebel:
7. Neck Release
4. Humming

Victim:
5. Butterfly Tapping
1. Physiological Sigh

Saboteur:
6. Grounding
4. Humming

Seeker:
3. Hand-to-Heart
8. Self-Talk

Performer:
2. Orienting
8. Self-Talk

Innocent:
3. Hand-to-Heart
2. Orienting

Creator:
7. Neck Release
6 Grounding

Lover:
5. Butterfly Tapping
3. Hand-to-Heart

Magician:
6. Grounding
1. Physiological Sigh

1 The Physiological Sigh

One of the fastest ways to calm overwhelm.

How to do it:

- Slow inhale through the nose → second short inhale → long slow exhale through the mouth.

This signals the brain that you are safe, lowers stress hormones, resets the breath and supports emotional clarity. Use it anytime you feel a surge of emotion.

Best for Archetypes
Controller – releases hyperfocus and tension
Caretaker – interrupts over - responsibility loops
Saboteur – calms anxiety - driven impulses
Victim – grounds spiralling helplessness

Best Learning Styles
Auditory – follow guided breathing rhythms
Kinesthetic– feel breath physically reset the body

2 Orienting to the Environment

When emotions rise quickly, your attention often collapses inward.
This practice gently brings you back into your body and your environment.

- Look around the environment and rest your eyes on three neutral objects.
- Name what you see. Let your breath follow what feels comforting or steady.

This signals the nervous system: "Nothing bad is happening now. I can stay present."

Best for Archetypes
Rebel – softens vigilance
Controller – interrupts hyper-focus
Victim – reduces threat perception

Best Learning Styles
Visual – uses the environment as a cue
Reading / Writing – follow a simple checklist of cues to notice

3 Hand-to-Heart Hold

- Place one hand on your heart and one on your belly.
- Hold gentle pressure and breathe slowly.
- Notice your body soften.
- Notice the warmth of your hands.
- Let yourself feel held.

Deep touch helps your system return to a state of calm.

Best for Archetypes
Outsider – reduces dissociation and brings presence
Caretaker – reconnects with self instead of others
Seeker – anchors spiritual/emotional exploration

Best Learning Styles
Kinesthetic– hands-on, body-oriented
Visual – imagine light or warmth moving through the chest

4 Humming or Vocal Toning

Humming, chanting, or long vowel sounds ie "mmm" or "ommm."relax the vagus nerve in the chest and throat. This helps the body shift into a state of connection and calm.

Humming during journaling or ritual work can reduce emotional overwhelm.

Best for Archetypes
Seeker – deepens intuition
Rebel – releases trapped expression
Saboteur – reduces internal agitation

Best Learning Styles
Auditory – responds well to vibration and sound
Kinesthetic– feels the vibration physically

5 Butterfly Tapping

Cross your arms over your chest, resting your hands on your upper arms or shoulders, and gently tap from side to side in a slow, rhythmic pattern. This bilateral motion helps soothe emotional overwhelm and re-engages the nervous system with a sense of calm and safety.

Best for Archetypes
Victim – softens overwhelm, restores inner steadiness
Saboteur – interrupts spiralling or self-attacking thoughts
Caretaker – brings comfort inward rather than outward

Best learning styles
Kinesthetic– grounding through hands-on movement and rhythm
Auditory – the gentle tap sound becomes a regulating cue

6 Grounding Through the Feet

Place both feet firmly on the floor and feel the weight of your body dropping down into the earth. Notice the sensation of contact, pressure, temperature, and support beneath you. This practice draws energy out of the mind and back into the body, anchoring presence and calming restlessness.

Best for Archetypes
Rebel – stabilises scattered energy and impulsive reactions
Saboteur – interrupts runaway thoughts and brings clarity
Outsider – creates a sense of belonging in the present moment

Best learning styles
Kinesthetic– benefits from physical grounding and embodied awareness
Visual – can enhance the exercise by imagining roots or light extending through the feet

7 Slow Neck Release + Side Glances

Gently tilt your head to one side, feeling the lengthening through the neck and shoulder, then repeat on the other side. Pair the stretch with slow side glances- moving only the eyes while the head stays still. This combination releases stored tension, signals safety to the vagus nerve, and helps shift the body out of freeze or hypervigilance.

Best for Archetypes

Controller – eases rigid holding patterns and over-control
Outsider – softens freeze, numbness, or emotional distance
Rebel – releases guarded postures and defensive readiness

Best learning styles

Kinesthetic – benefits from slow, intentional physical movement
Visual – settles the system through peripheral vision engagement

8 Compassionate Self-Talk

Speak warm, reassuring phrases aloud or write them gently on the page. Think of the tone you would use with a frightened child or a dear friend. This practice mimics safe social connection, reduces shame, and provides the nervous system with cues of comfort, validation, and belonging.

Best for Archetypes

Caretaker – supports learning to give to the self what is given to others
Victim – rebuilds inner safety and emotional grounding
Seeker – anchors emotional sensitivity and increases internal stability

Best learning styles

Auditory – responds strongly to soothing, spoken reassurance
Reading / Writing – benefit from writing and rereading compassionate scripts

Winter Solstice

Solstice Stillness Micro Practice
Solstice Ritual for Calm, Gratitude and Grounding
Learning Type Adaptations

The altar holds stillness, rest, and quiet hope. This is a time to pause, reflect, and honour darkness as a place of renewal. Keep the altar simple and spacious, allowing the returning light to be the clear focal point.

One central candle (white, gold, or red) to represent the return of the light
Evergreen elements (pine, fir, cedar, or holly) for endurance
A stone or piece of wood to symbolise stability and grounding

'Winter Solstice'
www.TeannaTaylor.com

Winter Solstice

Calming the System and Creating Inner Stillness

Solstice Stillness Micro Practice

The Winter Solstice, also known as Yule, arrives as the longest night of the year and marks a quiet celestial turning point in which the returning light first begins its slow and graceful ascent. Its name comes from the Latin word solstitium, meaning "sun standing still."

Across cultures and throughout history, this time has been honoured as a natural pause in which the world becomes hushed, the days draw inward, and the landscape settles beneath the deep darkness of winter. This shift in the season gently reminds us that we are part of the same rhythm, and that we, too, are invited to soften our pace and replenish ourselves after a year filled with movement, effort, and emotional weight. Even a few minutes spent breathing slowly, sitting quietly, or creating a small moment of calm can help the body release tension and allow the mind to find a sense of ease.

The days that surround the Solstice often carry a great deal of emotional charge, as the nearness of the Christmas season can bring together family expectations, social obligations, disrupted routines, and a general sense of overstimulation. This combination can stretch the nervous system in ways that make deeper inner work feel almost inaccessible. It is not a sign of weakness or lack of discipline; it is simply the body protecting itself when the world becomes loud and demanding.

For this reason, the Solstice is best understood not as the beginning of intense

Allow this Solstice to become a sacred threshold, a tender opening through which you can restore your strength, recalibrate your energy, and step with ease into the next phase of your unfolding journey.

Think of this time as a long and compassionate exhale after many months of doing, a slow return to your own centre, and a gentle welcome back to yourself.

The Science of Calming the Nervous System

After periods of heightened stimulation (Christmas preparations, social gatherings, emotional conversations), the nervous system often remains in a sympathetic (fight-or-flight) state longer than we realise. You may feel tense, easily triggered, overwhelmed, anxious, fatigued, or emotionally reactive.

Engaging in soothing practices activates the parasympathetic nervous system, the part of your body responsible for rest and restoration. This system slows the heart, deepens the breath, steadies emotions, and sends a clear message throughout the body: "you are safe."

"Nature has already given us the perfect timeline for growth. It whispers to us through the seasons"

Teanna x

Winter Solstice

A Solstice Ritual for Calm, Gratitude and Grounding
(This can also be found as a guided meditation on my website)

This ritual is designed for the busy days before Christmas, when emotions run high and energy runs low. It is gentle, simple and soothing, something you can do even in a full household or a crowded schedule.

- Find a quiet space, even if it is only a corner of a room or a moment alone in your car, bath or garden. Sit comfortably and allow your shoulders to drop, your jaw to soften, and your breath to settle.

- Close your eyes and imagine the long night of the Solstice as a blanket of stillness wrapped around you. Allow the darkness to feel safe, warm and protective, a space where you do not need to perform or produce anything.

- Place a hand on your heart and take three slow breaths. With each inhale, feel your body gathering soft strength. With each exhale, release a little of the tension you have been carrying.

- Whisper a gratitude for what has supported you this year. It might be a person, an experience, a challenge that shaped you, or simply your own resilience. Let the gratitude rise naturally, without forcing it.

- Acknowledge the stress you feel without judgment. Say quietly within yourself, ***"I am doing my best, and it is enough"***

- Allow that truth to settle into your body like a gentle weight.

- Light a candle if you have one and it's safe to do so. As the flame rises, imagine it carrying the first hint of the returning light. Let it symbolise your hope, your rest, and your intention to move through the coming days with steadiness.

- Sit for a final moment with your eyes closed, feeling both the darkness that holds you and the light that guides you forward. When you are ready, blow out the candle or simply open your eyes with a slow exhale.

Learning Type Adaptations

If you wish to take this practice deeper, you can, via your learning type.

Visual / Creative Learners

- Light a single candle and watch the flame as you breathe, or
- Imagine your thoughts dropping like snowflakes into stillness, or
- Draw a simple "calm meter" from 1–10 and mark where you land each day.

Auditory Learners

- Hum quietly or chant a soft sound (mmm or ahh) to vibrate the vagus nerve,
- or whisper a grounding affirmation:

  "I am safe. I am softening. I am steady",
- or Listen to a slow, rhythmic sound: rain, ocean waves, crackling fire.

Kinesthetic / Somatic Learners

- Wrap yourself in a blanket and rock gently, or
- Place your feet flat on the floor and press down firmly (grounding), or
- Take a slow walk, noticing how your feet meet the earth.

A space to anchor what arose.

Reading / Writing

- Let your writing regulate you, keeping sentences short. Complete this prompt once per day:

"Today, my body is asking me for… I release… I welcome…

Monday

Tuesday

Wednesday

Thursday

Friday

Saturday

Sunday

Why you should <u>NOT</u> Set Life Changes on 1st January

Many people feel compelled to reinvent themselves the moment January arrives, yet the truth is that most resolutions fade by mid - February, not because we lack willpower, but because we often choose a moment that is out of harmony with the natural world. The cultural pressure to begin the year with immediate transformation creates a sense of urgency that clashes with the body's need for rest, recovery, and quiet integration, and when a single lapse occurs, many feel they have failed before their intentions have even taken root. This is why it can feel almost impossible to begin meaningful practices of change or manifestation at this time of year, as though you are attempting to summon growth in soil that is still frozen.

We often forget that our lives unfold within rhythms much older than modern expectations. For thousands of years, time was guided by the movement of the sun, the phases of the moon, and the turning of the seasons. The earliest Roman calendar began in March, aligning the new year with the first signs of returning light and renewal. Over centuries, the calendar was repeatedly altered for administrative and political reasons, until the Gregorian calendar eventually fixed January 1st as the beginning of the year. This system, created for organisation and governance rather than for human well-being, places a new beginning at the heart of winter, a season that naturally calls for reflection, gentleness, and restoration rather than initiation.

This disconnection explains why many people feel stuck or discouraged during January, even when surrounded by self-help tools, motivational advice, or the promise of a fresh start. We are often trying to change during a moment when our bodies and minds are naturally quieter, slower, and more tender.

On a biological level, January is a recovery period. The body often holds the lingering effects of December's stimulation and stress. Hormones such as cortisol and adrenaline may still be elevated, creating what some describe as astress hangover that manifests as fatigue, low motivation, or a sense of emotional heaviness. Sleep routines tend to be disrupted by late nights, travel, and irregular rhythms, while shorter days in the Northern Hemisphere disturb the natural balance of serotonin and melatonin. These shifts contribute to sluggishness and can heighten symptoms of seasonal low mood. The immune system, taxed by rich food, alcohol, disrupted rest, and reduced sunlight, becomes more vulnerable, making illness far more common. Even digestion and metabolism are recalibrating, working to restore balance after a period of indulgence and irregularity.

Psychologically, January brings a gentle but noticeable crash after the heightened energy of the holiday season. Weeks of anticipation, celebration, and emotional stimulation are followed by a sudden stillness, and the contrast can create an unexpected sense of emptiness or flatness. Motivation naturally dips during this time, which makes ambitious resolutions feel even more difficult to sustain.

Rather than seeing this as a failure, we might view it as a reminder that January is not designed for grand beginnings. It is a month of quiet restoration, a time to allow the nervous system to settle and the spirit to rest after a long and demanding year. When we honour this rhythm, we understand that meaningful intentions often flourish more naturally once the energy of spring emerges, which is why setting goals or shaping new habits in March often feels more aligned, stable, and nourishing.

By recognising the disconnect between our biological rhythms and the modern calendar, we free ourselves from the belief that change must begin on the first day of the year. Instead, we can return to a more grounded and compassionate approach, one that honours the wisdom of the seasons and supports change in a way that feels steady, sustainable, and deeply aligned with the natural world.

"When we allow ourselves to wait for the right moment, we step into change not with force, but with flow."

Teanna x

Week 1 Date_______________

First Quarter Moon

Regulation and Safety - Calming the System

The First Quarter Moon marks the true beginning of your winter journey, arriving at a moment when nature is already slowing, softening, and drawing inward. This phase opens a quiet threshold in the seasonal rhythm where the old energetic cycle has loosened its grip and the new one has not yet taken form.

The energy of this week invites steadying, grounding, and gentle preparation. It asks you to settle your body, clear space in your inner world, and create the sense of safety you will need for the deeper emotional work to come.

Before turning toward your shadow, your nervous system must first feel supported and resourced enough to meet what rises. Without this foundation, inner work can feel overwhelming or confusing rather than healing.

True shadow work does not begin in the mind. It begins in the body.

When the nervous system is unsettled, the brain leans into protection, narrowing its focus toward vigilance and survival. In such a state, emotional openness becomes difficult, and reflection loses clarity because your system is simply trying to keep you safe.

This is why your journey starts here, with regulation. When you calm your body, you guide yourself out of the familiar patterns of fight, flight, fawn or freeze and into a steadier inner landscape where presence becomes possible.

From this grounded place, you can meet yourself gently, with curiosity rather than fear, and with compassion rather than pressure.

Remember, you can at any time use the techniques explained in the previous chapter - Supporting Your Nervous System

Practical Exercise
Learning Type Adaptations

Each of the following practices are designed to bring your body into safety, soften tension, and support emotional steadiness. As you learnt from the Learning Type excercise, you can be more than one type, so choose as many as resonate with you and repeat at least three times this week - the more you do, the calmer your system will become.
d guide your breath into a slow, even pace.

Reading / Writing Learners
Grounding Through Words

- Sit comfortably and take a few steady breaths. Then write a short grounding statement that reflects safety in the present moment.
-

You might write:

- "In this moment, I am safe."
- "My body is supported."
- "I am here, and nothing is required of me right now."

Read your words slowly, either silently or out loud, and notice how your body responds. Repeat the statement a few times, allowing the meaning to settle rather than analysing it.

Visual Learners

Colour-Breathing Grounding

- Sit quietly and imagine a soft, calming colour -such as blue, lavender, rose, or pale green - filling your body as you inhale.
- As you exhale, imagine a darker colour - black, navy, dark green, or deep purple -leaving your body, symbolising tension or emotional heaviness.

Allow the colours to shift naturally as your body softens and your breath slows.

Auditory Learners

Sound-Anchor Breathing

- Find a gentle, steady sound to focus on - this could be soft music, a ticking clock, white noise, or the sound of your own breath.
- As you inhale, notice the sound fully.
- As you exhale, allow your body to settle into its rhythm.

If it feels supportive, hum softly or exhale with a gentle sigh. Let the sound anchor you in the present moment and guide your breath into a slow, even pace.

Kinesthetic / Somatic Learners

Grounding Through Gentle Pressure & Movement

- Stand or sit comfortably with your feet making full contact with the floor.
- Press your feet down gently and notice the support beneath you.
- Place one hand on your chest and one on your belly, applying light, steady pressure. Take slow breaths, allowing your body to respond to the contact.
- If it feels helpful, add a small, slow movement - a gentle sway, a shoulder roll, or a subtle rocking motion. Let the movement be rhythmic and unforced.

This practice uses physical sensation and motion to signal safety to the nervous system, helping the body settle and return to the present moment.

A space to draw or anchor what arose.

Week 2

Full 'Wolf' Moon

Meet Your Shadow - The Inner Journey Begins

Meeting Your Two Wolves
Learning Style Adaptations and Reflection
Archetype Quiz
Archetype + Learning Style Adaptations
Reflection
Gratitude
Restoration
Working with Your Archetypes

A candle (white, silver, or blue)
A small stone, bone, or symbolic object (to represent the wolf)
A piece of paper and a pen
A quiet indoor space

Wolf Moon (Strength and Intuition)
The altar now holds quiet strength and awareness.
Keep space open-nothing crowded.

Add - without removing the base
A second candle (silver, white, or blue) to reflect moonlight
A wolf symbol (image, carving, or simple tooth/feather substitute)
Obsidian or hematite for protection and grounding

"Strength in the Stillness"
"Meet Your Two Wolves"

Week 2

Date_______________

Full Moon - Wolf Moon

Meeting the Shadow

The Full Moon illuminates not only the landscape around you, but also the inner terrain that lives quietly within, and this week becomes your first true descent into shadow work, inviting you to meet the parts of yourself that have lingered just beneath your conscious awareness, waiting for a moment of safety and clarity to be seen. Under the bright lunar glow, nothing remains fully hidden, and everything becomes available for gentle witnessing, not through force or confrontation, but through honest recognition and compassionate presence.

This is not a time for pushing yourself toward dramatic breakthroughs or demanding transformation; instead, it is an invitation to acknowledge the inner figures, emotional patterns, and protective strategies that have shaped how you move through the world.

Meeting your shadow requires courage, yet it is equally an act of deep compassion, for the parts you discover are not wrong or broken-they emerged in moments when you needed protection, adaptation, or emotional survival, and they carried you through experiences long before you had the capacity to understand them.

This week encourages you to explore these dynamics with curiosity, allowing you to see that your shadow is not an enemy but an unrecognised guide, one that has been trying in its own way to keep you safe.

Under the clarity of the Full Moon, these forgotten parts of yourself become easier to approach, and you can begin forming a relationship with them that feels steady, kind, and rooted in understanding.

The Wolf Moon is named from the haunting sound of wolves calling across snow-covered forests, as they seek connection, communicate with their pack, and orient themselves within the vastness of winter. During this time, scarcity could draw wolves closer to human settlements, reminding earlier communities of both the wild beauty of the natural world and the shared need for endurance in difficult months.

Historically, this moon symbolised perseverance, resourcefulness, and the importance of conserving strength through harsh conditions. Communities understood that survival required unity and cooperation, reflecting the behaviour of wolf packs, which rely on each other for warmth, protection, and support. The Wolf Moon therefore carries the energy of resilience, adaptability, and the fierce wisdom required to thrive even when the world feels stark and demanding.

In spiritual and metaphysical traditions, the Wolf Moon is seen as a powerful gateway to listen to your intuition, to reflect on what you have endured, and to acknowledge the lessons that have shaped you.

This moon also invites you to reconnect with your inner wildness, reminding you that wolves are symbols of instinct, courage, and primal intelligence. Their presence teaches you to honour your natural rhythms, to trust the wisdom held in your body, and to embrace the parts of yourself that refuse to be diminished by expectation or fear. Winter may mirror scarcity and uncertainty, yet the Wolf Moon gently encourages trust in the larger cycles of life, urging you to lean into your strength and to believe in the quiet power that resides at your core.

During Week One, you spent time calming your nervous system, settling your energy, and creating a foundation of inner stillness. Now, under the illumination of the full moon, you are invited to meet the parts of yourself you usually keep hidden-the fears that whisper beneath your thoughts, the patterns you avoid, and the emotions you have not yet allowed space to fully feel. Just as wolves embody both the wild and the wise, you too carry a complex interplay of instinct, vulnerability, and inner strength.

The Wolf Moon teaches that shadow work is not about choosing one part of yourself over another; it is about recognising the presence of both your fear and your courage, your wounded self and your empowered self, your instinct to protect and your instinct to expand. This week marks the moment you step through the doorway of true inner work, guided by lunar light and your growing willingness to know yourself more deeply.

The Two Wolves Within

There is an old story that says that inside every person lives two wolves.

One is fear, scarcity, anger, and doubt.
The other is courage, truth, intuition, and compassion.
The one that wins, the story says, is the one you feed.

Yet the deeper psychological truth is gentler and more profound:

Both wolves must be acknowledged,
for both carry messages born from different chapters of your life.

Your shadow wolf took shape through pain, fear, or unmet needs,
while your light wolf formed from resilience, wisdom, and hope.

Shadow work is not about starving one and feeding the other;
it is about bringing them into harmony,
so that you are no longer ruled by fear,
nor disconnected from your strength.

Under the Wolf Moon,
these two wolves rise to meet each other -
and in doing so,
they invite you to meet the full truth of who you are .

Practical Exercise

Meeting Your Two Wolves

(This can also be found online as a guided meditation)

1. Prepare Your Sacred Space
   - Dim the lights
   - Light a candle
   - Sit comfortably, feet grounded
   - Have your workbook and a pen nearby

2. Slow Your Breath
   - Inhale for 4
   - Hold gently for 2
   - Exhale for 6
   - Repeat until you feel your body soften

3. Close your eyes
   - Visualise the Two Wolves
   - To your left: the Shadow Wolf - the part of you shaped by fear, wounds, unmet needs, or old stories.
   - To your right: the Light Wolf - the part shaped by resilience, wisdom, intuition, and strength.

   - Let both wolves come into focus without judging them.

4. Ask Each Wolf a Question - Trust your first impressions. Do not overthink.

Shadow Wolf
What are you protecting me from?
What do you fear will happen if you let go?
What pain are you still holding?

Light Wolf
Where am I stronger than I realise?
What truth am I ready to step into?
How can I guide you forward from here?

5. Dialogue Between the Wolves

- Invite them to speak to each other.
- What does the Light Wolf want the Shadow Wolf to know?
- What does the Shadow Wolf need in order to feel safe?

This is the beginning of integration.

6. Write What Emerged

- Use the reflection space below.
- Words, images, phrases-whatever appeared.

Practical Exercise
Learning Type Adaptations

Now that you have begun to meet, or are gently beginning to meet, your shadow in the form of the shadow wolves, it is time to explore this inner encounter more deeply through the lens of your unique learning type. This step is important because each of us processes experience differently, and the way we learn determines how we integrate, soothe, and balance the emotions and insights that rise during shadow work. When you understand how your mind and body naturally take in information, express emotion, and make meaning, you give yourself the tools to weave your shadow work into your life in a way that feels aligned, steady, and supportive.

Your learning type becomes a guiding thread, offering clarity on how you can best approach the material that surfaces, how you can hold yourself through discomfort, and how you can anchor new awareness in a way that strengthens your transformation rather than overwhelming it.

Just as the wolves within you carry both instinct and wisdom, your archetype and learning style work together to help you navigate this journey with compassion and confidence.

In a previous exercise, you discovered your learning type or the blend of learning types that feels most natural for you, and it is important to remember that many of us embody a combination rather than fitting neatly into a single category. You are welcome to explore all of the practices if you wish, allowing yourself to experiment with how each one feels in your body and mind, and noticing which approach helps your inner world open with the greatest sense of ease, clarity, and emotional resonance.

Visual / Creative Learners

- Draw your two wolves: colours, shapes, size.
- Notice which appears clearer or larger.
- Observe how they shift after the ritual.

Kinesthetic / Somatic Learners

- Place one hand on your heart (light) and one on your belly (shadow).
- Let your body guide the dialogue.
- Note which areas tighten, soften, or warm.

Auditory Learners

- Speak your answers aloud.
- Write nothing until after you have vocalised it.
- Record a 1–2 minute voice note naming each wolf.

A space to draw or anchor what arose.

Reading / Writing Learners

- Complete these prompts:
  - My Shadow Wolf told me…
  - My Light Wolf reminded me…
  - What I now understand is…

All Learning Types - Reflection Space

After completing the meditation exercise(s), reflect and sum up:

- What did the Shadow Wolf reveal?
- What did the Light Wolf reveal?
- Where do both wolves agree that you are ready to grow?
- How did your body respond to the ritual?

Practical Exercise

Archetype Quiz

Identify your dominant + hidden shadow patterns

Now that you have begun to understand the learning style that supports your emotional unfolding, you are ready to take this journey one step deeper by exploring the archetype that shapes the way you move through life. Your archetype is the energetic pattern or inner identity that influences how you respond to challenges, how you express your gifts, and how your shadow forms and reveals itself. While your learning type shows you how you process and integrate your experiences, your archetype helps you understand why certain patterns arise, where your strengths live, and how your inner world naturally seeks balance.

Working with your archetype allows you to recognise the deeper forces that guide your instincts, your fears, and your intuitive wisdom. It offers a language for understanding the roles you play within yourself and within the world, making your shadow work more meaningful, more grounded, and more personal. Just as you may embody more than one learning type, you may resonate with more than one archetype, and exploring these patterns can help you see your inner landscape more clearly.

Answer the questions overleaf honestly. Choose the option(s) that feel most true to your natural tendencies, not who you wish to be. Do not overthink - your first instinct is usually the most revealing. You may find that you have more than one option per question. This is perfectly ok, as you may respond slightly differently to two different situations. So, if two or three options resonate per question, tick them all. Its the total that counts.

1. When life feels overwhelming, your first instinct is to…

☐ A) Help someone else
☐ B) Take control
☐ C) Escape into creativity
☐ D) Hope someone will guide you
☐ E) Seek closeness
☐ F) Read the situation symbolically
☐ G) Withdraw and observe
☐ H) Put on a confident mask
☐ I) Push back or disrupt
☐ J) Shut down emotionally
☐ K) Search for meaning
☐ L) Freeze or feel helpless

2. Your core fear in relationships is…

☐ A) Not being needed
☐ B) Losing control
☐ C) Not expressing your true self
☐ D) Becoming overwhelmed
☐ E) Not receiving love
☐ F) Being mistrusted or misread
☐ G) Being misunderstood
☐ H) Being unworthy behind the mask
☐ I) Losing freedom
☐ J) Failing
☐ K) Losing your sense of purpose
☐ L) Being hurt

3. When someone criticises you, you tend to…

☐ A) Try to fix the relationship
☐ B) Defend firmly
☐ C) Critique yourself harder
☐ D) Feel confused or naive
☐ E) Feel emotionally exposed
☐ F) Analyse their motives
☐ G) Retreat into thought
☐ H) Hide behind a role
☐ I) Argue or challenge
☐ J) Believe they are right
☐ K) Look for the deeper lesson
☐ L) Feel small

4. What drains you most?

□ A) Conflict
□ B) Chaos
□ C) Creative blocks
□ D) Harsh energy
□ E) Emotional distance
□ F) Stagnation
□ G) Crowds
□ H) Judgment
□ I) Restrictions
□ J) Expectation
□ K) Routine with no meaning
□ L) Emotional pain

5. When you want something, you usually…

□ A) Put others first
□ B) Plan and take charge
□ C) Dream and visualise
□ D) Feel unsure how to start
□ E) Chase emotional intensity
□ F) Manifest or ritualise it
□ G) Analyse the situation
□ H) Perform or impress
□ I) Follow your impulses
□ J) Hold back out of fear
□ K) Seek spiritual alignment
□ L) Doubt you can have it

6. Under intense stress, you secretly…

□ A) Overgive
□ B) Micromanage
□ C) Shut down creatively
□ D) Become dependent
□ E) Cling to others
□ F) Become suspicious or controlling
□ G) Disappear
□ H) Pretend everything is fine
□ I) Act out
□ J) Freeze
□ K) Escape into ideas or spirit
□ L) Collapse

7. Your inner child learned that survival meant…

☐ A) Being helpful
☐ B) Being responsible
☐ C) Being imaginative
☐ D) Being protected
☐ E) Being loving
☐ F) Being wise
☐ G) Being quiet
☐ H) Being impressive
☐ I) Being wild
☐ J) Being invisible
☐ K) Being curious
☐ L) Being wounded

8. Your emotional style is…

☐ A) Empathic
☐ B) Controlled
☐ C) Creative
☐ D) Innocent or childlike
☐ E) Intense
☐ F) Transformative
☐ G) Observing
☐ H) Performed
☐ I) Expressive
☐ J) Avoidant
☐ K) Expansive or transcendent
☐ L) Heavy or overwhelmed

9. Your greatest strength is…

☐ A) Compassion
☐ B) Leadership
☐ C) Creativity
☐ D) Hope
☐ E) Intimacy
☐ F) Transformation
☐ G) Insight
☐ H) Adaptability
☐ I) Courage
☐ J) Survival instinct
☐ K) Wisdom
☐ L) Sensitivity

10. Your greatest weakness is…

☐ A) Self-abandonment
☐ B) Control
☐ C) Self-criticism
☐ D) Avoidance
☐ E) Overattachment
☐ F) Manipulation or illusion
☐ G) Isolation
☐ H) Inauthenticity
☐ I) Impulsivity
☐ J) Sabotage
☐ K) Dissociation
☐ L) Victim mentality

11. You lose yourself when…

☐ A) Someone needs you
☐ B) Things fall apart
☐ C) You cannot create
☐ D) You feel unsafe
☐ E) Connection breaks
☐ F) Your intuition is dismissed
☐ G) Life becomes too loud
☐ H) You feel judged
☐ I) You feel restricted
☐ J) The stakes are high
☐ K) Life feels meaningless
☐ L) You feel powerless

12. You gain power when…

☐ A) You support others
☐ B) You take charge
☐ C) You express creatively
☐ D) You feel safe
☐ E) You bond deeply
☐ F) You transform a situation
☐ G) You go inward
☐ H) You step into visibility
☐ I) You break rules
☐ J) You prepare for danger
☐ K) You seek truth
☐ L) You are believed

13. Your comfort zone is…

☐ A) Caring for others
☐ B) Structure and control
☐ C) Creativity
☐ D) Safety
☐ E) Emotional closeness
☐ F) Spiritual growth
☐ G) Solitude
☐ H) Acceptance from others
☐ I) Change and movement
☐ J) Low stakes
☐ K) Exploration
☐ L) Familiarity

14. What do you hide most?

☐ A) Anger
☐ B) Vulnerability
☐ C) Imperfection
☐ D) Doubt
☐ E) Desire
☐ F) Power
☐ G) Needs
☐ H) True self
☐ I) Discipline
☐ J) Ambition
☐ K) Uncertainty
☐ L) Hope

15. When faced with change, you…

☐ A) Support others
☐ B) Create structure
☐ C) Reimagine creatively
☐ D) Feel lost
☐ E) Seek closeness
☐ F) Trust your intuition
☐ G) Observe and reflect
☐ H) Adjust your mask
☐ I) Jump in
☐ J) Freeze
☐ K) Look for meaning
☐ L) Panic internally

Tally your answers!

A's	B's	C's	D's	E's	F's	G's	H's	I's	J's	K's	L's

If you end up with an even score, return to the questions and notice the second response you would most likely choose. This usually reveals the underlying pattern beneath your first instinct.

A Caretaker → helping, overgiving, compassion
B Controller → control, structure, leadership
C Creator → imagination, creativity, blocks
D Innocent → safety, hope, guidance
E Lover → closeness, attachment, emotional depth
F Magician → symbolism, ritual, transformation
G Outsider → withdrawal, observation, solitude
H Performer → masks, visibility, judgment
I Rebel → disruption, freedom, rule-breaking
J Saboteur → self-criticism, fear, freezing
K Seeker → meaning, truth, exploration
L Victim → helplessness, collapse, overwhelm

This is not a personality label. It reflects a protective pattern that developed for survival, not a fixed identity. With awareness, these patterns can soften, integrate, and transform.

Your highest score reflects your Primary Archetype - the pattern that most often steps in to protect you when life feels challenging.

Your second-highest score represents a Secondary or Supporting Shadow. This pattern often operates more quietly or unconsciously, yet it can strongly influence your reactions and choices. In many cases, this is the archetype you least identify with - but one that shapes behaviour from behind the scenes.

Both archetypes matter. Together, they offer a fuller picture of how you learned to survive and adapt.

My primary archetype is:______________________________________

My secondary archetype is: ___________________________________

My tertiary archetype is:______________________________________

Moving Through Your Archetypes and Learning Types

Now that you have discovered both your learning type and your archetype, it is important to move through the next steps in a way that honours your inner rhythm.

Shadow work unfolds most naturally when you begin by creating space within yourself before you attempt to process or transform anything.

As you begin to weave your learning type with your archetype, you create a path that is **uniquely your own** - a guide for understanding how you move through your shadow, how you process emotion, and how you return to balance. This pairing shows you not only what you are working with, but how to work with it in a way that feels natural, grounded, and supportive.

Your archetype reveals the emotional patterns, instincts, and protective strategies that shape your inner world. Your learning type reveals the pathways through which insight becomes embodied, integrated, and transformed. When the two come together, your healing becomes clearer, more compassionate, and entirely aligned with who you truly are beneath roles, habits, and expectations.

You are not meant to dive straight into the exercises without first grounding, softening, and preparing your inner landscape.

You will begin with the **Reflection, Gratitude, and Restoration** prompts for your **primary archetype**. These practices gently open the doorway to your inner world, allowing your nervous system to settle, your emotions to become accessible, and your awareness to deepen. Reflection invites you to notice what has been shaping you without judgment. Gratitude softens the heart, creating emotional warmth for the deeper work ahead. Restoration replenishes your energy and reminds your body that it is safe to explore your inner world.

Together, these three practices create the quiet inner soil from which true transformation grows.

Begin by working with your primary archetype. Turn to its page, explore its qualities, and then find the practices connected to your learning type or types. Allow the two to meet without pressure. Once you have fully explored your primary archetype and come to balance, you will be ready to meet the deeper layers of your inner world through your secondary archetype.

You may notice that your secondary archetype carries a different emotional tone - one that feels more tender, raw, or revealing. This is natural because for many people, the secondary archetype is where the shadow quietly lives.

Why the Secondary Archetype Reveals the Shadow

Your primary archetype is the part of you that you recognise easily. It represents the strengths you use most often, the patterns you have permission to express, and the identity that feels familiar both to you and to others.

Your secondary archetype, however, often formed in response to experiences where you felt unsafe, unseen, or misunderstood and carries the qualities you learned to soften, silence, or mask. This is where the deeper wounds, unmet needs, and protective behaviours often sit - woven into the emotional imprint of your shadow.

Exploring this archetype with gentleness allows you to meet the parts of yourself that have been patiently waiting for acknowledgement. These parts are not broken; they have simply been carrying more than their share of your emotional history.

The Role of the Tertiary Archetype

Your tertiary archetype may influence you in subtler ways. It is not the driving force of your behaviour, nor the container of your deepest wounds, but it may appear in specific situations - during transitions, creative processes, moments of uncertainty, or relationships where different versions of you emerge.

This archetype can reveal unexpressed gifts, dormant strengths, or patterns that appear only under certain conditions. While it does not require the same level of focus as your primary or secondary archetypes, understanding it adds nuance to your self-awareness and helps you recognise the quieter threads of your story.

Why this order?

You have the most clarity and the most emotional stability within your primary archetype, so exploring it first gives you grounding before moving into the more vulnerable work your shadow may ask of you within your secondary type.

Once your system feels steady, then your secondary archetype should be explored next - this layer holds the deeper emotional imprints, and approaching it after your primary archetype ensures the work unfolds safely and at a pace your nervous system can hold.

Your tertiary archetype can be explored last, offering perspective once the main layers have been integrated.

Summary of Your Discoveries So Far

You have now uncovered two essential pieces of your inner landscape: **your archetypes and your learning type.** Together, they form a powerful foundation for the shadow work that follows.

Take a moment to acknowledge what you have already moved through. You have explored the deeper patterns that shape your emotions, your instincts, and the stories you have carried for years. You have also recognised the ways you learn, process, and integrate your experiences, giving yourself permission to grow in alignment with your natural rhythm rather than against it.

This is already profound progress.

- Understanding your archetypes reveals what you are healing.
- Understanding your learning type reveals how you heal best.

Bringing them together creates a pathway that is uniquely tailored to you - one that honours your emotional needs, your nervous system, and the truths held within your shadow.

In the next section, we will take these discoveries and begin **Moving Through Your Archetypes and Learning Types,** gently guiding you through your primary archetype first, then your secondary, and eventually any tertiary influences. This approach ensures that your journey remains grounded, safe, and aligned with your capacity.

For now, breathe deeply, soften your shoulders, and acknowledge the truth of where you stand: You have already begun to shift. You have already stepped into a new level of self-awareness. And from this place, the deeper layers of shadow work can unfold with ease, clarity, and trust.

You are ready for the next step.

Reflection Space

A Gentle Warning Before You Begin

Shadow work can stir old emotions, memories, and protective patterns.
This is normal, but it can sometimes feel intense.
If you notice yourself becoming overwhelmed, anxious, or unsteady:

Pause immediately.
Step away from the work.
Breathe.
Return to grounding or self-soothing practices.

You never need to force revelations or push through discomfort.
There is no prize for moving quickly.

If challenging emotions persist or feel unmanageable, please seek support from a trained therapist, counsellor, or mental health professional.

Shadow work is powerful, but it is not meant to replace professional care.
Your emotional safety comes first - always.

"Go gently.
you are your own safe place now."

Move slowly, honour your limits, and prioritise your well-being above anything written on these pages.

The Caretaker

You move through life with a heart that feels deeply and instinctively, often sensing what others need before they have the words to express it. You are naturally attuned to emotional shifts, subtle cues, and the unspoken dynamics in a room, and you offer care and support with genuine warmth and generosity. Helping, soothing, and nurturing others feels like second nature to you, and people often gravitate toward your calm, steady presence, trusting you to hold space when emotions run high.

Over time, caring for others became a form of safety. You learned that maintaining harmony and tending to the emotional needs around you could reduce conflict and create a sense of stability. When those around you are settled, you feel more able to relax. **Your compassion is a powerful gift,** yet it can quietly drain your energy when you lose sight of your own needs or place yourself last. Beneath your giving nature lives a tender fear that saying no might disrupt connection, disappoint others, or threaten the sense of belonging you deeply value.

Integration invites you to recognise that your worth is not tied to how much you give. Learning to receive support, honour your limits, and set gentle boundaries allows your care to flow from fullness rather than exhaustion. When you include yourself in the circle of care, your nurturing becomes balanced, sustainable, and rooted in self-respect. In this way, your kindness remains a source of strength, nourishment, and genuine connection, for others and for yourself, without costing you your own wellbeing.

Shadow Expression

People-pleasing
Overgiving and emotional exhaustion
Self-abandonment
Fear of conflict
Seeking worth through usefulness

Core Need

To honour your own needs, practice boundaries, and receive care.

Practical Exercise

The Caretaker / Pleaser Shadow

Reflection

- Where have you given more than you truly had, and what did that create for you?
- What emotions arise when you think about your own needs?

Practical Exercise

The Caretaker / Pleaser Shadow

Gratitude

- What moments of kindness or connection nourished me this year?
- What am I grateful to myself for surviving, tending, or carrying?

Practical Exercise

The Caretaker / Pleaser Shadow

Restoration

- What would help you receive comfort without giving anything in return?
- What small space can you create today that is just for you?

Integration

To integrate the Caretaker archetype is to understand how caring for others became the path to connection and safety.

There was a time when emotional harmony mattered deeply. Tension, conflict, or disconnection felt threatening, and you learned to sense the needs of others before they were spoken. You noticed moods, shifts, and unspoken feelings, and you responded instinctively. Offering care helped soothe the environment. Helping others helped relationships stay intact.

- This archetype protected you by keeping the connection alive.
- By being attentive, supportive, and emotionally available, you created a sense of belonging and usefulness.
- Care became a way of ensuring that bonds did not break.
- Being needed meant being valued.

And for a long time, this strategy brought closeness and meaning, but over time, the cost of this protection became clearer.

You may notice that your attention moves outward automatically, even when you are depleted. You may feel responsible for others' emotions, or uneasy when someone is upset around you.

Receiving care can feel uncomfortable, and asking for support may bring guilt or hesitation. Your nervous system learned that giving was safer than needing.

Through this work, you have begun to see that your care was not excessive; it was adaptive. But the conditions that required constant attunement have changed. What once kept connection intact may now be quietly eroding your own sense of self.

Integration begins subtly.

At first, you may feel discomfort when you pause instead of helping, or when you allow someone else to sit with their feelings without intervening. You may notice anxiety when you name your own needs, or a reflex to minimise them. This is not selfishness emerging; it is your system learning a new balance.

Slowly, something shifts.

Learning Type Adaptations

For balancing giving with receiving, restoring boundaries, and nurturing self-worth.

Visual Learner

Energy In and Energy Out Diagram

- Begin filling each column below with the situations, people, responsibilities, habits, and emotional patterns that either consume your energy or restore it.
- Use colour to show how much energy each item requires or gives back. Let darker or heavier tones represent the things that drain you, and lighter or brighter colours represent what nourishes you.

This visual practice helps you clearly see where your energy is leaking and where it is being replenished, giving you a compassionate map of the balance you are seeking.

What drains me	What nourishes me.

Reading and Writing Learner

Boundary Rehearsal Script

- Write three simple sentences below, which you can use to say 'no' with clarity and kindness. These phrases do not need to be dramatic or confrontational. They simply need to express your truth. An example might be, **"My plate is full, but thank you for thinking of me."**
- Write a few variations that feel natural in your own voice.

Practising them on paper prepares your nervous system to use them in real life.

When you rehearse boundaries gently, you show your inner Caretaker that saying no does not remove love or connection. It simply makes space for your well-being.

Auditory Learner

"My Needs Matter" Self-Holding Meditation

- Sit comfortably and cross your arms over your chest so each hand holds the opposite arm, as though you are giving yourself a gentle hug.
- Take a slow breath in, and as you exhale, repeat aloud,

  "I am worthy of the care I give."
- Feel the words move through your chest and shoulders as your body softens beneath your touch. Repeat the phrase several times, allowing it to sink into your heart.

This meditation is a quiet reminder that your needs are real, your energy is sacred, and you deserve to receive the same tenderness you offer so freely to others.

Kinesthetic / Somatic Learners

Self-Compassion Touch Ritual

- Find a warm blanket or shawl and wrap it gently around your shoulders.
- Let the fabric rest against your skin, creating a sense of warmth, comfort, and safety.
- Sit quietly for a moment and allow yourself to feel held.

This simple ritual teaches your body what it feels like to receive comfort without earning it, proving to your inner caretaker that rest, warmth, and softness are not luxuries; they are essential forms of nourishment that restore the heart.

A space to anchor what arose.

All Learning Types

For the Caretaker, small acts of receiving and gentle boundary setting are most effective when practised consistently over time. You may begin with one simple receiving practice or one small boundary each week and repeat it for the full lunar cycle of twenty-eight days. This gives your heart and nervous system time to adjust to the idea that your needs matter just as much as the needs of those around you.

If you find this work healing, you may continue it throughout the winter season, allowing your sense of worthiness and inner balance to strengthen gradually.

The purpose is not to withdraw from others or to harden your heart. It is to show your inner Caretaker that nurturing yourself is not selfish. It is a necessary act of replenishment that allows your generosity to remain sustainable, steady, and honest.

The Controller

You navigate the world by creating order, taking charge, and holding everything together - often long before anyone else realises support is needed. Control has become your armour. Structure helps you feel safe, precision reassures you that things will not fall apart, and responsibility gives you a deep sense of purpose and identity. You are often the one others rely on, the steady presence in uncertainty, the person who steps forward when things feel uncontained or unpredictable.

Your greatest strength is leadership - your natural ability to organise, direct, plan, and protect. You see what needs to be done and move toward it with clarity and resolve. Yet your deepest challenge lies in learning when to soften your grip, when to trust the process, and when to allow life to unfold without managing every detail.

Beneath your drive to lead is a tender part of you that learned long ago that chaos was unsafe, that stability had to be created rather than assumed, and that being in control was the only way to prevent things from going wrong.

Integration invites you to discover a different kind of strength - one that does not rely on constant vigilance, but on inner trust. As you learn to loosen control in small, intentional ways, you create space for support, collaboration, and rest. You do not lose your power when you let go; you refine it. Your leadership becomes more spacious, more flexible, and more sustainable, rooted not in fear of disorder, but in confidence, presence, and grounded authority.

Shadow Expressions

Perfectionism
Micromanaging
Over-responsibility
Suppressing vulnerability
Difficulty delegating / trusting others
Belief that safety = control

Core Need

To soften control and feel safe without being in charge.
(Trusting the process, allowing imperfection, releasing the armour)

Practical Exercise

The Controller / Warrior Shadow

Reflection

- Where have you held everything together this year, and how has that felt in your body?
- What moments of rigidity or pressure are you ready to acknowledge without judgment?

Practical Exercise

The Controller / Warrior Shadow

Gratitude

- What are you grateful to yourself for managing so well?
- Who supported you, even in small ways, when you allowed it?

Practical Exercise

The Controller / Warrior Shadow

Restoration

- What can you release today that softens your nervous system?
- What part of you is asking to rest from responsibility?

Integration

To integrate the Controller is to understand how responsibility once became synonymous with safety.

There was a time when stability could not be assumed. Things felt unpredictable or fragile, and someone had to stay alert, plan ahead, and hold everything together. You became that someone. Control was not about power, but prevention - if you stayed organised and prepared, fewer things would fall apart.

This archetype protected you by creating order where there was uncertainty. It taught you competence, leadership, and reliability. For a long time, being capable meant being safe.

Over time, however, the cost appeared. You may notice constant vigilance in your body, difficulty resting, or anxiety when you are not in charge. Letting go can feel risky, even when nothing is wrong. Your system learned that safety came after everything was handled - yet everything is never quite finished.

Through this work, you begin to recognise that the conditions requiring constant control have shifted. What once protected you now quietly exhausts you.

Integration does not come from forcing relaxation or surrender. It begins with small pauses - allowing others to step in, noticing that the world continues, and letting your body learn that safety no longer depends on holding everything together.

Gradually, steadiness arises from within. Leadership softens into discernment. Control becomes presence. Strength becomes something you inhabit, not something you prove.

Life begins to feel less like something you must manage, and more like something you can stand within.

Learning Type Adaptations

For softening control, building inner trust,
and allowing support without losing strength.

Visual Learners

The Soften the Edges Map

The large circle represents your life as a whole. Within this circle, begin shading areas where you notice yourself holding too tightly, whether through perfectionism, overplanning, constant responsibility, or the need to manage outcomes. As you shade, use softer colours or lighter pressure to symbolise your intention to release just a little of the weight you carry. Allow the act of drawing to become a visual meditation, helping you see clearly where your energy feels rigid and where gentleness is needed. This simple map becomes a compassionate reminder that not everything requires your control in order to be safe.

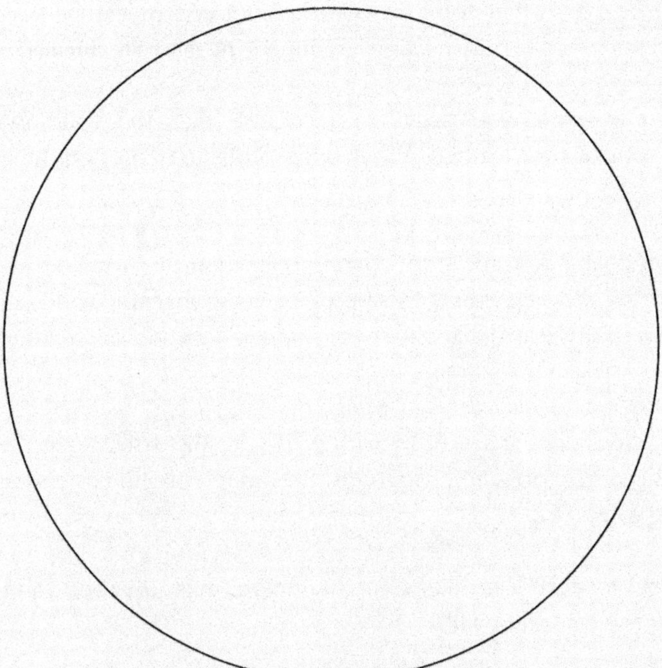

You may choose to add small words or symbols in the circle to guide you, such as work, relationships, family, health, emotions, or responsibilities. These are optional and simply offered to help you identify where control gathers in your life.

Auditory Learners
Surrender Mantra Repetition

- Find a quiet moment where your breath can settle, and repeat the mantra aloud in a slow and steady rhythm:
  "I release what is not mine to hold. I soften into trust."
- Speak it until you feel the tension in your voice begin to melt, and your breath begins to flow more naturally.
- If it supports you, record yourself saying the words and listen back, allowing your own voice to guide you into a state of surrender.
- Let each repetition gently loosen the inner grip you keep on life, reminding you that you are allowed to rest and that not everything requires your vigilance.

Kinesthetic / Somatic Learners
Shoulder Armour Release

- Stand or sit comfortably and take a slow breath in as you lift your shoulders toward your ears, feeling the familiar tension your body holds when you are trying to stay in control.
- As you exhale, let your shoulders drop completely and release a long sigh, imagining that the armour you have worn for so long is falling away piece by piece.
- Repeat this several times until you feel warmth or softness begin to move through your upper body.

This physical release mirrors the emotional release you are cultivating, reminding you that surrender can be felt not only in the mind but also in the body.

A space to anchor what arose.

Reading / Writing Learners

"What If I Let Go"

- Write ten sentences beginning with the phrase,

  "If I loosened control by five per cent, I could…"
- Allow the thoughts to come without judgment. You may write about emotional freedom, more spacious relationships, deeper rest, or unexpected joy.

This prompt encourages your mind to imagine what becomes possible when you ease your grip just slightly. It helps you see that letting go is not a loss of power but a softening that creates space for support, trust, and flow.

The Creator

You move through life with imagination, originality, and a deep need to express what lives inside you. Creativity is not just something you do - it is how you process emotion, make sense of experience, and bring meaning into form. you are inspired by possibility and driven to create something uniquely your own.

Over time, creation became intertwined with self-worth. When your work was praised, you felt seen; when it was criticised or unfinished, self-doubt crept in.

This can lead to perfectionism, avoidance, or fear of sharing your work at all. Beneath your creative drive lives a vulnerability around being visible and judged.

Integration invites you to create without attaching your value to the outcome.

Your expression does not need to be perfect to be meaningful. As you allow creativity to flow freely, it becomes a source of nourishment rather than pressure. Your art, in whatever form it takes, becomes a bridge between your inner world and the outer one.

Shadow Expression
Perfectionism
Creative paralysis
Fear of visibility
Harsh self-comparison
Abandoning ideas too soon

Core Need
To express freely without the pressure of perfection

Practical Exercise

The Creator / Expression Shadow

Reflection

- Where did you silence or doubt your creativity this past year?
- What ideas or expressions did you want to come through you, and what held you back?

Practical Exercise

The Creator / Expression Shadow

Gratitude

- What creative sparks, inspirations, or visions are you grateful for?
- Where did you allow yourself to imagine, dream, or express freely?

Practical Exercise

The Creator / Expression Shadow

Restoration

- What creative practice brings you back into flow without pressure or perfection?
- What simple expression reconnects you to joy, colour, or possibility?

Integration

To integrate the Creator archetype is to understand how expression became your way of making sense of the world.

There was a time when feelings, experiences, or ideas lived too loudly inside you. Creating gave them form. Art, words, movement, or imagination became a way to translate what could not be easily spoken. Creation helped you feel alive, understood, and connected to something meaningful.

This archetype protected you by giving shape to inner experience. Through expression, you found relief, coherence, and identity. Making something tangible helped you feel less alone with what you carried. For a long time, creativity was both refuge and lifeline.

But over time, the cost of this protection emerged.

You may notice pressure around expression, fear of being seen, or cycles of inspiration followed by harsh self-criticism. Creation can become entangled with worth - what you make begins to feel like proof of who you are . Your nervous system learned that expression mattered because it kept you visible, valued, or intact.

Through this work, you have begun to see that creativity itself was never the problem. The pressure came from needing it to mean something about you.

Integration unfolds through play.

At first, creating without outcome or audience may feel empty or unsettling. You may feel resistance when there is no clear purpose or validation attached. This is not a loss of creativity - it is your system learning a new relationship with expression.

Gradually, something opens.

You rediscover curiosity. Pleasure. Movement without judgment. Creation becomes an experience rather than a performance. Your body relaxes as expression returns to being a process, not a verdict.

Learning Type Adaptations

For releasing perfectionism, unlocking flow, and expressing truth without fear.

Auditory Learners

- Hum or chant a simple melody with no structure or goal.
- Let your voice meander until it feels expressive rather than "good."

Kinesthetic / Somatic Learners

- Use your hands to create movement: shaping clay, tearing paper, tracing patterns in the air.
- Let your body lead without thinking.

Visual / Creative Learners

- Draw or sketch something tiny and imperfect - a swirl, a shape, a colour patch.
- Allow it to be unfinished.
- Let your eyes enjoy the rawness.

A space to draw or anchor what arose.

Reading/Writing Learners

- Do a 3-minute free-write titled: ***"What wants to express through me?"***
- No editing. No rereading. Just flow.

The Innocent

You move through life with openness, sensitivity, and a desire for safety and goodness. you are naturally hopeful, trusting, and inclined to see the best in people and situations. Your gentleness brings lightness and sincerity into the world.

Over time, innocence became a way to cope with overwhelm. When life felt too harsh or unpredictable, retreating into simplicity or dependency offered comfort.

While this protected your heart, it may also have left you feeling unprepared for complexity or conflict. Beneath your optimism lives a quiet fear that the world is too much to face alone.

Integration invites you to pair hope with resilience. You do not lose your softness by becoming stronger. As you learn to meet reality with both openness and discernment, your innocence matures into wisdom.

You discover that safety can come from within, allowing you to remain tender without becoming fragile.

Shadow Expression

Avoidance and overwhelm
Dependence on others for certainty
Difficulty facing emotional intensity
Retreating into simplicity
Fear of responsibility or complexity

Core Need

To build inner safety so they can face life with grounded confidence

Practical Exercise

The Innocent / Safety Shadow

Reflection

- When did you feel overwhelmed this past year, and what tender part of you was seeking safety?
- Where have you avoided responsibility or truth because it felt too big to hold?

Practical Exercise

The Innocent / Safety Shadow

Gratitude

- What moments reminded you of hope, purity, or softness?
- Where did your gentle heart guide you with honesty or trust?

Practical Exercise

The Innocent / Safety Shadow

Restoration

- What helps you feel safe, nurtured, and supported in your body?
- What simple, childlike ritual soothes your nervous system and brings relief?

Integration

To integrate the Innocent is not to lose hope, but to understand how hope once kept you safe.

There was a time when the world felt overwhelming or unpredictable. Believing in goodness, simplicity, or positive outcomes helped soften fear and made life feel manageable. Optimism offered relief when reality felt too complex or heavy to hold.

This archetype protected you by preserving openness. By holding onto hope, you stayed emotionally alive and avoided becoming hardened or closed. Seeing the good allowed you to keep moving forward when trust felt fragile.

Over time, the cost appeared. You may notice discomfort with conflict, avoidance of difficult truths, or a tendency to minimise pain - your own or others'. Disappointment can feel especially sharp, as though it breaks something delicate. Your system learned that hope equalled safety.

Through this work, you begin to recognise that innocence is not naivety. It was protection. But the part of you that stayed hopeful may not yet know that you are now capable of holding more complexity than before.

Integration unfolds through gentle discernment. Acknowledging difficulty may feel unsettling at first, as though it threatens safety. Grief or resistance can arise as truth comes into view. This is not the loss of innocence - it is its maturation.

Gradually, hope becomes steadier. You learn that truth and kindness can coexist, and that safety does not require denial.

As the Innocent integrates, openness becomes grounded clarity. You remain trusting and gentle - without being unprotected.

Learning Type Adaptations

For building inner safety, easing overwhelm, and strengthening gentle resilience.

Auditory Learners

- Create a soft reassurance mantra and repeat it aloud:

  "I am safe. I can meet this moment gently."

- Say it slowly until your nervous system responds.

Visual / Creative Learners

- Imagine a glowing circle of light around your body.
- See it as a cocoon of softness and protection.
- Let the image grow warmer with each breath.

Kinesthetic / Somatic Learners

- Hold something soft - a blanket, warm cloth, or plush texture.
- Let your body feel comfort directly through sensation.
- Breathe slowly as your system settles.

A space to anchor what arose.

Reading/Writing Learners

- Write down three things that make you feel safe.
- Then choose one and describe how you can bring more of it into your daily routine.

1

2

3

The Lover

You move through life with passion, devotion, and a deep longing for connection. You experience intimacy intensely and are highly attuned to emotional closeness, affection, and bonding. Relationships are not just important to you; they are a primary way through which you understand yourself, find meaning, and feel alive. You love deeply, invest wholeheartedly, and often give your full presence to those you care about.

Over time, attachment became a source of security. When the connection felt uncertain or fragile, holding tightly offered reassurance and stability. You may have learned that closeness was something to protect or preserve, especially if it once felt threatened or inconsistent. This can sometimes lead to over-identification with relationships, fear of separation, or a tendency to lose yourself in the emotional world of another. Beneath your longing lives a quiet concern that without connection, you may lose your sense of self, your purpose, or your place in the world.

Integration invites you to balance intimacy with autonomy. Love does not require self-abandonment, nor does closeness have to come at the cost of your individuality. As you learn to stay rooted in yourself while opening your heart to others, your relationships begin to feel more secure, reciprocal, and nourishing. Your capacity for love deepens, no longer driven by fear of loss, but grounded in wholeness, self-trust, and emotional presence.

Shadow Expression

Overattachment or obsession
Emotional fusion
Losing yourself in relationships
Fear of abandonment
Difficulty self-soothing

Core Need

To build inner emotional stability so connection does not replace self-connection

Practical Exercise

The Lover / Attachment Shadow

Reflection

- When did you cling, crave, or reach for connection out of fear rather than love?
- Where have your emotions revealed unmet needs or deeper truths?

Practical Exercise

The Lover / Attachment Shadow

Gratitude

- What experiences of intimacy, affection, or connection warmed your life this past year?
- How did you allow yourself to feel deeply, even when it was vulnerable?

Practical Exercise

The Lover / Attachment Shadow

Restoration

- What helps you self-soothe and return to emotional balance?
- What gentle ritual restores your heart to softness and safety?

Integration

To integrate the Lover is not to stop longing for connection, but to understand how closeness once became the place you felt most alive and most safe.

There was a time when connection meant everything. Being chosen, desired, or emotionally close brought warmth, grounding, and meaning. Love was regulating - it helped your nervous system settle and gave you a sense of belonging. Through intimacy, you felt real.

This archetype protected you by anchoring you in a relationship. Emotional bonding and devotion helped you survive loneliness, instability, or uncertainty. For a long time, closeness made the world feel coherent.

Over time, the cost emerged. You may notice anxiety when distance appears, difficulty holding your own needs, or a tendency to merge emotionally. Separation can feel destabilising rather than neutral. Your system learned that closeness equalled safety.

Through this work, you begin to recognise that attachment was not weakness - it was adaptive. But the conditions that once required holding on may no longer be present. What once protected you may now limit your sense of inner ground. Integration unfolds through self-connection. Turning toward yourself may feel unfamiliar at first. Space can stir unease. This is not loss - it is your system learning a new anchor.

Gradually, steadiness grows within. Connection remains deeply important, but it no longer defines your existence. Love flows without gripping.

As the Lover integrates, intimacy becomes spacious. Desire becomes choice rather than need.

You do not love less.
You love more securely.

Learning Type Adaptations

For emotional grounding, deep self-connection, and soothing attachment patterns.

Auditory Learners

- Speak your emotions aloud in a gentle tone: ***"Right now, my heart feels…"***
- Name what arises without judging it.

Visual / Creative Learners

- Imagine a warm light expanding from your chest in slow waves.
- See it moving outward, then returning inward, balancing connection and self-connection.

Kinesthetic / Somatic Learners

- Place both hands over your heart and breathe deeply.
- Sway gently or rock your body to soothe your emotional system.

A space to anchor what arose.

Reading/Writing Learners

- Write a letter to yourself beginning with: ***"I am here for you."***
- Let the words become a dialogue between your wise self and your tender heart.

The Magician

You move through life with insight, intuition, and a heightened awareness of unseen patterns. You naturally perceive connections beneath the surface of events, sensing meaning, symbolism, and possibility where others may not. You are drawn to transformation, healing, and inner change, often feeling called to understand how things work beneath appearances. Your mind and spirit are attuned to energy, intuition, and the subtle forces that shape experience.

Over time, intuition became a way to navigate uncertainty. When reality felt confusing, unpredictable, or overwhelming, retreating into ideas, visions, or inner worlds offered clarity and a sense of control. This inner realm became a place of safety and understanding. Yet when intuition is not grounded, it can blur the line between insight and illusion, leaving you disconnected from your body or everyday life.

Beneath your power lives a quiet fear that your gifts may be misunderstood, judged, or even misused - by others or by yourself.

Integration invites you to anchor your intuition into embodiment. Your power becomes most potent when it is lived, not just perceived or imagined. As you learn to ground your insights into action, presence, and integrity, your ability to transform becomes clear, ethical, and deeply rooted. You discover that true magic is not about escaping reality, but about engaging with it fully - trusting your wisdom while remaining connected, responsible, and present in the world around you.

Shadow Expression
Illusion or manipulation
Overinterpreting signals
Hiding or withholding truth
Distrust of others' motives
Distortion of intuition

Core Need
To use their insight and power with grounded honesty and clear intention

Practical Exercise

The Magician / Transformation Shadow

Reflection

- Where did you distort your power, hide your truth, or manipulate outcomes out of fear?
- What transformations unfolded this year, and what did they reveal about you?

Practical Exercise

The Magician / Transformation Shadow

Gratitude

- What moments of insight, synchronicity, or manifestation shaped your path?
- Where did your inner alchemist guide you toward healing or clarity?

Practical Exercise

The Magician / Transformation Shadow

Restoration

- What helps you return to integrity and grounded truth?
- What ritual reconnects you to your deepest power in an honest, gentle way?

Integration

To integrate the Magician is not to diminish your power, but to understand how inner knowing once became the place you felt most in control.

There was a time when the outer world felt confusing or unsafe. You learned to turn inward, to sense patterns, meanings, and possibilities others could not see. Insight and intuition created coherence when reality felt fragmented.

Understanding brought stability. Perception brought power.
This archetype protected you through meaning-making.

By trusting inner vision over surface appearances, you learned to navigate uncertainty and transformation. For a long time, this inner mastery helped you feel oriented and capable.

Over time, the cost emerged. You may notice a tendency to remain in ideas rather than action, or to retreat inward when life feels demanding. Insight can become distancing. Transformation can stay conceptual rather than lived. Your system learned that understanding was safer than full participation.

Through this work, you begin to recognise that intuition was never meant to replace experience - it was meant to guide you into it. What once protected you may now keep you slightly removed from your own life.

Integration unfolds through embodiment. Bringing insight into action may feel slow or grounding at first. Reality can feel heavier than vision. This is not a loss of magic - it is its maturation.

As the Magician integrates, wisdom becomes lived rather than imagined. Intuition remains sharp, but anchored. Power no longer sits above experience - it moves through presence.

Your magic does not fade.

It takes form.

Learning Type Adaptations

For grounding intuition, transforming shadow gently,
and anchoring inner power into embodied truth.

Auditory Learners

- Speak an intention aloud, slowly and with clarity:
  "I choose to use my insight with honesty and grounded purpose."
- Let your voice carry the energy of alignment.

Visual / Creative Learners

- Visualise roots growing from your feet into the earth.
- Then see a soft light rising up your spine, aligning intuition with grounding.

Kinesthetic / Somatic Learners

- Place your palms together at your heart and press gently.
- Feel the steadiness of your own strength.
- Breathe until your body feels centred.

A space to anchor what arose.

Reading/Writing Learners

- Write down a truth you have avoided.
- Then write: ***"My intuition becomes clearer when I stand in honesty."***

The Outsider

You move through the world with a quiet depth, often observing life from the edges rather than standing at the centre. You are thoughtful, reflective, and naturally inclined toward introspection, finding meaning in solitude and inner exploration.

While others may rush toward connection, you instinctively step back, watching, analysing, and processing before deciding whether it feels safe to engage.

Over time, withdrawal became a form of protection.

You learned that staying unseen, unheard, or emotionally distant could shield you from misunderstanding, judgment, or overwhelm. Solitude offered clarity and control, allowing you to regulate your inner world when external environments felt too loud or demanding. Yet this self-protection can slowly turn into isolation, leaving you feeling disconnected even when you long for belonging.

Beneath your reserve lives a tender fear that being fully seen may lead to rejection or emotional exposure you are not prepared to hold.

Integration invites you to reconnect gently, without forcing closeness or abandoning your need for space. You do not have to choose between solitude and connection; both can coexist. As you learn to step toward others in small, safe ways, you discover that belonging does not require self-erasure. Your depth becomes a bridge rather than a barrier, allowing you to be both rooted within yourself and meaningfully connected to the world around you.

Shadow Expression
Withdrawal, avoidance, isolation
Emotional repression
Overthinking
Feeling misunderstood
Fear of being seen

Core Need
To feel safe while being visible
and authentically connected

Practical Exercise

The Outsider / Thinker Shadow

Reflection

- When did you retreat this year, and what were you protecting at the time?
- Where did you long for connection yet hide away?

Practical Exercise

The Outsider / Thinker Shadow

Gratitude

- What quiet moments brought you a sense of peace?
- What qualities of yours - sensitivity, depth, wisdom - are you grateful for?

Practical Exercise

The Outsider / Thinker Shadow

Restoration

- What helps you feel safe enough to simply be yourself?
- How can you create a gentle connection without overwhelming your system?

Integration

To integrate the Outsider is to understand how separation once became the path to safety and self-preservation.

There was a time when closeness felt unpredictable or overwhelming. Belonging carried conditions, and difference carried risk. The Outsider learned to step back, to observe rather than participate, to remain on the edges where they could not be consumed or rejected. Distance became protection.

This archetype safeguarded the self through autonomy and detachment. By relying inwardly and minimising dependence, they maintained a sense of control and integrity. Not needing others meant not being hurt by them.

Over time, the cost emerged. You may notice a tendency to withdraw when connection deepens, discomfort being seen or known, or a belief that true belonging is reserved for others. The nervous system learned that aloneness was safer than attachment.

Through this work, it becomes clear that withdrawal was adaptive, not a flaw. It formed in response to environments where difference was not welcomed, or safety was inconsistent. But the conditions that required distance have changed. What once preserved the self may now limit connection.

Integration begins gradually. There may be unease when staying present instead of retreating, or when allowing others to move closer without explanation or performance. This is not weakness; it is the nervous system learning that connection can coexist with safety.

Slowly, the Outsider discovers a new position: not outside, not merged, but in relation. Solitude becomes a choice rather than a defence. Belonging is no longer earned by disappearing.

As the Outsider integrates, individuality remains intact. Connection becomes possible without self-abandonment.

The Outsider learns they were never meant to vanish to belong.

Learning Type Adaptations

For gentle reconnection, easing withdrawal, and inviting safe belonging.

Kinesthetic / Somatic Learners

Doorway Step Exercise

- Stand in a doorway and place one foot inside the room and one foot outside. Notice how this posture feels. One side represents visibility and stepping forward, while the other represents safety and retreat.
- Take a slow breath and gently shift your weight so both feet rest evenly on the threshold. This is the place where openness meets protection, where expression and solitude can live together.
- Practise finding this middle ground as a physical reminder that you do not have to choose between hiding and exposing yourself. There is always a space in between where you can remain connected and still feel safe.

Auditory Learners

Voice Visibility Practice

- Find a quiet moment and record yourself speaking one truth you usually keep hidden. It does not need to be dramatic or overwhelming. It might be a feeling, a need, a desire, or a gentle admission of something you usually keep inside.
- Play the recording back and simply listen.

Hearing your own voice speak your truth allows you to witness your authenticity in a safe, private way before sharing it with others. With time, this practice can help soften the fear of being misunderstood or unseen, because you are teaching your nervous system that your voice can exist in the world without danger.

Visual Learners

Light in the Cave Drawing

- In the space below, sketch a simple cave, a quiet inner space that represents the part of you that retreats for safety.
- Inside the cave, draw a small light glowing gently at its centre.
- Each time you do something that feels vulnerable, honest, or slightly outside your comfort zone, return to this drawing and softly shade the light outward. Watch how it expands over time.

This visual practice helps you see, clearly and compassionately, that every act of openness makes your inner world brighter without forcing you into harsh visibility. Your cave remains a sanctuary, and the growing light shows that safety and expression can coexist.

A space to draw or anchor what arose.

Reading and Writing Learner#

Micro Exposure Journal

- Create a short list of five tiny ways you could allow yourself to be seen. These might include asking a question in a group, expressing a preference, sharing a thought online, sending a message, or speaking up in a meeting.
- Choose one each day and gently check it off.

Small acts of visibility build self-trust far more effectively than big leaps. This journal serves as a reminder that you can choose moments of connection without sacrificing your need for safety and space.

Done

The Performer

You move through the world by adapting, expressing, and shaping yourself to meet what is expected or admired. you are expressive, responsive, and often highly aware of how you are perceived. Your ability to read a room, adjust your presentation, and connect through performance is a powerful social gift.

Over time, performing became a form of safety. You learned that being liked, impressive, or entertaining could secure approval and reduce the risk of rejection.

While this skill allows you to navigate many environments with ease, it can slowly pull you away from your authentic self.

Beneath the polished exterior lives a tender fear that if the mask slips, love or acceptance might disappear.

Integration invites you to soften the performance and return to authenticity.

You do not need to earn belonging through effort or image. As you allow yourself to be seen without rehearsal, your expression becomes more honest and more freeing. Your creativity remains, but it is now rooted in truth rather than survival.

Shadow Expression
Performing instead of expressing
Approval seeking
Emotional masking
Shapeshifting to avoid rejection
Feeling unseen behind the role

Core Need
To feel safe showing up as their authentic, unfiltered self

Practical Exercise

The Performer / Mask Shadow

Reflection

- When did you hide behind a mask this past year, and what were you afraid others might see?
- Where did you perform instead of expressing your authentic truth?

Practical Exercise

The Performer / Mask Shadow

Gratitude

- What parts of yourself found the courage to show up honestly, even in small ways?
- Where did your creativity or adaptability support you in meaningful ways?

Practical Exercise

The Performer / Mask Shadow

Restoration

- What helps you exhale and let the mask soften or fall away entirely?
- What gentle practice brings you back into authenticity and inner presence?

Integration

To integrate the Performer is to understand how being seen once required careful shaping.

There was a time when acceptance felt conditional. You learned to read expectations and adjust yourself accordingly. Being engaging, capable, or impressive helped you belong. Approval brought safety. Performance became a way to stay connected without risking rejection.

This archetype protected you through adaptation. You learned how to communicate, express, and present yourself in ways that were welcomed. For a long time, this allowed you to move through the world with relative ease.

Over time, the cost appeared. You may notice distance from your own emotions, a sense of being known but not fully met, or effort where ease could exist. Expression can feel managed rather than spontaneous. Your system learned that authenticity required caution.

Through this work, you begin to recognise that performance was not vanity - it was protection. But the environments that once demanded constant adaptation may no longer define your life.

Integration unfolds through honesty. Letting yourself be unfiltered may feel exposing at first. Anxiety or vulnerability can arise when you speak without shaping yourself in advance. This is not weakness - it is your system learning that being real can now be safe.

Gradually, expression softens. You begin to feel met rather than evaluated. Creativity deepens. Belonging comes less from effort and more from presence.

As the Performer integrates, the connection no longer requires performance.

You are not loved for who you present.
You are loved for who you are.

Learning Type Adaptations

For authenticity, expression, and softening the mask.

Auditory Learners

- Speak a single truth out loud, gently and without polishing it.
- Say: "In this moment, I feel…" and let your voice express the emotion without filtering or managing tone.
- Notice how honesty sounds when you do not practice it.

Kinesthetic Practice

From Performance to Presence

- Stand or sit comfortably. Let your posture be natural - no "good posture," no adjustment.
- Take three slow breaths and notice any impulse to prepare, perform, or hold yourself a certain way.
- Gently say aloud (or silently): ***"I am allowed to be as I am."***
- For 2–5 minutes, allow your body to move or remain still without intention.
- This might look like:
  - shifting weight
  - stretching
  - sitting quietly
  - resting your hands on your body
- There is no correct expression. If you notice an urge to make the movement look a certain way, simply pause and return to sensation.
- Close by placing one hand on your chest or abdomen and noticing your breath

Visual / Creative Learners

- Stand before a mirror and soften your facial expression.
- Look at your eyes and imagine removing a layer of "performance" with each exhale.
- See the person beneath the role with compassion.

A space to anchor what arose.

Writer / Reader Practice

Letting the Mask Rest

- Prompt (write slowly, without editing):
  - When did I first learn that being liked required effort or adjustment?
  - What parts of myself do I usually edit before sharing?
  - In which situations do I feel most "on," even when I'm tired?
  - What do I fear might happen if I stopped managing how I'm perceived?
  - What might connection feel like if I didn't have to earn it?

Then complete this sentence gently, several times if needed:

If I didn't have to perform to belong, I might allow myself to…

- Read your words back once, quietly. Notice any warmth, resistance, or relief in your body.

You do not need to act on what you wrote - awareness is enough.

The Rebel

You move through life with a fierce instinct for freedom and authenticity. You are sensitive to constraint, quick to notice injustice, and deeply resistant to anything that feels limiting or imposed. Your energy is bold, original, and alive, often pushing against norms that feel false or restrictive. You are driven by an inner need to live on your own terms, even when that path feels uncertain.

Over time, rebellion became a form of protection. You learned that compliance could cost you your sense of self, and that staying true to your instincts was safer than fitting into expectations that felt suffocating. Defiance offered you space to breathe and a sense of power in environments where you may have felt controlled or unseen.

Yet this protective stance can sometimes turn into reactivity, impulsiveness, or a resistance to structure that might actually support you.

Beneath your fire lives a tender fear that if you soften or commit, you might lose yourself or be trapped again.

Integration invites you to discover that freedom does not disappear within structure when it is self-chosen. You are not here to be contained, but you are also not meant to stand alone in constant opposition. As you learn to channel your instinctual energy with intention, your rebellion transforms into courageous authenticity. Your fire becomes a force for creation rather than resistance, allowing you to move through the world with both independence and grounded purpose.

Shadow Expression

Impulsivity
Defiance for defiance's sake
Rejecting structure
Restlessness
Sabotaging stability

Core Need

To express freedom with grounded direction and self-chosen structure

Practical Exercise

The Rebel / Nonconformist Shadow

Reflection

- Where did you resist or push back this year, and what was the deeper need beneath it?
- What choices felt reactive rather than true?

Practical Exercise

The Rebel / Nonconformist Shadow

Gratitude

- What moments of freedom or expression felt deeply aligned?
- What are you grateful to yourself for exploring or daring?

Practical Exercise

The Rebel / Nonconformist Shadow

Restoration

- What helps you settle into warmth instead of intensity?
- Where can you allow ease without feeling confined?

Integration

To integrate the Rebel archetype is to understand how resistance became a form of self-preservation.

There was a time when conformity felt dangerous. Expectations, rules, or authority may have demanded parts of you that felt false or unsafe to surrender. You learned that compliance came at the cost of authenticity. So you resisted. You challenged. You pushed back. Defiance became a way to stay alive inside yourself.

This archetype protected you by preserving your autonomy. Your instincts, originality, and inner truth remained intact because you refused to be shaped by forces that did not honour you. Your fire kept you moving. It kept you awake. It kept you from disappearing.

But over time, the cost of this protection became apparent.

You may notice that opposition has become automatic. Commitment can feel constricting even when it is self-chosen. Structure may feel suspect, and stability may stir restlessness. Your nervous system learned that freedom required vigilance, and that standing still could mean being trapped again.

Through this work, you have begun to see that not all containment is a threat. The environment that once required resistance no longer exists in the same way.

Yet your system continues to respond as though it does.

Integration begins with discernment.

At first, choosing structure may feel uncomfortable. Pausing instead of reacting may feel like a betrayal of self. You might experience agitation when things slow down, or anxiety when you commit to something lasting. This is not loss of freedom - it is your system learning a new relationship with choice.

Slowly, something changes.

You begin to feel autonomy without opposition. Structure becomes something you shape rather than fight. Your energy moves from reaction into direction. The fire that once burned against the world begins to illuminate your path forward.

Learning Type Adaptations

For grounding intensity, directing fire, and transforming resistance into purpose.

Visual Learners

Creative Freedom Board

- In the space below (or on a separate piece of card) create a small collage that represents your authentic, soul-driven freedom.
- Gather or draw images that speak to the kind of life you truly want to live, not the reactions that arise from resistance or frustration, but the desires that come from your inner truth.

This is not about rebelling against rules or breaking away from expectations. It is about capturing the essence of the freedom that feels nourishing and aligned. As you add each image or colour, let it remind you that your deepest freedom comes from choosing what expands your spirit rather than what you feel compelled to resist.

Auditory Learners
Impulse Check In Voice Note

- Before acting on a strong impulse, pause for a moment and record a short voice note with the question: **"Do I want this because I genuinely desire it, or because I am avoiding something?"**
- Listen to your own voice as you ask the question, and notice how your body responds.

This simple practice helps you separate true desire from reactive rebellion. It invites honesty without judgment and teaches your nervous system that you can pause without losing your fire. Over time, this builds a deeper connection to your inner compass and allows your choices to come from intention rather than escape.

Kinesthetic / Somatic Learners
Body Led Movement Ritual

- Stand comfortably, close your eyes if it feels right, and allow your body to move freely for one minute.
- Let your movement be completely intuitive, guided by sensation rather than thought.
- After the minute has passed, bring your hands to your belly, take a deep breath, and ask yourself softly, **"What does freedom feel like in my body?"**

Do not search for the answer. Let it arise naturally as a sensation, a word, a feeling, or a subtle shift. This ritual reconnects you to the truth that freedom is not just a concept or an impulse. It is a physical experience, a grounded sense of expansion that begins within.

A space to anchor what arose.

Reading and Writing Learners

Your Way Agreements

- Write three personal agreements that you genuinely want to live by. These are not rules imposed by others or expectations from the outside world. They are self-created structures that support your creativity, your freedom, and your growth. They might be practices that help you channel your energy, boundaries that protect your autonomy, or gentle commitments that keep you grounded.

When structure is chosen rather than forced, it becomes a foundation that strengthens the Rebel rather than restricting them.

Let these agreements be promises you make to yourself, born from empowerment rather than constraint.

The Saboteur

You move through life with a keen awareness of risk, consequences, and what might go wrong. You are perceptive, cautious, and deeply attuned to potential threats, often sensing danger before others do. This awareness has helped you survive difficult moments, making you adaptable and quick to retreat when something feels uncertain or unsafe.

Over time, self-doubt and hesitation became protective strategies. By delaying action, lowering expectations, or stepping back before fully committing, you learned how to shield yourself from disappointment, failure, or rejection.

While this instinct once kept you safe, it can quietly hold you back, leaving you stuck in cycles of procrastination or self-sabotage. Beneath this pattern lives a fear that trying fully might expose you to pain you do not know how to recover from.

Integration invites you to build trust in yourself slowly and gently. You do not need to rush into risk or force confidence. Instead, healing comes from taking small, deliberate steps and noticing that you can survive uncertainty. As you begin to honour your caution without letting it lead your life, your inner protector relaxes. What emerges is a steadier sense of self-belief, where discernment replaces fear, and your intuition becomes an ally rather than an obstacle.

Shadow Expression
Procrastination
Quitting early
Fear of success or failure
Minimizing goals
Staying "safe" but stagnant

Core Need
To build self-trust through small, safe steps forward

Practical Exercise

The Saboteur / Doubter Shadow

Reflection

- When did fear stop you this year, and what were you afraid would happen?
- What dreams or desires have you kept close but not acted on?

Practical Exercise

The Saboteur / Doubter Shadow

Gratitude

- What small steps did you take that you have not yet acknowledged?
- What are you grateful for in the way you have protected yourself?

Practical Exercise

The Saboteur / Doubter Shadow

Restoration

- What is the part of you trying to protect you from?
- What do you actually need right now instead?

Integration

To integrate the Saboteur is to understand how hesitation once kept you safe. There were times when trying fully carried real risk. Hope led to disappointment, effort led to failure, or visibility led to pain. Your system learned that pulling back before the stakes rose was safer than entering and losing. Delay, distraction, or doubt became ways to protect you from emotional harm.

This archetype protected you by reducing exposure. By postponing action or lowering expectations, you preserved a sense of control. If you never fully entered, you never fully failed. For a time, this kept you emotionally intact.

Over time, the cost emerged. You may notice cycles of motivation followed by paralysis, frustration with yourself, or a sense that you are capable but unable to move. Your nervous system continues to respond as though effort equals danger, even when the threat is no longer present.

Through this work, you begin to recognise that fear is not evidence of incapacity - it is memory. The conditions that required withdrawal have changed, but your system has not yet updated.

Integration unfolds through patience. Small steps may initially trigger anxiety. Resistance can arise just as momentum builds. This is not self-sabotage failing to loosen; it is your nervous system recalibrating.

Gradually, trust forms through experience. You act and discover that the feared outcome does not arrive. Mistakes become survivable. Movement becomes possible again.

As the Saboteur integrates, caution turns into discernment. Action no longer feels dangerous - it feels deliberate. You are no longer frozen at the edge of possibility.

You are moving forward, carefully and consciously, with growing confidence.

Learning Type Adaptations

For meeting fear with compassion, building confidence, and dissolving self-doubt.

Visual Learners

Fear Web Diagram

- Draw a circle below, write a goal or desire you truly care about inside, something that feels meaningful but also slightly intimidating.
- Around this centre circle, begin drawing smaller circles or shapes that represent the fears, doubts, or limiting beliefs that hold you back. These might include fear of failure, fear of success, fear of being judged, fear of change, or fear of losing control.
- Once the web is complete, gently draw a line through each fear and write a softer, kinder belief beside it. For example:
    - Fear: *"If I fail, it will prove I'm not capable."*
    - Softer belief: *"I am allowed to learn as I go, and mistakes do not erase my capability."* or,
    - Fear: *"If I succeed, I will be judged or expected to do more."*
    - Softer belief: *"I can choose my pace and boundaries, even when things go well."*

This practice helps you visually transform fear into compassion, and shows you that you can hold your dreams without letting fear dictate your choices.

Auditory Learners

Courage, Breath and Affirmation

- Find a quiet space and sit comfortably. As you inhale, silently or aloud say the first part of the affirmation, **"I can do small things…"**
- Feel your breath rise as you invite courage into your body. As you exhale, finish the sentence, **"…without fear controlling me."**
- Let the breath fall gently as you release tension from your shoulders and chest.
- Repeat this for several rounds, allowing the words and the breath to settle into your nervous system.

This simple rhythm helps rewire the fear response by showing your body that action can be gentle, manageable, and safe.

Kinesthetic / Somatic Learners

Cutting the Rope Ritual

- Hold a small piece of string or thread in your hands.
- Take a slow breath and name one fear or limiting belief that has been holding you back.
- Feel the weight of that fear in your body, not to overwhelm yourself, but to acknowledge its presence.
- When you are ready, use scissors to cut the string and imagine the fear loosening its hold on you. You do not need to force anything to change.

This ritual simply signals to your subconscious mind that you choose to release even a small part of the fear that has kept you tethered.

It is a physical, symbolic gesture of freedom, courage, and new beginnings.

A space to draw or anchor what arose.

Reading and Writing

One Per Cent Daily Action Log

- Choose one very small step you can take each day toward a goal or change. This step should take no more than two minutes and should feel so achievable that your mind cannot argue with it.

As you complete these tiny actions, your mind begins to understand that progress does not require pressure or perfection. It teaches you that small, consistent movements build trust, confidence, and momentum.

This practice is especially powerful for The Saboteur, who often freezes when a step feels too big.

My goal/change is:

How Long Should You Practise This For?

This practice works best when you continue it every day for one full lunar cycle, which is around twenty-eight days. As a month of tiny, achievable actions gently retrains the mind to feel safe with progress, especially if you tend to freeze or hold back when steps feel too big.

If you find the practice comforting or motivating, you may extend it through the winter season or repeat it whenever fear begins to slow you down. The purpose is not to push yourself but to help your inner Saboteur discover that small, consistent movements can create trust, confidence, and steady momentum.

The transformation builds quietly, one day and one gentle action at a time.

	Done
1	◯
2	◯
3	◯
4	◯
5	◯
6	◯
7	◯
8	◯
9	◯
10	◯
11	◯
12	◯
13	◯

Done

14

15

16

17

18

19

20

21

22

23

24

25

26

27

28

29

30

31

The Seeker

You move through life guided by a deep longing for meaning, truth, and expansion. You are naturally drawn to questions of purpose, spirituality, and what lies beyond the surface of everyday life. Your inner compass is always searching for something more - more understanding, more connection, more depth - and this curiosity brings richness and vision to your world.

Over time, seeking became a way to cope with restlessness or dissatisfaction. When the present moment felt heavy, limiting, or unclear, turning toward what was beyond it offered relief and hope.

Yet this constant reaching can sometimes pull you away from the here and now, leaving you disconnected from your body or from the life unfolding in front of you.

Beneath your searching lives a quiet fear that if you stop moving forward, you might be left with emptiness or stagnation.

Integration invites you to anchor your wisdom in the present moment. Meaning does not disappear when you slow down; it deepens. As you learn to ground your vision into lived experience, your seeking transforms into embodiment. You discover that what you have been searching for is not somewhere else - it is revealed when you fully inhabit where you are.

Shadow Expression

Escaping into spiritual ideas
Chasing meaning but avoiding embodiment
Idealism
Difficulty staying present
Chronic searching

Core Need

To ground their wisdom into the body, the moment, and real-life action

Practical Exercise

The Seeker / Escapist Shadow

Reflection

- When did you drift this year, and what were you trying to escape?
- What insights or longings have shaped your journey?

Practical Exercise

The Seeker / Escapist Shadow

Gratitude

- What spiritual or intuitive experiences brought meaning to your life?
- What are you grateful to yourself for discovering or questioning?

Practical Exercise

The Seeker / Escapist Shadow

Restoration

- What grounds you gently into your body?
- What simple ritual brings your energy back into the present moment?

Integration

To integrate the Seeker is not to abandon the search for meaning, but to understand why seeking once felt necessary.

There was a time when the present moment felt insufficient. Life may have felt narrow, flat, or disconnected from something you sensed must exist beyond what you could reach. Looking ahead or elsewhere offered hope. Seeking became a way to stay alive to possibility when what was here felt limiting or incomplete.

This archetype protected you. Curiosity, imagination, and longing gave you direction when the ground beneath you felt uninspiring. For a long time, movement itself sustained you.

Over time, however, the cost of constant seeking may have appeared. You may notice restlessness when things settle, dissatisfaction with the ordinary, or discomfort with stillness. Your system learned to stay slightly ahead of itself; always reaching, rarely landing.

Through this work, you begin to see that seeking is not only curiosity, but a strategy your nervous system used to avoid stagnation or emotional weight. What once helped you endure may now pull you away from intimacy with your own life.

Integration unfolds through slowing down. At first, presence may feel uncomfortable. Emptiness, resistance, or boredom can arise where momentum once lived. This is not failure; it is learning how to remain.

Gradually, meaning begins to arise from lived experience rather than distant horizons. Purpose feels less like something to find and more like something to inhabit. Longing softens into presence.

As the Seeker integrates, you realise the path you were searching for has been forming beneath your feet all along.

Learning Type Adaptations

For grounding vision, returning to embodiment, and transforming searching into becoming.

Auditory Learners

Rooting Mantra Practice

- Find a quiet space where you can breathe deeply and let your attention settle into your body.
- Repeat the mantra slowly, either aloud or in a soft whisper: **"I return to my body. I root into the now."**
- Allow each repetition to draw your awareness downward, helping you reconnect with the present moment and inviting your spirit to settle gently into your physical form.
- Let the words become an anchor that brings you back to yourself whenever your thoughts drift into the realms of possibility, imagination, or anticipation.

Kinesthetic / Somatic Learners

Barefoot Grounding Ritual

- Stand on the earth or on a stable floor with bare feet, allowing the soles of your feet to make full contact with the ground beneath you.
- Soften your knees and breathe slowly as you imagine a steady current of energy flowing downward.
- Visualise roots gently extending from the bottoms of your feet, reaching into the soil or the foundation below you.
- Feel yourself held, supported, and connected to the present moment.

This ritual helps you return from the realm of dreams and ideas to the grounded reality where your visions can take shape.

A space to anchor what arose.

Reading and Writing Learner

Completion Journal

- Write a simple list of five things you once began but never finished. These may be projects, practices, intentions, ideas, or personal commitments that were left waiting for your return.
- Choose one item from the list that feels both manageable and meaningful.
- Then write a short reflection explaining why bringing this to completion represents spiritual growth rather than loss.

Completion is a form of grounding. It teaches the Seeker that wisdom is not only gathered but embodied through follow-through and closure.

1 ____________________

2 ____________________

3 ____________________

4 ____________________

5 ____________________

Reflection

Visual Learners

Earth and Sky Balance Chart

This practice helps you bring harmony between your spiritual vision and your grounded actions.

- In the Sky box, list your spiritual pursuits and inspirations. These might be meditations, rituals, intuitive ideas, or dreams. Add simple imagery, such as stars or clouds, to represent your inner expansion.
- In the Earth box, write the practical actions that support your daily life and help bring your visions into form. These might include routines, small tasks, body care, planning, or commitments. You can add grounding symbols like roots, stones, or leaves.
- When both boxes feel visually balanced, you have created a gentle reminder to live with one foot in the heavens and one firmly on the earth.

Return to this chart whenever you need to reconnect vision with action.

Sky

Earth

The Victim

You carry emotions with profound intensity, shaped by experiences that left you feeling hurt, abandoned, or unsupported. You feel deeply, remember vividly, and respond from a place of raw honesty. Life may have taught you that pain arrives without warning and that safety cannot be assumed. As a result, your nervous system often stays alert, scanning for signs of threat, disappointment, or loss.

Over time, helplessness became a way to survive. When circumstances felt too overwhelming to change, surrendering control may have been the only option available to you.

This pattern can linger, making it difficult to trust your own power or believe that things can turn out differently. Beneath this vulnerability lies a quiet grief for the support you needed but did not receive, and a fear that pain will repeat itself if you hope too much or reach too far.

Integration invites you to reclaim your energy slowly and compassionately. This is not about denying your pain or forcing strength where it does not yet exist. It is about recognising that survival itself is evidence of resilience.

As you learn to meet your emotions without collapsing into them, you begin to feel your inner strength returning. You discover that vulnerability and empowerment can live side by side, and that your sensitivity, once honoured, becomes a source of truth, connection, and quiet courage.

Shadow Expression

Helplessness
Emotional overwhelm
Blame and collapse
Dependence on rescue
Feeling stuck in old wounds

Core Need

To feel protected, validated, and supported while reclaiming personal power

Practical Exercises

The Victim / Survivor Shadow

Reflection

- When did you feel overwhelmed or small this past year, and what memory did it echo?
- What emotions have you been carrying quietly inside me?

Practical Exercises

The Victim / Survivor Shadow

Gratitude

- What support, comfort, or softness touched you this past year?
- What are you grateful to your past self for enduring or surviving?

Practical Exercises

The Victim / Survivor Shadow

Restoration

- What would comfort your inner child right now?
- What helps you feel safe enough to exhale?

Integration

To integrate the Victim is not to deny your pain, but to understand how helplessness once made sense.

There were times when you did not have power. Circumstances felt overwhelming, support was absent, or resistance only increased harm. Your nervous system learned that effort did not equal safety. Collapse, freezing, or withdrawal were not weaknesses - they were survival.

This archetype protected you by conserving energy. By yielding rather than fighting, you avoided further injury. Sensitivity became awareness. Endurance became quiet strength. For a long time, this strategy helped you survive what could not be changed.

Over time, the cost appeared. You may notice lingering powerlessness even when choice exists, or a tendency to shut down when challenged. Your body may respond as though danger is still present, even when it is not.

Through this work, you begin to recognise that the conditions requiring collapse have shifted. What once protected you may now limit movement, agency, and self-trust.

Integration unfolds gently. Moments of choice may feel unfamiliar at first. Grief, anger, or sensation can arise where numbness once lived - signs that feeling and capacity are returning.

Gradually, small experiences of strength emerge. You choose differently. You remain present. Your system learns that movement does not automatically lead to harm.

As the Victim integrates, vulnerability no longer equals helplessness. Sensitivity remains, but collapse softens. Power returns as steadiness.

You are standing again - slowly, carefully, and in your own time.

Learning Type Adaptations

For reclaiming inner strength, soothing overwhelm, and shifting from pain to empowerment

Visual Learners
Inner Child Timeline

- In the space below, draw a simple line that represents your life from childhood to the present moment. Begin marking the moments where emotional injuries, disappointments, or significant hurts occurred. There is no need for detail, only a gentle acknowledgement.
- Then add small symbols beside these moments to represent the strengths you gained along the way. These might be stars for resilience, hearts for empathy, leaves for growth, or any shape that feels right to you.

This visual practice helps you witness your story with compassion, reminding you that even in difficult times, your inner child developed strengths that now live within you.

Auditory Learners
Compassion Reparenting Phrase

- Sit in a quiet space where you feel safe and supported.
- Place a hand on your chest or belly and speak softly to the younger part of yourself.
- Repeat the phrase, **"I hear you. I will not abandon you again."**
- Allow the words to sink into your body at a pace that feels natural.
- Say them again and again until you feel a shift, a softening in your breath or your shoulders or your chest.

This simple phrase begins the process of reparenting, showing the wounded inner child that the adult version of you is here now, steady and present, offering the safety that was not available in the past.

Kinesthetic / Somatic Learners
Heart Holding Practice

- Sit or lie down in a comfortable place and hold a pillow, a blanket, or a soft cushion to your chest.
- Wrap your arms around it as though you are holding something precious.
- Begin to rock your body gently from side to side for one minute.
- Let the movement be slow and soothing.

This simple physical gesture allows the body to feel what the heart has long needed: warmth, holding, and reassurance. It sends a message of safety to your nervous system and offers your inner child the comfort they may never have received.

A space to anchor what arose.

Reading and Writing Learners

Letter of Power Retrieval

- Take a moment to breathe deeply before you begin writing.
- Then let the adult you speak directly to the child you.
- Begin with the sentence, **"Here is what I can give you now that no one gave you then…"**
- Allow the words to flow without pressure. You might offer love, protection, stability, validation, comfort, or understanding. You might offer the freedom to cry, to rest, to play, or to be imperfect.

This practice reconnects you with the power you have now, reminding your inner child that they are no longer alone. It is a gentle retrieval of the strength and safety that were missing when you needed them most.

All Learning Types
Final Reflection
To End This Wolf Moon Week

Before you move forward, take a moment to pause and settle into everything you have uncovered so far. Meeting your archetypes, exploring your shadow wolves, and witnessing the patterns that shape your inner world is powerful work, and it deserves a space to breathe.

Often, discovering your primary and secondary archetypes brings an immediate moment of recognition; an inner oh yes, a soft exhale through the body, a sense that something long-hidden has quietly stepped into the light. These archetypes do not judge you; they reveal you. They offer language for the emotional instincts you have carried for years, and they illuminate why certain wounds feel familiar, why certain reactions arise without thought, and why certain healing paths feel more natural than others.

Use the space below to reflect gently on any emotions, memories, sensations, or insights that surfaced during this process. You may wish to journal freely, capture fragments of understanding, or sit with the feelings that move through your body. Let this be a space without pressure - only honesty, compassion, and curiosity.

Let this reflection be a gentle bridge between who you have been and who you are becoming. There is no right way to capture your experience. Just honour whatever rises, knowing that this moment of honest witnessing is part of your integration.

Summary

“Shadow work
does not begin in darkness
- it begins in truth.“

You allowed yourself to stand in that truth with a rare and quiet kind of bravery. Most people spend their entire lives circling their discomforts, avoiding their deeper layers, or distracting themselves from the parts of their inner world that feel too tender to touch. But you did something different. You chose to meet yourself with honesty, curiosity, and compassion, and that choice alone marks a profound moment in your healing.

As you pause now, take a slow breath and notice how your body feels. Perhaps there is a softening, a stirring, or a sense of quiet recognition. These sensations are signs that your inner world is adjusting to being seen, acknowledged, and cared for. Next week, we will move more deeply into this process through the Mirror Gaze practice - a powerful yet gentle technique that helps dissolve resistance and allows you to see yourself with clarity and tenderness.

For now, let yourself rest inside the spaciousness you have created. Be kind to yourself - not only to the parts you find easy to love, but also to the parts that are learning to trust you again. Shadow work is not about dividing yourself into “good” and “bad.” It is about learning to hold all of you with care.

Rest
Soften
Trust the process
You have begun beautifully

Full Moon Ritual

Connecting with intuition and steady inner resilience
during the deepest part of winter.

Place the candle at the centre (if using one)
Set the stone or symbolic object beside it.
Light the candle and take several slow breaths, allowing your awareness to settle.

Close your eyes and imagine a quiet winter night. The air is clear. The world is still. This is a time for listening rather than action.

Name Your Strength - On the paper, write one quality that helps you endure challenging seasons. This may be courage, patience, boundaries, discernment, or trust in yourself.

Hold the paper and ask yourself silently:
"When do I know this strength is guiding me?"
Notice any sensations, memories, or feelings
that arise without trying to analyse them.

Anchor the Strength
Fold the paper and place it beneath the stone. This represents your strength being grounded and accessible, even when unseen.

When you are ready, place a hand on your heart and say:
"I trust the strength that lives within me.
I listen, I endure, I move with awareness."

Extinguish the candle if used

Aftercare - Keep the stone nearby/on your altar for the lunar cycle as a reminder of your inner guidance.

Why this ritual works - This ritual engages symbolic action and intuitive reflection, helping the brain integrate inner strength as a lived experience rather than an abstract idea. It aligns with the Wolf Moon's themes of awareness, endurance, and trust in instinct.

Going Deeper - Week by Week

How to Use the Weekly Exercises

Now that you have grounded yourself through reflection, gratitude, and restoration, you have created the inner stability needed for deeper shadow work. Your mind is clearer, your body more at ease, and your emotions steadier and more supportive. you are no longer entering this work from a place of tension or urgency, but from a space of grounded awareness.

What comes next invites you to move slowly into the deeper layers of your winter journey. The weekly exercises and full moon rituals will help you uncover what has been hidden, release what no longer serves you, and prepare the inner soil for the new beginnings of spring. Move gently. You have already done the hardest part by arriving here with openness and trust.

Each task focuses on one small, meaningful step, allowing you to explore your inner world without becoming overwhelmed. I have customised each task for your learning type so you can approach this in the way your mind integrates best. But still approach each week with curiosity rather than pressure. The exercises are meant to meet you where you are , not pull you into places you are not ready to go.

Some weeks may feel easy, others tender, and some may bring insights that take time to process. Move slowly, breathe deeply, and return to the practices that ground you whenever you need them. You do not need to complete each exercise perfectly or all at once. What matters is your willingness to show up for yourself in small, steady ways.

Each weekly exercise is a small step into the shadow, offering you gentle ways to explore what you have been avoiding, carrying, or suppressing. You will not be asked to force anything to change. Instead, you will be invited to witness, understand, and release at a pace that honours your emotional wellbeing. Combined with the powerful energy of the full moons, this winter journey becomes a time of honest self-discovery and deep inner healing.

Week 3 Date_______________

Last Quarter Moon -

Mirror Soft-Gaze: Seeing Yourself Clearly

The Last Quarter Moon brings a natural turning inward. It is a quieter lunar phase that encourages reflection and softening, making it the perfect container for meeting your own reflection with gentleness.

This week invites you into a practice of seeing yourself without judgment or analysis. Through soft-gaze work, you shift from evaluating your reflection to simply being with it, allowing hidden emotions to rise in their own time.

This practice helps you recognise the layers of self you usually overlook: the tiredness, the longing, the resilience, the sadness, the determination.

Much of shadow work is about being willing to truly see yourself - to meet the version of you that has been waiting for acknowledgement.

The Last Quarter Moon encourages humility, honesty, and tenderness. It helps you release the habit of self-scrutiny and replace it with presence.

The Science Behind Mirror Soft-Gaze

Softening your gaze in the mirror gently signals the nervous system to shift from a state of vigilance to a state of safety. When the eyes relax, the brain interprets this as a cue that there is no immediate threat. This activates the parasympathetic nervous system, the branch responsible for calm, connection, and emotional processing.

In moments of stress or self-judgment, the sympathetic nervous system (the fight–or–flight response) becomes dominant, making us hypercritical, tense, and emotionally guarded. But when your gaze softens, your facial muscles release, your breath slows, and your vagus nerve sends calming signals throughout the body. In this state, the prefrontal cortex (the part of the brain responsible for insight, compassion, and emotional regulation) becomes more active.

This creates an ideal internal environment for shadow work. Rather than reacting with self-criticism or avoidance, your brain becomes more open to curiosity, acceptance, and gentle self-awareness.

Practical Exercise

Learning Type Adaptations

Mirror Soft-Gaze

Sit in front of a mirror and soften your gaze until your features blur slightly. Instead of analysing what you see, allow yourself to feel what is present. Then follow the prompts for your learning type.

Auditory Learners

Speak softly to the part of you that appears

- Try saying: ***"I see you. I'm willing to know you."***
- Listen to your tone as you speak. Notice shifts in emotion, tenderness, or resistance. Your voice becomes a bridge between the conscious mind and the shadow.

Kinesthetic Learners

Trace Your Face in the Mirror

- Run your fingertip slowly along the outline of your face while breathing softly.

This grounds your nervous system and creates somatic safety as you meet yourself.

- Feel the warmth of your skin, the shape of your expression, and the presence of your body.

Visual / Creative Learners

Draw the Emotion you see

- Instead of writing, let colours and shapes express what appears in your reflection. Notice which colours you reach for instinctively, and allow the page to become a visual mirror of your internal state.

A space to draw or anchor what arose.

Reading / Writing Learners

- Use the Three Reflection Questions:

1. What emotion do you see?
2. What is it protecting?
3. What does it need?

Let your answers be short, honest, and gentle. Do not overthink - just respond to what arises.

Week 4

Date_______________

New Moon

Emotional Transparency

The New Moon is the darkest point in the lunar cycle, a time of stillness and inner listening. This week encourages you to turn your attention toward your emotional landscape. Rather than trying to change your feelings or understand them intellectually, you simply notice what is present. This is foundational work. Emotional awareness is the doorway through which the rest of your shadow work will pass.

Many of your patterns were formed before you had language for your feelings. Learning to recognise and name your emotions now allows you to bring clarity to places that once felt confusing.

This week, you create a gentle space inside yourself where emotions can be acknowledged rather than suppressed, so as you learn to recognise the signals your emotions send, you also learn how to respond to them with sensitivity and care.

The Science Behind Emotional Awareness

Emotional awareness is one of the most powerful foundations of shadow work, as it teaches your nervous system that your inner world is safe to explore and feel. When you take a moment each day to recognise and name what you are experiencing, the brain shifts from survival mode into calm presence.

Neuroscience reveals that simply naming an emotion can reduce its intensity by soothing the amygdala and activating the parts of the brain responsible for clarity and regulation.

Emotions always begin in the body before the mind interprets them, so by gently noticing what you feel and responding in a way that matches your natural learning style, you strengthen the pathways that allow you to understand yourself with compassion instead of judgment.

Did you know?

You have between 80,000 and 90,000 thoughts each day, and these thoughts can evoke hundreds of emotional states. Some emotions pass through you in just a few seconds, while others can linger for days, weeks, or even months. Understanding this helps explain why emotional work is not about controlling your thoughts, but about learning how to gently regulate and support your inner world as it moves.

Emotional awareness changes your brain:

✔ Naming an emotion reduces amygdala activation
Research shows that "affect labelling" reduces emotional intensity by up to 50%, calming your threat response.

✔ The prefrontal cortex becomes more active
You shift from reaction to response, increasing clarity and self-control.

✔ The vagus nerve strengthens
This improves emotional regulation, grounding, digestion, and your overall sense of safety.

✔ Stored or suppressed emotions begin to move
Once named, emotions no longer need to shout for your attention.

✔ Shadow parts feel acknowledged
When your emotional landscape becomes safe to explore, the deeper layers of your psyche begin to trust you.

This is why emotional naming is foundational in shadow work: You cannot heal what you cannot acknowledge.

Practical Exercise

Daily Emotional Awareness Practice

Your emotions are not random; they are signals from your nervous system.

Each one carries information:

- Fear points to a need for safety.
- Sadness points to a need for support or release.
- Anger points to a boundary crossed.
- Joy points to alignment.
- Numbness points to overwhelm or exhaustion.

When you learn to recognise your emotions without resistance, the shadow begins to open gently.

This daily practice helps you build that awareness in a soft, daily rhythm. Over time, it teaches your body that feeling is not a threat but an invitation to heal, making this exercise the most important step in preparing for deeper shadow work in the weeks ahead.

1. Pause for one minute each day
   - Sit quietly
   - Breathe slowly
   - Let your body settle

2. Ask three questions - gently, without forcing:

1. What am I feeling right now?
2. Where do I feel it in my body?
3. What might this emotion be asking for?

You do not need to fix anything. Awareness is enough.

3. Record it using your learning-type method (over leaf)

4. Close the practice with a breath
   - Place a hand on your heart or belly.
   - Tell yourself: "Thank you for feeling. I'm listening."

Practical Exercise

Learning Type Adaptations

Auditory Learners

- Name your emotion out loud - "I feel frustration in my chest."
- Record a short audio journal each day

The 3 Questions

1. *What am I feeling right now?*
2. *Where do I feel it in my body?*
3. *What might this emotion be asking for?*

A space to anchor what arose.

Kinesthetic Learners

Do a 30-Second Body Scan

- Close your eyes and slowly scan your body from head to toe.
- Notice where emotion lives - your chest, stomach, throat, shoulders, or jaw.
- Place your hand gently on that area.

This simple touch brings grounding and somatic safety, helping the body release tension and soften emotional intensity. Use the diagram below to record your findings - marking a place each day - over time, you will see a pattern of where you hold emotions in your body.

The 3 Questions

1. *What am I feeling right now?*
2. *Where do I feel it in my body?*
3. *What might this emotion be asking for?*

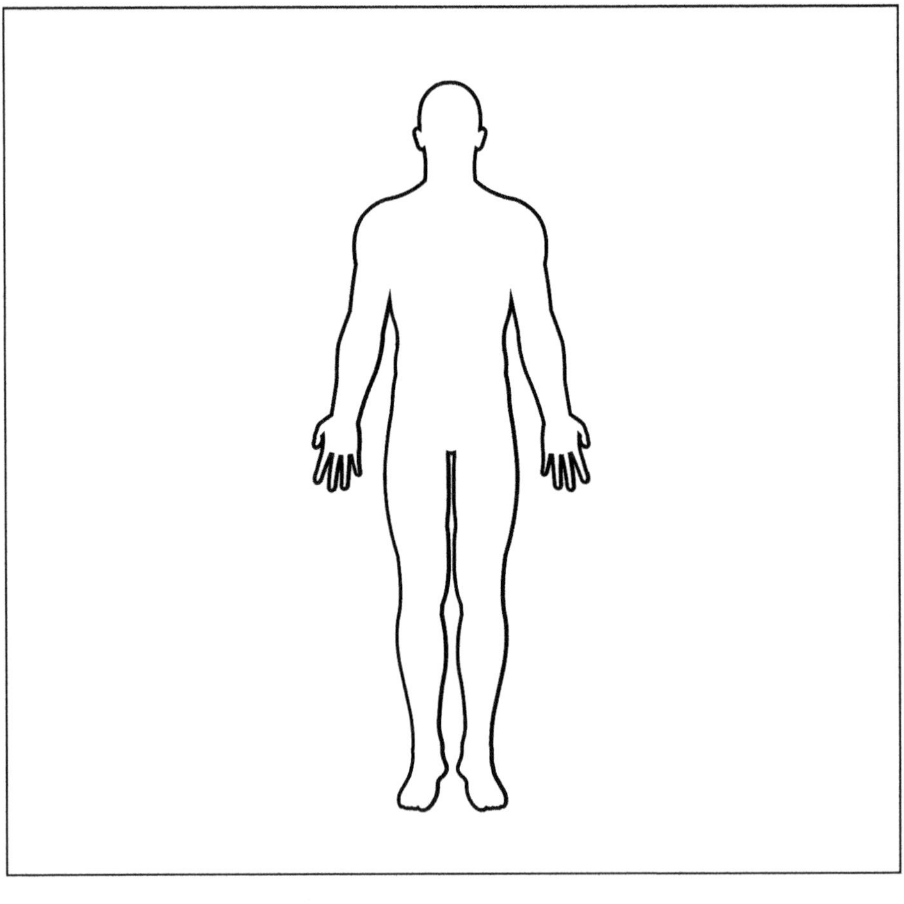

Visual / Creative Learners

- Colour-code your emotions eg

Red = anger
Blue = sadness
Green = fear
Yellow = joy
Grey = numbness

The 3 Questions

1. What am I feeling right now?
2. Where do I feel it in my body?
3. What might this emotion be asking for?

Mark where you feel emotion in your body

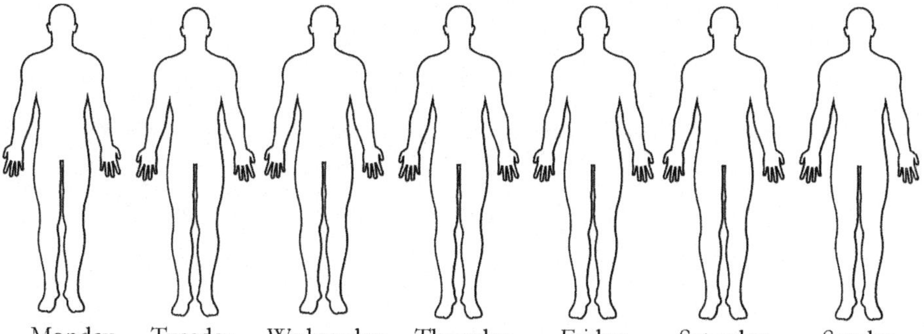

Monday Tuesday Wednesday Thursday Friday Saturday Sunday

Reading / Writing Learners

Use an Emotion Wheel

- Use the one below or print an emotion wheel from my website and have a copy nearby. Use it to identify the exact feeling instead of settling for broad words like "fine," "tired," or "stressed."
- Choose the most precise emotion, then journal, overleaf:
  - This emotion feels like…
  - It might be signalling…

This helps you articulate your emotional experience with precision and gentleness.

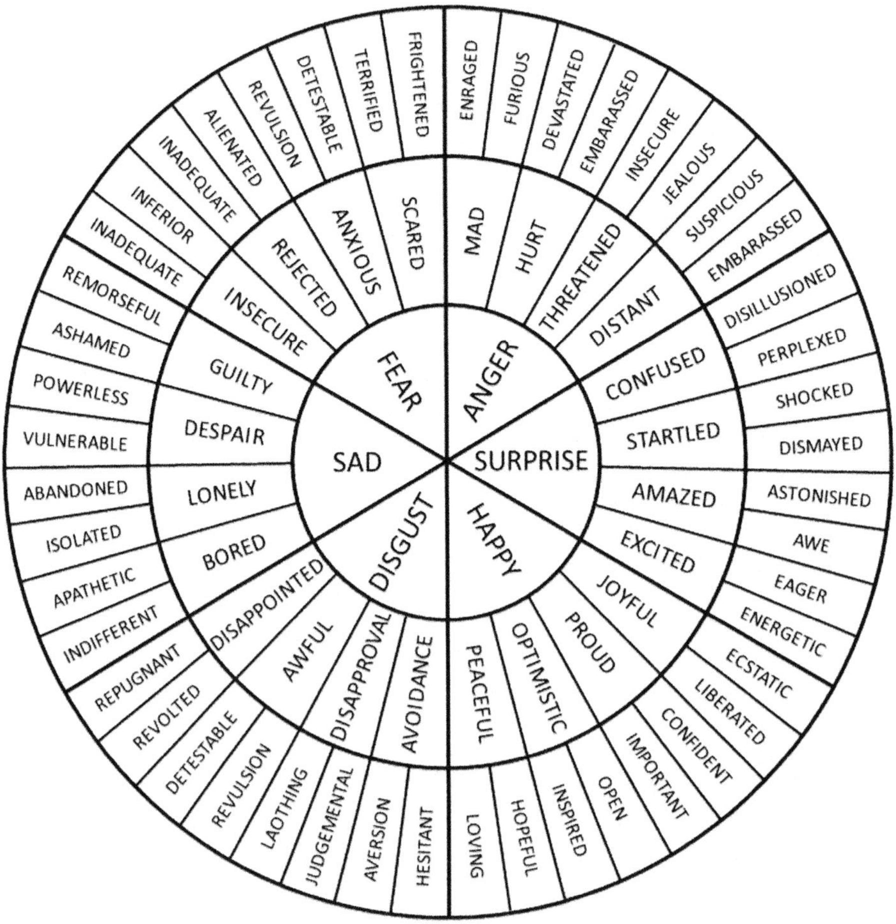

Monday

This emotion feels like... ______________________________

It might be signalling... ______________________________

Tuesday

This emotion feels like... ______________________________

It might be signalling... ______________________________

Wednesday

This emotion feels like... ______________________________

It might be signalling... ______________________________

Thursday

This emotion feels like... ______________________________

It might be signalling... ______________________________

Friday

This emotion feels like... ______________________________

It might be signalling... ______________________________

Saturday

This emotion feels like... ______________________________

It might be signalling... ______________________________

Sunday

This emotion feels like... ______________________________

It might be signalling... ______________________________

Practical Exercises

Archetype - Specific Processing

Each archetype has its own way of reacting when a feeling rises to the surface. These prompts help you see how your inner patterns influenced your emotional response this week so you can meet yourself with compassion rather than criticism.

The Caretaker

You instinctively move toward supporting others even when your own feelings need attention. Ask yourself:

- Which emotion did you minimise because someone else's needs felt more important than yours?
- Where did you silence yourself in order to keep the peace?

The Controller

You often respond to emotion by tightening your grip on order, structure or prediction because control feels safer than uncertainty. Ask yourself:

- Which emotion made you want to manage, organise or contain everything around you?
- What deeper fear or need were you trying to stabilise through control?

The Creator

You translate emotions into ideas, projects, or expression, sometimes bypassing the raw feeling itself. Ask yourself:

- Which emotion did you turn into something productive or creative?
- What feeling wants to be felt before it is expressed?

The Innocent

You may move away from emotions that feel heavy or complex, preferring optimism or simplicity. Ask yourself:

- Which emotion felt too difficult or unsettling to acknowledge?
- What truth might you be protecting yourself from seeing fully?

The Lover

You experience emotions through connection, attachment, and closeness to others. Ask yourself:

- Which emotion arose around connection, distance, or longing?
- What fear surfaced when closeness felt uncertain or threatened?

The Magician

You seek understanding and insight when emotions feel destabilising, retreating into inner worlds or concepts. Ask yourself:

- Which emotion did you try to transcend or rise above?
- What feeling wants to be grounded in your body rather than transformed?

The Outsider

You tend to retreat, detach or observe from a distance when emotions feel overwhelming or misunderstood. Ask yourself:

- Which emotion made you pull away or feel separate from others?
- What part of you feared that expressing this feeling would not be accepted?

The Performer

You manage emotions by shaping how you appear, staying composed, or performing strength. Ask yourself:

- Which emotion did you hide, soften, or perform around?
- What do I fear might happen if I showed how I truly feel?

The Rebel

You often react with defiance or resistance when a difficult emotion touches a deeper wound or old restriction. Ask yourself:

- Which emotion made me want to push back, resist or reject the situation?
- What truth or vulnerability was hiding beneath the urge to rebel?

The Saboteur

You often interrupt your own progress when emotions become uncomfortable, familiar or threatening to your sense of identity. Ask yourself:

- Which emotion made you want to step back, avoid or undo your own growth?
- What fear was trying to keep you safe by stopping you from moving forward?

The Seeker

You interpret emotions as signals for deeper meaning, insight or spiritual significance, yet you may escape into reflection rather than feel the emotion fully. Ask yourself:

- Which emotion did you try to analyse instead of simply experiencing it?
- What feeling is asking to be felt rather than understood?

The Victim

You may feel powerless or overwhelmed when big emotions rise, especially when they echo old wounds or experiences of helplessness. Ask yourself:

- Which emotion made me feel as though I had no choice or no voice?
- What part of me was asking to be heard, supported or protected?

"You do not have to banish your shadow. You only have to bring it home."

Teanna x

Week 5 Date______________

First Quarter Moon

Meeting the Inner Protector or Going Deeper with Archetypes

The First Quarter Moon carries a steadying energy that supports reorientation, clarity, and the strengthening of inner foundations. As the Moon begins to build toward fullness, the psyche becomes more alert and more capable of meeting itself with honesty.

Over the last month, you have already engaged in meaningful depth work - you should have identified your primary and secondary archetypes, noticed recurring patterns, or begun to see parts of yourself that were previously hidden.

For some, this process has felt illuminating and expansive;m for others, it may have felt slow, emotionally charged, confusing, or unexpectedly difficult.

If this work has felt challenging, there is nothing wrong with you - and nothing wrong with the process.

Very often, when we delve deeper into the layers of the psyche, a protective response becomes active. These responses are known as **Inner Protectors**. They are not personality traits or flaws, but nervous system strategies that formed early to keep you safe when choices, language, or support were limited.

Inner Protectors operate automatically through the body. When something feels unfamiliar, intense, or threatening to existing patterns, the nervous system may respond through **fight, flight, freeze, or fawn.** You might notice this as resistance, overthinking, withdrawal, emotional numbness, irritability, caretaking, or a sense of being stuck. These reactions are not signs of failure - they are signs that something important is happening.

Up until now, much of the work has focused on archetypes - symbolic patterns of identity, meaning, and becoming. Archetypes help us understand who we are and how we move through the world. Inner Protectors operate at a different layer. They are concerned not with meaning, but with safety. When a protector is active, the psyche is oriented toward survival, which can make archetypal shadow work feel overwhelming or inaccessible.

This week is not about undoing what you have already explored. It is about creating the conditions that allow that work to deepen. By learning to recognise and acknowledge your Inner Protectors, you give the nervous system the reassurance it needs to soften. When protectors feel seen rather than challenged, they no longer need to work as hard. Choice begins to return.

Everyone has all four protector responses. One may have learned its role earlier and worked longer than the others. Becoming aware of this does not take you backwards - it allows you to move forward with greater steadiness, clarity, and care.

This week invites you to pause, orient, and create internal safety. From this place, the deeper layers of archetypal shadow work can continue to unfold - not through force, but through trust.

"Every inner protector was once a solution, formed in a moment when safety was not guaranteed."

Teanna x

Practical Exercises

Choosing How to Work This Week

This week offers two equally valid pathways. The invitation is not to choose the "right" one, but the one that best supports your system right now.

You may move between these pathways over time - even within the same week, as this is not a linear process.

Decision Checklist: Which Pathway Supports You Today?

Read through the statements below and notice what resonates most in your body, not just your mind.

You may benefit from Pathway One (Protector Support) if you notice:

□ Resistance, avoidance, or procrastination around the work
□ Feeling emotionally overwhelmed, shut down, or numb
□ Overthinking, distraction, or difficulty staying present
□ Strong emotional reactions or irritability
□ A sense of being "stuck" or disconnected from insight

You may benefit from Pathway Two (Archetypal Deepening) if you notice:

□ A general sense of steadiness and emotional availability
□ Curiosity rather than urgency or fear
□ Ability to reflect without becoming overwhelmed
□ A felt sense of capacity to explore shadow material
□ Interest in going deeper with primary and secondary archetypes

If you resonate with both lists, start with Pathway One.

Safety always supports depth.

Pathway One
When an Inner Protector Is Active
(Stabilising and Creating Safety)

Inner Protectors are not archetypes or personality traits. They are **nervous-system responses** - instinctive strategies that emerge in moments of perceived threat. When safety was uncertain, the body learned one or more ways to respond automatically: to **fight, flee, freeze, or fawn**. These responses shaped four protector families:

- The One Who Pushes Back (fight)
- The One Who Moves Away (flight)
- The One Who Goes Still (freeze)
- The One Who Moves Toward (fawn)

Each protector expresses itself through behaviours such as control, withdrawal, perfectionism, anger, caretaking, humour, compliance, or silence. These expressions may resemble familiar archetypes, but they are different in nature. Archetypes describe patterns of identity and meaning; protectors describe how the body learned to survive. They are not who you are - they are what you learned to do.

These strategies were once adaptive and protective, helping you navigate emotional overwhelm, instability, or unmet needs. Over time, however, they can become rigid patterns that limit emotional healing, authentic connection, and inner freedom.

This week's work is not about dismantling these protectors, but about recognising them as allies that have been working hard for a long time. When their purpose is acknowledged, and reassurance is offered, they begin to soften. The protector shifts from reacting out of fear to working in partnership with the adult self. This creates the internal safety needed for deeper shadow work in the weeks ahead, because true transformation can only occur when the nervous system feels safe.

Practical Exercises

Inner Protector Discovery Quiz

Which Protector Learned Its Job First?

How to take the quiz:
Read each question and choose the answer that feels most true instinctively. Choose the option that reflects what you actually do under stress. There are no wrong answers - each response points to a protector that once kept you safe.

Keep track of the letter you choose most often (A, B, C, D, etc.).

1. When conflict arises, you tend to:
A. Push back or take control
B. Get busy or mentally check out
C. Go quiet or shut down
D. Smooth things over

2. As a child, safety often meant:
A. Being strong or right
B. Being fast, clever, or unavailable
C. Being unnoticed
D. Being liked or needed

3. Under stress, your body usually:
A. Tenses and braces
B. Becomes restless or jittery
C. Feels heavy or frozen
D. Softens and scans others

4. When emotions feel intense, you:
A. Argue, organise, or assert
B. Distract yourself or escape
C. Withdraw or numb out
D. Caretake or reassure

5. You feel most threatened when:
A. You lose control
B. You feel trapped
C. You feel overwhelmed
D. You feel rejected

6. In relationships, you often:
A. Lead or set boundaries
B. Keep moving or avoid depth
C. Stay distant
D. Adapt to others

7. When criticised, you:
A. Defend or counter
B. Deflect or leave
C. Shut down
D. Apologise

8. Rest is hard because:
A. You must stay alert
B. Stillness feels unsafe
C. You lose energy
D. Others may need you

Tally your answers!

A's	B's	C's	D's

Mostly A

The One Who Pushes Back (Fight)

Your strength kept you safe. Now it is learning how to rest without danger.

Protective orientation:
Against threat

Core belief:
"I stay safe by meeting force with force."

Protective behaviours may include:
Anger, control, perfectionism, criticism, intensity, confrontation, and taking charge.

Body signals:
Tension, heat, bracing, jaw or fist clenching.

When overworked:
Rigidity, reactivity, burnout.

Mostly B

The One Who Moves Away (Flight)

Your movement kept you safe. Now you are learning how to stay without fear.

Protective orientation:
Away from the threat

Core belief:
"I stay safe by getting out."

Protective behaviours may include:
Avoidance, busyness, distraction, overthinking, restlessness, emotional evasion

Body signals:
Restlessness, shallow breath, scattered energy.

When overworked:
Anxiety, inability to settle, emotional bypassing.

Mostly C

The One Who Goes Still (Freeze)
Your stillness protected you. Now you are learning gentle return.

Protective orientation:
Out of threat awareness

Core belief:
"If I don't move or feel, nothing can hurt me."

Protective behaviours may include:
Withdrawal, numbness, dissociation, silence, collapse, passivity.

Body signals:
Heaviness, low energy, fog, slowed response.

When overworked:
Depression, isolation, disconnection from desire.

Mostly D

The One Who Moves Toward (Fawn)
Your care created safety. Now you are learning to include yourself.

Protective orientation:
Toward others

Core belief:
"I stay safe by keeping connection."

Protective behaviours may include:
People-pleasing, caretaking, adapting, appeasing, emotional vigilance.

Body signals:
Softening, leaning in, hyper-attunement.

When overworked:
Resentment, exhaustion, loss of self.

The Science Behind the Inner Protector

Your Inner Protector is not a flaw - it is a survival response shaped by the nervous system. When the brain senses threat, the amygdala activates quickly, triggering fight, flight, freeze, or fawn responses before conscious thought. These responses once helped you survive emotional overwhelm or lack of support, but over time, they can become automatic patterns.

When you meet your Protector with awareness and compassion, the prefrontal cortex (responsible for regulation and choice) re-engages. The nervous system settles, and protective reactions begin to soften.

These protectors formed when choice was limited. Awareness allows them to work with the adult self rather than from fear. The body learns a new message: *I am safe now.* With repetition, old pathways gently rewire, creating space for more grounded, intentional responses

Practical Exercise

Learning Type Adaptations

Reading / Writing Learners

- Write a Letter to Your Protector. Begin with: ***"I see you. I know you are trying to keep me safe."***

Then answer these prompts:

- When does my protector take over?
- What fear is underneath its behaviour?
- What would I like my protector to know about who I am now?
- What new way of protecting would feel gentler, calmer, or wiser?

Kinesthetic / Somatic Learners

Embodied Soothing Practice

- Place one hand on your heart and one on your belly.
- Slow your breath until your shoulders drop.
- Then gently speak: ***"I am safe now."***
- Next, take one small movement that represents softness - unclenching your jaw, lowering your shoulders, stretching your hands open.
- Let the body signal safety to the mind.

Auditory Learners

A Dialogue With Your Protector

- Sit quietly and speak aloud to the part of you that reacts first. Ask it:
    - "What are you trying to protect me from?"
    - "When did you first learn you had to do this?"
    - "What do you need from me now?"
- Then speak back as your calm adult self:
    - ***"I hear you. Thank you for protecting me. You are not alone anymore."***

Visual / Creative Learners

Draw Your Protector

- Close your eyes, feel where tension lives in your body, and imagine the shape, colour, or form of your protector. Then draw it without judgment.
- After drawing, ask:
    - What does this form protect me from?
    - What is it afraid will happen if it lets go, even briefly?
    - What would help it feel safe right now?

A space to draw or anchor what arose.

Practical Exercises

Explore Your Archetypes

Identify your primary and secondary archetypes, and respond to the prompts below using your preferred learning style. You may also wish to explore your tertiary archetype if it feels supportive.

Choose Your Learning Style:

Writer / Reader
Write your answers down, then read them back to yourself.

Auditory
Record your answers and listen back to them.

Kinesthetic / Somatic
Walk, move, or gently stretch while speaking your answers out loud.

Creative
Express your answers through drawing, collage, poetry, movement, music, or symbolic imagery. Let meaning emerge without forcing words.

The Caretaker

- Whose feelings or needs are you prioritising over your own?
- What emotion of yours needs attention?
- What would it feel like to include yourself in your care?

The Controller

- What outcome are you trying to prevent or manage?
- What feels unsafe about allowing space instead of control?
- What might become possible if control softened?

The Creator

- What wants to be expressed but feels unfinished or blocked?
- What fear arises around visibility or imperfection?
- What would it feel like to create without outcome or approval?

The Innocent

- Where do you seek safety through simplicity, hope, or trust?
- What reality feels hard to face?
- How can discernment coexist with openness?

The Lover

- Where do you hold back from fully opening or receiving?
- What feels risky about intimacy, desire, or pleasure?
- What part of you longs for a deeper connection?

The Magician

- Where do you believe change is possible - or impossible?
- What power do you underestimate or misuse?
- How might you work with reality rather than trying to control it?

The Outsider

- What fear leads you to withdraw or stay on the edge?
- What does distance protect you from?
- What could connection offer that isolation cannot?

The Performer

- Where do you feel pressure to be seen, impressive, or acceptable?
- What happens when you stop performing?
- Who are you when no one is watching?

The Rebel

- What rule, expectation, or authority feels threatening?
- What part of you refuses to conform - and why?
- What freedom are you truly longing for beneath the resistance?

The Seeker

- What unknown are you hesitant to meet?
- What question keeps returning without resolution?
- What truth are you circling but not yet entering?

The Saboteur

- What success, stability, or intimacy feels unsafe?
- What do you fear you might lose if things go well?
- How could safety expand rather than shrink your life?

The Victim

- What part of you feels small, powerless, or overwhelmed?
- When did this belief first take hold?
- What strength or support have you forgotten you possess?

A space to draw or anchor what arose.

Pathway Two

Archetypal Shadow Deepening

(When the System Feels Settled)

Up to this point, you have already identified and explored your primary and secondary archetypes, and you may have noticed patterns in how you lead, relate, protect, desire, or withdraw. In this pathway, the focus shifts from identification to relationship: how these archetypes interact, where tension exists, and what has been held in shadow.

Shadow archetypes are not "negative" or wrong. They are often parts of the psyche that have been disowned because they felt unsafe, unacceptable, or incompatible with earlier environments. When the nervous system is regulated enough, these aspects can be approached with curiosity rather than defence.

This pathway invites you to deepen awareness without forcing insight. If at any point the work feels overwhelming or activating, you are encouraged to return to Pathway One. Moving between pathways is part of the work, not a disruption of it.

Core Focus

- Deepening relationship with primary and secondary archetypes
- Noticing shadow qualities without trying to resolve them
- Exploring identity with curiosity rather than self-judgment
- Allowing meaning to emerge slowly and symbolically

! A Gentle Reminder

If archetypal work begins to feel overwhelming, confusing, or emotionally charged, this is often a signal to return to Pathway One. This is not a step backwards - it is an act of self-trust.

If at any point the work feels too intense to manage on your own, please seek the support of a trained health or mental health professional. Asking for help is a sign of care, not failure.

Practical Exercise

Learning Type Adaptations

Choose the learning type that supports you best this week

Reader /Writer Learners

Archetypal Dialogue

Begin by writing the name of your primary archetype at the top of the page, and your secondary archetype beneath it. You may wish to divide the page into two sections, giving each archetype its own space.

Allow each archetype to speak in turn, responding to the same prompts. Write in the first person, as if the archetype itself is speaking through you.

Explore the following questions with each voice:

- **What do you want me to understand about you?**
- **What do you need in order to feel expressed or respected?**
- **What do you fear might happen if you were fully seen?**

Write continuously without editing, correcting, or censoring. Do not aim for clarity or coherence. Let the words arrive as they are.

If the voices overlap or contradict each other, allow this. Insight often emerges through contrast rather than resolution.

When you finish, pause before rereading. Notice any shifts in emotion, body sensation, or perspective. Meaning will reveal itself in its own time.

Visual Learners
Archetypal Mapping

Using drawing, symbols, colour, shapes, or collage, represent your primary and secondary archetypes on a page. Work intuitively rather than conceptually. Let images, marks, or placements arise without needing to explain them.

Place both archetypes on the page and pay attention to where they appear. Include the space between them—this is as meaningful as the figures themselves.

As you work, gently explore:

Which archetype feels closer, larger, or more dominant?

- Notice scale, colour intensity, or position on the page.

What exists in the space between them?

- Is it empty, crowded, tense, fluid, guarded, or open?

What feels hidden, distant, or emerging?

- Look for faint marks, unfinished edges, shadows, or areas drawing your attention.

There is no need for artistic skill or visual coherence. This is a symbolic process, not an aesthetic one. Meaning often reveals itself through shape, distance, and colour rather than conscious interpretation.

When complete, take a moment to view the page as a whole. Let the image speak before you try to understand it.

Kinesthetic / Somatic Learners
Archetype in the Body

Begin by gently bringing one archetype to mind, primary or secondary - allow the archetype to be present and notice how it shows up in the body.

Turn your attention inward and explore:

Sensation

- What physical qualities are present?
- You might notice tightness or softness, warmth or coolness, heaviness or lightness, contraction or expansion. Let the sensations be as they are, without trying to change them.

Breath

- Observe how the breath responds.
- Is it restricted or flowing? Shallow or deep? Held in certain areas or moving freely? Notice without forcing the breath to adjust.

Posture and Movement

- Sense the body's shape.
- Is there an impulse to curl, brace, lean forward, pull back, stand tall, pace, or remain still? You may allow small, slow movements if they feel supportive.

If it feels natural, place a hand on the area where the archetype is most present. Let the warmth and contact offer reassurance rather than correction.

Stay with the experience for a few moments. If sensations become too intense, confusing, or numb, pause. Ground yourself by feeling your feet, noticing the support beneath you, or orienting to the room around you. You can return to the exercise when the body feels settled again.

This practice is not about pushing through or resolving anything. It is about building awareness and safety, allowing the body to be included in understanding the archetype rather than being overridden by it.

A space to anchor what arose.

Auditory Learners
Archetypal Moment

Choose a recent situation where one archetype was clearly present. This does not need to be dramatic - ordinary moments often reveal the most.

Begin by speaking aloud about the situation, as if describing it to a trusted listener. Let your voice move at a natural pace.

Explore the following prompts verbally:

Which archetype was leading in this moment?

- Name it gently. Notice how it sounds to say it out loud.

Where was the secondary archetype?

- Was it supporting, competing, quiet, or waiting in the background?

What choice did this dynamic create or limit?

- Describe what became possible, and what felt closed off.

As you speak, focus on what happened, not why it happened. Stay with tone, sequence, and lived experience rather than analysis or judgment.

If it feels helpful, record your reflection and listen back. Notice not only the words, but the emotion, pauses, and shifts in your voice. Often, meaning emerges through hearing yourself rather than thinking harder.

This practice invites understanding through sound, rhythm, and resonance—allowing insight to arise as you listen.

A space to anchor what arose.

Summary
Reorientation and Safety

Week Five invited you to slow down and listen more closely to how your inner world responds to depth and change. Some of you spent this week tending to Inner Protectors - noticing where fight, flight, freeze, or fawn responses became active and offering them reassurance. Others continued exploring archetypal patterns, deepening your relationship with primary and secondary archetypes from a place of relative steadiness. (you may have done both)

Both paths were part of the work.

Whether you focused on regulation or exploration, the intention of this week was the same: to strengthen internal safety and restore choice. By noticing how your nervous system responds, you create space to engage inner material with greater awareness rather than automatic reaction.

You may have discovered that protectors soften when they are acknowledged, or that archetypal insight deepens when the body feels safe. You may also have moved between these experiences, learning that regulation and depth are not separate processes, but interwoven.

Week Five was not about arriving anywhere. It was about preparing the ground.

The awareness you have developed here - of how you protect yourself, how you respond to challenge, and how your inner system seeks safety - creates the conditions for what comes next. As we move toward the Full Moon in Week Six, this foundation allows deeper truths to surface without overwhelm, and old patterns to be released with compassion.

However, this week unfolded for you; it has served its purpose.

The paths now rejoin - and the journey continues.

Week 6

Full Moon - Snow Moon

Breaking Old Self-Contracts

Discovering Your Old Contracts
Learning Type Adaptations
Archetype Adaptations
Nervous System Integration
Releasing Old Contracts
Creating New Contracts
Snow Moon Activation

Stillness and Reflection
The altar becomes calm, reflective, and minimal, like a snow-covered landscape

Layer/add: the cloth with a lighter fabric (white, cream, pale grey)
Add clear quartz, selenite, or amethyst
Include a bowl of water (or reflective surface)
Remove: Any items that feel heavy or overly symbolic

For the Old Contract Melt
Rice paper is the best, but normal thin paper will work
Pens, Bowl and Water

Meditation Online
"Holding the Quiet"
www.TeannaTaylor.com

Why We Have Contracts

As you begin to uncover your old self-contracts and gently release the emotional weight attached to them, you may notice that a space opens inside you, not as an absence or loss, but as something quietly alive and receptive, a fertile inner ground where new understanding and more empowered agreements can eventually take root.

Before moving too quickly to fill this space, it is important to understand why self-contracts exist at all, and why it is natural for more than one to surface as awareness deepens, because every human nervous system is organised around the pursuit of safety, especially in early life when safety is not logical or verbal, but deeply emotional and relational.

As children, we learn how to survive not by reasoning, but by sensing, watching, and adapting to the moods, expectations, boundaries, and availability of the adults around us, and from these experiences the psyche quietly forms inner agreements - emotional vows and unconscious promises - about how to behave, who to be, and what to suppress to belong, to avoid harm, or to remain connected.

These agreements often take the form of simple, powerful beliefs such as I must stay quiet to stay safe, I must be useful to be loved, I must stay small to avoid conflict, or I must stay in control so nothing falls apart, and while they may now feel limiting or outdated, they once served a real and necessary purpose.

- These contracts helped you belong when belonging felt uncertain.
- They helped you minimise pain when you had little power to change your environment.
- They helped you navigate circumstances you did not choose.

For this reason, it is important to meet them with respect rather than urgency, because self-contracts are not signs of failure or weakness, but evidence of adaptation, intelligence, and care for survival.

However, these same agreements can begin to restrict rather than protect, quietly shaping your confidence, influencing your boundaries and relationships, narrowing what you believe is possible, and limiting the choices you allow yourself to make, until they function like invisible walls around your potential rather than supports beneath it.

It is common to recognise more than one self-contract during this process, as different agreements are formed in response to different moments, relationships, and needs. This layering is not something to correct or resolve immediately, but something to approach with discernment and care.

If more than one contract becomes visible, it is wise to work with one at a time, beginning with the one that feels most active in your body and daily life right now, rather than the one that seems most significant intellectually, allowing yourself to stay with it long enough for understanding and softening to occur without pressure to move on.

Only when you feel resourced, grounded, and strong enough should you consider exploring another contract, and even then, it is always appropriate to pause, return to grounding, or step away entirely if the work begins to feel overwhelming, because integration happens through repeated experiences of safety, not endurance.

As an old contract loosens, the space it leaves behind does not need to be filled immediately, and there is no requirement to rush toward a new agreement, because this open space is where choice begins to reappear, and where the nervous system learns that it is no longer bound by rules formed under earlier conditions.

In time, and at a pace your system can trust, new contracts may begin to form consciously, rooted not in survival, but in clarity, self-respect, and present-day truth, allowing you to move forward not by reacting to the past, but by choosing how you wish to live now.

Approach this work as winter itself moves - slowly, patiently, and with respect for what has carried you this far - knowing that releasing one contract at a time, and only when you are ready, is not avoidance, but wisdom.

Week 6

Date______________

Full Moon - Snow Moon

Breaking Old Self-Contracts

The Snow Moon is a time of illumination, culmination, and truth revealed. This phase brings what has been working beneath the surface into clear view, not to judge it, but to make a conscious choice possible. Over the past weeks, you have laid important groundwork. You explored your primary and secondary archetypes, noticing patterns of identity, desire, and shadow. In Week Five, you were invited to pay attention to how your nervous system responds - whether through ease and curiosity, or through the activation of Inner Protectors whose role has always been to keep you safe.

This matters now.

Many of the self-contracts we carry - the silent agreements about who we must be, what we are allowed to want, or how we must behave to stay safe - were formed in moments when choice was limited. They are rarely conscious decisions. More often, they are upheld quietly by protectors working in the background.

The Snow Moon illuminates these contracts.

Self-contracts can sound like:

- I must stay quiet to be accepted.
- I am responsible for everyone else's emotions.
- I cannot trust anyone.
- I am not allowed to want more.

Many of these agreements are held in place by Inner Protectors - fight, flight, freeze, or fawn responses that once kept you safe. They were adaptive at the time. They shaped your reactions, your sense of identity, and the archetypal roles you learned to inhabit. Even when the original conditions changed, these contracts often remained.

The Snow Moon invites you to meet these contracts with honesty and gentleness. This is not a week for forcing change or dismantling defences. It is a week for recognising the moment in your life when these agreements felt necessary - and acknowledging the intelligence behind them.

When a self-contract is seen clearly, it begins to loosen.

When it is understood compassionately, it begins to soften.

When it is released consciously, it creates space for truth, freedom, and new possibilities.

Breaking a self-contract is not an act of rebellion or rejection. It is an act of compassion - a recognition that the person you once were did what they needed to survive, and that the person you are now has more choice.

This is one of the most transformative moments of the winter journey. As the Snow Moon illuminates your emotional landscape, you are invited to step out of inherited stories, outdated roles, and limiting identities. By releasing what no longer belongs to you, you prepare the ground for what comes next.

Before a new story can be written, the old one must be gently laid down.

The Science Behind Breaking Old Self-Contracts

Self-contracts are emotional and behavioural agreements formed during earlier stages of life when your younger self needed safety, acceptance or stability. They arise not through conscious choice but through repeated emotional experiences that teach the nervous system what is required to survive. A contract may have been created in childhood when love felt conditional, or during stressful periods when you learned to stay quiet, agreeable or invisible to avoid conflict or rejection. These unconscious agreements become embedded in neural pathways through repetition and emotional reinforcement, shaping how you respond to yourself and the world.

A self-contract often becomes an internal rule that governs your behaviour under stress. It might sound like, "I must be perfect to be loved," or, "My needs do not matter," or, "It is safer to stay small," or, "I must take care of everyone else to prevent abandonment." These are not logical beliefs but emotional truths formed by a younger version of you who coped as best they could. At the time, the contract kept you safe or connected. Yet the nervous system does not automatically update these old agreements, and what once protected you can later restrict you, influencing your confidence, boundaries and relationships.

"True awareness is becoming conscious of the subconscious."

Teanna x

When a self-contract is brought into awareness, the brain begins a process known as cognitive restructuring. Old neural pathways that maintained the contract weaken, while new pathways linked to more accurate and empowered beliefs strengthen. This process is amplified when emotions are engaged, which is why rituals and full moon ceremonies often feel so transformative. The emotional intensity signals the brain that change is happening, making it more receptive.

As you recognise the contract and thank it for its past role, you are consciously releasing it, thus reclaiming the space once occupied by fear or limitation.

Breaking a self-contract does not mean rejecting your past; it means understanding that you are no longer living in the circumstances that created it. You can say, with compassion, "I am no longer that child, and I no longer need this contract to survive." In that moment, you step into your adult self with greater clarity and choice.

Releasing an old contract creates room for a new one, a conscious agreement rooted in self-worth and truth. This is where deep transformation begins, not through force but through freedom.

Discover Your Old Contract

A self-contract is not a contract you consciously chose; it was formed by a younger version of you, usually during moments when you needed love, protection, acceptance or safety. Before you can release an old contract, you must be able to recognise it. If that feels a little overwhelming, the good news is even if you do not realise it, your old contract has already been speaking through the last few weeks. This is made up of:

- The emotions that repeat
- The behaviours you use to cope
- The stories you tell yourself
- The patterns you fall into
- The archetypes you identified
- The protectors you identified
- The way your body reacts under stress

Now we just need to identify the contract with clarity and compassion.

The following page has a list of the original contract clues from your archetype, but for these to truly be met and transformed, they need to be fine-tuned to you and your journey.

As before, each learning type discovers their contract differently, so read back through weeks 1 - 5 and complete the following prompts - if they become hard to complete, jump forward to your learning type excercise and complete this and then return here to complete the prompts.

To summarise: this week aims to find your original contract and break it

Tools available:

- Journal prompts to walk you through the process
- Predictable archetype clues
- Learning style exercises to help with the discovery in your way

Practical Exercise

Reflection: Archetypes, Protectors and Emotional Contracts

Using your archetypes and protectors, reflect on the prompts below. Move slowly. Insight emerges through honesty, not effort.

1 Follow the Emotional Thread

Every self-contract is rooted in an emotional survival strategy. Begin by reviewing your reflections from Weeks 1–5.

Then consider:

- **Which emotions keep showing up most often?**

(e.g. sadness, fear, anger, shame, disappointment, overwhelm)

- **Which feelings do you tend to avoid, suppress, or override?**

You may recognise internal rules such as:

- "It is not safe to be angry."
- "Sadness is unacceptable."
- "I must stay strong no matter what."

Write what emerges:

My repeating emotional pattern is:

____

____

____

____

____

____

____

____

2 How Do I Keep Myself "Safe"?

Every protective behaviour exists for a reason.

Each one points to a deeper, often unconscious vow, such as:

- "If I keep everybody happy, I will not be hurt."
- "If I stay in control, nothing bad will happen."
- "If I stay small, I won't be judged."

Reflect and write:

My protective behaviour is:

This behaviour exists because I once believed:

3 Return to the Childhood Rule

This is the heart of the old contract.

Ask yourself gently:

What version of me felt most acceptable to the adults around me?
What emotion was I punished, ignored, or shamed for expressing?
What did I learn I had to be in order to feel loved or safe?

4 The Forbidden Emotion

Some emotions become marked as unsafe, forbidden, or too much.

Which emotion feels this way for you?

You are not looking for blame or certainty - only understanding.

These patterns once protected you. Seeing them clearly is the first step toward choosing differently.

Practical Exercise

Archetype Specific Contract Clues and Prompts

Use your primary archetype as an anchor, as each one carries a predictable old contract. The prompt questions help reveal the hidden promise you made long ago-and what you are now ready to release.

The Caretaker

Your contract is often formed around earning love through giving.

Old Contract: "My needs do not matter."
Clue: You apologise for having needs, feelings or limits.

Prompts

- Who taught you that your worth was measured by how much you give?
- Where did you learn that prioritising yourself is selfish?
- What contract binds you to meeting everyone else's needs before your own?
- What part of you fears being abandoned if you stop overgiving?

New Contract Seed

"My needs matter as much as anyone else's. I deserve nourishment too."

The Controller

Your contract is often formed around safety, certainty, and self-reliance.

Old Contract: "I must manage everything to stay safe."
Clue: You tighten, plan or take charge when anxious.

Prompts

- What situation taught you that you must always be in control to avoid being hurt?
- Where did you learn that vulnerability equals danger?
- What contract have you kept that says, "It is safer if I handle everything myself"?
- What belief is stopping you from receiving help freely?

New Contract Seed

"I can be safe and supported without controlling every outcome."

The Creator

Your contract is often formed around expression, visibility, and fear of judgment or failure.

Old Contract: "I must only create if it is perfect or approved."
Clue: You delay, abandon projects, or hide your work.

Prompts

- When did expression become linked to approval or outcome?
- What happened the last time you were seen or criticised?
- What contract says, "If it's not exceptional, it's not safe"?
- What part of you wants to create simply because it exists?

New Contract Seed

"I am allowed to create without permission or perfection. Expression is enough."

The Innocent

Your contract is often formed around safety, goodness, and the avoidance of complexity or pain.

Old Contract: "If I stay hopeful and uncomplicated, I will be protected."
Clue: You avoid conflict, denial, or difficult truths

.

Prompts

- When did simplicity feel safer than discernment?
- What truth feels too heavy to hold?
- What contract says, "If I don't see it, it can't hurt me"?
- How has avoidance disguised itself as positivity?

New Contract Seed

"I can face reality and still remain open-hearted. Awareness does not destroy my goodness."

The Lover

Your contract is often formed around attachment, connection, and the fear of abandonment.

Old Contract: "I must be desirable, needed, or available to be loved."
Clue: You overextend emotionally or lose yourself in relationships.

Prompts

- When did love become something you had to earn or maintain?
- What part of you fears being alone or unchosen?
- What contract says, "If I stop giving, I will be left"?
- Where have you confused attachment with intimacy?

New Contract Seed

"I am worthy of love without self-abandonment. I can stay connected and stay myself."

The Magician

Your contract is often formed around control, insight, and the belief that awareness alone keeps you safe.

Old Contract: "I must understand everything to prevent harm."
Clue: You stay in your head, analysing, anticipating, or trying to foresee outcomes.

Prompts

- When did knowledge or insight become a form of protection for you?
- What are you trying to prevent by staying one step ahead?
- What contract says, "If I can see it coming, I won't be hurt"?
- What feels risky about not knowing or not controlling the outcome?

New Contract Seed

"I can trust life without mastering it. I am safe even when I don't have all the answers."

The Outsider

Your contract is often formed around self-protection and invisibility.

Old Contract: "I do not belong."
Clue: You detach before others can reject you.

Prompts

- When did you first feel you did not belong?
- What moment taught you to stay small or quiet to avoid rejection?
- Which contract says, "It is safer if no one sees the real me"?
- Where do you still hold back parts of yourself out of fear of being misunderstood?

New Contract Seed

"I belong where my truth is welcome. I am safe to be seen."

The Performer

Your contract is often formed around visibility, approval, and being valued for how you appear.

Old Contract: "I must be impressive to belong."
Clue: You feel anxious when not seen, validated, or applauded.

Prompts

- When did being noticed become necessary for connection?
- Who did you need to perform for in order to feel valued?
- What contract says, "If I stop performing, I will disappear"?
- Who are you when no one is watching?

New Contract Seed

"I belong even when I am not performing. My presence is enough."

The Rebel

Your contract is often formed around resistance and self-preservation.

Old Contract: "If I soften, I will lose myself."
Clue: You resist expectations, even supportive ones.

Prompts

- Who first tried to control, restrict, or silence you?
- What situation taught you that saying yes meant losing yourself?
- What contract says, "I must resist everything or I will be trapped"?
- Where are you rebelling out of habit rather than truth?

New Contract Seed

"I choose my path with clarity, not resistance."

The Saboteur

Your contract is often formed around fear of success, visibility or change.

Old Contract: "Good things are not safe for me."
Clue: You undo progress or create chaos at the edge of success.

Prompts

- When did striving or succeeding lead to pain, judgment, or loss?
- What moment taught you that getting what you want is unsafe?
- What contract says, "It is better to stay where I am than risk failure or disappointment"?
- Where do you hold yourself back because an old belief still whispers caution?

New Contract Seed

"I am safe to grow, succeed and expand beyond my past."

The Seeker

Your contract is often formed around searching, longing and the fear of settling

Old Contract: "I must keep striving to be enough."
Clue: You move goalposts, never feeling complete.

Prompts

- What moment taught you that contentment meant stagnation?
- Where did you learn that you must always be moving, changing or improving?
- What contract says, "I cannot rest because something better might appear"?
- What part of you fears choosing a path because it feels final?

New Contract Seed

"I am allowed to find fulfilment where I am. I can seek and still belong."

The Victim

Your contract is often formed around helplessness and emotional overwhelm.

Old Contract: "I am powerless to change things."
Clue: You feel stuck even when options exist.

Prompts

- What early experience made you feel powerless?
- Who taught you that your voice did not matter?
- What contract binds you to believing you cannot change your circumstances?
- Where do you underestimate your strength because an old story still leads?

New Contract Seed

"I am capable, resilient and able to choose differently now."

Optional - Learning Style Adaptations

Exploring the Childhood Contract

Complete the following exercise for **both your primary and secondary** archetypes. You may notice different rules, emotions, or body responses for each. This contrast is important.

Visual Learners

- Draw the version of you from childhood or adolescence that is most connected to the archetype you are exploring.
- Add words, symbols, or labels that describe what you learned you had to be in order to feel accepted or safe.
- When you finish, pause and observe:
    - Which word or label feels the heaviest?
    - Which one draws your attention again and again?

Do not analyse. Let the image communicate.

Auditory Learners

- Say the following sentence aloud, filling in the blanks instinctively:

"I learned I had to ______ in order to ______."

- Repeat it slowly.
- Listen closely to your voice.
- It may hesitate, soften, tighten, or speed up at the truth.

Space to note what came up is overleaf.

Kinesthetic / Somatic Learners

- Stand and speak each sentence aloud, one at a time:
  - "I must be perfect."
  - "I must stay small."
  - "I must stay strong."

- As you say each one, notice your body.
  - Where does it tighten?
  - Where does it brace, collapse, or hold?

Your body will respond most strongly to the sentence that holds the original contract.

Do not analyse. Let the image communicate.

Space to note what came up is overleaf.

Reader / Writer Learners

- Set a timer for five minutes and free-write the following sentence:

  "***When I was young, I believed I had to…***"
- Write without stopping. Do not edit or soften.
- Let the words arrive before your mind tries to organise them.
- The contract reveals itself through repetition, tone, or urgency.

Closing Note

These beliefs were once intelligent adaptations.
You are not trying to erase them, only to see them clearly,
so new choices become possible.

A space to draw or anchor what arose.

Sum it up - your answers
here directly reveals the original contract.

Write it as a sentence:

I learned I had to ____

____

____

in order to feel____

____

____

This sentence is your self-contract.

Take a moment to self sooth if needed.

Sum it up - your answers
here directly reveals the original contract.

Write it as a sentence:

I learned I had to ____

____

____

in order to feel____

____

____

This sentence is your self-contract.

Take a moment to self sooth if needed.

Snow Moon Ritual: Releasing the Old Contract

Letting go of outdated beliefs, roles, or inner agreements
with gentleness rather than force

Ritual Steps

Place the bowl of water at the centre
If using a candle, light it and take a few slow breaths, allowing your body and mind to settle. This is a ritual of softness, not effort.

On the rice paper, write what you are ready to release. This may be a belief, pattern, expectation, or role you once needed but no longer serves you.

Write simply, this is not a story, just an agreement you are done carrying.
Examples: ***"I must always be strong."***
"My worth depends on productivity."
"I am responsible for everything."

Hold the paper in your hands for a moment. Acknowledge that this contract once had a purpose and thank it for what it offered, without judgment.

Gently place the rice paper into the bowl of water and watch as the words soften, blur, and dissolve. Do nothing else - just observe.
Let the melting mirror the Snow Moon's quiet release,
where nothing is forced, and everything changes in its own time.
As the paper disappears, imagine space opening within you.
Not emptiness - but calm, clarity, and breath.

When you are ready, close by placing a hand over your heart and say
"What no longer serves me is released with kindness.
I make space for what is true."

Extinguish the candle if used

Aftercare - The water can be poured into the earth, a plant, or down the sink with intention, symbolising the return of the old contract to the wider cycle.

Why this ritual works - This ritual engages symbolic action, sensory awareness, and witnessed release, all of which help the brain process letting go more effectively than thought alone. Watching the words dissolve allows the nervous system to experience release as safe, gradual, and complete, perfectly aligned with the Snow Moon's energy of quiet transformation.

Week Six Summary

Week Six has been about illumination rather than action. Under the Snow Moon, you were invited to see more clearly the self-contracts that have quietly shaped your inner world, not to judge them or force them to change, but to recognise when and why they were formed. You explored how these agreements once served survival, how they may now limit choice, and how awareness itself begins to loosen their hold.

You may have worked with one contract, noticed several, or simply recognised patterns without naming them fully. All of these experiences are valid. This week was not about resolution or completion, but about creating the conditions for release by meeting the past with honesty, compassion, and respect for your nervous system's pace.

Whether something shifted dramatically or subtly, the work has already begun to do what it needs to do.

As the journey moves into Week Seven, the focus gently turns toward what becomes possible once old agreements begin to soften. Rather than breaking or discarding the past, you will be invited to listen for new language, new choices, and new ways of relating to yourself that emerge naturally from the space created. What comes next is not about forcing a new direction, but about allowing a more truthful one to take shape.

Week 7 Date_______________

Last Quarter Moon

Integration and Gentle Recalibration

The Last Quarter Moon marks a natural turning point in your winter journey. After the deep emotional release of the Snow Moon and the powerful work of identifying and dissolving an old self-contract, this lunar phase invites you into a quieter, more reflective space.

Transformation rarely happens all at once; it unfolds softly, layer by layer, as the mind and body adjust to the shift that has taken place. This week is not about doing more work or uncovering more shadow.

It is about listening inward with tenderness and allowing the changes you initiated to settle into your nervous system so they can become part of your lived experience.

When you released your old contract, you created a shift in identity. Even when this shift is positive and liberating, the nervous system needs time to integrate it. Old beliefs may briefly surface again, not because you have failed or because the release "didn't work," but because your inner world is reorganising itself around this new foundation. Think of this week as the gentle recalibration that allows your new truth to take root. You are learning how it feels to move without the old weight you once carried, and this requires softness, presence and patience.

During this integration phase, subtle insights may rise to the surface. You may become aware of behaviours that no longer fit the person you are becoming, moments where the old contract tries to reappear out of habit. All of this is normal. Integration is not linear; it is a conversation between the past you have released and the self you are stepping into. The more compassion you bring to this process, the easier it becomes for your new identity to stabilise.

This week is a time to observe rather than analyse, to deepen rather than push, to soften rather than strive. Instead of asking yourself to uncover something new, allow yourself to feel into what is already shifting. Support yourself with rest, reflection and grounding practices.

The Science Behind Integration

Much of who we are is shaped gradually. By the mid-twenties, the brain's core patterns are largely established, and by the mid-thirties, many responses, beliefs, and habits feel automatic. This is not a flaw; it is how the nervous system conserves energy. Becoming conscious of the subconscious takes time, repetition, and patience.

When you release an old self-contract, the emotional weight it carried does not disappear instantly. These beliefs were held not only in memory, but in neural pathways formed through years of repetition. In the days or weeks that follow, the brain may revisit familiar thoughts, emotions, or reactions as it updates its internal maps.

This is not regression.

It is memory reconsolidation - the process by which old emotional associations are reviewed, softened, and gradually replaced with new information.

After a meaningful release or ritual, the nervous system often enters a period of recalibration. The amygdala, which governs emotional memory and self-protection, may briefly activate old patterns as it reassesses safety without the context it once relied on. At the same time, the prefrontal cortex (responsible for insight, perspective, and conscious choice) begins strengthening the new narrative you are introducing.

This is why trigger awareness is so important, and why we will be exploring it next week.

For now, rest and reflect if you need to.

We will be creating new contracts in the spring, but for the moment, allow the space to remain open. As you practise self-compassion and integration, you may notice aspects of the following process unfolding. These stages do not always occur in a linear order, and you may move back and forth between them. They are offered as a way to understand what can take place within the nervous system over time, not as steps to complete or achieve.

How Integration Often Unfolds

1. An old narrative is activated
The amygdala signals "danger," and familiar emotional memories may surface. The body shifts into protection mode (fight, flight, freeze, or fawn).

↓

2. Memory enters a recall window
When a memory is remembered, the brain briefly becomes open to change. Emotional patterns loosen, creating space for new information.

↓

3. New meaning or perspective is introduced
Adult awareness, compassion, and context soften the emotional tone of the memory. What once felt absolute begins to feel negotiable.

↓

4. New neural pathways begin forming
The prefrontal cortex supports calm reflection and choice. Emotional intensity may decrease, even if gradually.

↓

5. Body-based practices support integration
Speaking, writing, drawing, or moving help anchor the new understanding in the nervous system. The body begins to register: I am safe now.

↓

6. New responses strengthen over time
With repetition:
Old pathways weaken
New pathways strengthen
Reactions soften
Identity becomes more flexible
The shadow integrates

↓

7. A new orientation emerges
I respond from who I am today, not from old wounds.

Optional Integration Reflection

Take a moment to settle your body before reading on.

You do not need to analyse or fix anything right now.

If you have noticed old thoughts, emotions, or reactions resurfacing, pause and remind yourself: **this is not a step backward.**

Your nervous system is learning how to move without something it once relied on.

What arises now is not a failure of change, but evidence that change is underway.

- You might gently ask yourself:
    - What feels unfamiliar or tender in this space of release?
    - Where do I notice sensations in my body when old patterns arise?
    - Can I meet this moment with curiosity rather than judgment?

There is no requirement to respond differently yet. Awareness alone is enough.

If emotions feel heightened, offer yourself reassurance.

- Place a hand on your body if it helps.
- Slow your breath.
- Let your system know it is safe to rest.

Integration happens quietly, often beneath conscious effort.
What is being reorganised does not need your force - only your presence.

For now, allow the space to remain open.
Nothing new needs to be decided.

Nothing needs to be filled.
We will return to conscious choice in time.

Until then, let this be a period of listening, softness, and trust.

Week 8

Date_______________

New Moon

Mapping Your Triggers

The New Moon arrives as a quiet companion on your winter path, offering a soft space for introspection and gentle truth. This lunar phase invites you to begin again with clarity and honesty, not by setting intentions but by opening your awareness to the deeper patterns that shape your emotional world. After the integration of last week, when your inner landscape was recalibrating around the release of an old contract, the New Moon brings a fresh moment of inward stillness that supports the next step in your shadow work journey.

This week is dedicated to understanding your emotional triggers, not as signs of weakness or flaws, but as tender indicators of unhealed places within you. A trigger is a moment when the past reaches into the present and asks to be acknowledged. It is a sudden emotional shift that reveals where an old wound, unmet need or outdated belief is still active beneath the surface of your awareness.

Triggers often arise around themes of rejection, abandonment, control, criticism, uncertainty or vulnerability. They may show up in your relationships, your self-talk, your reactions or your body. Although they can feel overwhelming in the moment, triggers are not enemies. They are messengers carrying vital information about the parts of you that are most ready for healing.

The New Moon's quiet energy makes it easier to observe these patterns with compassion. There is no pressure to fix anything or to understand everything all at once. Instead, this is a week of gentle awareness. Where you map your triggers, and you begin to see the emotional patterns that have shaped your reactions for years or even decades.

As you do this, you gain insight into what you protect, what you fear and what you long for. This simple act of noticing begins to restore your ability to choose how you respond rather than react out of habit or old conditioning.

As you move through the week, allow your observations to be soft and unforced. Pay attention to moments of tension in the body, shifts in mood, the urge to withdraw or defend yourself, or feelings of irritation, sadness or fear that seem larger than the moment warrants. These experiences reveal where the shadow is speaking. And as you listen with kindness, you begin to loosen the grip of old patterns and create space for new responses to emerge.

This work is not about eliminating triggers; it is about understanding them so you can meet your inner world with presence instead of reflex.

Awareness brings choice. Choice brings freedom. And freedom brings healing. The New Moon supports this process with its quiet, receptive light, offering you a stillness in which your inner truth can finally rise to the surface.

Move gently. Pay attention. Trust what you discover. Your triggers are not obstacles. They are guideposts on the path to your deeper self.

The Science of Trigger Mapping

A trigger is the nervous system's rapid response to a perceived threat, often rooted in past experiences. When something in the present resembles an old emotional wound, the amygdala activates before the logical mind has time to interpret what is happening. This can create a surge of emotion, physical tension or an instinctive behavioural reaction. These responses are automatic because they originate in neural pathways formed during earlier experiences, many of which were created when you were young and did not yet have the emotional or cognitive tools to process them.

Mapping your triggers allows the prefrontal cortex (the part of the brain responsible for insight, reasoning and emotional regulation) to engage again. By naming the trigger and observing the emotional reaction without judgment, you interrupt the automatic survival response and bring awareness back online. This shifts the brain from reactivity to reflection, creating a moment where you can choose your response instead of being carried by old patterns.

The act of recognising and naming a trigger also supports memory reconsolidation, a process through which old emotional associations are softened and rewritten in the presence of new information and emotional safety. Over time, this reduces the intensity of the trigger and strengthens new neural pathways that are based on conscious choice rather than past pain.

As your awareness grows, your nervous system learns that the emotional danger associated with the trigger is no longer present, and the body gradually stops reacting with the same intensity or speed.

Trigger mapping, therefore, becomes not only an emotional practice but a neurological one. It helps the brain update its internal model of the world and the self, transforming patterns of fear and protection into patterns of clarity and empowerment. Through this work, the shadow becomes less threatening and more understood, and you move steadily toward wholeness.

Common Triggers by Archetype

(Awareness, not expectation)

You may recognise some of these, or none at all. They are offered as reference, not instruction.

The Caretaker

Commonly triggered by:

- Others' distress, disappointment, or emotional withdrawal
- Being perceived as selfish or unavailable
- Conflict where needs are expressed directly
- You may notice urges to fix, soothe, explain, or over-give

The Controller

Commonly triggered by:

- Uncertainty, unpredictability, or last-minute change
- Situations where others appear unreliable or careless
- Feeling out of control, misunderstood, or dependent
- You may notice tension, overthinking, or a need to manage outcomes

The Creator

Commonly triggered by:

- Criticism, comparison, or being seen before feeling ready
- Creative blocks, deadlines, or pressure to perform
- Fear of failure or of work being dismissed
- You may notice avoidance, perfectionism, or sudden loss of motivation

The Innocent

Commonly triggered by:

- Conflict, harshness, or emotional complexity
- Loss of certainty, safety, or optimism
- Being confronted with difficult truths
- You may notice withdrawal, denial, or a pull toward positivity at all costs

The Innocent
Commonly triggered by:

- Conflict, harshness, or emotional complexity
- Loss of certainty, safety, or optimism
- Being confronted with difficult truths
- You may notice withdrawal, denial, or a pull toward positivity at all costs

The Lover
Commonly triggered by:

- Distance, rejection, or perceived disconnection
- Ambiguity in relationships
- Feeling unwanted, unseen, or emotionally unsafe
- You may notice heightened sensitivity, longing, or fear of abandonment

The Magician
Commonly triggered by:

- Not knowing, ambiguity, or lack of clarity
- Situations that cannot be explained, predicted, or understood
- Feeling powerless despite awareness
- You may notice over-analysis or a retreat into thinking

The Outsider
Commonly triggered by:

- Feeling excluded, overlooked, or misunderstood
- Group dynamics or social expectations
- Pressure to belong or conform
- You may notice withdrawal, detachment, or self-isolation

The Performer
Commonly triggered by:

- Being unseen, unacknowledged, or unappreciated
- Failure, embarrassment, or loss of approval
- Silence where validation was expected
- You may notice a push to perform, please, or prove worth

The Rebel
Commonly triggered by:

- Rules, authority, or imposed expectations
- Feeling controlled, restricted, or misunderstood
- Loss of autonomy or choice
- You may notice defiance, resistance, or impulsive reactions

The Saboteur
Commonly triggered by:

- Success, progress, or things going "too well"
- Commitment, visibility, or increased responsibility
- Fear of loss, exposure, or change
- You may notice procrastination, self-criticism, or sudden disruption

The Seeker
Commonly triggered by:

- Feeling stuck, limited, or confined
- Routine, repetition, or lack of novelty
- Being asked to commit or settle
- You may notice restlessness, distraction, or a pull toward escape

The Victim
Commonly triggered by:

- Feeling powerless, blamed, or unsupported
- Overwhelm, injustice, or unmet needs
- Situations that echo past helplessness
- You may notice collapse, hopelessness, or withdrawal

Rememeber

Triggers are not failures.
They are signals that something familiar is being touched.

Awareness does not eliminate triggers immediately,
but it creates space; and space restores choice.

Practical Exercise
Shadow Trigger Mapping

Mapping your triggers helps restore choice. When a trigger is named and understood, the conscious mind can return. This creates space for new response patterns, rather than automatically repeating old emotional reflexes.

Triggers are not flaws or overreactions. They are learned responses - signals that once helped you adapt, protect, or belong. By mapping them, you begin to relate to them with clarity instead of confusion.

Choose one or two recurring triggers, i.e., emotional reactions you find difficult to control, predict, or fully understand.

Step 1: Identify the Trigger
Describe what happens, as simply and neutrally as possible.
Focus on the external event, not the interpretation.

Examples:

- "When someone ignores my message."
- "When plans change unexpectedly."
- "When I feel criticised."
- "When I'm interrupted while speaking."
- "When someone pulls away emotionally."

There is no need to explain or justify your response.
Just name the moment that activates it.

Step 2: Name the Emotional Reaction

What arises first in your body or emotional field?

Common initial reactions include:

- anger
- panic
- withdrawal
- shame
- defensiveness
- sadness

If more than one emotion appears, choose the strongest or earliest one.

You may find it helpful to use an emotional wheel to locate more precise language. Often, the first emotion is layered - for example, anger may sit on top of fear, or withdrawal may mask shame.

There is no "correct" emotion to find.
Accuracy matters more than insight.

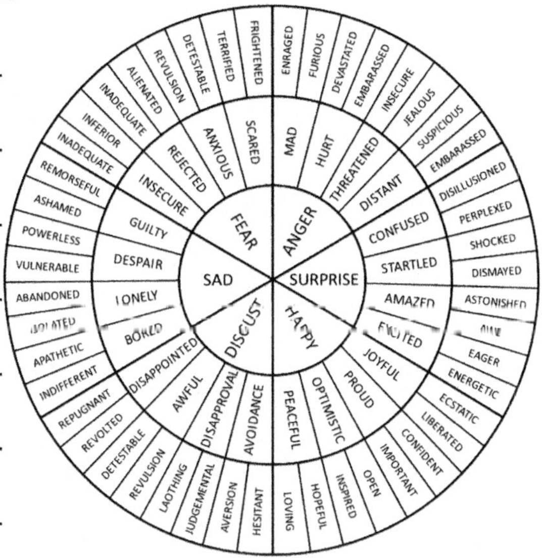

Step 3: Map the Body Response

Where do you feel the reaction in your body?

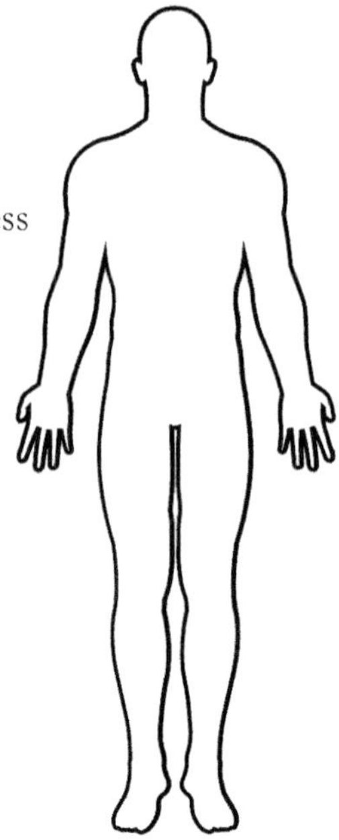

When a trigger activates, the body responds before the mind can explain it. Noticing physical sensations helps interrupt the automatic loop and brings awareness back into the present moment.

You might notice:

- tightness in the chest
- jaw clenching
- a dropping sensation in the stomach
- heat in the face
- tension in the shoulders or neck

There is no need to change the sensation.
Simply notice where it lives and how it feels.

Step 4: Find the Root Scar

Ask gently: ***"What is this really reminding me of?"***

Triggers often echo earlier experiences where your system learned to protect itself. You are not trying to relive the past - only to recognise the pattern.

Possible themes may include:

- childhood rejection
- betrayal or broken trust
- being unseen or unheard
- carrying responsibility too young
- loss of control or unpredictability

Let the answer arise naturally. If nothing comes, that is okay. Awareness will deepen over time.

Step 5: Translate the Trigger into a Need
Every trigger is a need asking to be met. When the need is named, the nervous system no longer has to shout for attention through emotional reactivity.

Examples include:
- "I need reassurance."
- "I need clarity."
- "I need autonomy."
- "I need respect."
- "I need to feel important or valued."

Choose the need that feels most accurate, not the one that sounds most reasonable.

____

____

____

____

____

____

____

Step 6: Create a Soft Response
A response that supports your nervous system and matches how you process experience

Choose one or two practices that feel natural to you. You are not trying to fix the trigger - only to help your system settle enough to restore choice.

Kenithtic / Somatic Learners
- Take 3–5 slow breaths, lengthening the exhale
- Place a hand on your chest, belly, or heart
- Gently press your feet into the floor
- Stretch your shoulders, neck, or jaw
- Wrap yourself in a blanket or hug a pillow

Message to the nervous system: "I am here. The body is safe."

Visual / Creative Learners

- Picture the trigger softening or moving away
- Visualise a protective boundary or calming scene
- Draw or colour a symbol of safety (light, leaf, star)
- Write the trigger on paper, then add a grounding image beside it
- Imagine the emotion changing colour, shape, or intensity

Message to the nervous system: "I can see this without being overwhelmed."

Auditory Learners

- Listen to calming music or white noise
- Hum, sigh, or tone gently
- Speak reassurance to yourself in a steady voice
- Count your breaths aloud
- Read grounding words or affirmations out loud

Message to the nervous system: "I am being guided and supported."

Reader / Writer Learners

- Write a short description of what just happened, without analysis
- Complete this sentence in writing:
- "Right now, I am feeling ___, and I need ___."
- List three facts about the present moment to anchor yourself
- Write a compassionate note to yourself as if you were a trusted guide
- Read a grounding passage, affirmation, or familiar text
- Journal for five minutes with the intention to observe, not resolve

If helpful, you can keep a dedicated trigger journal where patterns, needs, and responses are tracked over time.

Message to the nervous system: "This exper
held safely."

You do not need to use every method.
One small, consistent soft response is enougl
Over time, these moments create space, and :

A space to draw or anchor what arose.

Archetypes Shifts

As the old contract and triggers soften and intragrat, you may notice subtle or sometimes confusing shifts in how you respond to the world, and it is natural to wonder whether this means your archetypes are changing, disappearing, or being replaced, especially if patterns that once felt defining begin to loosen or behave differently.

Archetypes themselves do not vanish or transform overnight, because they are not habits or behaviours that can be switched off, but deep patterns of meaning and orientation that shape how you perceive, interpret, and move through life, often formed early and reinforced over time.

What does change is **how those archetypes are expressed.**

When an archetype is held in place by an old self-contract, it is often confined to its protective or shadow expression, operating in service of safety rather than choice. As an old contract softens and a new one begins to take root, the archetype is no longer required to work in the same way, and the system begins to reorganise.

This can feel unfamiliar at first, not because something is wrong, but because the nervous system is learning a new baseline.

Below are examples of how this shift may appear across different archetypes.

Examples of Archetypal Shifts After Integration

The Caretaker may notice that care is no longer compulsive or draining, but offered more selectively, with clearer boundaries and an emerging ability to receive support as well as give it.

The Controller may still value structure and clarity, but with less urgency, finding it easier to tolerate uncertainty without feeling the need to manage every outcome.

The Creator may feel less blocked or perfectionistic, allowing expression to happen more freely, even if it is unfinished, imperfect, or shared only privately.

The Innocent may begin to hold complexity without losing openness, becoming more discerning while still retaining hope and gentleness.

The Lover may experience connection with less fear of loss, noticing a growing ability to stay present in relationships without self-abandonment or over-attachment.

The Magician may rely less on constant insight or foresight, allowing mystery and not-knowing to exist without anxiety, and trusting that understanding can unfold in its own time.

The Outsider may still value autonomy and perspective but feel less compelled to withdraw, finding ways to remain connected without losing a sense of self.

The Performer may feel less dependent on visibility or approval, experiencing a quiet sense of worth that does not require constant affirmation.

The Rebel may continue to value freedom and authenticity, but express these qualities with less reactivity, choosing alignment over opposition.

The Saboteur may begin to allow success or stability without immediately undermining it, noticing a growing tolerance for things going well.

The Seeker may still feel drawn to growth and meaning, but with less restlessness, finding that curiosity can coexist with presence and commitment.

The Victim may continue to honour pain and vulnerability, while also recognising capacity, agency, and the ability to respond rather than collapse.

Sometimes, as one archetype releases its role as the primary protector, another may come forward more clearly, not as a replacement, but as a rebalancing that reflects increased safety, support, or inner capacity.

It is also important to understand that noticing old archetypal patterns returning does not mean that releasing the old contract did not work. Learning is not linear, and the nervous system often revisits familiar responses while testing whether change is safe.

The purpose of this work is not to eliminate parts of yourself, but to allow them to function with more flexibility and choice, so that identity is shaped less by survival and more by conscious participation in the present.

Over time, we will create new contracts, and others will appear naturally as these are embodied gently, archetypal expressions naturally mature, becoming more balanced and responsive to who you are now rather than who you once needed to be.

Nothing essential is lost in this process.
What changes is the grip of the past.

What You Might Notice in Daily Life

You might notice that you pause more easily before reacting, even if only for a moment, and that this pause creates a sense of choice where there once felt like none. Situations that previously triggered urgency, withdrawal, or over-efforting may still arise, but with slightly less intensity or duration.

You may find yourself catching old patterns earlier - recognising a familiar urge, thought, or emotional pull before it fully takes hold. This awareness does not always stop the pattern, but it often shortens its grip and reduces the sense of being overtaken by it.

You might also notice moments of neutrality where you once felt charged, or moments of clarity where you once felt confusion. Some responses may feel unfamiliar or quieter than before, which can initially feel unsettling, especially if you were used to strong internal reactions guiding your decisions.

At times, old behaviours or emotional responses may return briefly, particularly during stress, fatigue, or periods of change. This does not mean the work has undone itself. It reflects the nervous system, testing whether new ways of responding are truly safe and available.

You may also experience increased sensitivity - not as fragility, but as awareness - noticing when something feels misaligned more quickly, or when rest, boundaries, or self-care are needed sooner than before.

Above all, you may notice that growth feels less like pushing forward and more like settling in. Decisions may feel quieter. Boundaries may feel simpler. Choice may feel less dramatic and more natural.

These are signs of integration.

If You Feel Unsettled

If you notice a sense of unease, emotional activation, or disorientation as this work integrates, pause here. Feeling unsettled does not mean something has gone wrong. It often signals that old patterns are loosening and the nervous system is adjusting to a new way of responding.

This is an invitation to return to grounding rather than to analysis.

You are encouraged to revisit the grounding techniques shared earlier in this book and choose one that aligns with how you learn best, or the archetype that feels most active in that moment. These practices were offered not only for moments of distress, but for times of transition, when the familiar begins to shift.

If the feeling persists or intensifies, it is always appropriate to pause the work, seek additional support, or return to rest. Listening to your limits is part of integration, not a step away from it.

You can come back to this work when your system feels ready again.

Integration is rarely loud. It often arrives as ease where effort once lived, or as steadiness where urgency once ruled.

Looking Ahead: Self-Compassion

As this phase of integration settles, the work naturally turns toward self-compassion. When old contracts loosen and familiar patterns shift, what is often most needed is not more insight or effort, but kindness - the steady, regulating presence that allows change to be held rather than managed.

Self-compassion is not a reward for doing the work well, nor a technique to apply when things feel difficult. It is the foundation that allows integration to continue safely. As you move into the next week, the invitation is to meet whatever arises (clarity, discomfort, relief, calmness or uncertainty) with the same gentleness you have been cultivating throughout this journey.

Nothing more is required.

"Compassion
is not
something to achieve.
It is something
to practice returning to."

Teanna x

Week 9

Date_______________

First Quarter Moon

Self-Compassion

The First Quarter Moon introduces a gentle rising energy - a subtle shift from inward reflection toward steady movement and emotional support. After the deep awareness that came from exploring your triggers last week, this phase invites you to soften once more and tend to your inner landscape with kindness.

Shadow work requires courage, but it requires compassion even more. Without compassion, reflection can turn into self-judgement, and emotional discovery can harden into shame. Compassion is what allows insight to be held safely, rather than used against yourself.

This week, you are invited to meet yourself with tenderness. Instead of pushing through your feelings or analysing them from a distance, the practice is to offer warmth and understanding to the parts of you that carry pain, fear, or uncertainty.

Self-compassion is an internal gesture that signals to the nervous system that it no longer needs to hide or defend itself. It is the quiet reassurance that says, I see you. I am with you. You do not have to go through this alone.

Compassion transforms shadow work because it dissolves the very thing that keeps the shadow hidden: shame. Shame contracts the body and closes the heart. Compassion softens the body and restores a sense of safety.

The First Quarter Moon offers a natural container for this practice. Symbolically, it represents gentle growth and renewed strength- not through force, but through steady, intentional care. You do not need to feel confident, resolved, or fully healed.

This week begins with small moments of kindness, offered to your younger self, your present self, or the parts of you that still carry old wounds.

As the week unfolds, notice how compassion shifts your inner world. It may bring tears, relief, quiet understanding, or simply the sense of being held. There is no right response. Each of these is a meaningful step in the process of healing.

The Science Behind Self-Compassion

Self-compassion activates neural pathways associated with safety, regulation, and emotional integration. When you offer kindness to yourself, the brain reduces activity in regions linked to threat detection and self-criticism, particularly the amygdala. As this threat response softens, stress hormones such as cortisol decrease, and survival-based reactions lose intensity.

At the same time, compassionate attention supports activation of the vagus nerve, which plays a central role in calming the nervous system and fostering a sense of connection and emotional openness. This shift helps the body move out of defence and into a state where healing and integration are more accessible.

Research in affective neuroscience also shows that self-compassion engages the brain's caregiving system, releasing oxytocin - a hormone associated with bonding, trust, and emotional warmth. This biochemical response signals safety, allowing difficult emotions to be approached without overwhelm. As a result, the prefrontal cortex, responsible for insight, perspective, and emotional clarity, becomes more active, supporting thoughtful and grounded responses rather than automatic reactions.

In this way, compassion becomes a powerful internal support for shadow work. It does not bypass difficult material, but creates the conditions in which it can be met safely. Over time, repeated experiences of self-compassion help reshape emotional patterns, gradually replacing pathways rooted in fear or shame with those that support acceptance, resilience, and care.

"The parts of you that hurt the most are the ones that waited the longest for your love."

Teanna x

Practical Exercise

Self-Compassion Practice -
Softening the Inner Critic and Neutralising Shame

For this practice, find a warm, quiet space where you feel relatively at ease. You are invited to write a compassion letter to yourself - not as an exercise to complete, but as an act of care. Speak to yourself as you would to someone you love who is struggling, using words that carry tenderness, understanding, and patience.

As you write, you may choose to support your body as well as your mind. You might place a hand on your heart, wrap yourself in a blanket, slow your breathing, or use any gentle, soothing gesture that helps your nervous system register safety.

There is no right way to do this. Let the pace be slow, and allow pauses when they arise.

Through this simple yet meaningful act of kindness, you begin to soften the inner critic and loosen the grip of shame.

When you feel ready, you may choose to deepen this practice by exploring one of the following exercises aligned with your learning style. You are welcome to select just one, or to explore more than one if that feels supportive. There is no requirement to do everything - follow what feels most steady and nourishing for you.

The word - Shame

Before beginning, it may help to pause with the word shame, as it can carry weight.

Shame is not a sign that something is wrong with you.

It is a quiet belief, often formed early, that certain parts of us must stay hidden in order to feel safe or loved. It arises not from failure, but from moments when understanding or care was missing.

Shame often moves subtly, showing up as self-criticism, withdrawal, or a gentle turning away from ourselves.

When it appears, it does not need to be challenged or fixed, but met with kindness.

Compassion offers what shame never had - warmth, presence, and safety.

When care is extended inward, the body softens, and the need to hide begins to ease.

Compassion Letter

Practical Exercise

Learning Type Adaptations

Reading / Writing Learners

Turn Your Letter Into a Dialogue

Expand your compassion letter into a gentle written conversation between Light You and Shadow You.

- Ask questions, respond with empathy, and allow the shadow part to express what it needs.

This creates clarity, emotional depth, and a written bridge toward integration.

Auditory Learners

Read Your Compassion Letter Aloud

- Read your letter aloud slowly.
    - Notice how your tone changes as you speak and how your body responds to your own kindness.

Your voice becomes a healing frequency, signalling safety and acceptance.

Kinesthetic / Somatic Learners

Wrap Yourself in a Blanket While Reading Your Letter

- Hold your compassion letter and wrap yourself in a warm blanket, shawl, or robe.
- Read the letter slowly while feeling the physical sensation of comfort and safety. Let your body absorb the message: ***I am worthy of gentleness. I am safe to be seen.***

A space to anchor what arose.

Visual / Creative Learners

Draw a Gentle Self-Portrait of Your Shadow

- Create a simple drawing (stick figures are absolutely welcome) representing the part of you that you are offering compassion to.
- Let the image be soft, gentle, and free of judgment.
- You might add colours, symbols, or shapes that express how this part feels.

This visual connection helps your shadow feel seen and embraced.

Week 10

Full Moon - Worm Moon

Discovering Your Core Values

Identifying Your Core Values
Learning Type Adaptations

A stone
One candle (green, brown, or white)
A small piece of paper and a pen

Worm Moon (Core Values and Space)
The altar should reflect foundations, not decoration.
Empty space is intentional - this mirrors underground movement and unseen preparation.

Transform rather than add:
Clear the altar back to only a few key items
Add a small bowl of soil, seeds, or a stone resting on the earth
Place written core values folded beneath a stone or bowl

"Beneath the Surface"
www. TeannaTaylor.com

Week 10

Date______________

Full Moon - Worm Moon

Discovering Your Core Values

The Worm Moon arrives as winter begins to loosen its grip and the first signs of movement stir beneath the surface of the earth. Though the landscape may still appear quiet, the ground is alive with beginnings. The soil softens. Subtle shifts occur underground. Life prepares to rise. This Full Moon mirrors a similar awakening within you.

After weeks of reflection, release, understanding, and compassion, you are now ready to reconnect with what truly matters to you.

Shadow work clears what once obscured your inner landscape. With greater clarity, you may begin to notice the values that have always lived at your core; not as rules or expectations, but as guiding principles that quietly shape your sense of meaning and direction. Values are not goals to achieve or roles to perform. They are the truths that help you recognise when your life is aligned, and when it is not.

When you live in accordance with your values, decisions tend to feel clearer, relationships more grounded, and your inner world less conflicted. When values are obscured or compromised, you may experience confusion, tension, or a sense of disconnection from yourself.

"Values offer a compass -
not to dictate your path,
but to orient you toward what feels true."

The Worm Moon is a powerful time for this work because it represents renewal before visible growth. It is a moment of preparation rather than action, making it an ideal time to ask:

- What do I stand for?
- What matters most to me now?
- What needs to be honoured so I can grow in the months ahead?

Understanding your values also supports deeper integration of the shadow. Many old wounds, triggers, and self-contracts form around unmet or compromised values. If you value honesty but learned to stay silent, the shadow may carry grief. If you value connection but learned to self-abandon, the shadow may carry resentment. Naming your values helps bring coherence to these inner tensions, not by erasing them, but by offering context and meaning.

This week's work may bring clarity, relief, or the quiet recognition of yourself returning. Your values are the roots from which new intentions will grow as spring approaches. Honour them gently. Let them inform your choices and guide the direction you are beginning to sense.

This Full Moon marks a turning point - where winter's healing begins to orient toward renewal.

The Science of Values Clarification

Clarifying your values engages neural circuits associated with meaning, motivation, and behavioural regulation. When you reflect on what truly matters to you, the brain activates areas of the prefrontal cortex linked to decision-making, emotional alignment, and personal integrity. This supports greater coherence between thoughts, feelings, and actions, reducing internal conflict and strengthening psychological resilience.

Values work has also been shown to reduce stress. Research indicates that reflecting on core values can lower cortisol levels and support emotional regulation by reinforcing a stable sense of identity and purpose. When the brain feels anchored in meaning, challenges are more likely to be experienced as manageable rather than overwhelming.

From a behavioural perspective, values act as internal anchors. They help organise emotional and cognitive responses, making it easier to navigate decisions and relationships with clarity and awareness. When actions align with values, reward pathways associated with satisfaction and motivation become more active, supporting steadier habits and long-term change.

Within shadow work, values provide direction rather than pressure. As old patterns, wounds, or limiting beliefs surface, values help the nervous system orient toward what feels safe, true, and life-giving. They offer a compass for healing - not to dictate behaviour, but to guide integration and prepare the mind and body for new ways of living as spring approaches.

Did You Know?

Reflecting on your core values activates areas of the brain linked to meaning, clarity, and emotional regulation. When your nervous system feels anchored in what truly matters to you, stress responses soften, and decision-making becomes steadier. Values don't add pressure - they reduce it.

Values vs Conditioning

It can be helpful to distinguish between values and conditioning, as they often sound similar but feel very different in the body.

Values are inner truths that feel grounding and life-giving. They tend to create a sense of clarity, alignment, or quiet steadiness, even when choices are difficult. Values guide you toward how you want to live, not who you should be.

Conditioning develops in response to expectations, rules, or survival needs. It often carries urgency, fear, or obligation, and may feel heavy or constricting. Conditioning tells you how to behave in order to stay safe, accepted, or avoid discomfort.

A simple way to tell the difference is to notice how your body responds.

Values usually bring a sense of expansion or calm.
Conditioning often brings tension or pressure.

This week's work is not about choosing the "right" values, but about recognising which principles feel true to you beneath learned rules and expectations.

"Your core values
are not goals you choose.
They are the truths you return home to."

Teanna x

Values List Examples

Connection and Relationships
Love
Belonging
Trust
Loyalty
Intimacy
Community
Compassion
Empathy
Support

Self and Inner World
Authenticity
Self-respect
Self-worth
Inner peace
Emotional safety
Integrity
Honesty
Alignment
Balance

Growth and Learning
Growth
Healing
Curiosity
Wisdom
Awareness
Learning
Reflection
Self-understanding

Freedom and Autonomy
Freedom
Independence
Autonomy
Choice
Sovereignty
Personal space
Flexibility
Stability and Security
Safety
Security
Consistency
Reliability
Groundedness
Stability
Trustworthiness

Expression and Creativity
Creativity
Self-expression
Play
Inspiration
Imagination
Beauty

Purpose and Meaning
Purpose
Meaning
Contribution
Service
Legacy
Responsibility

Respect and Boundaries
Respect
Dignity
Equality
Fairness
Boundaries
Mutuality

Presence and Way of Being
Presence
Mindfulness
Patience
Acceptance
Gentleness
Ease

Strength and Courage
Courage
Resilience
Perseverance
Confidence
Empowerment

Justice & Ethics
Justice
Fairness
Equity
Accountability
Integrity
Responsibility
Truth
Moral clarity
Ethics
Human dignity
Non-harm
Advocacy

Practical Exercise

Values Identification Practice

A Quiet Return to What Matters

This practice is not about choosing values you think you should have or defining yourself for the future. It is about noticing what already feels true beneath roles, habits, and expectations.

- Find a quiet moment. Move slowly. You may pause at any point.

Step One · Settling

- Begin by bringing your attention to your body
    - Notice your breath without changing it
    - Allow your shoulders, jaw, and hands to soften
- You are not trying to arrive anywhere. You are simply creating enough space to listen.

Step Two · Remembering Alignment

- Gently reflect on the following questions. There is no need to answer quickly or completely.
    - When in my life have I felt most like myself?
    - When have my actions felt honest, grounded, or quietly right?
    - What qualities were present in those moments?
    - Write down any words, phrases, or images that arise. These may be simple or unexpected.

____

____

____

____

____

____

____

Step Three · Noticing What Matters

- Now consider moments of discomfort or inner conflict.
    - When have I felt drained, resentful, or disconnected from myself?
    - What felt compromised or unhonoured in those moments?
    - What value may have been ignored or suppressed?
- Often, what hurts points toward what matters.

Step Four · Distilling Your Values

- Review what you have written and circle or highlight words that feel alive, steady, or resonant in your body. You may notice themes such as honesty, connection, freedom, care, creativity, integrity, or presence.
- From these, gently choose three to five values - not as labels, but as touchstones. These are not rules. They are reminders.
- You may phrase them as single words or short statements, for example:
    - Honesty
    - Compassion
    - Authentic expression
    - Meaningful connection

Trust what feels simple and true.

Step Five · Listening to the Body

- For each value, pause and notice:
  - Does this feel grounded or pressured?
  - Does my body soften, expand, or tighten?
  - If a value feels heavy or forced, set it aside. It may belong to conditioning rather than truth.

Step Six · Closing

- End by placing a hand on your body or taking a slow breath.
  - You do not need to act on these values yet.
  - For now, it is enough to recognise them.
  - Let them rest with you as winter continues to loosen and new growth quietly prepares beneath the surface.

Practical Exercise

Learning Type Adaptations

Visual / Creative Learners

Values Mandala

- Use the mandala and in each petal, write or symbolise one of your core values - words such as truth, freedom, compassion, creativity, grounding, courage, or peace.
- Allow colours, shapes, or simple symbols to represent each value intuitively. There is no right or wrong way to do this. Let your body and imagination lead rather than your thinking mind.

This visual mandala becomes a sacred reminder of what your life is built upon - the principles that orient you when you feel uncertain, triggered, or disconnected.

If a value draws you toward a darker colour, this does not mean it belongs to conditioning. Dark colours often represent depth, protection, strength, mystery, or seriousness. What matters is not the colour itself, but how the value feels in your body.

You might gently ask:

- Does this value feel chosen, alive, and supportive?
- Or does it feel heavy, imposed, or tied to obligation?
- Trust your internal response more than symbolic rules.

Values can be quiet, deep, and powerful - just like darker hues.

Reading / Writing Learners

Write Your Top 3 Values and Why They Matter

- List your top three values. For each one, write a few sentences exploring what it means to you.

You may find it helpful to reflect on:

- Where did this value first emerge in your life?
- How does it guide your choices or behaviour?
- When have you abandoned or compromised it?
- How might your life change if you honoured this value fully?

Write without censoring or correcting yourself. Let clarity arise through language rather than perfection.

This written exploration helps translate values from abstract ideals into lived orientation, creating greater alignment between what you believe and how you live.

Auditory Learners

Speak Each Value Aloud and Listen for Resonance

- Read each potential value out loud, slowly and with intention. Leave a small pause after each word.

As you speak, notice how your body responds:

- Which value feels warm or settling
- Which creates tension or contraction
- Which feels true, even if it scares you
- Which feels hollow, distant, or inherited

Your voice activates the nervous system differently from silent thought. When spoken, values move from concept into lived experience.

After each value, gently ask yourself:

- "Does my body soften or brace when I say this?"
- "Would I choose this even if no one else expected it of me?"
- "Does this feel like truth — or like obligation?" *A space to anchor what arose.*
- "Is this value energising, or does it drain me?"

There is no need to decide immediately. Let the sound of your own voice guide you. Our voice often tells the truth before the mind catches up.

Kinesthetic / Somatic Learners

Assign Each Value a Symbolic Movement

For somatic learners, values are best understood through the body. Instead of analysing them, allow your body to express each one.

Create a small physical gesture, movement, or posture that represents each value. Keep it simple and intuitive.

Examples:

- Integrity → stand tall with a long spine
- Compassion → place a hand gently over the heart
- Growth → take a slow, intentional step forward
- Peace → soften the shoulders and exhale
- Courage → widen your stance and ground your feet

Repeat each movement slowly, pairing it with the value name if that feels supportive.

As you hold each posture or movement, gently ask yourself:

- "Does my body feel more grounded or more tense here?"
- "Does this movement feel natural or forced?"
- "Do I want to stay in this posture, or pull away from it?"
- "Does this value bring strength, softness, or pressure?"

Let the answers come through sensation rather than thought.
Let the body memorise your values.

When values are anchored somatically, they become lived rather than conceptual. Over time, these movements can become quiet, embodied reminders - helping you return to alignment in moments of stress or choice.

A space to anchor what arose.

Full Moon Ritual

This ritual honours what supports us beneath the surface - our core values

What you will need

A stone
One candle (green, brown, or white)
A small piece of paper and a pen
Quite Space

Ritual Steps

Take three slow breaths, feet on the floor, hands resting gently.
Light the central candle (if using) and name the intention:
"I create space for what truly matters."

In quiet reflection, write one core value that feels essential right now
(such as honesty, compassion, courage, balance)
Keep it simple; this is about what is foundational, not aspirational.

Fold the paper with intention and place it beneath the stone,
and then place it on your altar

Imagine space opening within - like tunnels in the earth -
allowing clarity, integrity, and alignment to flow.

When you are ready, close by placing your hand on your heart and saying:
"What I honour beneath the surface shapes what grows above."

Extinguish the candle if used.

Aftercare - Leave the paper buried under the stone through the lunar cycle - you can plant it outdoors later if you wish. Let the ritual continue quietly over time.

Why this ritual works - This practice supports values-based living, a concept used in modern psychology and therapy. By physically grounding values in soil, the brain associates them with stability and support rather than effort or pressure, mirroring the Worm Moon's unseen but essential work beneath the earth.

Week 11 Date______________

Last Quarter Moon

Making Space -Holding the Threshold

The Last Quarter Moon marks a natural clearing phase, arriving as winter prepares to come to rest. This is a moment of release, not to create immediate movement, but to hold the space between what has been and what is quietly forming. It is a threshold week - where less is carried forward, and nothing new is yet required.

After the clarity of the Worm Moon and the reconnection with your values, this week invites you to notice what no longer fits the person you are becoming. Much of the deeper work has already taken place beneath the surface. Now, the invitation is simply to allow what feels heavy, outdated, or unnecessary to be gently laid down.

Making space is not a dramatic act. It may be physical or internal - a drawer cleared, a belief softened, a routine released. What matters is not the size of the action, but the intention behind it. Even small shifts can bring a sense of relief, as the nervous system responds to the easing of pressure.

This week is not about minimalism or productivity. It is about choosing one place in your life that feels cluttered or misaligned and offering it gentle attention. In doing so, you are not stepping into spring yet. You are allowing space to remain open, so what has already changed can settle and integrate.

The Last Quarter Moon supports reflection and closure. As you make space, notice what arises, and meet it with care. Let this clearing be the final tending of winter - a quiet act of self-respect before stillness returns.

Making space does not require explanation or justification. You do not need to know what will fill this space, or when. Trust that the pause itself is meaningful. In nature, nothing rushes to replace what has fallen away. The space is part of the process.

As this week comes to a close, allow yourself to rest in what has been released and what has not yet arrived. You are standing at the edge of a new season. There is nothing to prepare for now. Simply remain here, steady and open, and let winter finish its work.

The Science Behind Making Space

Creating physical or emotional space reduces cognitive load and eases pressure on the nervous system. When the brain perceives clutter, unresolved tasks, or emotional overload, it activates networks associated with vigilance and tension, particularly in the anterior cingulate cortex. This can keep the nervous system in a low-level state of alert, making it harder to rest, focus, or process emotions clearly.

When you tidy a space, simplify your environment, or set a boundary, the brain receives cues of order and completion. This supports greater activity in the prefrontal cortex, which enhances clarity, emotional regulation, and decision-making. Small acts of organisation or release can also stimulate dopamine, creating a quiet sense of satisfaction and reinforcing feelings of ease rather than effort.

On an emotional level, making space reduces unconscious triggers. Objects, environments, and unfinished tasks often carry subtle emotional associations. When these are released or brought into order, the nervous system experiences relief, as if something it was holding can finally be set down.

Within shadow work, making space supports integration. As old beliefs and patterns soften, the brain benefits from a sense of openness rather than accumulation. Creating space - physically or symbolically - helps the nervous system settle, making you more receptive to the integration of winter's work and the gentle growth that spring will bring.

Did You Know?

Clearing even a small physical or emotional space can signal safety to the nervous system. The brain often interprets simplicity and order as relief, allowing attention to soften and emotional processing to become easier.

Practical Exercise

Learning Type Adaptations

Choose one exercise only. This week is about easing pressure, not creating effort. If none of the exercises feel right this week, resting in awareness is enough.

Visual / Creative Learners

Before-and-After Photo Ritual

- Choose one drawer, one shelf, one box, something small and manageable.
    - Take a "before" photo.
    - Clear, cleanse, organise, or simplify the space.
    - Take an "after" photo.

Seeing the transformation visually helps your brain recognise change and internalise the feeling of spaciousness. This creates a ripple effect, making you more open to emotional and energetic clearing as well.

Auditory Learners

Sacred Sound Clearing Ritual

- Create a playlist of calming, grounding, or cleansing music.
- As you clear your chosen space, let the sound guide your breath and rhythm.
- Music anchors the ritual, turning it from "chores" into a sacred act of renewal.
- Allow the soundscape to hold you in a gentle, slow-flowing pace as you release what is no longer needed.

Optional enhancement: Ring a bell, chime, or soft tone when you finish as a way to "seal" the space with clarity.

Kinesthetic / Somatic Learners

The Physical Clearing Itself Is the Tool

For tactile learners, the movement matters more than the symbolism.

- Let the clearing be slow, grounding, and mindful:
  - Feel the textures
  - Notice the weight
  - Sense the release
- Track your breath as you move objects out and create space

The body learns through action, and this physical ritual signals to your nervous system: "I am ready for something new."

A space to anchor what arose.

Reading / Writing Learners

Sacred Writing Clearing Ritual

As you clear your chosen space, pause intermittently to write short phrases or sentences about what you are releasing. This may include physical clutter, emotional residue, outdated roles, or lingering thoughts connected to the space

You might write:
"This no longer serves me."
"I release what feels heavy here."
"I make room for clarity and ease."

Let the act of writing slow your movements and focus your attention. Language becomes the anchor, turning practical tidying into a conscious ritual of release. When the space feels complete, write a final sentence that reflects the quality you are inviting in - such as calm, creativity, rest, or openness.

Optional enhancement: Tear up, recycle, or safely discard the pages you wrote on as a symbolic act of clearing, then write one final line to "seal" the space, such as "This space is now held with intention."

“"Making space
is
not about
clearing your home;
it is about
clearing the places
where your
energy
has been
silently
held hostage."”

Teanna x

Week 12 Date_______________

New Moon

Integration - Bringing your Shadow Self and Light Self into harmony

The New Moon brings the final and most tender moment of the winter journey. It is a phase of quiet beginnings, invisible growth, and gentle rebirth. Nothing is yet visible, yet everything is stirring beneath the surface. Winter has done its sacred work. You have reflected, released, rested, discovered, softened, and clarified. Now your inner landscape is ready to integrate all that has been uncovered over the past twelve weeks.

Integration is the moment when understanding becomes embodiment. It is where insight settles into the body, the nervous system, and the way you meet life. Shadow work reaches its purpose not through analysis alone, but through integration - when reclaimed truths are allowed to live within you. This week invites you to bring together all aspects of yourself: shadow and light, past and present, fear and courage, so they may coexist without conflict. Integration is not perfection. It is wholeness.

The New Moon supports this process through stillness and renewal. It offers a sacred pause before the energy of spring begins to rise. In this pause, you are not asked to fix, change, or improve anything.

Integration requires gentleness rather than effort. It asks only that you sit with yourself as you are, allowing the parts that surfaced during winter to find their rightful place within you.

This week's practice helps you recognise both what has softened and what is quietly emerging. It is an opportunity to honour the strength that carried you through this season, the wisdom that revealed itself, and the clarity that now rests within you.

Integration is the final movement of winter - the moment before intentions are set, visions are formed, and new growth begins.

Let this be a time of stillness.
Let your breath slow.
Let your heart soften.

Trust that the seeds tended in darkness are preparing to rise. Nothing needs to be forced. Your only task is to allow.

Integration is the gentle alchemy that turns healing into transformation.

The science of integration

Integration occurs when emotional learning is stored not only as insight but as a new pattern within the brain. During this process, the hippocampus and prefrontal cortex work together to consolidate emotional memories, reorganise neural pathways, and create greater coherence between different regions of the brain. What was once fragmented begins to form a unified inner narrative, reducing internal conflict and supporting emotional stability.

When experiences are met with acceptance rather than judgment, the brain strengthens pathways associated with self-compassion, emotional regulation, and resilience. At the same time, activity in areas linked to fear and self-protection (particularly the amygdala) begins to soften. As reactivity decreases, the nervous system can rest more often in states of safety and connection.

Integration also supports neuroplasticity, the brain's capacity to form new connections and release outdated emotional patterns.

When shadow and light are held together without opposition, the brain no longer experiences inner differences as threats. Instead, they are recognised as parts of a coherent whole. This increases psychological flexibility and allows change to take root gradually and sustainably.

From a nervous system perspective, integration completes the work of winter by grounding healing in a parasympathetic state. This creates a stable internal foundation, preparing mind and body for the rising energy of spring, where intention, creativity, manifesting, resolutions, dreams and movement can emerge with greater ease.

Did You Know?

Integration often happens quietly. The brain continues to reorganise emotional learning during rest and reflection, even when you feel "nothing is happening." Stillness allows new patterns to settle without effort. If it feels like nothing changed, trust that integration often unfolds beneath awareness - subtle shifts today become steadiness over time. When the nervous system feels safe, the mind becomes coherent, and the soul finds its rhythm; this is how healing completes its cycle and prepares to become lived.

Practical Exercise

Learning Type Adaptations

Visual / Creative Learners

Shadow and Light Merge Drawing

- Draw your Shadow Self on one side of the page and your Light Self on the other.
- Then draw them:
  - Shaking hands
  - Standing side-by-side
  - Or merging into one balanced figure

This imagery symbolises unity and acceptance.

- You are visually affirming: ***"Both parts belong. Both parts deserve a voice."***

Auditory Learners

Shadow–Light Dialogue Out Loud

- Write one shadow belief and one light truth below;
- Read your written dialogue aloud.
- Then improvise responses:
    - What does the shadow say?
    - What does the light say back?
    - What reassurance or truth emerges?

Hearing the conversation powerfully activates emotional processing, making both sides feel acknowledged.

Kinesthetic / Somatic Learners

Heart–Belly Integration Breath

- Place one hand on your heart (Light Self) and one hand on your belly (Shadow Self).
- Breathe slowly:
  - Inhale into the belly (honouring the shadow)
  - Exhale through the heart (bringing compassion)
- Let your breath move between the two, weaving them together.

This somatic practice helps your body understand that both parts can coexist safely.

A space to anchor what arose.

*"Integration is not
the absence of shadow.
It is the dance between the light
you show the world
and the truth you carry within."*

Teanna x

Reading / Writing Learners

Split-Page Shadow vs. Light Journaling

The left-hand side is your shadow voice, and the right-hand side is your light voice

- Let them speak to each other.
- Allow honesty on both sides.
- Let the dialogue evolve until both parts feel heard.

This written conversation becomes a bridge between fear and truth.

Shadow Voice	Light Voice

Embracing Winter's gifts as we move into spring

As winter draws to a close, it leaves you with quiet gifts: stillness, introspection, and a deeper relationship with your inner wisdom. This season has asked you to slow your pace, soften your expectations, and turn inward toward the quieter places within yourself. In winter's darkness and silence, you have met aspects of your shadow, listened to emotions that once lay buried, and gently released patterns that no longer served you. Like the earth resting beneath frost, you allowed yourself to pause, restore, and heal.

Throughout these months, you learned to honour your needs, to sit with truth rather than resist it, and to cultivate the inner safety required for real transformation. This work has taken courage. You faced what was once hidden, tended to your inner landscape with care, and rediscovered your own resilience. Winter has not been empty or barren; it has been a sacred preparation, quietly creating fertile ground beneath the surface.

As you transition toward spring, you carry this wisdom with you. The clarity, steadiness, and emotional strength you cultivated now form the foundation for what comes next. Spring does not ask you to rush forward. It invites you to awaken gently, to trust the natural momentum of renewal, and to allow what has been growing unseen to begin its ascent toward the light.

Spring is a season of emergence. Action returns, but not through pressure or urgency. Instead, it arises through inspired movement: small, meaningful steps that honour what you have learned and who you have become.

As the balance shifts from inward listening to outward expression, may you move forward with a softened heart and a clearer sense of purpose. Let winter's gifts remain with you, not as something left behind, but as a quiet strength you carry into the season of becoming.

Author's Note

Content Note

The following Author's Note contains personal reflections on chronic and hidden illness, prolonged isolation, passive-aggressive relational harm, severe neurological pain, loss of cognitive function, suicidal vulnerability, and the absence of care during periods of crisis. These experiences are shared with honesty and care, but may be activating for some readers.

Please read at your own pace. It is okay to pause, skip this section, or return to it later. If strong emotions arise, consider reaching out to a trusted person, therapist, or local crisis support service for additional support.

Your well-being comes first.

For many years, I believed healing would arrive through care - through being seen, supported, and restored by others.

Winter taught me something different.

It taught me that healing does not arrive through force. That stillness carries its own intelligence. That reflection, silence, and waiting are not signs of failure, but responses shaped by deep, embodied wisdom. I learned that transformation does not always look like progress. Sometimes it looks like stopping.

I believe deeply in working with seasonal energy - in listening to the natural rhythms of rest, release, and renewal that shape both the earth and the psyche. And yet life does not always move in neat cycles.

There are times when everything halts, when forward motion is no longer available, and when the season you enter does not match the calendar.

For me, this took the form of a winter that lasted nearly ten years.

This unfolded during a period when I was also caring for four children under the age of five - a reality that quietly shaped every decision, every limitation, and every moment of endurance.

That time was marked by near isolation, chronic illness, and a gradual narrowing of the world around me. I lived with hemiplegic migraine, survived a stroke, and navigated a marriage shaped by passive-aggressive harm that slowly eroded my sense of safety and self. My body and mind became unreliable in ways I could not control.

There were periods when I had no stamina, no clarity, and at times no language at all - moments when thought itself fractured and words disappeared.

Migraine, especially hemiplegic migraine, is not "just a headache." It is a neurological event that can strip language, movement, and thought. There were days - and sometimes longer - when the only option was to lie completely still, unable to tolerate light, sound, or touch, waiting for sensation and pain to pass. In those moments, there was no strategy, no insight, no plan - only endurance.

At the beginning of my illness, I believed doctors would cure me. That I would be listened to, understood, and guided back to myself. That belief made sense, but was not reality. Before my health collapsed, I worked in complex systems, large-scale projects, and process re-engineering. I was used to analysing, deciding, and leading. Yet by this stage, I could not even decide what bread to buy. The way I had once solved problems was no longer available to me.

There were also times when the care I needed was simply not there. When I was most vulnerable, frightened, and at times suicidal, those who might have offered comfort did not know how to reach me. There were no hugs, no holding, no steady presence - only brief gestures that could not meet the depth of what I was living through. I share this not to assign blame, but to name a reality many endure quietly: sometimes support is absent at the very moment it is most needed.

In that absence, my archetypal protectors stepped in. The Controller and the Caretaker did not emerge as strength or competence, but as necessity. When the external structure failed, something in me tried to create order. When no one could care for me in the way I needed, something in me attempted to do that care internally. This was not empowerment or choice - it was the nervous system responding to abandonment, pain, and uncertainty.

There were times when I had no mind, no stamina, no coherent thought process, and no language. Human resources were not available to me then. What remained was not strength in the way we usually describe it. What remained was tenacity - and a soul that continued to listen.

When cognition, strategy, and external support were unavailable, I listened in the only way I could. Not through logic or analysis, but through something quieter - a sensing, a responsiveness beneath thought. This is where spirit returned.

As a child, I had this way of listening. Over time, I closed it down. During my long winter, it re-emerged - not as certainty or instruction, but as gentle orientation. I can speak with spirit, not dramatically or as belief, but as a quiet dialogue that remained open when everything else had closed. This spiritual awakening was not serene or elevated. It was messy, disorienting, and deeply human. It did not replace the psychological or the neurology work; it ran alongside it, offering presence where answers were unavailable.

As some capacity slowly returned, so did the ability to see more clearly. What I had not been able to question while I was unwell - because survival required all available energy - began to come into view. In that space, I started to recognise relational patterns I had previously normalised or overlooked, including passive-aggressive behaviours that had quietly undermined my sense of safety and self-trust.

This book remains grounded in psychology - in nervous system regulation, integration, and trauma-informed self-inquiry. The spiritual layer will be explored more fully in another work. For now, it is enough to name that it existed, and that it helped me endure when nothing else could.

I share this not to explain myself, but to stand in truth.

This work is not written from stacked qualifications, degrees, or certificates. It is written from lived experience - from shadow-faced honesty, from long seasons of collapse and return, from a body that has known profound limitation and a psyche that learned how to listen. Parts of this story are still settling. And yet I can now tell most of it without emotional charge. That, more than anything, taught me that facing the shadow works.

I am deeply aware that for many people living with chronic illness - especially illness that is hidden, misunderstood, or minimised - words like growth, renewal, or even healing can feel distant or meaningless. This work is not offered as a cure, a solution, or a promise that insight will change what must be endured. It is offered as a way of meeting life as it is, with greater kindness, safety, and coherence, even when circumstances do not improve.

Sometimes the work is not about becoming better, but about becoming gentler. Sometimes winter does not end, and the wisdom lies in learning how to live within it.

My intention is not to teach you something new. It is to help you remember - what your body already knows, what your nervous system has been protecting, and what your inner wisdom reveals when it is met with patience and compassion.

If this journey resonates, it is because truth recognises itself.
If it helps, then it has already meant something.

With warmth

Teanna x

Acknowledgements

This workbook is the result of years spent listening to the quiet rhythms of the seasons, the cycles of the moon, and the deeper movements of the human heart. It would not exist without the people who, in different ways and at different times, walked alongside me through this journey.

To the many thousands of people whom I have held space for through readings, workshops, meditations, books, and seasonal gatherings: thank you. Your courage, honesty, and willingness to engage deeply with this work have shaped and refined it far beyond me, and it has been an honour to witness the ways you have grown and bloomed in your own lives.

To John and MJ, who walked the spiritual path with me during a time of awakening and unravelling, thank you for your companionship, presence, lessons, and shared listening. That season mattered beyond words.

To my teachers, mentors, and the writers whose wisdom appears in the bibliography, thank you for illuminating the landscapes of psychology, neuroscience, quantum physics, energy, spirit, and soul. Your work has informed and supported my own, and I am grateful for the paths you have made visible.

To my friends and loved ones, especially Sarah, Ruth and Kristtiina, who offered presence during difficult seasons, thank you. And to the many others who showed up in quieter ways: through words, silence, or simply staying. Your steadiness made space for reflection, writing, and quiet continuation.

And to my children, whose presence shaped the seasons of my life in ways both seen and unseen, thank you. You were part of the rhythm that carried me forward, even when words were scarce.

And finally, to the part of myself that stayed, the part that endured illness, navigated loss, and continued to listen even when certainty was absent. Thank you for your persistence, your gentleness, and your capacity to remain open. This book is for you, and for everyone walking their own path of becoming.

As the final book in this seasonal series, this work marks a natural resting point in my own story, not an ending, but an understanding. Winter has allowed the question of why this path unfolded as it did to settle into coherence. From here, the movement turns naturally toward spring, toward living, creating, and becoming, carrying this understanding forward rather than leaving it behind.

About the Author

Teanna Taylor is a meditation facilitator and guide of seasonal wisdom, energy work, and embodied transformation.

Her work was shaped through a long initiation - marked by profound illness, including recovery from a stroke and a decade-long journey with hemiplegic migraine. This extended period of stillness, uncertainty, and deep listening drew her inward when the outer world fell away. Through meditation, somatic awareness, and nervous system attunement, she began to heal and rediscovered an ancient truth: that healing unfolds when we learn to move in rhythm with the body, the psyche, and the cycles of nature.

Blending neuroscience, psychology, astrology, quantum principles, and ancestral spiritual traditions, Teanna's work bridges the seen and unseen. She holds spaces where the nervous system softens, intuition reawakens, and the soul remembers its own timing.

Through her books, retreats, seasonal rituals, and guided meditations, she has walked alongside thousands as they reconnect with inner wisdom, release old patterns, and return to a deeper sense of belonging within themselves.

Teanna is the author of Unlock Your Cosmic Flow and the Seasonal Workbook Series. And co-creator of the mindfulness tool SCAN (Still, Chill, Aware Now)

She lives in the UK, listening closely to the turning of the seasons, and devotes her life to guiding others back to the quiet truth that was always within them.

Also available by Teanna Taylor

Unlock Your Cosmic Flow

Living in Harmony with Nature's Rhymes

Cosmic Flow - Spring Workbook - Sow the Seeds of Success
Cosmic Flow - Summer Workbook - Cultivate Your Dreams
Cosmic Flow - Autumn Workbook - Harvest and Release

www.TeannaTaylor.com

Lunar Calendar

2026 Moon Phases Calendar

Jan	3:○, 10:◑, 18:●, 26:◐
Feb	1:○, 9:◑, 17:●, 24:◐
Mar	3:○, 11:◑, 19:●, 25:◐
Apr	2:○, 10:◑, 17:●, 24:◐
May	1:○, 9:◑, 16:●, 23:◐, 31:○
Jun	8:◑, 15:●, 21:◐, 30:○
Jul	7:◑, 14:●, 21:◐, 29:○
Aug	6:◑, 12:●, 20:◐, 28:○
Sep	4:◑, 11:●, 18:◐, 26:○
Oct	3:◑, 10:●, 18:◐, 26:○
Nov	1:◑, 9:●, 17:◐, 24:○
Dec	1:◑, 9:●, 17:◐, 24:○, 30:◑

2027 Moon Phases Calendar

Jan	7:●, 15:◐, 22:○, 29:◑
Feb	6:●, 14:◐, 20:○, 28:◑
Mar	8:●, 15:◐, 22:○, 30:◑
Apr	7:●, 13:◐, 20:○, 28:◑
May	6:●, 13:◐, 20:○, 28:◑
Jun	4:●, 11:◐, 19:○, 27:◑
Jul	4:●, 10:◐, 18:○, 26:◑
Aug	2:●, 9:◐, 17:○, 25:◑, 31:●
Sep	7:◐, 16:○, 23:◑, 30:●
Oct	7:◐, 15:○, 22:◑, 29:●
Nov	6:◐, 14:○, 21:◑, 28:●
Dec	6:◐, 13:○, 20:◑, 27:●

2028 Moon Phases Calendar

Jan	5:◐, 12:○, 18:◑, 26:●
Feb	3:◐, 10:○, 17:◑, 25:●
Mar	4:◐, 11:○, 17:◑, 26:●
Apr	2:◐, 9:○, 16:◑, 24:●
May	2:◐, 8:○, 16:◑, 24:●, 31:◐
Jun	7:○, 15:◑, 22:●, 29:◐
Jul	6:○, 14:◑, 22:●, 28:◐
Aug	5:○, 13:◑, 20:●, 27:◐
Sep	4:○, 12:◑, 18:●, 25:◐
Oct	3:○, 11:◑, 18:●, 25:◐
Nov	2:○, 9:◑, 16:●, 24:◐
Dec	2:○, 9:◑, 16:●, 23:◐, 31:○

2029 Moon Phases Calendar

Jan	7:◑, 14:●, 22:◐, 30:○
Feb	5:◑, 13:●, 21:◐, 28:○
Mar	7:◑, 15:●, 23:◐, 30:○
Apr	5:◑, 13:●, 21:◐, 28:○
May	5:◑, 13:●, 21:◐, 27:○
Jun	4:◑, 12:●, 19:◐, 26:○
Jul	3:◑, 11:●, 18:◐, 25:○
Aug	2:◑, 10:●, 16:◐, 24:○
Sep	1:◑, 8:●, 15:◐, 22:○, 30:◑
Oct	7:●, 14:◐, 22:○, 30:◑
Nov	6:●, 13:◐, 21:○, 28:◑
Dec	5:●, 12:◐, 20:○, 28:◑

2030 Moon Phases Calendar

Jan	4:●, 11:◐, 19:○, 26:◑
Feb	2:●, 10:◐, 18:○, 25:◑
Mar	4:●, 12:◐, 19:○, 26:◑
Apr	2:●, 11:◐, 18:○, 24:◑
May	2:●, 10:◐, 17:○, 24:◑
Jun	1:●, 9:◐, 15:○, 22:◑, 30:●
Jul	8:◐, 15:○, 22:◑, 30:●
Aug	6:◐, 13:○, 21:◑, 29:●
Sep	4:◐, 11:○, 19:◑, 27:●
Oct	4:◐, 11:○, 19:◑, 26:●
Nov	2:◐, 10:○, 18:◑, 25:●
Dec	1:◐, 9:○, 18:◑, 24:●, 31:◐

2031 Moon Phases Calendar

Jan	8:○, 16:◑, 23:●, 30:◐
Feb	7:○, 14:◑, 21:●
Mar	1:◐, 9:○, 16:◑, 23:●, 31:◐
Apr	7:○, 14:◑, 21:●, 29:◐
May	7:○, 13:◑, 21:●, 29:◐
Jun	5:○, 12:◑, 19:●, 28:◐
Jul	4:○, 11:◑, 19:●, 27:◐
Aug	3:○, 10:◑, 18:●, 25:◐
Sep	1:○, 8:◑, 16:●, 24:◐, 30:○
Oct	8:◑, 16:●, 23:◐, 30:○
Nov	7:◑, 14:●, 21:◐, 28:○
Dec	7:◑, 14:●, 21:◐, 28:○

CONTRACT: IMPOSSIBLE

By the same author

ANOTHER DAY, ANOTHER JACKAL

END AS AN ASSASSIN
– André Warner, Manhunter Vol I

I KILL
– André Warner, Manhunter Vol II

THE MAN WHO HUNTED HIMSELF
– André Warner, Manhunter Vol III

REACTION OF THE TIGER
– André Warner, Manhunter Vol IV

SHE KILLS
– Liza Power, Vigilante

SPANISH ROCK
– André Warner, Manhunter Vol V

BLOOD RED AND BARDOT

André Warner, Manhunter – Vol VI

CONTRACT: IMPOSSIBLE

LEX LANDER

Kaybec Publishing

Published in 2020 by Kaybec Publishing
441 Avenue President Kennedy
Suite 1003
Montreal
Québec
H3A 0A4

ISBN: 978-1-989030-10-3 (mobi)
ISBN: 978-1-989030-11-0 (epub)
ISBN: 978-1-989030-09-7 (Paperback)

Printed and bound by Kindle Direct Publishing

I

ONE WOLFF IN ANOTHER WOLFF'S CLOTHING

Chapter One

They always came in pairs.

Their cover was so natural, so cleverly choreographed, I almost mistook them for what they were pretending to be. Two couples, white Caucasian, casual dress, chatting in group on the sidewalk in Avenue Jules Janin, voices raised and animated as after a few drinks. Beside them a car with a running engine and an open driver's door. The scene was cleverly set. One couple dropping another couple off outside their apartment after an evening out as a foursome. What could be more commonplace?

Since moving in to my swank hotel in Paris' still fashionable 16th *arrondissement* two weeks back, I had avoided a predictable pattern of behaviour. I had dined out most evenings at different restaurants, occasionally with a girl from an escort agency, occasionally with an acquaintance, at other times alone. Once in a while I travelled by cab; mostly I went on foot, varying my itinerary as much as the street layout allowed. One route bordered the Seine, another straggled through a park, a third – tonight's choice – along respectable tree-flanked streets on the fringe of the diplomatic district. Of the three, the park option was the loneliest, the natural choice of a hit man. Tonight's more populous route should have been the safest, the one where I was most likely to be off my guard.

It was a balmy evening for mid-April Paris, a cloud-free night but no stars on view thanks to the light pollution that blights all major cities in this twenty-first century. The sidewalk was wet. Away across the Seine the mutter of a storm in retreat. It was past midnight and traffic was light in this backwater of a street, hemmed in by high-class apartments ancient and modern and walled yards with private entrances.

When the foursome baled out of the car, a so-ordinary Peugeot sedan with silver paintwork and French licence plates, I was still fifty metres

distant, too far to read the number. Vigilant as ever, I might have slowed a little, just to play it safe and allow extra seconds to assess and compute the risk factor. Because every encounter had its risk factor. On a scale of 1 to 10, where 1 is zero risk, these two couples represented a 3 or at most a 4.

As I drew closer the animated conversation continued, interspersed with laughter; one girl, a tall, runway-thin brunette, was giggling too much, her speech high-pitched and breathy, as if she were tipsy. Beyond the foursome, another man and woman were walking towards me. She was in an evening gown and had her arm tucked through his; he was in a tux and smoking. All these details and others registered with me but contained no overt warnings.

The oncoming couple reached the foursome before I did, and I heard an exchange of voices, what sounded like an apology from one of the guys, and the couple were allowed to proceed, albeit in single file. All so, so normal.

The apologetic guy then glanced at me as I approached. He was talking as he glanced, fluent in French, and he carried on talking without taking his eyes off me.

Still nothing out of the ordinary about his behaviour or that of the rest of the group. Except that the tall woman was no longer doing her giggly-squealy act; she was standing still – so still and in such contrast to her previous routine, it triggered a tiny alarm bell in my brain. There was an air of expectation about her, like a compressed spring waiting to be released. My personal risk indicator was rising. Less than twenty metres now separated us. The 75 on the licence plate, denoting central Paris, was now legible. The couple who had been forced into single file were now passing me, absorbed in each other.

The guy in the group who had been watching me flapped a vague salutation.

'Say, do you speak English?' he called out. His accent was Transatlantic. A few seconds ago they had all been speaking French like natives.

The wrong note. Why hadn't he waited until I reached them to ask the question? That was when the smell of ambush became overpowering.

The instinct that had kept me alive all these years as a contract killer went onto red alert. I was about to pass a parked SUV. I made an immediate ninety-degree sidestep, to dart behind the SUV. Screened from the foursome by its bulk, I crouched and freed the little Boberg automatic from its ankle holster.

A pounding of feet on the sidewalk. I flung myself flat as the thud of a silenced gun accompanied the clang of a bullet slamming into the back door of the SUV. It had originated in the opposite direction from that of the group who, I now realised, were red herrings. The other couple were the hit team. On their side I was unprotected, but even as a second, then a third shot whined off the paving, I was rolling under the SUV which, fortunately for me, had just enough clearance.

By now I had lined up the Boberg – tiny, powerful, accurate – and was primed for action. The gun wasn't silenced. When I started using it, the noise would rouse the neighbourhood. I would have to hit hard and move fast, because gunshots mean phone calls to the police.

Legs were all I could see of the four red herrings, all on the move into the Peugeot. Their job done, they were out of it. The lone couple had taken cover behind the next car in line, hidden from my sight, horizontal as I was. One or both of them pumped several wild shots my way, too high to do any damage, but not by much. The guy's head popped up above the hood, and I let fly a couple of rounds, but my aim was too hasty to do more than score the car's fender and give the bastard a fright.

He was savvy enough to know when he had lost his advantage. No pro who tried to take out another pro and failed would stick around for a second go. Like fouling up the first service at tennis; the second was nowhere near as fast, never as deadly.

The doors of the car with the 75 plates slammed. An engine stuttered into life, tyres squealed, mufflers burbled. Farther along the street another engine woke up as the lone couple joined in the retreat. Both sets of noises quickly faded into the Paris night. A rectangle of light flared in an apartment across the street. A window opened. A male voice demanded to know what was going on 'down there'. I lay still, confident that I was invisible to him. By now silence had revisited the street. The

guy at the window cursed in a different language and shut the window with emphasis.

I slithered out from under the life-saving SUV. The backs of my jacket and pants were soaked, and the fronts were smeared in muck from the underside of the vehicle. Not that sartorial issues figured high on my menu of worries in the wake of this attempt on my life. The fact that the attempt had been made, and I had survived it was now history. What preoccupied me above all else, as I made tracks back to the dubious sanctuary of my hotel suite, was who and what was behind it.

* * * * *

It was well over a year since my last contact with *Il Sindicato,* my erstwhile regular employers-cum-brokers until we fell out over my unauthorised killing of a major client. Since then, a Damocles-threat had hung over my head, although it had never been more than hinted at, and of late I had become ever more hopeful they would leave me in peace.

This new development suggested my hopes were founded on quicksand. Sure, I had enemies out there. You don't knock off fifty people without somebody, someplace, getting hacked off about it. The victims' family, friends, business associates, all with cause to avenge violent death. In the main, even if they suspected who placed the contract, they had no knowledge of who was responsible for the act of slaying. It was inevitable though that snippets would trickle out into the public domain, be it by accident or by design and with malice aforethought.

I had no means of determining who wanted me removed. The only clues the group had left behind were a handful of spent shell cases in the gutter and around and about. Without access to a forensics laboratory this detritus would have been valueless to me.

Literally clueless, I could only speculate. Or perhaps not quite. Later that morning, with the sun up and warming my room at the Hotel Hameau de Passy on the street of the same name, I called Giorgio du Poletti, senior executive at *Il Sindicato*, my long-time mediator. A man I

used to think of as a friend, but who had proved he was a 'company man' through and through, when I put his loyalties to the stress test.

He was slow to pick up. A voicemail finally cut in and invited me to leave my name, the reason for my call, and a number to call back. It was Sunday, so maybe he was at church. Despite his involvement in big crime, he was a practising Catholic and a regular attendee at his local church in Antibes. Just another of the many paradoxes about him and his contemporaries.

Although he knew me by my real name, André Warner, I used my permanent pseudo to leave a message, in case of prying ears.

'Henley,' I said. 'I need to speak. Call me back to save me having to drive down to the Côte d'Azur to make a personal visit.'

The threat was to guarantee he would return my call. Were I to appear in person at his swish split-level home overlooking the Med, I wouldn't be welcome. Meanwhile, my stomach was grumbling a protest. I put in place the usual precautions against my room being searched in my absence and went down to breakfast.

* * * * *

My short layover in Paris was in part for the pleasure of renewing my acquaintance with that still most cultured of European capitals, but mostly to do business. My business was killing, and the man I was meeting the morning after the ambush had money to spend on a person's or persons' demise.

It sometimes seemed to me that I passed most of my nights in hotels of variable quality and most of my days meeting dubious characters in bars and eateries, ranging from sleazy to Michelin-starred. My periodic retirements hadn't prevented the word from circulating among the denizens of the dark side of the world that I was a gun for hire. What troubled me most was that the more people knew about me and the services I provided, the greater the prospect that the word would filter through to Interpol or Europol *et al.* Becoming infamous was not the same as becoming famous.

Notwithstanding the drizzly skies that had quenched the morning

sun, not to mention the unseasonably low temperatures, we sat outside at the Café Montespan, a short leg-stretch from my hotel. A faded awning kept us dry, and the traffic drowned our voices, making us secure against eavesdroppers.

My contact didn't come up with much of substance.

'I know you by reputation, of course,' was one of his early lines. 'Also that you're semi-retired but can be tempted back into active service if the deal is right.' He pronounced it 'roight'.

His name was Donovan, and his brogue attested to his Irishness or his talents as a mimic. He was large, but not fat, in his fifties and dressed like a vacationer, in chinos and a polo shirt. Regular features and, take away the receding hairline and bare crown, passably good-looking. His surmise that I could be 'tempted back', was not wrong. It depended on my state of mind at the time and the attractiveness of the proposition. Money alone wouldn't cut it.

'Well then,' Donovan said with a touch of irritation, when I failed to respond. 'Is it true?'

I could have played it obtuse, but I decided on openness.

'That I'm still in the market?' My sigh wasn't all theatrical. 'It's not out of the question.'

Unusually for a preliminary meeting with a client, we didn't progress much further, and he was shy about the details. After a short exchange about my availability, geographical constraints, and fee – $500,000 US, fifty percent down – we were done.

'I'll be in touch,' he said, knocking back his *pastis*, and leaving a 10-euro bill under the glass.

A tip of the head and he was off, striding down the Rue de la Pompe like a man with a mission accomplished.

* * * * *

It is said that classical music appreciation is a pastime of the 'elite'. I disagree. But if it's true – and who decides these things? – then I'm an unashamed, paid-up member of that club.

As I swung my Aston Martin Vantage, a mode of conveyance as

elitist as they come, off the Boulevard Périphérique and linked up with the Autoroute du Soleil to head south, I slid a CD into the slot of the player and my choice was inarguably classical – Vivaldi's Autumn.

The initial rush of strings, uplifting and stirring the soul, with all its little intricacies and switches in direction, is designed to keep you in a state of alertness until, three minutes in, the pace slows dramatically, and what was vigorous and stimulating becomes lilting and dreamy. Music to doze by, if it weren't too magnificent a piece to miss. Plus, I was driving.

Ahead of me lay six hours of *autoroute* to Montelimar. Not to visit the nougat vendors in that town, but because it was a comfortable stretch to drive, and the town is blessed with a pleasant traditional hotel – the Château les Oliviers de Salettes. The chateau in question is of 16th century vintage and the olive trees after which it's named of similar antiquity. The other attraction is a gastronomic restaurant worth fasting for. La Petite France is in a cul-de-sac in the heart of Old Montelimar. The owner is a Mme Le Poitier, a *grande-dame* of the old school, by which I mean she respects and cossets her clientele and manages, without any hint of familiarity, to make you feel at home.

'*Vous êtes chez vous, cher Monsieur*,' she had cooed at me, on the occasion of my premier visit. Since when I had made a ritual of stopping over in Montelimar when travelling north to south and vice versa, to renew my acquaintance with her simple but so tasty cuisine.

Chez moi or not, on this benign evening in May, I insisted on a table in a corner, by the door to the kitchen, with my back to the wall. And the Boberg in my belt instead of in the ankle holster.

* * * * *

As I was pulling away from the toll booth to rejoin the *autoroute* next morning, my cell phone burped. A familiar number replaced the GPS image. The cell was connected to Blue Tooth, so I stabbed the speak button on the dash and responded with a neutral 'Yes?'

'Ah, André,' Giorgy said, almost gushing.

'Hello, Giorgy.'

'Are you well, my friend?'

I bipped the gas pedal to dart around a lumbering tanker and settled down in front of it before answering.

'Sorry, I'm on the Soleil and had to deal with a traffic issue. I'm good, thanks. You?'

A chuckle. 'Oh, I am always well, apart from signs of rheumatism and the usual hay fever.'

His wife, Dolores – French, *chic*, loyal – was well too, and the Antibes weather was delightful, and business continued to be profitable.

'How can I assist you?' he enquired, with the niceties behind us. 'It's quite a while since we spoke.'

Now for the crunch.

'You can assist me by telling me if some of your dogs have been let loose on me again.'

I had no expectation of his coming clean. That wasn't how the game was played, *Sindicato*-style. Nobody ever came clean. What I hoped for, was that some nuance in his voice would help me sort out facts from equivocation. Plus, if he were feeling charitably disposed towards me, a hint of a hint of who was out to get me.

I was doing a hundred and forty kph and a Porsche ripped past me as if I were parked. Czech plates. I had no opinions on drivers from Eastern Europe except to note that they were among the quickest on the highway.

'Has there been a … er, an incident?' Giorgy said, without a ripple in his tone. Even the hesitation was manufactured to disarm, make it sound so much more natural.

'Three guys, three women, in Paris in the small hours yesterday morning.'

I could sense his yawn. Also manufactured, as if I were suffering from a persecution complex.

His tongue-clicking came over clear as crystal.

'You don't think we had anything to do with it, do you?'

'Well … if you didn't, that just leaves me a hundred or so other suspects.'

Another chuckle, mellifluous and warm.

'Do not worry, my friend, on this occasion we are not planning your demise. That's not to say that a member of the Syndicate isn't, mind you.'

There it was. That subtle whiff, insubstantial as smoke in the breeze, of a line I could pursue. No use asking him to enlarge. He had said all he was likely to say, and I would have to make of it what I would.

The conversation was effectively over. He had betrayed no confidences, broken no oaths. He was as clean and gleaming as a newly shined shoe. Our goodbyes were non-committal. He had once professed to be a true friend. I had doubted that then, and I still had doubts.

Puzzle still unsolved, I drove on to the Franco-Spanish border, slowing down as I crossed it but not required to stop. My next overnight pause would be my yacht, *Seamist II*, berthed at Sitges to the south of Barcelona. Tomorrow, the final leg to Malaga, to conclude the sale of my bar-restaurant, The Golden Palm. To bring to an end my tenure in the hospitality trade, freeing me up to converge on who was out to burn me, and why.

Chapter Two

My restaurant was in good shape. The exterior repaint I had sanctioned in my absence had fixed the tired look, and the new terrace furniture and solar roof transformed it from typically Spanish, i.e. careworn and grubby, into an inviting place to drop in, be it for nothing more than a coffee, a coke, or a cut-price, barely profitable *menu del dia.*

Fernando, my manager-cum-Man Friday, and José, waiter-cum-gofer were both on the ball and between them could handle English and German, as well as their native Spanish. The newly recruited third member of the staff, a Swedish girl named Elvira, all freckled cheeks, obligatory blonde locks, and a winning smile, was already proving an asset – according to Fernando, who regarded all comely females as assets. His choice of outfit for her predictably included a low neckline and a high hemline. She didn't seem to mind, and for sure her virtues were bound to pull in a few extra male voyeurs. On very short notice she was already flirting with me. I took her aside and insisted on a proper employer-employee relationship. She wasn't offended. She didn't give up either.

My first and second days back passed without event. No couples showed up bearing arms and I began to believe I had sufficiently muddied my traces, at least for now.

I wasn't due to sign my ownership away until the next weekend, and as my agenda for the days, weeks, and months to come was blank, I was happy to help behind the counter and prepare salads in the kitchen, where Juan-Felipe, the chef, was producing his usual selection of *paellas, pascaitos fritos, pistos* and *polbos*, and his speciality from the north of Spain, *fabadas Asturianas.*

It was early evening of the second day of my return when the woman entered the restaurant and my life. She could have been any age between

thirty and a well-preserved mid-fifties. In a cluster around her, like a protective screen, were four teenage-ish kids, two of each sex. Most Spanish eat after 9.00pm, so a showing before 7.00 labelled her party as non-Spanish.

Several tables were laid for dining on the terrace. The sinking sun was dispersing the storm clouds over the hills to the west, and the temperature was just about right. The kids were allowed their say and predictably opted for *al fresco*. They spoke French, so communication was not a problem for me, though I guessed Elvira would struggle with it. It turned out okay though, as the woman had passable English, and so did two of the kids.

While José handed out the menus, I performed my usual 'mine host' routine, welcoming them in French, and offering complimentary aperitifs. The woman ordered a sherry, the boys beers, the girls juices of different hues. While an underemployed Fernando prepared them, I studied the group discreetly from behind the bar. The kids addressed the woman as '*maman*', which made her probably over forty. The absence of a *papa* intrigued me in a vague, passing-the-time fashion, no more. The mother had worn well for her years and multiple pregnancies. Her figure was slender, no tummy to speak of, and with brown eyes that were just the right size for her small face. Same colour hair, worn short but not mannish. Good quality apparel – tailored pants, one of those shirt things that ties at the waist, a sweater with the sleeves looped over her shoulders – and a discreet display of jewellery. The boys both dark-haired, the older girl blonde, the younger sandy. Age range fourteen to twenty, all of them good-looking, all dressed to suit their individual tastes. The chatter was animated, Parisian French, with plenty of laughter. Their drinks came. They ordered their food. I took off to lend an extra pair of hands in the kitchen. Later, when Fernando went to serve their starter courses, I tagged along to wish them '*Bon appétit*!' All the youngsters thanked me but only the mother caught my eye; not merely caught but held it for several seconds until I looked away as if she had caught me out in some indiscretion.

Back in the steamy kitchen, my first thought was not that she was hitting on me in front of her family, but that she was the vanguard of a

hit squad. Mistrust of all off-key behaviour goes with my professional territory and the recent fracas in Paris had made me doubly alert and triply suspicious.

With the chatter and laughter of the family entering the open door of the kitchen, I prowled around, wondering and worrying. Whoever was after me would have figured that a seemingly normal family would make an ideal scouting party. In that respect a replay of the Paris ambush. The kids could be presumed innocent of any involvement. As for the mother, she didn't look the type to be mixed up in villainy, but over the years I had come to mistrust looks alone as a reflection of a person's moral etiquette.

To get my mind off negativity, I went upstairs to the apartment and made sure my weaponry was accessible. The SIG was too bulky to wear in the restaurant, but the Boberg wasn't. I strapped on the ankle holster and practised a few fast draws from a seated position.

The Boberg XR9 is a quirky little piece. Five inches long, ultra-light, made to a bullpup format with the firing chamber behind the trigger, and a magazine in which you load the bullets nose-down. The preferred calibre is 9mm, and as it can be a bit hissy about ammunition it's best to stick with the manufacturer's recommendation.

Few handguns are compact enough to allow concealment in an ankle holster, but the Boberg is one of that select group. That or a cuff extension that ejects the gun into your waiting hand. The drawback to the cuff version is that you have to wear a jacket to conceal it.

Duly armed and dangerous, I meandered back downstairs. A few early diners had swelled the numbers, but nobody that made me twitch with paranoia. I sat down at a small table in the corner of the terrace, by the open door that led to the bar. The sky was darkening and the solar-powered outdoor lighting in full bloom. I opened the newspaper I had collected en route as a prop.

The woman and her youngsters were well into their main course. She had abandoned hers, the knife and fork forming a V on her plate to signify she had finished. She was sitting back, a glass of white wine held by the stem, her gaze fixed on the dying sun. Then, as I studied her agreeable profile, her head turned towards me, and once again we

locked stares. A corner of her mouth twitched – a half smile, friendly or mocking, it was hard to gauge. I nodded to her and switched on a full smile.

'Are you the owner?' she asked in French, her voice raised to carry across the unoccupied table between us and counter the chatter of her kids.

'I am,' I answered in French, my other natural tongue. 'Are you staying around here?'

'Yes. We're at the Molina.'

The Molina was a somewhat faded boutique hotel a few doors down, with a beachside terrace. Inexpensive but clean and friendly.

'When you've finished, if you feel like a change of company, come and join me for a *digestif.* On the house, naturally.'

'*D'accord,*' she responded coolly, no affected coyness at all. In my experience, Frenchwomen, especially those of a certain sophistication, don't get all snooty about being hit on. They just deal with it.

'In a few minutes then?' I said, and she nodded and transferred her attention back to the young set; the two girls, who were facing me, were suddenly taking an interest in proceedings. The younger, who was about fourteen, stared at me wide-eyed and not entirely innocently; her sister, who could have been a year or two older, gave me a sultry once-over followed by a haughty toss of her head, putting me in my place as a glorified bartender. Typical Parisienne in the making. Full of icy froideur one minute, raging nympho the next.

It was coming up to nine o'clock, dark, and a chill had descended on the terrace when the Frenchwoman left her kids to mosey over to my table. She was wearing the sweater by now. I proposed we go indoors and she agreed with a ghost of a smile.

I guided her to a corner table in a dimly lit alcove. The adjoining restaurant area was still busy, but we had the bar to ourselves apart from a madly-in-love couple in the shadows of the opposite corner, making the most of their semi-privacy and a meal of each other.

'Jack Henley,' I said, proffering a hand. As ever, when I wasn't convinced of someone's innocence, I used my *alter-nomen*, my bogus identity whose pedigree was almost as solid as the genuine me.

'Sophie Morais,' she said. For a woman she had a firm grip. We sat down opposite each other at the little square table. 'You are English?'

'Half.'

'And the second half? You speak French like a native but you have an unusual accent.'

'Québecois. On my mother's side.'

She nodded. 'I see.'

Fernando had berthed alongside the table to enquire after our desires. Mme Morais settled for San Pelegrino water.

'I'll share it with you,' I said, and ordered a 75cl bottle between us.

'You are the owner of this place?' she said, while we were awaiting delivery of our refreshment.

'Not for much longer. I've sold it. Move out next Saturday.'

'What a pity. What will you do?'

'When I've sold it?' It was a reasonable question. 'Oh, I don't know. Kill time, I guess.'

'Kill ... *time*?' It didn't translate well. She frowned. She had a nicely shaped but sulky mouth, designer-built for expressing disapproval. Then she said something that made me uneasy about her all over again, just when I was beginning to accept her at face value.

'Is that all you will kill?'

If Fernando hadn't set a tray down on the table as she spoke, I might have given myself away. The distraction, small though it was, put the dialogue on hold while he opened the bottle with a flourish worthy of a Grand Cru, and slopped the fizzing contents into two glasses.

He performed his usual stiff little bow that was not much more than a forward tilt of the head and left us alone.

I clinked Mme Morais' glass with mine. 'You were saying?' Though I recalled word for word what she had been saying.

Her shrug was elegant. 'I don't remember.'

'How about you?' I said, to force a switch of subject. 'These are your children?'

'Yes.' A real smile now, the smile of a proud parent. 'I have that good fortune.'

'Your husband will be meeting you in Spain?'

She drank delicately from her glass, wrinkling her nose at the bubbles.

'My husband, the father of my sons, is dead.' Before I could gush the usual condolences, she added, 'It was a long time ago. There has been another husband since then.' A grimace. 'Unfortunately that one is still alive. As far as I know.'

'Oh.'

It wasn't often my chat skills let me down in the company of an attractive woman. But her cryptic 'all you kill' comment, had left me struggling to keep the party alive.

'We are on vacation,' she stated, helpfully bridging the void in our conference.

My tongue finally untwisted itself.

'Best time of year.'

We shot some more breeze, mostly about nothing of consequence now that I was on my guard.

The restaurant emptied. Her kids came to say goodnight. She didn't introduce them to me, or me to them. They all included me in their '*Bonne nuit, maman, bonne nuit, monsieur,*' though, evidence of their good breeding.

The young couple, having gone as far by way of sexual congress as the indecent exposure laws would permit, paid up and eloped. Now there was just me and the mystery woman, Mme Sophie Morais.

She glanced left and right, leaned across the table towards me, her manner conspiratorial.

'You *do* kill, don't you?'

* * * * *

Of late, I had been doing a lot of sleeping alone, and I was tiring of the novelty. No doubt, when I invited the delectable Mme Morais to share my table, the prospect of sharing a bed with her had been at the back of my mind. Or maybe at the front. She was pleasing enough to behold to inspire your average male stud to think wicked thoughts.

My aspirations had fizzled out when she fired that question at me –

only it wasn't a question. She *knew*. She knew about me and my line of work, and I was intent on finding out why it mattered to her.

'You've got me confused with somebody else,' I said, my voice level, my expression calm. Wriggling out of compromising situations had become second nature in a decade or more of fake IDs, false passports, and invented autobiographies.

'Not possible. John 'Enley, owner of the Golden Palm, in Malaga.'

No room there for mistaken identity.

'This is some kind of joke, isn't it?'

She shook her head, her eyes engaging mine.

'No joke, Monsieur 'Enley.'

Words of denial jammed in my vocal chords. A straight rejection was too simplistic. If she trusted her source of information, she would just assume I was playing it cautious, as would any real-live hit man.

The half-smile was back on her face; the other half was a searching gaze.

'You have nothing to say?'

'No comment, I think is the usual comeback.' I topped up both our glasses with San Pelegrino. 'Except that you are being a little indiscreet – if you really are looking for a killer.'

She cupped her face between her palms and let her jaw sag, giving an impression of being mildly horrified. If it was an act, it was a star performance.

'Looking for a killer!'

'Don't let it bother you,' I said, throwing in a grin to prove I wasn't taking it seriously. Like hell I wasn't. 'If there really is a killer called John Henley running a restaurant called the Golden Palm in Malaga, it's a king-size coincidence.'

She muttered under her breath and pushed her chair backwards, the feet scraping on the tiles.

'Do you take me for a fool?'

We got up simultaneously.

'Not a fool. Somebody with a big problem to solve, otherwise why would you need a … a hit man. I suppose that's what you're after?'

She made to leave but I grabbed her arm. She didn't pull free, just stood glaring at me.

'Would you like to talk about it?' I said.

She swallowed, hesitated, nodded.

Fernando chose that moment to roll up in case we needed refills. I waved him away but the window of opportunity had already slammed shut.

'Perhaps not,' she said, her tone decisive. She put out a dainty, ringless hand. 'Good night, Monsieur 'Enley, or whatever your name is.'

'Good night.' I was reluctant to let her go, and prolonged the handshake, hoping to send her a signal. It didn't connect. She extricated her fingers from mine and took off through the open doorway to be swallowed up in the night.

Now, three hours later, I was lying in my bed in the dark, brooding over her. The occasional vehicle passed by, its headlights traversing the wall, spotlighting the exquisite lithograph of a young girl by the Flemish artist Madou. Thinking about her, not so much because of her sexual allure, of which she had her fair quota, but because of the weird exchange of words. She had my name, the name of my restaurant, and she was expecting to meet a hit man. All pretty unequivocal to my thinking. She had a story to tell but in the end, she backed off telling it. Yet it must have been me she really wanted to meet. So why the reticence?

I eventually drifted off, awoke late and hurried round to her hotel. She and her family were long gone, destination unknown. Leaving the mystery unsolved.

* * * * *

His outfit was a three-piece summer weight grey suit complete with pocket watch and chain. Classy or pretentious, hard to judge which. His tie was burgundy, knotted with precision below a crisp white collar. A shade too sartorial for the venue – the Hilton Lake Como Hotel, at the southern extremity of the lake. My own choice of attire was more relaxed and appropriate: sport jacket, cords, no tie.

From where we sat, a floor below the pool terrace, we could gaze out over the shortest strand of the lake's Y, loomed over by the heights of the

Triangol Lariano to the right, the shoreline cluttered with a multitude of multi-millionaire properties, including that of George and Amal Clooney.

It was evening and I was dining on Sicilian red prawns tartare to Donovan's white truffle. In my extensive hotel experience, the in-house restaurant of the Hilton chain is not the in-place for gourmets, but I had no complaints over my dish. Donovan seemed satisfied too, now and again grunting in what I took to be approval as he munched.

He was overweight, but it wasn't flab. Former boxer was a possibility, though his vocabulary was a cut above that of your average pugilist. He had requested this second meeting, accepted the venue without demur, and had shown up ahead of me. I caught up with him at the bar, making short work of a Guinness. A black attaché case was propped against his stool.

Only when I was mopping the juices off my plate with some local bread did he open negotiations, which after all was the reason for my being here. Well, not quite the only reason.

'We're prepared to pay your price,' he informed me. As my price was non-negotiable, this concession didn't quicken my pulse.

'Who's we?'

'My associates and I.'

'You mean Mme Sophie Marais.' It was a long shot. His reaction was deadpan.

'Who?'

'Cut it out. Two weeks ago, I was approached by a guy, namely you, looking for a hit man. Last week a woman approached me, also looking for a hit man. This week I'm meeting up with a messenger boy looking for a hit man. Any connection, do you think?'

He didn't rise to it.

'You'll have to work it out yourself.'

I let it lie. Many contacts came through a go-between, though in such cases the principal usually stayed nameless and faceless.

'So what's the job?' I asked, dabbing my lips.

'Well, for that much money you can hardly expect to get him served up plucked and oven-ready.' A smirk teased one side of his mouth; the other side stayed horizontal and lipless.

He didn't elaborate, so I prompted him with an irritated 'Well?'

I didn't need his half-million bucks. I didn't need another death at my door. In fact, all I needed was to be left in peace, something that seemed to be as elusive as Will-o'-the-wisp, whoever the hell he was.

'There's a catch … nobody knows where he is.'

It wouldn't be the first contract that had required me to play detective.

'Finding people goes with the territory, as often as not. Where was he last seen?'

'Budapest,' he said promptly.

I nodded. 'I did some work there once.' I burped into my napkin. Those prawns had been a gastronomic masterpiece. 'When was this?'

'Therein lies a problem. The most recent sighting was 2008. June, to be precise.'

His brogue was less pronounced today. His mode of speech bespoke an educated man. It made me curious how and why he was mixed up in hiring a contract killer.

'June 2008,' I said reflectively. 'Eleven years ago. You think he's still there?'

An elegant shrug.

'Who knows? Part of the payment is for finding out.'

From our elevated position, the lake's surface was so calm as to appear matt. The sun, hovering over some low hills on our left, was too far past the meridian to create any light reflection. If I had painted the lake just as it was, backseat artists would have scoffed at my lack of skill and advised me to add reflection and ripples.

'It's a tall order,' I mused. 'It could take months. He could be dead.'

He drained the last dregs of Guinness from his glass.

'You could be right.' He glanced sidelong and flagged a passing waiter. The man came over. He had a stiff-backed gait, as if he were balancing a trayload of drinks.

Donovan ordered another Guinness, maybe to bolster his Irish credentials, or because he genuinely liked the stuff. My choice was a modest Toscana Rosso wine, a dense full-bodied red. I was already on my third glass.

'I presume you have a photograph – a recent photograph.'

He cleared his throat. 'A photograph certainly. Recent, no; in fact, it dates back to 2008. It was taken in …'

'Budapest?' I finished for him, like an offstage prompter feeding lines to an actor. 'That's logical if he hasn't been seen in public since then. Is it a good resemblance?'

'See for yourself.' He fished an envelope from his inside jacket pocket and passed it over. With some misgivings, I opened it and slid out a grainy colour shot of two men, seated at a table out of doors.

'The one on the right,' he said, which wasn't helpful as the one on the right was in profile: long nose, eye colour anybody's guess, mouth just a mouth; blond hair worn long and rather unkempt; age anything from thirty to fifty; apparel just clothes, giving no clue to his dress tastes. A beer mug was halfway to his mouth.

The other guy, also blond but better groomed, was full frontal to the camera. His features were obscured by saucer-size sunspecs and a raised hand, as if he were shielding himself from the photographer. Fleetingly I wondered what had become of the camera-wielder.

'Is that it?' I asked, trying to extract something from the photo that wasn't there. 'This is the only photo?'

'The only one we have,' he said unhelpfully.

I studied the photo anew. Between the two heads was a sign that read DSESSZ B. Having a limited command of Hungarian – more accurately, not a single word – I couldn't pronounce it, let alone translate it, even if it was a complete word and not just a string of letters. Other than that, the photo contained no clues as to the whereabouts of the subjects.

'Is there any other information you can provide about him? His date of birth, his nationality, his tastes in women, cars, sports, for instance. Does he have any known relatives, friends, haunts, peccadilloes? How does he, or did he back in 2008, earn a living? Does he have a criminal record? Any special skills and talents, such as safecracking, housebreaking, mending sewing machines? Is he a boozer and/or a druggie?'

He frowned. 'A certain amount of data exists and will be provided,

but not until the contract is made.' A momentary hesitation. 'There is something else you will need to know.'

'Something else?' I raised eyebrows at him. 'You mean besides the lack of a decent photo and reliable knowledge of his whereabouts.'

He tossed the residue of his Guinness down his throat, burped behind two fingers, and set the glass down.

'Keep your sarcasm, Henley.' His voice was cold. Until now, emotion hadn't been his strong point, so I was surprised that I had ruffled his equanimity.

'I do beg your pardon. I was wondering if I was expected to find a guy who hadn't been seen for half a generation, and who looks like about a million other guys that I can see from a blurry photo. Now it seems there's more. You're spoiling me.'

His expression darkened.

'The other man in the picture is his identical twin brother.'

Lost for the right words to express my feelings, I expressed no feelings.

'Nothing to say?' He was regarding me behind another of his little smirks.

'Nothing that will make the job easier. In fact, I would say what you're asking is just about impossible. It's not even worth my while negotiating a higher price. Do you mind if I ask what he's done to upset you?'

His eyebrows shot up.

'Me? Not a thing. My principals are the ones who want him dead.'

Now it was principals, not associates.

'Question still applies. In plain English, what did he do to merit the death sentence?'

'Fair enough. They're keeping the details to themselves, but I understand it's about a sum of money that's theirs by right, but which he seems to have appropriated. A very large sum.'

'If it's so large, why wait eleven years to hire me, or somebody like me?'

'I'm not authorised to release that detail.' He fidgeted with his watch chain. 'It's a private matter.'

'Is getting the money back included in the deal?'

'There will be a bonus, a percentage of the amount recovered.'

I frowned. 'So he swindled your principals out of some cash. Is that all he's done?'

It wasn't enough for me that he was a bad guy who stole from bad people, if that's what happened. It could be he stole from the wicked to give to the good. If so, I was on his side.

'What is, or was, his racket?'

'At the time he was a money launderer for most of the big boys in Eastern Europe and Russia. He's also wanted for rape in Japan. They tried to extradite him, but there was no treaty between Japan and Hungary, so he's got clean away with that particular crime.'

I only ever accepted contracts on vermin. Money laundering didn't cut it, and I wasn't even sure about rape, considering the high percentage of alleged rapists whose victims were proved to have given consent.

'Are you not happy with his CV?' he asked.

'Anything to add to it? Anything nasty, I mean, and not based on the word of one witness.'

'Only rumours. He used to run a team of collectors whose job was to empty slot machines and ensure the bars that operated them didn't skim some of the profits.'

'Hmm. If they did skim the profits, what happened to them?'

His look was bleak.

'They were snuffed out. Not by him personally, you understand. He used paid help, people like you.'

If I was going to accept the contract, that plus the rape would have to suffice for now. It would mean taking a lot on trust – that the guy was, or used to be, in charge of an operation that occasionally murdered people for a minor misdemeanour.

'It's a bit thin for my liking,' I said. 'The evidence, I mean.'

He chuckled, blue eyes sparkling.

'I heard about your squeamish side.'

'Don't call it squeamish, call it selective. The ones I kill deserve to die.'

'Jack Henley, knight in tarnished armour.'

Let him mock. Mockery's cheap. My self-imposed code of practice was for my benefit, not my employers'.

'About the payment,' he said. 'It won't be your usual terms. We propose to hold on to your entire fee until you find him, just in case you don't. Then we'll pay the fifty percent up-front payment.'

Curious to hear how he was going to persuade me to accept such terms, I said, 'So you want me to work for nothing.'

The breeze teased the remnants of his hair, making him rush to tidy it with the flat of his hand. He fumbled for a pack of cigarettes – the pack was one of those lurid, anti-smoking designs with pics of diseased organs to deter the deterrable.

'Not quite,' he said, having lit up and taken a long drag, and to hell with his organs. 'We propose to pay an expense allowance of a thousand dollars a day.'

Well, well. This was a new angle. Not that it wasn't a fair enough proposition, if a shade unorthodox. If it took a year, I would earn $350,000 and have no need to touch my capital or commit a crime. On a grand a day, in Budapest, one of the cheaper capitals of Europe, I could live like a king.

'You accept the contract?'

'Not yet. Don't rush me. Do you have a dossier on him or do I have to memorise it all?'

He reached down for the attaché case at his feet, unzipped it and produced an A4 size padded envelope with a name and address written on it, but deleted with marker pen. He shoved it across the table. The postage stamp was French.

'It's all in there,' he said, pointing with his cigarette. 'Read and burn.'

'How will you know if I don't – burn it, I mean?'

'Good question. It's in your own interests. Nothing in that envelope incriminates me or my principals. Anyone could have typed and printed it. It might incriminate *you* though.'

Chapter Three

Donovan was only my first date of the evening. My second was female, name of Angela Renwick, pronounced Rennick. English, thirty-seven years old, and smart as a crossword-puzzle compiler. We had met in Gibraltar a month back when I was finishing up a job there, and struck up a platonic friendship. She had recently lost a husband, Lucas, from pancreatic cancer. She never talked about him. Nor was she over his death. I became a handy shoulder to cry on, a prop, a distraction. Despite the heartache she tried to hide with only limited success, I enjoyed her company. She made an attractive companion for evenings out, with her sandy bobbed hair that provided a flattering frame to her heart-shaped features. Her best facial asset was the eyes that were deep blue and deep-set, beneath eyebrows she declined to pluck. Her nose, in profile, had a bump at the tip and was, quirkily, the first thing I had noticed about her. Slight northern accent – she came from a village near Bolton. No children, no explanation, none required.

We spent a week doing things together in Gib, remaining platonic, until she had to return to her home in Devon, and I to the Golden Palm.

She owned an apartment in Laglio, the upper floor of a two-story building with an interrupted view of Lake Como, that she and her husband bought when such places were still affordable. The day before I left Spain, she had emailed to say she planned to spend a few weeks at the apartment, and would I care to join her for a short spell.

The invitation was innocent of sexual overtures. She wasn't in the market for a replacement for Lucas. I had a few twinges of regret about that, but had developed a respect for her that precluded getting in deeper unless she initiated it. She was good company and, importantly from a professional angle, no one knew of our friendship. As a last resort, her apartment could serve as a bolthole. Always useful.

* * * * *

I was travelling in my Range Rover Evoque in preference to the Aston Martin. It was less ostentatious and therefore less likely to attract attention, and you never could tell when the off-road capability might drive you out of trouble. The paintwork was silver grey, bordering on drab.

The reason for choosing the Evoque over a nondescript rental car was the hidden compartment behind the dashboard locker, where I kept a SIG P229 Legion auto pistol and two spare magazines. Spring clips kept the gun secure, and the interior was lined with foam padding to absorb movement.

It was close to midnight when I parked up across the street from Angela's apartment and, carryall in hand, rang her front door bell. The door opened and there she was, the ceiling light picking out golden highlights in her hair.

'Hello, Jack. You're a bit late.'

'Sorry. Business meeting.'

We did the lips-to-cheek ritual. She seemed more reserved than usual, and we didn't talk much before she introduced me to my quarters and wished me good night.

The guest room was on the cramped side, thanks in part to the queen-sized bed. The rest of the furnishings comprised a night table, a bureau, and a built-in closet. A pair of coordinated prints alleviated the starkness of the pale green walls, and a rug by the bed took the chill off the ceramic floor.

In bed, the apartment and the street in the throes of small-hours stillness, I dipped into the dossier on my prospective target. He was American, name of Vincent Wolff. His twin was Victor. Cute on their parents' part, giving them similar names to go with their similar looks. Born in Sylvania near Savannah, Georgia. Ages fifty-one. Height, weight, hair and eyes colouring, it was all there, and all of it at least eleven years old. He/they might be fat slobs by now, bald, adorned with elaborate tattoos. Or dead.

Determining which twin was which threatened to be a major

hurdle. The dossier classed them as identical, no distinguishing marks. That would suggest that no one outside a close relative or lover could tell them apart. I might kill the wrong man. Afterwards, how would I prove to Donovan that I'd killed the right one? The whole twin issue troubled me.

Vincent's education was sound enough. He attended Savannah State University but dropped out after two years. Victor stayed on, majored in French and Italian. Despite failing to graduate, Vincent was recruited by Wells Fargo Bank, but they let him go "under a cloud" a year later. He dropped off the radar, surfacing in Canada after four years, in his mid-twenties.

That was the point in history when his movements became speculative. He was alleged to have been involved in a stock market scam that made him a rich man. Brother Victor teamed up with him and they moved across to Switzerland, became sorts of consultants in "financial services". Vincent married a Genevese heiress, name of Helène de Cardevac, and they started a family. It was beginning to sound as if he became respectable. It didn't last though. Whispers were circulating about his operating as a fence for a Swiss racketeer. You would think that racketeers were a non-existent breed in that haven of staidness, but in my experience the whole Swiss banking profession is a great big racket; they just call themselves bankers.

Vincent and his wife broke up in 2001, divorced the following year. Infidelity on both sides. Then came his second marriage. Another Frenchwoman, a *marquise*, which is in the upper echelons of the aristocracy. His activities spread to France, and continued unabated, still speculative and based on innuendo. Speculation and the Wolff twins seemed to be inseparable. Vincent split with his second wife in 2008. Just upped and decamped, relieving her of several paintings and most of her precious jewellery. What happened to the kids, of which there were then five, all sub-teen, wasn't recorded. No further reference to this phase of his biography, except that he and Victor left Switzerland.

They surfaced next in Budapest. Vincent's abandoned wife set a local PI on him, and at a guess this unfortunate was responsible for the dodgy photos. Nobody knows for sure because two days after he was hired his

remains turned up floating in the Danube, struck down by a lethal case of lead poisoning.

It was three o'clock. I yawned, knuckled my eyes to keep the lids from drooping. A boat hooted out across Lake Como; partygoers letting off steam, likely as not. No shortage of that breed in this playground of mega-rich. In Angela's unfashionable little enclave on the Via Torregia Alta all was quiet.

I returned to my homework, seeking clues and pointers. The Budapest photo suggested that the twins had stayed in harness. But eleven is an awful lot of years and either of them could be long gone, long dead, or no longer recognisable.

As contracts go, it stank. Likelihood of success, close to zero. Without massive resources, such as only the state could provide, finding Vincent Wolff would be an impossibility.

If it was impossible, it wasn't for me. Even at a thousand daily dollars in expenses. I dumped the dossier on the floor, doused the reading light, and was asleep without counting a single sheep.

* * * * *

It was a fine morning. High streaks of cloud like aircraft contrails dimmed the sun, but it was windless and warm. Angela and I went for a pre-breakfast jog along the Veccia Regina which runs beside the lake and leads down to the minuscule harbour and, beyond it, the supermarket. I wore regular shorts and a T-shirt without logos; Angela's shorts were black lycra, the kind that are almost indecent when viewed from behind and in motion; she screened what she termed her 'wobbly bits' from male scrutiny with an oversize T-shirt.

We passed the pink-stuccoed frontage of the Hotel Plino, then the Osteria Vecchio Milo, where an old guy hunched over his breakfast coffee at an outside table, flapped a greeting. After the *supermercato* came the cemetery with its shrines to local notables topped by the pyramidic monument to the renowned philanthropist Dr. Joseph Frank. The lake with its moored boats and the steep hills on the opposite shore popped into view at intervals in the gaps between the lakeside villas.

After covering about two kms, we U-turned by a row of truncated lime trees, cropped to provide shade, and jogged back, making a detour to the *supermercato* for croissants and eggs. We didn't chat as we jogged. Angela wasn't much of a conversationalist at best, and while running she preferred to control her breathing. It was fine and dandy by me. I was used to exercising alone. It was enough to appreciate the lakeside air in my lungs and on my face, and be grateful that my forty-plus-years old body was still functioning like a well-maintained machine.

Breakfast was on Angela's tiny balcony, where there was room for a round table barely the size of a bicycle wheel, and two uncomfortable iron chairs, selected for the lack of space they took up. Angela herself looked especially nice this morning. Not ravishing, not yet restored to happiness, just … nice, overused though that compliment is. The sort of woman you might pass in the street without noticing, yet who has a lasting quality that will survive into old age.

'So who was this mystery man you came here to meet?' was her first question of the day. She didn't ask many, so it was quite an event.

'A possible contract.'

To her, ignorant of the parlance of my trade, a contract was an innocuous enough term.

She nodded and broke a piece off her croissant, dipped it in the puddle of maple syrup on her plate.

'To do with investments?'

Two questions already. She must really be curious. Either that or something was cooking besides the eggs. I had led her to believe I was in the investment business, to account for my haphazard lifestyle. I led most of my women friends up that garden path.

'What else?' I looked past her across the lake where a yacht, similar type to *Seamist*, was trying to get some traction from a feather of breeze.

'Well …' Reticence was unlike her. Maybe she had bad news to impart.

'Speak out, Angie. You're among friends.' I touched her forearm, to show how friendly I was.

'Yes … yes, it's just that I'm a still a little bit frightened by a visit I had, the day before you arrived.'

That would account for her downbeat welcome the previous night. I let her take her time, which she did, munching a rag of croissant, her brow furrowed.

'Two men were here,' she blurted at last, after disposing of the last of the croissant.

'Selling insurance?' I quipped, regretting it when I saw she was seriously uptight about the incident. 'Sorry, I didn't mean to be frivolous. All right, two guys came knocking on your door. What then?'

She swallowed. 'They didn't just knock, they sort of forced an entry. I should have put the chain on before I answered the door … stupid of me. It's so quiet here, you don't think anything bad could happen to you.'

Her innocence in these days of global violence and mayhem was frightening.

'They didn't hurt you, did they?'

She shook her head. 'Not physically. Their attitude was threatening though, and they scared me shitless, if you'll pardon the expression. They … they were looking for a man. They said his name was Warner.'

Two tough guys looking for a man called Warner. I let this seep through my grey matter without hurrying it. Being looked for was on its own worrying enough. Worse than that though, they had my real name and had traced my new Lake Como hideaway.

I tried to squirm out from under.

'Do you know this Warner?' I said, maintaining my pretence to the last. If I was going down, I would go with guns booming and a defiant flutter of England Expects flags at the masthead.

She looked at me directly, her eyes troubled.

'They described him: wavy blond hair, very blue eyes, slightly hooked nose, just over six feet tall, well-built, need I go on?'

Sheltering behind a grim smile, I said, 'Sounds familiar.' I stood up. 'So my cover's blown. I'll pack and be out of your hair in fifteen minutes.'

'No!' She clutched my hand. 'No, Jack. I don't want you to go. Not like that, at any rate.' She hesitated. 'What … what I really want is an explanation. For you to tell me which identity is the real you – if either

of them are. And why you need it, what you do that makes such a deceit necessary.'

Angela was not a major feature in my life. In the month since we had met I had spent barely a week in her company. To walk away, leaving her clean and uninfected by my baggage, would have given me no more than a regretful twinge. Not only that, but I would have removed the threat to her by association that was the penalty of all who got too close to me. Wherever I travelled, perils of one kind or another lurked. Enemies were legion, and they didn't fight to any rule book.

Yet, at times the need to take someone into my confidence was so tempting that I succumbed to it and came clean. Well, fairly clean.

I sat down, pondered how much to reveal, how much to conceal. The sky had clouded over and it seemed as if the very air had become cold and hostile. In the garden below, a woman was hanging out washing, observed by a small dog with a tail that wagged non-stop. As always, the everyday, the commonplace, impacted on me, a reminder that there were people to whom violence and sudden death were only the stuff of newspaper headlines.

'Years ago, when I was young, I became an operative for MI6 –'

'MI6?'

I nodded. 'You know, the British Secret Intelligence Service? Spies and all that razzmatazz.' It rang over-dramatic even to my ears, like a corny line in a movie. 'Well, I quit after my first wife was killed because of my job.'

Angela clasped my hand in both of hers, her expression transformed from anxiety to sympathy.

'Oh, Jack …'

'It's okay, it's okay. It was years ago, fifteen years actually. Anyhow, I quit the service and moved on to new pastures. Now and again though, they haul me back to do some job or other that, usually in the cause of political expedience, they prefer to foist on an outsider.'

This was as close to factual as made no difference.

'As you can imagine, I make enemies. Some of 'em are arrested, some of 'em disappear. And some get away and come back to haunt me.'

'Haunt you? Oh, you mean these two chaps might be looking to

square accounts.' She chewed her lower lip, managing to do it very becomingly. 'You say some disappear. How do they disappear?'

I shifted my backside to extract more comfort from the iron chair. Also to buy a few seconds to construct an answer.

'Not my department. I seek, I find, I do not execute in any of the senses of the word.'

'Somebody does though? Execute, I mean.'

'Leave it, Angie. It's never a good idea to know too much about how the dark underbellies of government clean up their messes. All in the name of protecting the public and the safety of the realm.'

We talked on through the morning. All the while though, my mind was occupied with the defences I needed to erect in case her two callers dropped in for a cup of tea while I was in residence. The Boberg was in a hidden pocket in my carryall; the SIG was still stashed in its bespoke compartment under the dashboard in the Evoque.

In time the topic dried up. She accepted my explanation as far as I could tell and our friendship was none the worse for it. An ex-nurse, who did a stint with the army in Iraq, she was likely to have seen plenty of examples of gunshot wounds, so at least I could expect her not to fold at the sight of blood, should there be any letting.

'Let's go for a walk,' she proposed.

I was reluctant to step outside and put her in the line of fire. But to cry off on the grounds of safety would just frighten her more, and I chose to risk it.

'Just need to pee,' I said, and did just that, collecting the Boberg from my bedroom beforehand. It would have taken too long to strap on the ankle holster, so I slipped the gun inside my hip pocket.

Then I composed a very brief text message on my cell phone.

A year ago I had been doing a stint of press-ganged duty for Her Majesty's Secret Service that took me to Finland. A serious error of judgement, financially speaking. In fact, I couldn't think of an aspect of that mismanaged venture that had turned out right.

Except one. I had been introduced to a Finn named Granit, nicknamed Rocky. The appellation had proven apt. He was a rock – dependable, resourceful, and tough. His prowess had impressed me so

much that I was paying him a retainer to be at my beck and call, to come to my aid if summoned. Which I hadn't yet.

The unanswered questions about who was hunting me remained just that. It was only after Angela told me her unsettling tale that I thought of a suspect other than *Il Sindicato*. In the run-up to Finland I had occasion to get mixed up with a Russian oligarch and super-spy called Maxim Maximov. The details are unimportant. He was vengeful about my perceived failure – without justification as it happened – and desired my extermination. I had been presented with two opportunities to remove the threat for good. I passed on both of them, because of Maura Beck, an American woman whom I had fallen for and who returned my love – with strings attached.

The strings required that I bring to a close my killing ways and revert to a life of probity. It was, and still is, easier said than achieved. My continuation or not as a hit man was not a decision for me alone. The powers at *Il Sindicato* were averse, for reasons of security and credibility, to releasing me from their dominion. Maura's own well-being, and that of her daughter, Rebecca, came to be in jeopardy. But I digress. It was Maximov who was still at large, still omnipotent, with an army of gunmen to do his bidding and a long reach that extended across the European and Asian contents, up, down, and sideways.

The message I texted to Rocky was short but not sweet.

Hi. Check if MM has set dogs on me. A.

His acknowledgement was instant.

Roger.

Not a man to waste words.

* * * * *

Angie and I walked and chatted about normal stuff, much as usual. Later we even swam in the lake, though I was leery about being separated from the Boberg. Nothing happened outside of a van driving into a tree across from Angela's apartment just after we returned from the beach. Some busybody had summoned the police to check the driver's alcohol level. I stayed indoors. As I had no history with the *carabinieri* I had little to

fear, but by instinct I kept my distance from all representatives of law and order.

Tomorrow I would be leaving. I made a mental note to go over the Evoque for booby traps.

A text came through from Rocky while we were enjoying an aperitif on the terrace.

No hard evidence yet. Will stay on it. R.

Angela was naturally curious to know who was texting and why. With some misgivings I told her about Rocky and Maximov, staying as truthful as prudence allowed, inventing when it didn't. She absorbed these new episodes from my past with an eerie calm.

'Do you really have to leave tomorrow?' she asked as she made circles with the base of her early-evening wine glass.

I shrugged. 'A new job's just come up. I've more or less accepted it. It's true though, I don't have to start on it right away.' I smiled at her. 'It's mostly that I think you'll be safer without me around.'

'I shan't *feel* safer,' she retorted. 'Women on their own never feel completely safe.'

'I get that. But it's me these people are after, and if there's going to be shooting, it's better I'm far away from here.'

'Yes, I see that.' It was my guess she was torn between the desire to stay uninfected by whatever dirty doings I was involved in, and the atavistic need for the company and protection I could provide. After mulling it over behind a frown, she let it ride.

She took to her bed about eleven, leaving me with an Italian cops and robbers series to watch. After enduring a half hour of Italian dialogue without subtitles, I descended to the basement garage which served six apartments. The Evoque occupied a space allocated to another apartment, currently up for rent, and the purpose of my nocturnal jaunt was to inspect the car for explosive devices.

It was hot down there, and airless. I used a penlight to view the underside of the car and the engine compartment for attachments not specified by the manufacturer. All clear. The SIG, complete with spare magazine, was still in its padded nook. I slipped it down the back of my waistband, draping my untucked shirt over it.

Then the lights went out.

It might have been a power outage, but I took no chances, instantly assuming a crouch in the gap between my car and a white Alfa in the next bay. The SIG was in my hand with no conscious effort on my part, slide racked, safety off, good to go.

I held my breath and listened. My heart was thudding away, sweat already filming my forehead, the heat so thick you could cut it. Nothing stirred. If anyone was holed up in the parking garage, they were not about to broadcast their presence by making a move. They would wait me out. If they were top flight professionals, they would wait until dawn if that was what it took. The first move would have to be mine.

All the advantages lay with them. They knew where I had been standing less than a minute ago, and if their auditory senses were at least average, they would know I hadn't moved. All they had to do was direct a flashlight beam at my last position and I was as good as dead.

Unless it was only a power outage.

Minutes crawled by. These guys knew their business. They knew they had me on toast if I changed position and, in the long run, if I stayed put. I needed a diversion. The classic, beloved by moviemakers, is to toss an object to a far corner and wait for them to blast away at it in a frenzy of unprofessionalism. Two flaws in that ploy. I had no objects to toss, apart from the gun. And my enemies were too smart to be taken in. They had watched Hollywood detective movies too.

A diversion did take place though – from an unexpected quarter. The door to the stairwell opened inwards, projecting an oblong of light into the garage. A guy was crouching beside the door and the light fell across him. He twisted sideways to bring a machine pistol to bear on the newcomer. He was too slow by a heartbeat. From my prone position I pumped a series of aimed shots at him, the muzzle flashes creating a strobe light effect. None of my shots missed, leaving him with four bloody holes in his trunk. The person who had opened the door screamed – it was a woman – and a second gunman, given the choice of going for me or her, chose me.

After their failed attempt in Paris they had come better armed, the

second guy also being equipped with a machine pistol, and he expended half a magazine in my general direction. The noise in that basement was eardrum rupturing, the muzzle flashes blinding. Fortunately for me and for the Evoque, his shots went high as is often the case with an automatic weapon if you don't compensate for muzzle "climb". The terrified woman possessed enough savvy to slam the steel door shut. Darkness was restored, but I had pinpointed the second gunman's location. Still prone, I let go with my remaining ten shots, firing under the nose of the Alfa, protected by the front right wheel. A bullet makes a very distinctive sound when it enters flesh, compared, for instance, with entering masonry. It's like a slap, the flat of a hand against a cheek. By my reckoning, no less than five rounds slapped, the rest thudded or ricocheted.

If a third gunman had been around he would have joined in by now, his best opportunity being when I fired at the guy by the door. No more shots came though, and I left the Alfa's protection, confident there had only been two of them. Semi-blind from the gun flashes and semi-deaf from the shots, I groped and stumbled across the garage to the exit door. I dragged it open, expecting the woman who had saved my bacon to be gone, probably to summon the law. She hadn't. She was huddled in a corner of the stairwell, eyes wide with fright, hands pressed to her ears. Trembling from top to toe.

'Angie!'

Appalled at how close she had come to copping a bullet, and relieved that she hadn't, I knelt beside her. She stared at me, tried to speak but could only make noises in her throat.

'It's okay,' I soothed, holding her to me. 'It's finished.'

Her face buried in my chest, her arms wrapped around me tightly enough to restrict my breathing.

'Are … y-you all r-right?' she said with an effort at last, teeth chattering.

'Good as new. It's okay, it's over.'

For tonight maybe it was over. But for nights to come it manifestly wasn't. Someone was out for my blood. He, she, or they had let slip the hounds of retribution and like a coursing hare I would have to keep

running from them lest they caught up with me and ripped me limb from limb.

Metaphorically, that is.

* * * * *

Back in the apartment, I dealt with Angela's expected inquisition.

'Who were they?' she rightly demanded to know. She had recovered fast, was now more indignant than scared.

I couldn't answer her. I had raided their pockets for any clue as to their identities and origins. The absence of any incriminating paperwork pointed to a professional organisation, whichever side of the law they were on. One had a receipt from a local restaurant, a parking ticket, and an unused packet of Kleenex; the other had a car key fob and a receipt from a *parkhaus* in Germany dated last week. That could have meant he was German or simply that he had visited the country, maybe to receive instructions about me.

So I had nothing to go on, and admitted as much to Angela.

'It could happen again,' she pointed out, as if I weren't aware of that. 'Anytime, anywhere.'

'I've set some enquiries in train.' I yawned, stretched. 'Now all I can do is wait.'

'What – here?'

'No, don't worry, I'm not going to put you at risk. When I go, they'll stick with me.'

'I'm not bloody worried,' she retorted with some heat. 'Not for myself. It's *you* I'm thinking of.'

She went on to tell me how fond she was of me, and how I had become a major feature in her life.

'Nice of you to say so. But I can't just sit around and await developments. I've got two bodies to dispose of.'

Angela, far from insisting I report the attempt on my life to the police, volunteered her help.

'You can't,' I said, shocked. 'You'll be an accessory.'

'I'm already an accessory,' she said tartly, and thus ended all discussion.

The bodies went in the Evoque's trunk. The plan, impromptu as it was, was to dump them, guns and all, in Lake Como, along a secluded stretch between the Villa Laglio and the Ristorante Crotto dei Platani. I would have preferred to dump their car with them, but I had no idea where they had parked it, or of the make and colour, and if they were as professional as their actions had suggested, it wouldn't be close by.

Traffic was thin on the Via Regina, the principal highway north of Laglio. We pulled into a turnout on the chosen section of road, and listened for other vehicles. All was at peace. With me lifting the head-and-shoulders end and Angie taking the feet, we launched the bodies over the safety barrier into the deep, still waters of Lake Como. The weight of their guns would be enough to take them to the bottom. If it wasn't, nothing among their possessions connected them with me or Angela's address.

I continued to marvel at Angela's composure. She didn't speak, just followed instructions, as if it were a routine event.

Back to the apartment. I parked in the basement as before, and went in search of cartridge cases and spent bullets. I found all of my cases and what I hoped were all those of the second gunman. The bullets were less traceable. Some would be embedded in wood or brick. My final tally was twenty-eight. I piled them on the Evoque's front passenger seat for later disposal and returned to the apartment to pack.

Angela put pressure on me to change my mind.

'Don't go for my sake,' she said, looking cross, as I dumped my baggage by the door and took both her hands in mine.

'I'll keep in touch. As soon as I can make it, I'll be back. Promise. If the police come calling, play innocent. They've nothing to connect you with those guys.' I used my curled forefinger under her chin to lift her eyes to mine. 'You *are* innocent.'

'Dropping dead bodies in the lake isn't as innocent as all that.' Her sense of humour was still intact then.

'Thanks for your help, and for showing up when you did. You probably saved my life.'

We hugged goodbye. Lips brushed cheeks.

'Take good care,' she said, hanging on to my arms. 'Really good care.'

'You bet. The goodest.'

The door closed behind me with a certain finality. From there I moved fast and within a couple of minutes was on the road, driving with due care and attention through the sleeping town.

Destination Budapest.

Chapter Four

A new contract necessitated a false passport, plus supporting documents. Before filling that urgent need, I aimed to put space between Italy and me. Flying was quick but meant passport controls and credit card payments and computer entries – the all-incriminating traces. Going by road meant a tiring roundabout trip via Switzerland, Liechtenstein, and the length of Austria to Slovenia, my springboard for Hungary. But all borders were control-free to motorists and this was the deciding factor.

After a back aching night in the Evoque behind a closed filling station near the Swiss town of Lugano, I called my provider, Thierry Marceau, citizen of Marseille, and made certain arrangements. My French was good enough to justify a Walloon-Belgian ID, so I was to become Gilles Devreese. Preparation would take three days, plus a day to transport my new papers across two borders in a parcel of books.

I spent the rest of the day at the wheel, covering over eight hundred km. I went to ground in a small hotel in the Slovenian town of Pince, near the border with Hungary, there to await delivery of my papers by UPS. Nobody knew where I was headed, by what means, and by which route. Even Donovan only knew I would be in Budapest 'sometime next month'. If, for reasons unknown, he was two-timing me and was connected with the attempts on my life, he wouldn't be able to give away my whereabouts to the mastermind, be he Maximov or some other enemy from my grey past.

From Pince, I called Donovan and confirmed my formal acceptance of the contract. It was now binding on both parties. Arrangements were made for on-line transfer of the first thirty days' expenses to a bank in Monaco. The money would land in my account in a matter of hours. When my passport turned up on schedule, I would proceed on the final leg of my journey to Budapest.

* * * * *

The border point I had chosen to enter Hungary is known as the Pince-Torny-something crossing. Here, EU open borders notwithstanding, controls of sorts had been reimposed. Primitive by West European standards, and very police-intensive. The notorious Hungarian barrier, with its razor wire and electrification, only extends along the borders with Serbia and Croatia, even though the latter is now a member of the EU.

The border control guards weren't interested in me, a white man with a Belgian passport and an expensive car. They were on the lookout for illegal immigrants, non-white, non-Christian, and any who tried to cross were either turned back or, if they resisted, placed under arrest. The guards' inspection of my passport was fleeting, and didn't include a computer check. One of them addressed me in basic French, unsmiling but polite. He insisted on seeing inside the trunk, but not on opening my luggage. My other passports were secreted away with the SIG and the Boberg; to find them, they would have had to dismantle the car. It didn't happen. The guard handed the passport back and waved me on with a curt '*Allez*'.

So far, so to plan. I was inside Hungary and my arrival, even as Gilles Devreese, was not on the record. I could go about my impossible contract without suspecting every solo male of tailing me.

* * * * *

It didn't seem much of an abuse of my employer/s' generosity to spend the first two days establishing myself in Budapest, checking out watering holes and boltholes, while being paid $1000 per day. Why not?

My chosen hotel was the newly constructed Clark, located on a hill in Adam Clark tér, on the Buda side of the River Danube. My suite (no expense spared as long as my employer was funding me) overlooked a vast traffic circle, the river, and a stone suspension bridge. Checking out Budapest's places of interest on Google that first afternoon, I learned that the bridge is the Széchneyi Chain Bridge, named after a Hungarian engineer but designed by a British architect and opened in 1849.

On the opposite bank stands Pest, the greater part of the city by area, more bustling and less refined than Buda, with an allegedly thriving nightlife and underworld. A building with a spiked dome dominates the waterfront. Google identified it as the home of the Hungarian Parliament.

My first evening at the hotel, I prevailed on the front desk clerk to look up Wolff in the Budapest telephone directory. Not because I expected finding the guy to be that simple, but as the opening phase of the process of elimination. No Wolffs in the directory, which didn't surprise or discourage me. I asked the clerk to go a step further for a twenty-euro bill, and call the Information Service, in case Wolff was unlisted. No unlisted Wolffs either.

'Could you check the whole country?' I asked next.

He suppressed a frown. 'Only if you know the name of the town.'

'How about the Internet?' I was taking for granted the Hungarian on-line information service would be in Hungarian and therefore beyond my comprehension.

He hummed and hawed then admitted it might be possible.

I let him see a much larger denomination bill. His face cleared, like storm clouds parting to let a ray of sunlight through.

'I'll check with you tomorrow,' I said, with a winning smile, and continued on to the dining room.

* * * * *

Next morning at breakfast – an open toast sandwich with a selection of cheeses and salamis, rounded off by a fresh fruit salad – I handed a waiter a slip of paper on which I had written DSESSZ B, culled from the photo of the Wolff twins. His headshake was emphatic, but in his basic English he offered to check with Josep, who was older than him and had been born in Budapest.

Josep himself showed up bearing my paper. He was about sixty, with tired, crumpled features and an untidy haircut.

'It was bar long time ago,' he told me. 'Gone away.' He flapped his hand in a vague gesture to represent a departed bar.

'Okay,' I said. 'Thanks anyway.' I slipped him five-euros. It dived into his waistcoat pocket.

'Is new place now,' he said, pursing his lips as if to aid the thought processes. 'Funny name, like number. Twenty-five or seventy-five.'

I thanked him again, and he trundled off, collecting the odd item of dirty crockery en route.

The clerk's enquiries on the Internet had yielded no Wolffs. I stuffed the bill in his shirt breast pocket anyway, for goodwill's sake. The easy option having been ruled out, I consulted Google on my cell phone for the 25 Bar. No dice. I fared better with 75: it threw up the 77 Bistro & Bar. The map placed it in Saint Stephen's Square, in Pest. It was a starting point, I rated it no higher. If nothing else, I could submit a report on it to Donovan to justify my expenses.

Post-breakfast, I took advantage of the hotel's renowned gym facilities. A session of hard exercise was part of my daily regime and I worked out on the leg press, the pec deck, the triceps bar, the rowing machine, and the weight bench, culminating in thirty minutes on the treadmill with the gradient set at fifteen degrees. Punishing but satisfying.

A cold shower and a caffeine reviver later, I set out to explore. Several bridges, ancient and modern, link Buda with Pest. The nearest was the Széchneyi Chain Bridge I had observed from my room.

It made a pleasant stroll under a sky of blue with bursts of benign cumulus. Traces of an unpleasant miasma entered my nostrils as I hit the bridge. Back in the 1800s a traveller accused the so-called Blue Danube of "looking like a river, smelling like a drain". Or was it a sewer? Halfway across, I took a break, leaning on the steel handrail, ostensibly to watch the water traffic. It was sparser than I had expected, although plenty of boatware lined the banks, hooked up to little jetties. Pleasure craft mostly, including river cruisers with big viewing windows and two or three decks.

My non-ostensible reason for the break was to check my rear for unwanted adherents. June was still early in the season for the package tour trade, and promenaders were as thin on the ground as the boats on the water. This made it easy to spot any oddballs. When I recalled how

they had used couples as decoys in Paris, I couldn't rule out man and woman combos, or even small groups. I lingered awhile until everyone on both sides of the bridge within my range of vision had passed me. Then I retraced my steps to the Buda side and checked in both directions.

Nobody stood out, which on its own wasn't conclusive. A professional tail is hard to shake. All I could do was take the usual precautions and stay alert. Irritating. Inconvenient. But necessary.

A hearse went by at walking pace toward Pest, with an entourage of mourners' cars, slowing the traffic. I stepped up my own pace, overhauling the hearse and, on reaching the Pest end, dodged the stream of cars to cross some public gardens, the high spot of which was a metal sculpture of a twenty-foot tall woman, besieged by tourists taking pictures with their cell phones and tablets. From there I plunged into the warren of Pest, guided by my cell phone's Google map, and found myself in a long straight pedestrian street, with an unpronounceable name – like most streets in Budapest. A brisk walk brought me to St Stephen's Square, a tiled expanse of intricate circular designs, dominated by St Stephen's basilica, a white building with a central domed tower flanked by lesser towers. To the right of the square was a line of bars, identifiable from the clutter of tables lining the sidewalk. Above the bars, several levels of apartments with tiny balconies. Tourists were everywhere.

It was a tranquil place. No city bustle penetrated. Muted rock music issued from speakers someplace. From the open window of an apartment, three floors up on my left, came the tinkle of a piano at work. Some classical piece, hesitantly played, impossible to identify.

The 77 Bar & Bistro was midway along the square. I took the last vacant table outside, by some pink marble steps that led beneath an archway into the interior. A prominent 77 logo was reversed out on a white background of glass above the entrance.

I sat there for a few minutes before a waitress attended to me, fetchingly presented in a skimpy outfit, fronted by a tiny white apron to prove she really was a waitress.

'*Seeya,*' she said to me – if I heard aright – accompanied by a broad smile that emphasised her dazzling teeth. Her hair was near-black and done up in a ponytail.

I offered a moue of apology. 'Sorry, I don't speak your language.'

'That's all right,' she said, converting seamlessly to accented but otherwise impeccable English. 'What would you like?'

It was too early for liquor in my book. I settled for an *espresso.* She pecked at her electronic order pad with a silver-varnished fingernail.

'Anything to eat,' she enquired, keeping the smile going. If she was a typical Hungarian native I was already impressed.

'Not right now, thanks.'

She thanked me, checked around for other clients requiring service, and, seeing none, took off indoors. An agreeable aroma wafted out of the entrance and trickled up my nostrils. The only Hungarian dish I had ever knowingly tasted was goulash, but this was new to me. The sweet-pepper smell of paprika was in there, overlaid with garlic. Beyond that I was out of my depth.

I took professional stock of the other users in my vicinity. Two guys on their own, two women likewise, two women together. The usual cross section of mid-morning idlers enjoying their *Kaffee und Kuchen.* Any of them could have been enemy agents.

A male waiter brought my *espresso*. I restrained him from leaving and showed him the photo of the Wolff twins with the name behind them. His English was passable and he immediately exclaimed, 'Of course, it is taken here ten years or more past. Before they change the name.'

'You ever see these men?'

He shook his head. 'No, I only work here since last year.' His face brightened. 'The manager can know them. He is here many years.'

'Please ask him to come and see me,' I said.

If I had prodded his backside with a pitchfork, he couldn't have moved faster, bustling off, up the steps and into the interior. The manager was less responsive. A full quarter hour elapsed before a squat, square-headed man with a drooping moustache came down the steps. The young waitress who, I supposed, had been roped in to translate, trailed along behind him.

'Are you the person looking for some men?' the waitress asked, the smile more restrained but the aura still friendly, anxious to please.

'Yes.'

She rattled off a stream of what I assumed was Hungarian to the squat man, who scowled.

'This is Mr Ziffer.' She pronounced it carefully. 'He is the manager.'

I stood up, old-world-courtesy style, and extended my hand to Mr Ziffer. He accepted it with circumspection, as if I were offering him a stick of fizzing dynamite.

'Please sit down, both of you,' I said. 'May I buy you a drink?'

He grunted acceptance of my offer; the waitress declined, the smile now wistful. His drink ordered, Ziffer fired off what seemed to be a question.

'He asks why you look for these men,' the waitress interpreted.

Interesting. To ask 'why' before 'who' struck me as the inverse of what was natural.

'They are old friends who used to live here,' I replied smoothly. 'As I am here on vacation, I thought I would try to contact them.'

She translated. He grunted. His drink came, carried on a tray by another, less fetching, waitress. It consisted of a honey-coloured liquid in a small pitcher, with a wine glass in attendance. Ziffer waved the waitress away and filled the glass himself.

A pigeon touched down on the table, close to Ziffer. He swatted it and it took off, quick to infer that it wasn't welcome.

Ziffer swigged half the contents of his glass and stared moodily at me, like an undertaker sizing up a client for a coffin. I debated offering money, but decided that to bribe information out of him supposedly to contact a couple of friends would be overdoing it.

After a long lull, he mouthed more Hungarian at my interpreter. In amongst the jabber was what I took to be her name – Patricia.

'He asks to see the picture.'

I almost said, 'I thought you'd never ask.' Decided that British irony would fly right past him, even correctly translated.

He studied the photo at length, giving little nods and pursing his lips. He spoke to the waitress.

'He has never seen them before,' she passed on to me.

'Uh-huh. Is he absolutely sure … Patricia? That *is* your name, isn't it?'

'Yes, I am Patricia.' I later learned that the first 'i' was topped by an accent, like the French acute.

'Ask him if he is certain he hasn't seen these guys.'

She transmitted my request to Ziffer – at least, I had to assume she did. He gave me a dirty look in return, as if I were doubting his honesty.

His next utterance was longer.

'He will think more and try to remember if he has seen them,' Patricia conveyed to me. 'Where are you staying?'

'In Buda,' I said. Wary of providing more details, I added, 'In an apartment. I know where it is, but I don't remember the street name.'

When Patricia conveyed this to Ziffer, he grunted again, tossed back his drink, and heaved himself out of the chair. His farewell adieu was a single long word, unlike anything I had so far heard.

'Goodbye,' I said, and the girl's translation to Ziffer resembled his original to me, delivered in a more amicable tone.

'I am sorry he cannot help you,' she said, with a lift of her shoulders.

'No matter. I didn't expect much.' As she rose, I said, 'Do you live in Budapest?'

'Yes. Quite near here.' She blushed faintly, hesitated as if she wanted to say more. Instead, she gathered up Ziffer's pitcher and glass and hurried off indoors.

Which left me stumped and still devoid of leads and clues.

* * * * *

Rocky came through at last, as I was heading for the bathroom for my night-time ablutions.

M in USA. No contract placed. Enquires
continue until you say stop.
R

* * * * *

If it wasn't Maximov after my blood, it could be almost anybody from my murky past. Even Rik de Bruin may not have died from the wounds inflicted on him by Liza. He wouldn't be much use to a woman,

but that didn't make him less likely to be on the vengeance trail. More, come to think of it.

I set aside speculation on my enemies, as I lay between the sheets with Chopin's Nocturnes performed by the Chilean pianist Claudio Arrau, soothing me on my iPod, and gave speculation room to my encounter with Ziffer. Was it significant that he asked my reason for seeking the Wolffs, instead of asking who they were? Was it the instinctive correct sequence, first ask why, then who? Maybe it was a Hungarian custom.

Next I considered his attitude. Truculent, almost resentful. If he was busy and I had screwed up his daily routine, that might account for it. Either that or he was by nature a surly soul. In which case he could still be acquainted with the Wolffs or just be miserable by nature.

Chopin and Arrau transported me to sleep with the reading lamp still on and my kindle still unopened on the night table.

* * * * *

If I was to unearth any leads as to the whereabouts of either or both of the Wolffs, gumshoeing was an unavoidable chore. If I managed to locate Victor, he would serve as a conduit to Vincent, so I wasn't fussy which of them swam into my net. Victor would be sure to know where Vincent was, and if I had to rough him up a little to extract the knowledge, it wouldn't give me sleepless nights.

From the 77 Bar I worked outwards to other bars in and around St Stephen's Square: the Divino with its hundred-plus selection of wines, the Padthia wokbar, an island of calm in the big city noise, the St Andrea Skybar, a rooftop establishment with views of the wooded hill to the west of Buda, surmounted by a monument called the Liberty Statue – I found it on Google. Next came the Kör, with its homey ambience, the TG Italiano, whose terrace backed on to the basilica, and the Borkonhya, newly awarded a Michelin star and renowned for its fine Hungarian wines. Later in the day I inspected the Hummus, purported to represent the best value for money in Budapest, the Spoon, a moored boat downstream from the Chain Bridge, and the Boutiq Bar, cool and

gloomy, with acres of woodwork but a shortage of clients.

The only common denominator among these watering holes was that the photo of the Wolffs made no impact. A few of the interviewees pointed out that the bar in the picture no longer existed and was now the 77.

By evening I had called on over twenty eateries and drinkeries and advanced not an iota in my search. Though the head waiter at the Borkonhya – the Michelin star drew me back there – was initially promising.

I had bagged a table on the terrace for an early dinner and he came bustling over, inflated with self-importance. His opening shot was in English, before even checking my linguistic preference.

'Good evening, sir. Would you like to see the menu?'

'It would be a good way to begin our relationship,' I rejoined, which puzzled him until he unscrambled it and broke into a face-splitting beam

'Indeed, sir, indeed.'

He whisked the leather-bound menu and wine list from under his armpit and presented them to me. From the wine list I chose a Hungarian white, a 2013 Tokaj Furmint – undertones of honey, apricots, and fine oak. The maitre d' stood in attendance as I pored over the menu, all of it translated into English and German.

'Tell me,' I said, my finger hovering over the pike-perch fillet before moving on to settle on the trout with fennel and scallops, 'have you ever seen these men?'

With my free hand I dealt him the increasingly dog-eared photo. He studied it while I continued studying the menu, then, to my astonishment, said, 'They have eaten here.'

I had become so inured to negative responses, I reacted with disbelief.

'Are you sure? The photo's not very clear.'

'Quite sure. They were together. They look the same.'

I could have interpreted his 'quite' to mean totally or somewhat. Whichever, it was as close as I had come all day to a make.

'You mean they were twins.' I said.

'Yes, twins.' He returned the photo. 'One of them make big noise about his veal is too rare, so we make it well done and, he make bigger noise because it is too much done. He leave without paying.'

An oversight that was guaranteed to make him memorable to a maitre d'.

'How long ago was this?'

He made a thinking sound with his fleshy lips.

'More than one year. Perhaps even two years.'

So I was already doing better than Donovan, with his latest reported sighting of eleven years vintage.

'Have they been back since? Or either of them.'

'No, I never see them again.' He tapped the menu. 'Now, sir, if I might recommend ...'

Order placed, I fed him a 1,000 forint bill to circulate the photo among the staff, in case any of the evening shift were familiar with the Wolffs. It transpired to be a blind alley. Nobody had seen them, and the maitre d' himself had nothing more to contribute.

If either Wolff had still been living in or near Budapest no more than two years ago, the prospects of their still being here were a shade improved. Now I had credible testimony that they could have stayed for at least nine more years after the photo was taken, therefore it was likely they had ties here that couldn't be cut – business, family, or both. My task was no less impossible, but instead of climbing a mountain without ropes and pitons, I was now just without ropes.

The trout though was exquisite and fully justified the Michelin star.

* * * * *

On occasion in the past, I had been obliged to locate my target before taking him out, so all this back-and-forth searching was not new turf. I was being handsomely rewarded for my daily toil, so why complain? Budapest was a charming city, the climate was benign, and it was early summer, my favourite time of year. My hotel was comfortable and people seemed friendly – Ziffer excluded.

On the downside, I was alone, the language was impenetrable, the

work was boring, and I could see no prospect of a pot of gold with or without a rainbow's end.

The fourth morning of my search for clues dawned wet and windy. It was Sunday, day of rest to some. I didn't have to venture out, but lounging around the hotel on my own, unable even to understand the conversations that went on around me, was guaranteed to drive me to distraction. Better out, in the wind and the rain, than watching Hungarian TV.

Armed with a flimsy umbrella borrowed from the desk clerk, I braved the elements. In my belted raincoat I looked the part of a real-life gumshoe. St Stephen's square was sodden and bleak, with empty tables and chairs, some of which had been blown over. Only a handful of walkers out and about, all skulking under umbrellas of many colours. The wind was behind me, and pushed me along like a yacht under full sail, my umbrella threatening to turn itself inside out. I was passing by the 77 bar when a figure emerged from the entrance: female, a plastic waterproof around her shoulders, a magazine held over her head.

I spared her no more than a glance until she rushed up to me and grabbed my arm to slow me down.

'Hello,' she said. 'It is me, Patricia.'

It was, too.

'Oh, hello. Come on, let's get out of the rain.'

With me towing her, we scuttled under the awning of the 77. She confronted me, her face damp with rain, agitation in every rapid blink of her eyes.

'What's up, Patricia?' I said, unable to believe she was interested in me in the age-old way that makes the world go round. She looked to be about eighteen.

'Him – Ziffer – he was making lies. He knows those men you look for.'

'What!' I gripped her arms, tighter than I had intended, and she struggled to shake free of me.

'Sorry,' I said, letting her go and opening up space between us. 'How do you know this?'

'I cannot tell you now. He might see us, then for me it will come big

trouble.' She kept shooting nervous glances towards the interior. 'Meet me after I finish work.'

'Sure. Just tell me the time and place.'

She nibbled her lip. 'The Publin. Six o'clock tonight.'

I repeated it. Then she was gone, leaving me at once elated and suspicious. It had the smell of entrapment. Of Ziffer or someone higher up the hierarchical chain setting me up. Why would this girl be willing to risk spying on her boss and passing information on to me? Unless she was planning to sell it. That would make sense for her, and for me.

* * * * *

The clue to its function was in the name. The Publin was a Dublin-themed pub a few streets deeper into the warrens of Pest, in a courtyard named Madách Tér. Tér for terrace maybe, or square. The rain had taken a break and the sun was back in full blaze, but Madách Tér was in a shadow thrown by a wall of apartments on all sides. It was like being in a huge box with no lid. It had a few spindly trees and other cafes and bars at ground level, some with alcoves containing tables and chairs. Some of the tables were occupied; I chose the nearest to the open end of the courtyard.

A nearby clock struck the hour. At the sixth bong she came around the corner, hurrying, breathless. Her attire consisted of jeans with rips in both knees, and a white *señorita* blouse with lots of frills, worn off the shoulder.

She crashed into the chair opposite, very unladylike, and gasped out an apology.

'No worries,' I said. 'I didn't have anything better to do.'

Her uncertain smile told me she wasn't sure how to interpret that. A waitress came, nowhere near as attractive as mine, and we ordered some Hungarian beer that Patricia recommended.

'Let's talk,' I proposed.

She placed her purse in front of her and rummaged in it. Produced a folded slip of paper and handed it to me without a word.

I opened it. A name was written there. It meant zilch to me.

'Who's Laszlo Farkas?'

She edged her chair closer to the table and her head closer to mine. Unlike some famous paintings, she looked at least as good close up as she did at a distance. Her face was more or less classic oval, a touch heavy on the jawline; her nose was straight, her lips about the right size and shape for all purposes. Her eyebrows were sculpted black commas above cobalt-blue eyes that made a striking contrast with her almost-black hair, now worn loose and long and seductive.

'He is the man my boss called to tell him you are trying to contact Mr … Wilf?'

'Wolff,' I corrected.

'Ah, yes, sorry. Anyway, that is all.' She quaffed beer in big gulps like a man. 'What is your name?'

'Gilles.'

She frowned, also becomingly. 'That is a French name, no?'

'I'm from Belgium. We can speak French if you prefer.'

She didn't. 'I have some French but I like to practice my English. In the school I have learn English and German'.

'Can you remember exactly what your boss said to this … this Laszlo guy?'

'Not exactly, but it was like "a guy here at the bar asks about the Wilfs."'

'Wolffs. That's all?'

She shrugged her bare shoulders as if to say 'isn't it enough?'

It would have to be. It proved that people were interested enough in anyone nosing around after the Wolff twins to alert a watchdog, in this instance a guy called Laszlo Farkas.

I patted her hand, which was resting by her purse.

'You've been very helpful.' I felt in my hip pocket for the wad of Hungarian forints tucked away there and peeled off a twenty-thousand bill. Worth about forty US dollars.

She wasn't shy about accepting it.

'*Kosonom*,' she said, and translated it. 'That means thank you.'

'How do you spell it?'

'K-o-s-z-o-n-o-m. And all the 'o's have two dots above, like the German umlaut.'

I took out a pen and jotted it on the back of the note she had given me – *köszönöm*. The start of my Hungarian vocabulary.

The waitress returned and asked if we needed a refill. Patricia accepted, I passed. The sun had gone behind the apartment block on the opposite side of the terrace and the temperature went south too. Goosebumps were standing out on Patricia's bare shoulders.

A cell phone trilled. Not mine, which was on silent/vibrate. Patricia solved the source by plucking hers from her purse. She glanced at the screen, grimaced, put it to her ear anyway.

'*Ee-gen.*' Or that was how it sounded to my untrained ears.

She listened for a while, face and lips set, a groove of displeasure between her eyebrows. Not good news then.

The caller broke off his or her monologue and she charged in with a stream of Hungarian that did not sound complimentary or friendly. When she had done remonstrating she cut the call dead with a curt '*Caio.*'

The cell went back in her purse.

'My past boyfriend,' she explained. 'Is that correct English?'

'Ex-boyfriend is better. You obviously didn't want to talk to him.'

'It is finished between us. He will not accept it.'

I offered a sympathetic murmur, then said, 'You seem to be bright girl. Your English isn't bad at all. So why do you work as a waitress?'

'Many people speak English. I have none other qualifications. And the tips are very nice. Besides, it is not my only job.'

'Really?' I was in no rush to get after Lazlo whatever-his-name, and more than happy to sit here chatting to this rather lovely girl. It did my morale good.

'No. At weekends I also do porn.'

It wouldn't be strictly true to say I was shocked. A little surprised, as she didn't seem the type. If there is a type these permissive days. An acquaintance of mine, very non-PC, once declared 'Take my word, they're all up for it.'

'How do you mean,' I said, 'you *do* porn?'

'On the internet. I am a porn star here in Hungary. My name on-line is Tricia. I am eighteen and still in college.'

'You mean people *believe* you are eighteen and still in college?'

She nodded brightly. Not at all flustered by the deception.

Ah, the Internet. Purveyor of serious news, hard facts, and integrity.

'You not liking porn?' she said, interpreting my silence as disapproval and throwing in an exaggerated pout that would go down well in the kind of videos that feature porn stars.

'As much as the next man, I guess.'

Lines appeared on her very smooth forehead. 'I am not understanding. Who is this next man?'

A guy walked by, casting a not uninterested glance at Patricia. With her black hair down she was worth a glance or two.

'It's a fig– … a saying. It means I like it as much as any other man.'

'You watch it?'

Christ, she wasn't letting go.

'I've seen it. I don't spend hours ogling it. I prefer the real thing. A real woman.'

She gave a gurgle of mirth. 'I am a real woman. I also prefer everything real, especially sex.'

I had walked into that, without realising I was walking into it.

'You think I am too young for you?' she said, resurrecting the pout.

'Yeah, actually, even if you're older than eighteen. For the record, what's your real age, Patricia?'

'I am twenty-two.'

Better than eighteen. Still, I was pretty sure I didn't want to take a porn star to bed, knowing that she shared her body with an incalculable number of male performers, their couplings drooled over by a million voyeurs of both sexes.

She hadn't asked me for money yet, but I was sure she would. Years ago, during the epoch when my moral compass was to hell and gone, I would pick up the phone and summon a paid bed-mate to satisfy the demands of the flesh. My morals and my priorities had moved onward and upward since then. Paid sex was no longer in fashion. Maura was my true and only current love – period. Since she walked out on me, few women had entered my life for whom I felt real affection, and even they had been passing ships on the ocean, substitutes for the genuine article.

Girls like Patricia were cheap and easy to come by, even at my age.

'You think I want money, eh?'

'You mean you don't?'

'Some men have no need to pay. You are one of these.'

She had read my mind, only it seemed I hadn't read hers nearly as accurately.

Behind me there was a screech of a car braking to an abrupt halt. Raised voices, a plastic chair crashing to the floor. Patricia's lovely eyes were suddenly less lovely, as they widened in terror. I turned, slower to react than I should have been.

Three guys, big, muscular clones in T-shirts and jeans, armed with baseball bats. The Boberg was in the Evoque, too far away for a fast draw.

Two of the guys grabbed Patricia's arms and started dragging her, struggling and yelling, towards a blue SUV parked at the curbside, doors open. The third guy swung his bat at my head. As I jerked backwards and simultaneously tried to get up, my legs got tangled in my chair and I hit the paved terrace floor with a painful jar to my spine. The bat whistled past overhead, close enough for me to feel the wind of its passage.

Around us, other members of the café set were on the move – mostly out of the immediate area, though several braver souls were coming to Patricia's aid. But my attackers weren't there for a brawl. They had achieved their objective. They bundled Patricia into the SUV. The third guy quit trying to remove my head from my shoulders and scrambled aboard. The engine revved and they were off, doors slamming, still pursued by a trio of coffee drinkers who had a whole lot more guts than respect for baseball bats.

Furious and conscience-stricken at my lack of preparedness, I disengaged myself from the chair. The SUV was lost from sight.

'What's going on?' I said to the three, as if I hadn't already figured it out.

'Your friend was taken,' one replied, in US-accented English. 'We must call police.'

That would be the right thing to do. But questions would be asked,

explanations sought, that I couldn't answer. Not without compromising my mission. Not only that, but if anybody was going to go after Patricia it had to be me.

Lost for a course of action to take, I just stood by while the guy who spoke American-English used his cell phone to summon the law. If I hoofed it, I would become a suspect and the police would be after me too. If I stayed and brazened it out, I would need to concoct a cover story. How would it go? I met Patricia earlier in the day and asked her to join me for a drink. Classic boy meets girl, boy fancies his chances with girl, boy plies girl with drink to soften up her resistance. Never mind that the boy ought by rights to be married, settled in a nine-to-five job, providing for the open beaks of a brood of teenage kids.

So I resigned myself to spending a few hours with the police and sat down at the table Patricia and I had been using. Her purse was still there. Unlikely it would contain anything that would incriminate me. That left just the notepaper bearing the name of Laszlo somebody. I glanced around. The other customers, those who had remained, were in an animated discussion group, showing no interest in me. I opened the square of paper, committed the name to memory. With maximum discretion, I then shredded it into tiny pieces and scattered it to the breeze, hoping I wouldn't get spotted and fined for dropping litter.

The police eventually deigned to turn up. Their transportation was mostly white, with a diagonal blue stripe on each side bearing the word RENDÖRSÉG. If that meant police, it just emphasised anew what a weird language Hungarian is.

Two uniformed officers dismounted, began to harangue the Publin's clientele. The English speaker approached them, and a voluble exchange took place, with some arm-waving from the witness. The police appeared unmoved. After a minute or two of this, they all looked at me. I got up and prepared to be interrogated.

Their uniforms were the standard police blue over pale blue shirts. Their hats were baseball type, similar to those used by the military. They wore sidearms and nightsticks. One was tall with an old-young face, the other medium height, and much younger.

The tall cop could speak only broken English, his partner none. A

short conference ensued. The decision, communicated to me by the English-speaking guy, was to take him and me to headquarters for a friendly grilling. They frisked me, relieved me of my Devreese passport and my wallet.

Off we went in their shiny rendörség car, with the grill between the front seats and rear compartment, and doors that couldn't be opened from the inside. They were generous with their hee-haw siren, so we made it with no hold-ups.

The name of the street where our short journey ended was Akademia, among the few Hungarian words I had encountered whose meaning I could guess. The building was a square five-floor traditional block with a facade of stone cladding. Above the double front door was a coat of arms surmounted by an impenetrable inscription. I was getting used to the language in the sense that I expected to understand almost none of it. Once you accept that, you can relax and rely on interpreters.

Inside was cool and heavy on tiles and dark wood. We didn't report to the front desk, but were hustled down a corridor, dodging cops of both sexes going in the opposite direction.

For me and for my contract this represented a foul-up of major proportions. Police awareness of my presence in their city might restrict my manoeuvring room, even make it impossible for me to function – a new impossibility to add to the original one. Yet I had done nothing they could construe as illegal or even negligent. The initiative had come from the girl, I had just followed up on it.

They escorted the interpreter guy and me to separate rooms with INTERJÚ in white on a wooden plaque. I went in, assisted by a gentle push between the shoulder blades.

I was invited to sit on a straight-back chair in front of a shaky rectangular table, scarred with carved initials, cigarette burns, and other memorabilia. The door closed and I was on my own.

An hour later I was still on my own. Was this the preliminary softening-up process, Hungarian-style? It wasn't so long ago that Hungary was a police state. Even now, under the Viktor Orban regime, they were edging back towards that status, with creeping restrictions on a free press and free speech.

Behind me the door opened. Footsteps presaged the arrival of the man or woman who would be my interrogator. I maintained an attitude of relaxed long-suffering. So far, in Hungary, I was innocent of any crime except using forged ID documents. In fact I was a victim. My new girlfriend had been abducted and I wanted, no demanded, that the police initiate a search for her forthwith.

All that was in my head. The reality would be different: I would cause no upsets, thump no tables. I was a law-abiding Belgian with only tourism on my mind. Well, maybe girls just a little. I had only met the girl a few days ago, and the Publin was our first date, if you could even call it that.

A man in plain clothes came around the table to stand in front of me. Saturnine features, sallow skin, and hair that was receding in reverse, from the crown forwards.

'Monsieur Devreese. *Enchanté de vous connaître. Desolé pour l'inconvenient. Je m'appele* Inspecteur Beres.'

His French was fluid. As a "Belgian" I was happy to communicate in the same language. He pulled up a chair and sat facing me. He placed three items on the table at his elbow: a pack of cigarettes, a gold lighter, and a pocket recording device, an inch between each item.

'Now,' he said, still in French, forming a spire with his index fingers. 'Please describe to me what happened at the Publin Bar, including the name and address of the young woman who was abducted.'

'Right,' I said. 'But before I do, have you launched a search for her?'

'Not yet. We have no information. At the very least we need a name for the girl, a full description, details of the car, and the men who abducted her.'

He was right. The prospects of her being found by the police were slim anyway. Aside from that, it was my self-appointed job. More, it was an obligation, a question of honour. The girl was in deep shit because of me.

Before they would turn me loose, I had to make a statement. I made it. There was no reason to hide any details, even if I had many to hide. I omitted to mention the 77 bar and Mr Ziffer. Even if he was involved, it suited my priorities to keep him out of it. You couldn't guarantee the

police would make him talk. I could.

In my version of events, Patricia became a girl I had fallen into conversation with in the street. I invited her for a drink. She accepted. Less than ten minutes after we sat down a blue SUV – a Renault to judge from the diamond-shaped badge on the hatch door – drove up. Three guys got out, two of them grabbed Patricia. The third guy attacked me with a baseball bat. I fell over a chair. The SUV drove away. End of statement.

'Was there a fourth man?' Beres enquired. 'Perhaps a driver?'

It riled me that I couldn't answer. The constant need to be on the alert had honed my powers of observation over the years, made me good at registering and recalling details. Yet the truth was, I hadn't noticed.

I settled for 'It's possible.'

'It probably doesn't matter. Any theories why they took her? Was it because she was talking to you?'

This was dangerous ground that I didn't want the police stomping on. The trick was to steer Beres away from any suggestion of a connection between the snatch and Patricia's meeting with me. Otherwise, they might wonder about me and my motives for being in Budapest. They could hold me as a material witness or for my own protection, while they instigated enquiries with Interpol, Europol, and the like. At a pinch, they might even expose my fake identity or stumble on my persona non grata status with the German police. Germany was a country to avoid, ever since I did a job there and unknowingly left a live witness at the scene. The Swiss police arrested me for the crime, and illegally extradited me to Germany under escort by the *Bundespolizei Kriminalamt*. Their star witness, the politician's wife whose lover was my victim, declined to identify me because she had other plans, revenge for my killing of the boyfriend being uppermost.

Beres didn't work me over physically. He spent a solid two hours extracting every snippet of minutiae, down to what Patricia and I were drinking and the size of the tip. Meticulous wasn't in it. Not until he had pumped me as dry as an empty wallet, did he condescend to release me. He accepted my hotel key card as proof of my accommodation. He requested me not to leave Budapest without informing the police. My

effects were returned, and I was set free to get on with my business.

Next on my agenda was a friendly chat with Mr Ziffer, when I expected him to come clean about Patricia. If he didn't, I would have to apply what, in the nether world where I made my living, was euphemistically styled friendly persuasion.

Chapter Five

It was after nine when I reached the 77. The place was buzzing with clients and music and, it being a mild evening, people had spilled out onto the terrace. Patricia's abduction seemed so unreal, I half-expected to see her serving tables.

As I mounted the three steps into the interior, a waiter approached and addressed me. He might have been telling me I wasn't welcome here for all I knew. I waved him aside and threw in my hard man stare for good measure. He took the hint.

The drinks bar was tended by two girls and a young guy who, from his build, probably doubled as the bar bouncer. I homed in on a girl, dark-haired like Patricia, but less striking. She had just finished serving a client and came over to me with a wide smile that recalled my first encounter with Patricia.

Her greeting was the now familiar, '*See-ya*.'

My reply was the equally familiar, 'You speak English?' as I pulled up a stool.

She nodded. 'A little.'

I laid a 5000Ft bill on the wooden surface of the bar. 'I want to see Mr Ziffer.'

My request seemed to startle her.

'I am sorry. He not here. He not work tonight.'

I doubled the bribe. She looked worried rather than pleased at my generosity. It could be she was right to worry. If what happened to Patricia because of helping me was typical, Mr Ziffer was not a man to trifle with.

'Where does he live?'

She fired off a spate of Hungarian that didn't strike me as friendly, though as ever I didn't understand a single syllable. When I just stared

blankly at her, she darted across to where the husky guy was serving a customer.

Oh-oh. Even if I could have taken him, which was questionable, a pub brawl with the potential for more police intervention was not going to save Patricia. I snatched up the two bills, removing evidence of my presence, and hightailed it out of the 77 to lose myself in the still-thronged streets.

The only remaining option was to scour Budapest hoping to come across the abduction vehicle. As it would take a week to check every street in the city even if all the cars stood still, that brainchild died at birth. Now I was stymied until morning at the earliest.

Troubled and guilt-ridden, I returned on foot to my temporary lodgings.

* * * * *

My WhatsApp newsflash to Donovan, transmitted over breakfast, read as follows:

Contact made with employee at bar in photo, now
renamed. Employee subsequently snatched & present
whereabouts unknown. On credit side two leads to V to
follow up but on hold while I try to rescue employee.
Suspend daily expenses meanwhile if you wish.

While I was draining the last dregs of my coffee, his answer came through. All was noted, and he was even waiving the right to suspend my fee for now. Generous of him.

The sky was full of cloud and the clouds looked full of moisture as I stepped out across the Chain Bridge, as it is popularly known. If last night's waitress at the 77 had passed on my description, and if it was matched up with the guy who had questioned Ziffer and Patricia, the opposition could already be gearing up to deal with me. I now had to consider myself a target, which meant I could no longer stroll the streets of Budapest like an innocent tourist. I had to take steps to protect myself.

Carrying a gun, even as discreet a piece as the Boberg, was a massive

risk. The alternative, to go out and about with no protection other than my unarmed combat skills, wouldn't help me succeed in either my personal or my professional goals. The police were unlikely to kill me, the bad guys might. Acting on this hypothesis, I raided the secret compartment in the Evoque, which was parked in the hotel's underground garage, and sallied forth to do battle with my miniature armoury. Not strapped to my left ankle, but in the right pocket of my windbreaker. You never could predict when a fast draw might mean life over death.

A large hotel boat passed under the bridge as I neared the Pest side. Like a regular tourist, I lingered to watch it go by. A woman waved from the upper deck. I returned the gesture, affable soul that I am. She took a picture with a tablet.

I continued my stroll into Pest. Ten minutes later I was standing before the 77. I was dressed unremarkably in grey gabardine jeans and a maroon polo shirt with a Ralph Lauren logo. For a few minutes I observed the flow of clients and staff. A solitary waitress on duty outside, whom I remembered from the morning I met Patricia.

Inside, a girl behind the bar was chopping lemon slices on a board. Only two clients, female, sitting on stools at a high table, their heads close together, as if dispensing and receiving the latest scandal. Soft music filtered from a speaker over the door, French lyrics. I didn't make the mistake of talking to the help, I made for an arched opening beyond the bar as if I had every right to be there. A left turn took me into a short hall with a single door bearing a unisex washroom logo. Ahead, a flight of wooden stairs.

Fast and silent, I went up to the expected landing. Three doors here, one facing me, and one on each side. None of them marked.

To knock and wait for permission to enter would be to lose the element of surprise, which might or might not be decisive. I opened the door to my left and entered, hand in pocket wrapped around the Boberg, finger on trigger, slide racked, safety off. All for nothing. It was a store room, choc-a-bloc with cartons, tables and chairs, and wall-to-wall wine racks, all well stocked. No living beings.

Backing out into the hall, I tried the door opposite. This room was

an office containing the usual pieces of furniture and, at the desk, a woman of about fifty, with fluffy blonde hair, broad shoulders, and the face of a concentration camp guard. Her lavishly lipsticked mouth somehow made her more not less masculine.

She jabbered a few words at me. I grinned back at her.

'Sorry, I don't speak Hungarian,' I said in my best Queen's English.

'I said who the fuck are you,' she returned, in her best Anglo-Saxon.

'Ah. That's better. The fuck I am is someone looking for Mr Ziffer.'

She laid down the pen she was holding in her left hand. She interlaced her fingers; they sported enough rings to make up a set of brass knuckles. Well, gold knuckles.

'Is he expecting you?'

I perched on the corner of her mahogany desk.

'In a manner of speaking. Let's just say I don't think he'll be surprised to see me.'

Her hands were no longer linked. The faint sound of a drawer sliding open reached me. I pushed her in the chest, leaned over the desk and lifted out the revolver lying on top of some papers. It had a two-inch barrel, shaped grip, and chromed finish. The name Weihrauch was engraved on the frame, below the cylinder.

'Naughty, naughty,' I said. 'You weren't really planning to shoot little me, were you?'

She just glared. 'This is a legitimate business. You have no right to come barging in here and threatening me.'

'Shush,' I said, giving her a target's view of her own piece. 'Let's stay on good terms. You just take me to Mr Ziffer and leave us to our business, or …'

Her eyebrows, which were thick and didn't match her hair, collided over the bridge of her nose.

'Or?'

'Or I hit you over the head with this little German pistol of yours, tie you up, and find him without your help.'

Tough as she pretended to be, she went pale under her make-up.

'Who *are* you?' she asked again.

'A man with a problem only Mr Ziffer can solve.'

'If you make trouble for him, you'll be sorry. He has many important connections.'

'Including the police? That wouldn't surprise me. Maybe I should call Inspector Beres and ask him to come and give me a hand. We were having a chat about the 77 club only yesterday.'

She went a paler shade of pale. 'You know Beres?' Her voice was hushed, reverent; you'd have thought we were discussing the Pope.

I nodded. After all, it was no lie.

'We're like that.' I crossed my index and middle finger. That *was* a lie, but I wasn't destined for Heaven anyway, so an occasional untruth wouldn't on its own damn me to eternal hellfire.

She rose, her movements stiff, as if her joints were playing up. Up on her hind legs she was within an inch of my height. With those shoulders and her hefty build, she would need no special favours from me if it came to a punch-up.

'Come with me.'

As she went by me to the door, I kept plenty of space between us. I let her go ahead and she led me through the third landing door, into another office, bigger than hers and more luxuriously appointed, with dark panelled walls and a scattering of paintings. The occupant was my new acquaintance, Mr Ziffer, manager and abduction suspect.

He leapt out of his throne-sized leather chair as if a firework had gone off under his backside. The expected torrent of Hungarian expletives never materialised though; he just stood and stared. No surprise in his expression, just hostility. Perhaps his tea leaves had foretold my visit.

I made sure my borrowed firearm was on view.

'Good morning,' I said, and the woman obligingly translated for me.

'He has no English,' she said to me.

'No matter. Just tell him I want him to accompany me to the place where he's keeping Patricia.'

The woman shot me a puzzled glance. 'What are you talking about?'

'Patricia, the waitress who works here.'

'What about her?'

Ziffer was looking from me to the woman as each of us spoke. A

narrowing of his eyes at the mention of Patricia was the only reaction.

'She didn't show this morning, did she?' I said.

'No. Perhaps she is ill.'

'Or perhaps she is a prisoner of friends of Mr Ziffer.'

The woman, who seemed genuinely not to be in the picture, looked at Ziffer and socked it to him in words he would understand.

He sat down in his over-stuffed throne, shook his head and rumbled back at her, boss to employee.

'Tell him I know he's responsible for taking Patricia,' I said. 'Him and Laszlo Farkas.'

The mention of Laszlo Farkas visibly unsettled him. He squirmed and, avoiding my eyes, rattled off a long explanation, or instruction, or resume of what he had for breakfast.

The woman summarised this as 'He tells me to warn you that if you do not get out of here immediately you will not leave Budapest alive.'

I'd received more convincing threats over the years. They hadn't impressed me either.

'And I tell you to warn him that if he doesn't get his fat ass out of that chair and lead me to Patricia, he'll get a bullet in his foot. And that'll still leave five bullets for other parts of his anatomy.'

Whereas she had showed no concern over the possibility that I might meet an early demise, the prospect of her boss being shot galvanised her into a rapid fire monologue.

Ziffer's response was to look sulky and growl a few truculent syllables that didn't go down well with her, if the downward set of her over-lipsticked lips was an indicator.

To me, she said, 'He doesn't know what you are talking about,' adding, 'I am his wife.'

That accounted for the lengthy rant. I had thought she was being disrespectful to her boss, when all along she was just a wife nagging her husband. That aside, the image of this woman, built along Amazonian lines, married to the squat, swarthy Ziffer bordered on risible. The only feature they had in common was their ugliness. And possibly their nastiness.

This woman was not easily intimidated. She planted herself in front

of me and issued another dire warning about my prospects of attaining old age.

'Now, go, or you will be sorry.'

I pointed the gun at her and said, 'Bang, bang,' in case she'd forgotten who was giving the orders around here. 'Get behind the desk with your husband. If you're his wife, you must know where Patricia's being held.'

'I keep the accounts,' she snapped. 'I know nothing about it.'

Even if I accepted that she was an innocent party, her husband certainly knew everything about it.

The challenge for me was how to ensure their cooperation without having to shoot either or both of them. Tricky, tricky. I could force Ziffer to call whoever was guarding the girl and order them to bring her here, but how would I know what he was saying. His wife's translation couldn't be guaranteed reliable.

That was when I noticed a door in a corner of a windowless wall.

'Where does that lead?' I asked the woman. 'Outside?'

She hesitated which I interpreted as a yes.

'It is the back of the building,' she said grudgingly.

'Good. Now get down on the floor.'

She looked at Ziffer, spoke to him, and he replied with a spate of terse words. She knelt.

'Lie face down,' I ordered.

With a motion to Ziffer to move away from the desk, I went through its drawers. In the sixth and last I found what I had hoped to find – a roll of insulation tape.

'Tell him to tape your hands and feet,' I instructed the woman.

As she was passing this on to Ziffer, a knock came at the door. The Ziffers exchanged glances.

'It's only one of the girls,' the woman told me.

'Tell her to come back later,' I said, before they could use the interruption to their advantage.

The woman, now back on her knees, called out what I hoped was 'Come back later', and the response – 'Okay' – confirmed she hadn't tried to be clever.

She resumed her face-down position, allowing Ziffer to strap her up – wrists and ankles. I sent him to the furthest corner of the office and checked his handiwork. Keeping the gun within easy reach, I added a few more turns of tape.

I ordered the woman to convey my requirements to him. To avoid misunderstandings in the translation, I kept them basic: leave by the back door, pick up his car, drive me to the place where they were holding Patricia. Release her to me. Drama over.

The imponderables, such as how far we would have to drive, how secure was Patricia's prison, how many guards would be waiting to welcome me, would remain until we reached our destination. The Weihrauch revolver was not an ideal weapon for taking on this gang on their home territory. Six shots, no reloads, but with the Boberg as back-up I had at least an even chance.

My final act was to apply a generous amount of tape to the woman's mouth and continue around her neck. Using sign language with the gun, I motioned Ziffer to head for the door. It was locked but he didn't try and stall, just produced a key ring from his pocket and opened up. It accessed a metal platform with stairs, also metal. I pushed him out onto the platform. If he tried to make a break, I would be helpless to prevent it. The place was too public for shooting, even as a warning.

Ziffer descended the stairs, the muzzle of his wife's gun gouging the back of his neck as a deterrent. If anybody showed up in the small square courtyard below and Ziffer hollered for help, that would bring my rescue plan to a premature ending. Nobody showed up and my hostage didn't get cute. We made it to the bottom and out of the courtyard into a dingy passageway. Voices reached us from the street. I prodded Ziffer hard in the base of his spine. No point in making threats, he wouldn't have understood them, but a prod from a gun speaks a universal language.

We reached the end of the passageway. I slipped the gun into my hip pocket out of sight, my finger on the trigger as a comforter. A metal rail bordered the sidewalk, with several cycles chained to it. On the other side of the rail was a ramp to an underground garage, or *garász* in the local lingo. People pushed past us, intent on their own business and having no interest in ours. I reminded Ziffer I was still here, still armed,

and for all he knew crazy enough to put a bullet in him in front of a dozen witnesses. Maybe I should have rolled my eyes and drooled a little to convince him I was cuckoo.

My luck and Ziffer's cooperation held. We set off along the sidewalk to a door next to a jeweller's and entered. It led downstairs. A couple more doors and we were in the parking garage. Ziffer said something to me, but I could only shrug my incomprehension.

His car was a blue SUV. Maybe a coincidence. I didn't think so. He unlocked it and got in behind the wheel. I climbed in beside him and freed the gun from my pocket. Now came the tricky part. A driver under duress has the potential to upset his capturer by speeding up and slamming on the brakes. So, my first precaution was to fasten my seat belt. My second, was to prevent Ziffer from fastening his. Now, if he braked with intent to throw me against the windshield, he would spread himself all over the steering wheel.

'Get going,' I said, pointing the gun at his head and cocking the hammer.

He grunted his assent and fired up the engine. We reversed out of his parking space and drove towards what I took to be the exit. A sign fixed on a gantry read KIJÁRAT, which didn't resemble any of the translations of exit I had ever come across.

We stopped at a barrier. Ziffer flashed a card at the check-out and we drove through, past an unoccupied kiosk and up a ramp to filter into a slow-moving procession of vehicles. He drove without much road sense, nose to the tail of a battered station wagon, until we cleared the side street and entered a wide thoroughfare with multiple lanes. I kept the gun muzzle hard against his thigh, to make sure my message was sticking.

We crossed into Buda by the Chain Bridge. There, we joined a long straight avenue that reminded me of the Diagonale in Barcelona. Ziffer was prone to dart in and out of the traffic. He sweated a lot; I could smell it and see it on his forehead. I fiddled with the climate control to boost the airflow.

At a major junction we turned left onto a divided thoroughfare, becoming part of an endless river of traffic. Progress was slower here, but

as we entered suburbia it speeded up and before long we came to a six-lane freeway. An IKEA billboard flashed by on the right. Another sign on a gantry announced M7 Balaton Nagykanízsa. My knowledge of the geography of Hungary was hazy, but I was sure that Balaton, the great lake in the centre of the county, lay about a hundred kms west-ish of the capital. I consulted the GPS. We were heading south-west, which might suggest my geography was wrong, or that Balaton wasn't on our route.

I sank the muzzle of the gun deep into Ziffer's thigh, just keeping in practice. He flinched and tried to squirm away.

'No tricks, buddy, or I'll make you sorry.'

He couldn't understand, but I added some grit to the warning, to make sure he was taking me seriously. His head bobbed like a chicken's.

The rest of the journey was notable only for the boring scenery and lack of conversation. We stayed with the M7, Balaton repeater signs popping up at intervals overhead. I still half-expected Ziffer to try some tricky move, such as braking sharply or swerving, but his behaviour was impeccable. As long as I was strapped in and he wasn't, his freedom of action was zero.

An exit sign came up, and we slowed – Siofok, Sosto. The names meant nada to me. We veered away from the freeway and delved into an area of small individual houses, the majority finished in white with grey garbage bins at the entry to their driveways. After that I lost track of our direction, even with the GPS to help me. Lake Balaton appeared on the edge of the screen as an expanse of blue. A few turns and we were travelling alongside it, still in a residential area. The houses thinned out, became more sporadic, giving ground to open countryside.

'I hope you're not stringing me along,' I said to Ziffer

He paid no heed. Why should he worry? He was driving me to a destination known only to him, and even if Patricia was there, she was sure to have company, such as three or four beefy guys with experience in abducting girls. All I had was my two titchy guns. If they had guns too, titchy or otherwise, bullets were going to fly.

The sky was no longer blue, nor was the lake. Rain spattered the windshield. We were in a residential area again. On the right a green panel with a ship silhouette read Tihany. At an intersection, we swung

right on a road that ran past some apartments, then a row of trees, before coming to a port or, more precisely, a ferry terminal. At a small blue kiosk Ziffer bought a ticket. Another precarious moment. But he continued to play it straight. He no more wanted a public brawl than I did. Mixed up as he was in Patricia's abduction, not to mention his links to the dubious business dealings of the Wolff twins, he had more to fear from the police than me. Whereas, if he drove us to where Patricia was or wasn't being held, the reception committee could deal with me behind closed doors.

Ah, Warner, you Quixotic fool.

* * * * *

The house we came to, in the late afternoon under skies the colour of dishwater, was grand in size if not in style, like many individual properties I had observed in Hungary. White finish, grey tiled gable roof with a squat chimney stack, two floors, upper floor balcony with an awning extended over it, double garage with a room above. A panoramic window on the ground floor to exploit the view across the lake. On the gate a colourful notice read ELADO with a name and address beneath. For sale, for rent? In the gravel-surfaced driveway, three cars including another SUV, also a blue Renault.

Ziffer braked hard, the car sliding on the gravel. He killed the engine and sat there, gazing through the windshield, breathing through his nostrils in little snorts.

Nobody came to see who was visiting. In fact there were no signs of occupancy. Ziffer seemed content to wait. I took my cue from him. If any of his associates came out shooting, he was as much a target as me, so I felt as secure as any person who's just poked a stick in a hornet's nest.

The inability to communicate with this guy limited the extent of my control over him. I could brandish the gun, make neck-slicing motions, and shout at the top of my voice, but that would only get me so far. I could make him move by jabbing the gun in his back, or stop moving by restraining him. For the rest I was having to wing it.

Just as I was about to do some jabbing, half of the front double door

of the house swung inwards. A woman stepped onto the paved path. It was still raining but she was sheltered by a porch with a hanging basket of flowers at each corner. Her smile was more predatory than welcoming.

She was about fifty, mousey hair, small boned with eyes made huge behind black-rimmed glasses, and the smooth, wrinkle-free skin of a Barbie Doll.

Ziffer lowered the window on his side. She spoke to him, in his language not mine. His reply included the word *angol*, which I guessed meant 'English'. Then another word I recognised – Patricia.

The smile switched off. Her eyes swivelled towards me. Another exchange between her and Ziffer was short and sour. I nudged him with the gun, giving him permission to dismount.

As I stepped down, my feet crunching on the gravel, I made sure the woman could see I was holding a gun, therefore calling the shots. Or maybe not. Behind the drawn drapes a rifle might be trained on me right now.

'Who are you?' the woman snapped in flawless mid-west American English as I approached her, gun levelled.

'I've come for Patricia,' I said.

'Do you have an appointment?'

'No appointment, only a gun. And my hostage here.'

'The gun is unnecessary. As for your hostage …'

The trace of a sneer that accompanied the reference to my hostage suggested that Ziffer may not be worth much as a bargaining tool.

He and I were getting wet; the woman beckoned us under the porch.

'I am Sara Wolff,' she informed me, cool and composed, as if she were speaking to an invited guest. 'And you are?'

She almost sucked me in with her polite *froideur*. I wasn't about to divulge any of my identities, real or phoney. Then belatedly it hit me. Sara *Wolff*! Coincidence? The hell it was. It suited me not to reveal that the name meant anything to me, while my brain sorted it out.

'If you must call me something, call me Charles.'

'Very well, Charles. Would you like to come in and take some refreshment?'

The hallway extended the length of the house: tiled floor, the only piece of furniture a trapezium-shaped table, on which stood a Japanese bonsai tree in a blue pot; garish pictures adorned both walls.

With Sara Wolff in the lead, Ziffer in the middle, and me as tail-end Charlie, we walked down the hall to where it opened up on a living room, with a French door on one wall, filled with an outlook of Lake Balaton beneath ramparts of threatening clouds.

The furniture was all pine and Swedish-influenced, apart from a set of drums. The floor was darker, the elongated whorls in the grain suggesting oak. Random shaggy rugs with an irregular geometric pattern were scattered about. I had a sense it was a rented house, and the furnishings had come included.

The yard to the rear of the building, as viewed through another French door, was landscaped with no expense spared. Exotic trees and plants abounded. A tiled terrace surrounded a kidney-shaped pond, with sun beds and lounging chairs dotted about, the whole caboodle under the supervision of a patrolling Doberman whose big, black nose was nuzzling the glass.

I positioned myself with my back to the wall, facing two internal doors. Two-Gun Warner, braced for action.

'Do sit down,' Sara Wolff said, making a sweeping gesture to imply the choice of seating was entirely mine. It was weird. She behaved as if armed visitors were everyday occurrences, no more worthy of note than a pizza delivery boy.

'I'll stand if you don't mind. It's easier to shoot people from a standing position.'

Even that intentional dose of reality didn't faze her beyond a lifted eyebrow.

'Let's hope it won't be necessary,' she said, adjusting fast to the implied threat. She switched to Hungarian to fire a short, sharp fusillade at Ziffer, who responded with a snort and made to leave.

'Hold it!' I snapped. To Sara Wolff, 'He's my hostage. He stays.'

Her smile was sickly sweet. Her glasses reflected the light coming through the French door, so I couldn't see her eyes.

'Aren't I valuable enough to play that role?'

'In one sense, yes. But you see, I might really have to shoot you.'

That finally penetrated her cool defences. The homely act dissolved into a glare that would have stripped paint.

'I suppose you think that's funny.'

'Look, Mrs Wolff, let's cut out the small talk. Just fetch Patricia and I'll be on my way, no more questions asked.'

Ziffer piped up and I recognised the name Beres in his spiel. Sara Wolff didn't take kindly to what he told her. She gave him what smacked of a good old tongue thrashing, under which he succumbed like a miscreant schoolboy. It was obvious who was in charge here.

She crossed the room to a small round table with a white phone sitting on it. She pressed a single button and gained an instant response. God knows what she reported to the person on the line, as her side of the conversation was in Hungarian. When she came off the phone, she looked smug though.

'If you're planning any funny stuff, I should warn you I'm not playing games,' I said, seriously handicapped by my lack of Hungarian. 'If anybody steps out of line, they get shot.'

'Thank for the warning,' she said.

The two internal doors opened, more or less simultaneously, and two large males crowded in through each of them, all toting pump-action shotguns, with cut-down barrels.

'As you see, we too are well-prepared.'

Even outgunned as I was, I didn't cave there and then. I switched the revolver from my right to my left hand and tugged the Boberg from my pocket. As if it would make a difference.

'If there's going to be shooting, my first bullet's for you, Mrs Wolff.'

She shook her head and chuckled. 'Oh, Mr Charles, you've been watching too many Hollywood movies. The first shot from one of those shotguns will knock you off your feet. You won't get to pull the triggers of either of your toy guns.'

I was tempted to wing her there and then, if only to prove my guns weren't toys. Since suicide wasn't on today's agenda, I stayed my hand.

'Put the guns down, please,' Sara Wolff requested of me, in her soft, lilting voice.

Disarmed, I would be at her mercy. She would want to avoid killing me, but if my reading of her was accurate, she wouldn't hesitate to order her goons to disable me with a dose of buckshot.

I was paying the price of a failure to plan and predict. Unlike a contract hit, when I had days, weeks, or months to calculate my moves and research the ground, I had blundered into a well-organised outfit. My hero-to-the-rescue act may have boosted my ego and sense of righteousness, but it was also downright unprofessional, and no use at all to Patricia.

For now, Sara Wolff was in the driving seat and I might as well stop resisting it. I engaged the safety of the Boberg; the revolver didn't have one. With a crooked grin, I tossed both weapons into the nearest armchair.

'Thank you for averting unnecessary bloodshed,' Sara Wolff said, eyes sparkling with humour behind the severe rims. 'Please continue to co-operate while my men make you comfortable. I'll come and see you in a while and you can then explain the real reason for this invasion of our privacy.'

Chapter Six

The making-comfortable process Sara Wolff style involved a shotgun butt in the ribs and another in the kidneys, leaving me semi-incapacitated and only able to climb the wide staircase to the second floor with assistance from two of the heavies. They shoved me through a doorway into a room with no ceremony at all. I collapsed in a groaning heap. Whether through being out of practice, getting old, or over-confidence, I had walked myself into a deep dark hole. The only saving grace was that I had taken a major step forward in my search for the Wolff twins.

By prison standards my cell was luxurious. It was lit by a single square window set in the slope of the roof behind a steel grill, above head height. The only other exit was through the door I came in by, which had been locked and bolted behind me.

When I had recovered from my rough handling I dragged the bed, which was the only piece of furniture the room contained, across the room and stood on it. Postcard view. Or it would have been if the sun had been shining. Lake Balaton was still grey and choppy in the rain, the far shore invisible. A motor cruiser was slicing through the waves, making heavy weather of it.

I lay down on the bed, hugging my ribs and feeling sorry for myself. No obvious escape plan was forming in my mind. I would have to wait for an opening and go for it. Sara Wolff was sure to visit and follow up on her parting comment.

Sandwiches with a bottle of Theodora mineral water were brought up to me as evening set in. Two guards made the delivery, large and extra-large sizes, the large one with a tray, the extra-large model with a shotgun. Both with lurid tattoos on their forearms. They didn't speak.

'You understand English?' I tried on Large, as he set the tray down

on the floor and made to back out, covered by Extra-Large.

'Fuck off,' he said, grinning, and slammed the door almost on my nose.

* * * * *

After my bread and cheese supper I mooched around. I had nothing to keep me entertained, and it was a welcome break in the monotony when Sara Wolff came visiting just before dark. Even though I was expecting a certain amount of unpleasantness as she, with a little help from her friends, attempted to extract information that I was reluctant to part with. Large and Extra-Large accompanied her, complete with matching shotguns at the ready.

'Now then, Mr Charles alias Mr Devreese,' she said leaning against the wall and lighting a cigarette with a Zippo. 'Are you going to cooperate?'

I spread my hands. 'Yours to command, Mrs Wolff.'

'We checked your cell phone. It seems to have a password.'

They had confiscated my cell phone and my wallet. The two charge cards in my wallet both carried my identity of the moment, as did the driver's permit and EU medical card.

'Sure it does. One-three-five-seven.'

A flicker of surprise crossed her face. Almost immediately she resorted to a little ladylike snort.

'By parting with it so readily you're telling me I won't find any of your secrets on it.'

'Be my guest anyway.'

'Later, later. For now I have a couple of questions for you. Why did you come to Budapest?'

I sat down on the edge of the bed, trying to appear nonchalant, like a man with no secrets.

'Tourism.'

'Am I supposed to believe that? Do you normally go armed on vacation?'

'The world's a dangerous place these days.'

'Cut it out. I want the real reason and you're going to tell me, either voluntarily, or under duress, it's all the same to me.'

She inhaled and projected a plume of smoke at me; it didn't quite reach its target.

'Look, Mrs Wolff, why don't you save yourselves a lot of inconvenience and potential grief. Just turn the girl over to me. I'll leave and you'll never hear from me again. You can even keep the guns.'

She spoke to her companions in Hungarian. They broke into identical laughs like a double act. Large said a few words back to her.

'Mikel asks if you think we need your permission,' she translated.

She had a point. But letting them intimidate me wouldn't help my case. I had to tread a fine line between respect and insouciance, in the hope they would accept that I was harmless, and release me, with or without Patricia.

'So, if we let you leave you will not report to Inspector Beres, is that what you're saying?'

'You're American, aren't you?'

'If I am, so what? Sure as hell you're not Belgian as your passport says. If we add it all up – the fake passport and ID cards, the gun, your interrogation of Patricia – it comes to this: you're either with Interpol, or Europol, or you're a PI. You can tell us which it is here and now, or we're going to take you apart. And if that isn't enough to convince you to blab, we'll give Patricia the same treatment.'

Large and Extra-Large were grinning wolfishly, as if they understood English and were thrilled with anticipation about being turned loose on me.

'This much I'll tell you,' I said, with feigned reluctance. 'I'm not with any police organisation. It's strictly a private operation.'

Sara Wolff dropped her half-smoked cigarette on the bare wooden floor and ground it in with her sole, bearing out my view that the house was rented. Outside, darkness blanketed the land, dribbles of rain were rolling down the skylight. Inside, I was having to face up to the seriousness of my position. This wasn't a Mickey Mouse operation. If I handled these people wrongly, I could be taking a trip to the bottom of Lake Balaton without a diving suit.

Me and my chivalrous gestures. If I had left Patricia to her fate, I wouldn't be in this seedy little room, facing either a slow or a quick death, depending on how cooperative I was.

'If it's private, you're working for somebody. I want to know who.'

She meant 'whom' of course, but I didn't correct her.

'I can't help you. It was all arranged by phone, using code names. It was a guy, I can tell you that, probably Dutch, and he paid my fee up front.'

She nodded slowly. A nod of contemplation, not acceptance.

'What was your brief?'

'To trace Laszlo Farkas.'

That stunned her. She stood away from the wall, her face thunderstruck.

'You have been paid to find Laszlo?'

It was a blind. Farkas was just a lead that could well be false. By meeting Sara Wolff I might have circumvented the connection anyway.

'That's right. My job is to seek him and find him. No questions asked or answered. My quarries are usually criminal, but I don't need to know that, and it doesn't alter my methods.'

She began to pace. For her age she was in good shape physically. Extra-Large shuffled his feet, which were in proportion to the rest of him. He changed his grip on the shotgun, flexed his fingers.

'The question is, do I believe what you say,' Sara Wolff murmured, talking as much to herself as to me. 'Even if I do, even if we put you on a flight back to Brussels or wherever you came from, what's to stop you returning to Budapest to continue your search?'

'My word?' I suggested, which provoked a barking little laugh.

'Your word. Interesting proposal. If I knew you, and believed you to be an honourable man, your word might just have been enough.' A sneering smile. 'Then again, it might not.'

I got up off the bed. The two gunmen stiffened, their guns extended, fingers on triggers.

'Relax,' I soothed. 'I just want to stretch my legs.' I made a show of massaging my knees.

'If you find the person you're looking for, how do you report to your employer?'

'I don't. He contacts me, two or three times a week, at random.'

Sara Wolff was standing about three feet from the door, with her back to it, and therefore ideally positioned for my purposes.

'Contacts you how?'

'Usually by email,' I said. On the pretext of restoring circulation I stamped my feet a few times, edging closer to her. 'If you have a computer, I could show you his latest message.'

She perked up at that. She was still perked up when I lunged into her, prompting a startled squawk, and swung her round to place her between me and those nasty men with guns.

While I held her squirming body against mine with one hand, I fumbled for the door handle with the other. She bawled at Large and Extra-Large and they moved to intervene, unable to use their guns for fear of hitting her, but their muscle power more than adequate if I let them within touching distance. With all the strength I could muster, I launched Sara Wolff at them. Without lingering to see how it all turned out, I wrenched the door open and was out of that room like a sprinter leaving the starting block. To my rear a rumpus of crashing and banging and cursing as Sara Wolff and her oversized gofers ended up on the floor. I had bought maybe a ten seconds start, no more. I half fell down the stairs. If the two other guys I had seen earlier were still around, my escape attempt could yet come to an abortive end and, most likely, me with it.

At the foot of the stairs a door stood open; I lurched through it just as the first blast from a shotgun travelled down the stairwell, splattering the wall and missing my backside by not much. They weren't just acting tough.

I found myself in the living room. To the thunder of feet on stairs I cast around for a weapon or inspiration. The two pistols I had brought with me were lying on a cabinet. I grabbed them. Two-Gun Warner was back in business.

They came through the doorway side by side, comically getting stuck in their desperation to get at me. I used the Ziffer revolver to put a bullet in the woodwork over their heads. They gave up the contest to be first into the room. I ripped off two more shots, bracketing the doorway, and

asked them politely to drop the shotguns. With two corpses already debited against my account in Italy, I was averse to shedding more blood. Averse, but ready and able if it was between them and me.

They played it sensible. Their guns hit the floor with the clatter that heavy objects landing on wood tend to make.

'Now back off,' I snapped, taking a step towards them to underline the message.

They retreated into the hall with me pacing them. I slipped the Boberg into my pants pocket and stooped to collect a shotgun. It was a Mossberg, an inexpensive piece but functional enough. I kicked the other shotgun out of reach.

'On your knees,' I said.

Extra-Large complied at once. Large, taking his cue from his partner, did likewise.

Sara Wolff was still upstairs, staying away from the rough stuff. If she was on her cell phone rounding up reinforcements, I was far from home free. The next obvious step was to render these two *hors de combat* and make a break for it, using Ziffer's SUV. Of Ziffer himself there was no trace.

Before leaving though, I had another task to perform, namely to locate Patricia. After all, she was my reason for being here and I would hate to leave empty-handed.

I called up the stairs for Sara Wolff.

'Come on down or your two pet guard dogs will suffer.'

No reply. I didn't have the luxury of waiting for her decision. With the revolver I placed a bullet in Extra-Large's right bicep. He howled and clutched at the wound. Blood oozed between his fingers.

'Five seconds before the other guy gets it,' I called again.

'I'm coming, I'm coming,' she responded, still sounding composed and in control. 'No need to waste any more of your precious bullets.'

She descended the stairs, brazen as ever, as if she were still in charge of events. Extra-Large didn't even rate a sympathetic glance from her. He was moaning softly, blood still dribbling over the back of his hand in little rivulets.

'Where's Ziffer?' I demanded. 'And who else is here?'

'Ziffer's gone,' she said, her tone disdainful. 'There's no one else.'

'You'd better be telling the truth.' I gestured with the shotgun. 'Now, fetch Patricia.'

'If only it were that simple,' she said, with the sort of pitying smile you bestow on a disabled street beggar.

'It is, so don't make it complicated.'

'She's not here, so too bad, but I can't oblige you.'

My grip on the shotgun tightened. As a rule, I shrank from shooting women, even to wound, but I was ready to make an exception if she refused to co-operate.

'I don't believe you.'

A wall clock chimed the half hour, making me start in my keyed-up state.

'But it's true. Ziffer took her away.'

I fumed inwardly. If it was true, I was back where I started from. It would be a tough enough challenge merely to extricate myself from the quagmire I had tumbled in, let alone continue the hunt for Patricia. Based on the number of personnel I had encountered so far, the organisation to which Sara Wolff and Ziffer belonged was major-league.

I ordered the three of them into the living room, then retrieved my wallet and cell phone from the cabinet. My immediate need was a room with a lockable door.

'Upstairs,' I said, 'to the room you kept me in.'

With the woman in the lead we all traipsed up to the second floor. The key was in the door lock. I shepherded them into the room with the muzzle of the shotgun.

'Don't be in a hurry to break out,' I warned Sara Wolff. 'I'll be checking this place out in case you're lying about Patricia, so I'll be around for a while yet.'

She didn't thank me for my thoughtful advice. I shut and locked the door.

On this level were a number of other rooms. None was locked, a confirmation of sorts that Patricia was not on the premises. All the same I checked and made an interesting discovery. On a night table in what appeared to be the master bedroom – it boasted a four-poster bed, an

ensuite bathroom, and a walk-in wardrobe – was a colour studio portrait of a couple. The woman was Sara Wolff, minus specs, taken at a guess about ten years ago. The man was blond and profuse of locks and resembled the Wolff twins in the photo provided by Donovan. If Victor really was Sara Wolff's husband, it was probably him. It didn't advance my search for either twin. I smashed the frame on a corner of the night table and removed the portrait. At least I would come away from this little interlude with a useful addition to my limited but growing CV of the twins. If I came away at all.

As for Patricia, there was no evidence she had ever been in the building. After going through the whole of the rest of the house and the attached double garage, I went outside. The rain had eased off. The night was clear, with a panoply of stars and Venus presiding over the display away in the west. The moon was a sickle, to the left of Venus. Lake Balaton appeared as a furrowed field of gunmetal blue, sending endless lines of ripples to the shore, and the moon's reflection a shimmering silver sword bisecting its surface.

A car and an SUV stood in the driveway. They were recent vintage models, the kind that doesn't require a key to be inserted in the ignition. I had come across no key fobs in my prowl through the rooms. Hot wiring cars was a skill I had learned long ago from the Secret Service, but modern cars, stuffed with electronics, were not such easy meat. If my three prisoners had the fobs on them, it would be quicker to arrange a change of ownership – at the point of a gun to speed up the process.

I was about to turn around and re-enter the house when my attention was drawn to a jetty at the water's edge. Tied up beside it were a mid-sized motor cruiser with a fly bridge, and a speedboat, both white hulled. The jetty was illuminated with a dim light at the top of a pole, probably solar powered. It had to be the Wolff's private property as it was accessed from their yard. A light was burning behind a curtained oval porthole on the cruiser.

The boats were giving me ideas. I slunk along the edge of a lawn, staying in the shadows of a row of trees, as far as a short flight of steps up to the jetty. There I paused. All was quiet but for the hum of an air-conditioning motor around the side of the house. Music came to me

faintly from the cruiser. The shotgun was already primed. If I couldn't make my getaway by car, a boat would do equally well.

The jetty was the floating kind. Both boats were moored stern in, as is common practice. I stepped on the jetty and felt it shift beneath my feet. Unavoidable. The movement would have been transmitted through the mooring ropes to the boats themselves, giving away my presence if there was anyone on board the cruiser.

A glance behind reassured me all was clear in that direction. Sara Wolff and her fellow prisoners wouldn't find it easy to force an inward-opening door.

The cruiser was about thirty-five feet in length, a French-built Jeanneau Prestige 34 according to the scrollwork along the side of the hull. Scrollwork on the stern, trumpeted the boat's name – *Hullám Cimerje*. Three oval portholes on my side; the illuminated one was now in darkness. Whoever was on board was ready to welcome me.

The speedboat was the better bet as a means of escape. Enclosed bow, three rows of seats, it would be super-manoeuvrable and looked seriously fast. I stepped aboard, checked it for an ignition key. No surprise when I drew a blank. Two dashboard lockers proved equally barren.

I transferred to the motor cruiser, stepping onto the stern swimming platform. It dipped appreciably under my weight, another warning of my presence. The stock of the shotgun felt slick from the sweat of the palm of my hand. The tightest spots were those where your enemy was lying in wait, when you were out in the open and he was under cover, and armed and ready to kill you.

My experience and knowledge came mostly from sailing boats. Still, I could manage the basics – cast off, start up, and steer which was about all it would take to get me away from here and across to the other side of the lake. After that, events could look after themselves. Before that, I needed to clear the decks.

Inside the cabin, movement. A lowered voice. Two of them at least then. I stepped up to the cockpit, with its single seat for the helmsman and communal area with curved padded seating. To the right of the helm, steps descended into the hull. With the jetty light behind me, I would be in full silhouette when I entered the saloon.

Time didn't favour me. The longer I lingered on the boat, the greater the prospects of the Wolff woman and her goons forcing the bedroom door. As the two cars were still in the driveway, it wouldn't take them above a few seconds to conclude I was aiming to use waterborne transport. I had almost decided to take my chances on foot, and merge into the countryside, when whoever was below decks made the first move.

The skylight on the forward deck opened on its hinges. As it rose, the top half of a head rose with it, paused, was followed by the rest of the head plus shoulders. In the moonlight I made out a hand with a weapon attached to it. He fired the instant I hurled myself sideways behind the helmsman's seat. His gun was fitted with a sound suppressor, and its cough was lost in the crash of my body on the unyielding teak deck.

The shooter loosed off a succession of shots, wild and unaimed, making holes in the night but not in me. I stayed still, crouched in the gap in the communal space between two seats.

The sound of the skylight closing reached me. He hadn't emerged onto the foredeck while I was belly down, of that I was sure. His choices were to play safe and sit tight, or come out through the saloon door, gun blazing.

My commandeered Mossberg shotgun held five cartridges. I would need to make them count, as I had no reloads. The music was no longer playing. I listened to the slap of water against the hull, a familiar, almost soothing refrain from many days spent afloat on my yacht *Seamist*. The waiting game had begun – a game at which I had much practice. No good came from precipitate moves. In a duel of wits such as this, whoever was the more patient would win through.

In a stand-off, you needed to probe the mind of your adversary. He would be unsure if any of his bullets had struck home. If they had, was I disabled, or even dead? My failure to return his fire introduced an additional uncertainty into an already precarious contest. From my side, all he had done was give notice that he was armed but impulsive.

The flaw in my waiting stratagem was the presence nearby of Sara Wolff and the two goons, Large and Extra-Large. The longer I waited,

the greater the prospect of them escaping from the locked room. In the long run I was bound to lose.

Out in the woods beyond the house, an owl hoo-hooed. A car engine cranked down the road. The Wolff house was far from isolated, but other people would be no help to me. If I were to seek refuge with neighbours, I would just expose them to danger and complicate matters further. For once, waiting wasn't the answer. I had to break my rule and take the initiative. I had to win by subterfuge.

Making plenty of noise, I leapt on the navigation table beside the helmsman's position, and scrambled on the roof. As I crouched there, a shot bored a hole between my feet. I moved on, doing a sidelong dance as a second shot made another hole, even closer than before. I kept going, skipping to the left and right like a hunted man zig-zagging to disrupt the aim of a sniper.

The roof acquired four, five, six holes. The magazine of his gun might contain a dozen or more, of which he had now used eleven, including the five I had counted from his opening salvo. I was now at the bow and immobile, hoping to confuse him by the lack of movement. Another shot, like a sneeze, another hole. I yelled, simulating pain, and jumped over the side, parting company with the shotgun as I hit the water.

That Lake Balaton in early summer is a bloody cold stretch of water, I can personally testify. It got me moving, that's all I can say in its favour. Within a few seconds I could expect my adversary show up on deck. I swam at a frantic pace, towards the stern where I heaved myself onto the swimming platform. I was still on my knees, dripping, shivering, and panting, when he blundered out onto the deck already pumping lead with his silenced gun.

The revolver came to my hand like a well-trained dog. I fired and our bullets must have passed each other. His went over my head by some distance, mine chewed a piece of stuffing from the back of the helmsman's seat, beside his hand. There was another difference: while his shots were muffled, mine was noisy and likely to attract attention, which wasn't in my plan.

He paid for his profligate use of ammunition; his gun clicked empty,

and I hadn't even felt the wind of bullets passing. My revolver was empty too, so now we were even.

'Hold it there!' I barked. 'And tell your buddy to come out with his hands in the air, or you're one dead Hungarian.'

If it was Ziffer, I was wearing out my vocal chords for nothing. His response was unintelligible. The glow from the pole light fell across his face. It was Ziffer all right. I gazed upon his unlovely features, came up off my knees, and closed in on him. I needed to put him out of action to leave me free to deal with his companion, so I whacked him across the temple with the barrel of the revolver. Plenty of power and frustration went behind the blow and he subsided to the deck, out cold, blood oozing from a gash in his forehead.

'Come on out!' I yelled down the hatch, swapping the empty revolver for the Boberg. 'Your buddy's finished.'

If Ziffer's pal understood, he wasn't about to raise the white flag. No gunfire though, which was an improvement. Lights had come in a building along the shore, thanks to my unsilenced shooting. If the occupants summoned the police, I would have to do a lot of explaining to Inspector Beres.

While I wavered, a cry for help came from below decks, feeble and female.

'Help me,' the cry came again, stronger now, bordering on hysterical.

Suspicious that it could be a ploy to lure me into an ambush, I was tempted to wait for Ziffer to come round and use him as a hostage. Except that waiting was an unaffordable luxury.

In defiance of common sense and caution, I took a deep breath and clattered down the steps to the saloon, gun in hand, the rest of me an arm's length behind. My questing fingers touched a wall switch, and I shed light on the scene. The saloon was empty, except for fixtures and a scattering of shell cases on the carpet.

'Help me!'

It came from behind a closed door towards the bow. Based on my basic knowledge of the internal layout of motor cruisers of this size, it would give access to a forward cabin.

Three paces took me from one side of the tiny saloon to the other. I

grasped the door handle. Another deep breath before yanking on the handle, while stepping to the side to avoid being silhouetted in the doorway. The bow cabin was in darkness but the open door projected an oblong of yellow light across a double bed on which lay the naked, bound figure of Patricia.

Chapter Seven

They had gagged her, but she had somehow managed to yank the gag down from her mouth. Her face bore bruises and a runnel of dried blood from the corner of her mouth to her chin. Her body had come in for similar ill treatment: burn marks on her breasts and lower down.

'Oh, thank you, thank you,' she snuffled, as I tackled the knots in the cords that bound her wrists.

'Don't thank me, it's all my fault.'

The knots were tight and complicated, and it took a while to free her. The cords had bitten deep into her skin and left angry corrugations.

'I can't feel my fingers,' she moaned, massaging them weakly. I took over, none-too-gently manipulating hands and digits until she yelled with the pain of returning circulation. Never had the proximity of a naked girl made so little impression on me.

'Where are your clothes?' I asked.

'Over there.' She pointed with her nose at a small bundle of clothing, jeans on top, in a corner of the suite.

'We have to get away from here,' I said. 'Do you know where the key is?'

'The key? For the engine?'

'Yes.'

'I see hooks in the kitchen with many keys.'

While she continued the manipulation, I went in search of the key. The hooks did indeed contain many keys, but only two were the right size and shape. Both had tags without identification. I took them up on deck, stepping over Ziffer who was stirring. I decided he was supercargo and should be ditched. He wasn't as heavy as he looked, and I was able to heave him over the gunwale onto the jetty without straining a tendon. His landing made a satisfying thud on the boards.

I followed him over the side to unhitch the two mooring ropes. As the hull began to drift away from the jetty, I scrambled back aboard and got settled behind the wheel.

I crossed my fingers that one of the keys would fit, and it did. Dials and screens came alive. At a glance all looked normal. The fuel tank was well over half full. I skipped the pre-start check as a precaution I couldn't afford.

Twin throttles meant two power units, diesel at a guess. I twisted the key. As the engines rumbled into lusty life, I heard a shout from the direction of the house; a gunshot split the silence and chewed a piece out of the glass fibre top of the instrument panel. I ducked down and pushed the throttle levers forward. The boat responded like a greyhound leaving its trap and accelerated away from the jetty.

The shooting began in earnest, as if I hadn't had a bellyful tonight. The crunch of bullets into glass-fibre ceased as the shore receded at a high rate of knots. A glance over my shoulder provided a snapshot of the situation. Two figures had reached the jetty, the third was running back to the house. I remembered the sports boat bobbing beside the cruiser and cursed myself under my breath for not disabling it. The chase was only just beginning.

I estimated the distance to the south shore of Balaton as less than ten miles. At twenty knots I would be there in a half hour. If the speedboat was capable of thirty, they would overhaul me well before I made landfall. Best then to head longwise along the lake, and deal with Sara Wolff and helpers while out on the water and out of visual range of nosy observers. I might even lose them in the darkness.

Throttling back, I went in search of Ziffer's gun to augment my weaponry. It was in the footwell of the helmsman's position. A Walther PPQ, recognisable by its square trigger guard and ergonomic grip with its eleven-round magazine, minus whatever Ziffer had fired. The sound suppressor doubled the gun's length but was too useful to discard. I unscrewed it and threaded the gun through my belt and retired the silencer to my hip pocket where it made an impressive supplement to my manhood.

My hopes of evading my pursuers under cover of darkness were

dashed within minutes when I suddenly found myself in the spotlight, literally. I looked astern. The speedboat was closing fast. No escaping the beam of light, short of putting a bullet in the lens.

Patricia came up on deck, dressed as she had been for our meeting at the Publin: ripped jeans and the señorita blouse, no longer pristine white. The spotlight made her look anaemic. She flicked me an on-off smile, shielded her eyes against the beam of light.

'They come for us?' she said, a tremor in her voice.

'They do,' I confirmed. 'You'd better stay below. There's going to be shooting.'

Her hand flew to her mouth. '*More* shooting?'

My sentiments precisely.

I nodded. 'Get below.'

'No, I stay with you.' She was a wilful girl. No respect for her elders.

'Then get down.' I jabbed at the space between the seat and the navigation table. That much at least she managed to do without a debate.

An idea was taking shape in my mind. The speedboat had the advantage of pace and was using it. I had the advantage of size and bulk, and I wasn't using it. Glass-fibre hulls on boats of this size were tough, designed to stand up to the rigours of crashing waves. How would it stand up to a different kind of crashing?

On impulse, I swung the helm hard to starboard, sending Patricia tumbling halfway down the stairs with a startled squeal. The boat came round in a tight sweep, the port engine roaring as the prop came partially clear of the water. I juggled with the trim but by the time I had it sorted the turn was complete, and I was back on a straight course, aiming directly for the speedboat.

If I telegraphed my intentions too clearly, they were nimble enough to stay out of my way. I needed a feint. As a penalty kicker will try and deceive a goalkeeper as to the trajectory of the ball, so I had to get them to misjudge my probable line. Already they were re-routeing sharply to port, the spotlight staying on me as they presented their beam. Perfect for ramming. Except that I wasn't close enough and they could outrun and out-turn me at whim.

Their wake made an S as they crossed my bow and swung behind me. I ploughed on with no change of direction and they paced me on a parallel course, keeping the spotlight trained on the cruiser.

Patricia popped up beside me for a look-see.

'Get down!' I hissed.

As if to prove the value of my warning, a gun cracked and did new damage to the hull of the cruiser.

'Stop!' came the command through cupped hands from the guy seated behind the driver.

'Okay,' I yelled back. 'Don't shoot.'

I reduced the throttle settings and the engines quietened to a burble. With my speed down to a walking pace, I stuck up my hands in lieu of a white flag. They closed in, still wary, still ready to accelerate out of trouble. The guy who had shouted was training a rifle or shotgun on me.

They reduced their speed to match mine, and edging closer on a converging course.

'Turn off engine!' the guy ordered.

'Right.' My hand hovered over the ignition key. Both our motors were only idling now; the gap between us continued to close as their momentum carried them along. Below, cowering in the stairwell, Patricia stared up at me with frightened eyes. I tried for a reassuring smile, not sure it came off.

The speedboat drifted across my bow, only feet away. The rifle was still covering me. It was now or surrender. I dropped below the control panel, hauled the throttles back. From my crouched position I could see nothing, but I knew the rudder was dead ahead, so by hanging on the helm I was bound to steer a straight line. There was a scream, a shot, and a massive jolt as we crunched into the speedboat. The front of the cruiser reared up then tilted down, the engines racing for an instant, then we were through and past and charging along at speed. I got back in the seat, eased back on the throttles, and screwed round to check the effect of the impact on the speedboat. It was no longer recognisable as a boat; just two shattered pieces of glass-fibre, seat cushions, flotsam, and the heads of two swimmers. The stern section was the smaller piece, and this slid below the surface as I watched.

Patricia rose to stand beside me, hand over mouth in astonishment.

'You any good at lifesaving?' I asked.

'You make a joke, no?'

'I make a joke, yes. Let's go.'

Cries for help lingered in the air as we put distance between us and the collision scene. Then we were out of earshot.

* * * * *

As it turned out, we hadn't come through entirely unscathed. There was hull damage and we were taking in water. The goal now was to head for the nearest dry land, so I consulted the GPS and set a course for the ferry port at Szántód. I also slowed to a more sedate pace to reduce the inflow of lake water and started the pumps.

'Will we sink?' Patricia, beside me on the helmsman's seat, asked anxiously.

'It's possible. You could try looking for some lifejackets.'

'Okay.'

I patted her shoulder. 'Are you all right?'

She shrugged. 'A bit of pain … I will compete.'

'Compete?' I chuckled. 'I think you mean cope. You will cope.'

'Yes, sorry, my English is terrible.'

We chugged across the darkened water. I was on the alert for police boats or coast guard – if such a thing exists in landlocked Hungary. If the Wolff bunch made it back to shore, they might report their launch as stolen.

The shoreline became visible, the lights at the ferry terminal marking its position. Even with the pumps at full blast, we were well down at the bows, and the cruiser's handling was becoming sluggish. When I left the helm to check on conditions below, a foot of water was sloshing about the saloon. Patricia had unearthed two lifejackets and was already wearing hers. As I emerged from below, she handed me the other one.

'Looks like we won't need them,' I said, drawing her attention to the nearness of the shore.

I guided the boat alongside a concrete jetty and with the gentlest of

bumps we came to rest, the three beam fenders deadening the impact. Nobody was about. A ferry was parked on the opposite side of the jetty, but was in darkness.

Patricia proved what a resourceful girl she was by producing a cell phone from her jeans pocket and calling a cab.

'He's a good friend,' she explained when I expressed surprise that she had found a cabbie willing to turn out in the small hours. 'We know each other for many years. He will not ask questions.'

To me it seemed likely that even a 'good friend' would be just a wee bit curious, but her confidence settled my concerns, and we sat down to wait on a patch of grass by the terminal check-in. The village was well and truly asleep. A cat was complaining over the rooftops, that was all.

'How do you feel?' I asked, recalling the burns on her body.

'The burns sting a bit, but I am okay.'

She had plenty of spunk, considering all that had happened to her.

'Why did they do it? Hurt you like that.'

She gave me a puzzled look. 'To make me tell them what I tell you.'

'Did you tell them?'

'Sure.' She tossed her pretty head. 'You think I keep quiet for you? I don't know you. Anyway, they don't believe I only give you a name. They think there is more, so they keep hitting me and burning me.'

'If I get the chance, I'll pay them back.'

We stayed there on the grass, engaging in desultory chat, until her old buddy showed up in his Mercedes taxi. And she was right about him. His name was Elek and he didn't ask any questions. Just happy to charge me a small fortune.

* * * * *

A blustery morning, with pewter skies and a suggestion of rain. I awoke late and breakfasted late. Patricia didn't put in an appearance; I had secured a room for her at the Clark Hotel to keep her safe from Sara Wolff and her crowd. It wouldn't take them long to track us down, I was sure of that.

Meanwhile, I still had a job to do. I texted a partial update to

Donovan, just to keep him from getting agitated at the lack of news. Then I texted Rocky for the latest on his enquiries into the doings of Maxim Maximov, my sworn enemy and deadly with it. He was still scratching around but the feedback from Rocky's various sources was that Maximov had put out no feelers for me. I advised him to shut down the operation for now, just keep his ear to the ground and his nose twitching for whiffs of foul play.

While I was in the hotel gym, puffing and panting at the bench press, a call came through. As always, I checked the screen before answering. Donovan.

'Yes?' I said.

'You seem to have been busy,' Donovan said, which I interpreted as faint praise.

'In a manner of speaking. I gave you the bare bones, that's all. There are complications, and the biggest of them all is that they're onto me.'

'How the feck did that happen?' Brogue usurping the cultured Irish tones.

'If you must know, it happened because my enquiries gathered more fruit than I expected. You could say I'm a victim of my success.' If he saw the funny side of my whimsy, he kept it to himself. 'Anyhow, as I told you, because of my poking around, the girl who provided a lead was abducted, and I abandoned my digging for a while to save her from the wolves.'

'Let's hope there'll be no more playing knights in shining armour,' he grumbled. 'Now that you've salved your conscience.'

'That's my business. What my knightly act did was lead me to the wife of Victor Wolff. Supposedly. Goes by the name of Sara.'

'Holy mother of God! Are you serious?'

I glared at my reflection in the cell panel. 'Too right I'm serious. Finding out almost landed me in a coffin along with the girl.'

'Well, take more care going forward. Without you, the contract's a dead duck and we all lose out.'

'Yeah, me most of all.'

I used the stairs to get to the lobby where I bought a copy of the Washington Post and made for the elevators. As I thumbed the level 6

pad the doors of my chosen elevator slid open and Patricia stepped out, almost into my arms.

'Hey,' she said, a wide smile brightening her face, 'you've been exercising.'

She laid a hand on my arm while the elevator doors swished shut and it set off without me.

'Agh, you are all sweaty!' She snatched her hand away and wiped the palm on her jeans leg.

'It'll wash off. Had your breakfast?'

She shook her head.

'Go and get it. Charge it to Suite 605. I'll join you for coffee, then we need to talk.'

'What about?'

'Your future,' I said, deadly serious. 'Making sure you have one.'

She paled and her hand clutched my arm again, sweat or no sweat.

'You think I am in danger?'

God, she was incredible. Maybe yesterday's adventure was all in a day's routine to her. Internet star that she was, she would be conditioned to being abused by men.

'You're in danger all right. And next time they'll do the opposite of making you talk – they'll stop you talking for good!'

I left her with that vision to stimulate her appetite and boarded the elevator that had just returned to the ground floor. It whisked me upwards in company with a middle-aged matron cuddling a Pekinese that alternately yapped and growled at me. The woman regarded me with suspicion, as if the dog's hostility was a judgement on my character. Maybe it had a point at that.

* * * * *

The conversation over coffee with Patricia brought me to the point where I had to choose between abandoning her or spiriting her away to a place where the Wolff-Ziffer combo couldn't touch her. If only they realised they had little to fear from her. She had spilled all she knew and was no longer a threat to them and their misdeeds, whatever they might be.

From my multiple encounters with the criminal fraternity I could reliably predict that they would kill her, chiefly because they hadn't done with her when I interrupted their grilling. They would resume the torture unto death, because she had nothing more to give them. Life was never so cheap as in the milieu of the Milieu.

'Do you have parents in Hungary, or relatives who could take care of you?' I asked.

'No.' Peevish now, disinclined to cooperate.

'Right, then. I have an apartment in Spain next to the sea, and you can use it for as long as you like. Lots of sunshine. You'll get a great tan.' When she still looked unhappy, I threw my hands up in despair. 'For God's sake, it's not forever.'

'But my work! How can I make my life, I mean my living.'

'I'll give you enough money to last for a while, and send you more when it runs out.'

Even that failed to placate her. We argued for a while until finally she slumped in her seat, lower lip pouting, arms folded.

'It's not even safe for you to stay here another night,' I said, and I wasn't exaggerating.

She sniffed, produced a travel pack of Kleenex from her pocket and blew her nose with great gusto.

'I am grateful to you,' she said, examining the contents of the Kleenex like a fortune teller reading tea leaves. Apparently satisfied with what she saw, she dropped it in her empty cup. 'I will do as you say.'

'That's my girl. Just one thing – you can't go to your apartment. It's too dangerous.'

'But I must. There are things I need.' She wrinkled her brow as she tried to come up with some indispensable article such as lipstick, sun block cream, or a change of underwear. 'My passport! I cannot go without my passport.'

There she had me.

'Give me the address and your key, and tell me where to find it.'

* * * * *

The address was deep in the heart of Pest. A grubby alley of looming tenements. Kids playing in the street, unkempt women gossiping in doorways. Seen it all before, in every major city I had ever passed through.

Patricia's apartment was no. 414 on the fourth floor. No elevator. I went up the four flights of concrete stairs sprightly enough and wasn't too blown when I reached the top, emerging into a long corridor with a window at each end. A man was standing by the window on the left. Just standing, doing nothing more strenuous than leaning on the wall, hands in pockets. When I popped out of the stairwell, he glanced at me, and went back to doing nothing. He did it with great panache.

If he had been posted there to watch for Patricia coming home, he was due a long wait. I walked down the corridor towards him, passed three doors and stopped before 414. This was his cue to take notice and detach himself from the wall. It was enough to make me undecided whether to use the key, or knock and pretend I was just an innocent visitor. The pretence wouldn't make him go away, it would just put off the evil day when I would have to confront him. He didn't amount to much physically: puny build, narrow sloping shoulders, dark hair done up in a stubble through which pink scalp shimmered.

I shoved the Yale type key in the lock. As if it were a signal, the guy started towards me. He spoke, the ring of a challenge, his tone aggressive. From a more impressive physique it might even have been intimidating. I opened the door to 414: it stuck slightly against the frame, then I was in, with Mr Puny on my heels. I spun round as I entered the apartment. He was right behind me, stepping across the threshold. That was as far as he got. I rammed the door in his face, putting maximum force behind it. When I reopened the door, he was slumped against the door opposite, his nose reshaped and dribbling blood, his legs buckling. While I watched, he went down on his knees and toppled, slow and graceful, onto his face on the bare floor. His groan touched my heart.

The door off which he had rebounded – number 413 – opened and a fat man in shirt sleeves, suspenders, with a newspaper in his hand, stood and gawked at the prostrate form. His gawking shifted to me.

I nodded to him, dusted off my hands in a 'job done' pantomime, and closed Patricia's door on his bemused expression.

Her apartment was compact, to put it charitably. She had given me directions on where she kept her passport – in the kitchenette, under a silverware drawer insert. It was there, all right. From this document I learned that ÚTLEVÉL is Hungarian for Passport and URÓPAI UNIÓ means European Union. At this rate it wouldn't be long before I was fluent in the language.

I slipped the passport into my back pocket. I considered chucking a few clothes into a bag for her, decided against. As I had foreseen, Wolff and company were still after her. It proved to be a wise decision. In the corridor, Mr Puny, a bloody handkerchief to his nose, was sitting with his back supported by the door of 413, talking into an old flip-top cell phone.

He looked up, startled, when I reappeared.

'Bad boy,' I said, and kicked him in the head, adding ear injury to the nose injury.

He toppled once more, sideways this time. The cell phone clattered on the floor. I stooped to pick it up. A faint squawk issued from it. I activated the speaker.

'Estevan? Estevan?' None of my various names was Estevan, so it couldn't have been for me. I closed the flap, added the phone to my belongings on the grounds that it might contain useful numbers and cause inconvenience to Estevan.

Leaving the garbage in the corridor where I found it, I hit the stairs back down to the street, well pleased with the results of my visit. Patricia's passport was in my possession, and a member of the opposition had been disabled, albeit only temporarily. I was curious as to why the Wolff organisation was investing so much resource in trying make Patricia talk. Either they were paranoid about informants, or she knew more than she was letting on. No third reason came to mind, but that didn't mean there wasn't one.

Noble creature that I am, my priority now was to make the girl safe, not to pump her for more gossip and rumours. She had suffered enough on my account.

* * * * *

She would be leaving in the clothes she wore, together with her passport and my donation of a thousand euros for immediate expenses, with more promised once she arrived at her destination.

I drove her to Budapest Fenhegy Airport. The next flight to Barcelona with seats available was scheduled to leave at 7.55pm, so I hung about while she bought a carryall, some clothes and toiletries in the airport shopping mall.

At 7.20pm came the call for her flight. Her face was solemn as we said our goodbyes. She had changed in the rest room, swapping the jeans, blouse, and sneakers for a newly purchased summery dress with a printed design of yellow roses, and practical flat-heeled shoes. Her hair hung unrestrained about her shoulders. She was more than just pretty.

'I'm sorry, honey,' I said, sincerely repentant. Although I was doing all in my power to protect her, it was because of me she was in trouble.

'It's all right.' Her smile was a struggle.

'You have my cell number. Buy a pay-as-you-go phone and text me the number as soon as you arrive.'

She raised herself on her toes and kissed me on the mouth. It was a sisterly kiss, a sample to keep me hooked.

'Will you come soon?' she asked, slinging the bag over her shoulder. 'To Spain.'

'When I've finished my job here.'

No cause to tell her that might be weeks or longer. Or even never, if things turned sour.

'Hurry up then.' The sparkle in her eyes held a hint of come-hither. I reminded myself that this was no innocent maiden. The acts she performed on the Internet were likely to be more extreme than anything I had ever indulged in, even during my dissolute spell.

Off she went, turning at the gate for a cheery wave. Resolved to make the best of it, maybe even looking forward to an expenses-paid vacation in sunny Spain. A large part of me wished I was going with her.

Chapter Eight

The house overlooking the lake where I had spent a few uncomfortable hours had an unoccupied air. Drapes drawn, no cars in the driveway. No music or other evidence of human activity.

I had parked the car in a lakeside viewing area a half kilometre short of the Wolff residence, then proceeded on foot. It wasn't sunny, but it wasn't raining either. A small wood screened the site on the side of my approach and I used it to advantage, keeping to a path that wound through the mixed evergreen and deciduous. It enabled me to get close to the lot unseen. I was about to step out of the wood onto a stretch of careworn grass that ran alongside the driveway when I heard the pad of canine feet. Sure enough, the Doberman I had observed on my previous visit was on deterrent duty. It trotted past, tongue lolling, dripping saliva. It was decidedly male.

I watched it down the drive. At the point where the gravel of the drive became asphalt it stood, surveying the empty road and the meadowland beyond. A white van went by at speed with script and a logo on the side panel. The dog observed it, head swivelling to the right to keep it in sight. It made no move to go outside the lot, and I figured it was enclosed by an invisible electric fence.

Dogs as a species I can take or leave. I had no quarrel with this particular representative, but I needed to get inside the house, and the Doberman was clearly under orders to prevent such intrusions. The choice was between being savaged or doing the savaging myself. A classic no-brainer.

On this side of the house there was a door and a narrow rectangular window beside it. The lock was a mortise type, and I was expecting to have to prise it open, for which purpose I had brought a jimmy.

After a jaw-dislocating yawn or two, the dog padded past me,

oblivious of the intruder lurking in the undergrowth, and rounded the corner into the back yard. I didn't hang about to see if it was just trying to spoof me. I crossed the driveway to the door, SIG in right hand, jimmy in left. It isn't easy to tread gravel without crunching, but by placing my feet with care, I managed it. The jimmy made short work of the lock and I was inside before you could say 'Bite him, boy!'

The room was a utility room, complete with appliances, a sink, built-in work areas and cupboards, and an ironing board that folded flat against the wall. Beyond the sliding door was a kitchen with the usual fixtures, fittings, and equipment. The house was as hushed as a church on Monday morning. In the living room, all was as before. I went left into the entrance hall with its stag's head on the wall. On the trapezium table, beside the potted bonsai tree, lay two envelopes with franked postage stamps. I picked them up: the smaller of the two was addressed to a Mr L Farkas, the name on the other, I guessed, was the Hungarian equivalent of The Occupier.

The Farkas was puzzling. It was the name Patricia had written down for me. If the Wolffs were tenants, Farkas could be the owner. Hence the connection. I dropped the envelopes back on the table, retreated to the lounge and from there to a room at the back of the house, that seemed to serve as an office/study/library to judge by the desk and the bookshelves lining the walls. I was here to search for leads and an obvious starting point was the desk. It had seven drawers, none of them locked. They yielded miscellaneous correspondence, office oddments, and a selection of porno DVDs. Starring Patricia? No reference at all to the Wolff twins. The desktop computer was more likely to contain clues that I could use, but when I tried to fire it up I was blocked by a password.

Upstairs to my former prison. It too was unchanged from my brief stay. The tray of snacks they had brought me was still there, suggesting Sara Wolff was not house-proud, or they had cleared out in a hurry.

Downstairs again, in the kitchen, hunting for a personal address book. Another blank. The window revealed the Doberman pacing up and down. I noted its empty food dish and gnawed bone, and a bowl of

water big enough to paddle in. More evidence that Sara Wolff's absence was temporary.

I swore to myself. If I knew how long she would be away, I would stick around. Without that knowledge, it would make no sense. In fact, it would heighten the risk; she might return with her whole gang.

A quick exit was the only course now. The dog had flopped down by its empty dish to make a half-hearted attack on the bone. It seemed preoccupied. Just the same, I jacked a shell into the breech of the SIG. I wasn't sentimental about dogs.

So I left the house, ready for combat. Careful though I was retracing my steps across the drive, the dog's ears must have pricked up. The growl was an advance warning, but not by much. It came around the corner like a canine cannonball, skidding on the gravel, and launched itself at me as if it hadn't eaten for a month.

Running was out of the question. I did a fast sidestep the instant it entered my airspace, leaving it to hurtle past me. A whack with the jimmy across its hindquarters made it howl but didn't deter it. It fell, rolled over like a parachutist landing, and was coming back at me for a second go before I could get my feet moving.

This time I cracked it on the snout with all the force I could muster. It yelped, skidded to a halt and twisted round to snap at me, its jaws locking on the sleeve of my windbreaker. It worried at the sleeve, tearing it, snarling all the while.

Mindful of animal rights, instead of putting a bullet in it, I used the SIG to deliver a vicious blow to the space between its ears. Hurt, finally, it sank to earth in slow motion, my sleeve still gripped in its jaws. It took another rap, and another, before its eyes glazed over and the fight went out of it. A long-drawn out sigh, almost human, and it went limp, releasing my sleeve. Still breathing. Still dangerous if I didn't remove myself to the far side of the electric fence before it recovered.

I blundered back through the wood, sweaty and panting, and made it to the Evoque more or less intact – ruined windbreaker aside – and no further forward in my search for either or both of the Wolffs.

* * * * *

A change of hotel was next on my agenda. To ask the Clark front desk to find or recommend somewhere would be tantamount to leaving a forwarding address. So I drove over the river in search of accommodation and lucked out at the Corvinus, a great monolith of a place with a curved, colonnaded front. A porter escorted me to a fifth floor room with a fine outlook over the adjacent park with its canopy of trees, and a Ferris wheel rising out of them like an alien growth. Off-street parking came with a surcharge. So what, Donovan could afford it.

In the circular lobby I took the additional precaution of registering as John Henley. It was unfortunate that I had to use my alternative ID so early in my mission, but safer than checking in as Devreese. Then it was back to the Clark to collect my luggage.

The clerk asked casually where I was bound.

'Spain. I'll be sailing for the next few weeks.'

He printed out my account, placed it before me. I was doing a cursory inventory for room bar overcharges when a woman's voice hailed me from across the lobby.

'Jack! Jack Henley!'

I made myself ignore the summons. The Clark knew me as Gilles Devreese. If I responded to Henley, it might give them cause to wonder about me. Questions might even be asked, and if anyone came nosing around enquiring after Devreese, my alias might be exposed. When you use multiple identities, as I did, you get sensitive about publicising them.

So I carried on entering my card details in the processing machine, hoping it was some other Jack Henley the woman was calling, while my mind was sifting through the best courses of action if it wasn't. Which of course it wasn't.

As the machine dealt with my transaction, I half-turned with feigned disinterest towards the voice, and my heart skipped a beat. On a couch near the jewellery counter, sitting upright and looking querulous, was a woman I had left behind on the shores of Lake Como.

Before Angela could start gesticulating to attract my attention, or, worse, come rushing to greet me with a great display of affection, I made shushing motions with my hand, hidden from the view of the clerk.

Fortunately she received and understood my message even as she rose from the couch. She completed the act of rising but walked with apparent purpose towards a guy browsing at the bookstall. The help she had given me dumping bodies in Italy had testified to her resourcefulness; she had just proved she was fast on the uptake too.

I finished my business at the front desk. I wafted a tip-seeking porter away and hauled my valises across the lobby, the wheels rumbling on the honeycomb tiled floor. The Evoque awaited me at the curbside, flashers pulsing. As I was unloading the valises into the trunk, Angela came through the glass doorway, not hurrying, just behaving like a tourist in no hurry.

'Ignore me,' I cautioned as she approached, looking anywhere but at her and talking through a rictus grin like a third-rate ventriloquist. 'Take a cab to the Corvinus Hotel.' I spelled it. 'I'll meet you in the lobby there in about thirty minutes max.'

She had paused while I spoke, but didn't respond. A cab was pulling into the curbside, and she diverted towards it, making the change of course appear natural.

To reinforce the pretence of Angela being a stranger to me, I lingered at the Clark for another ten minutes, ranged over the newspapers, settling for *The Times* and *USA Today*. When I left, I drove twice around the traffic circle, the trees in the hub tossing in the wind that had sprung up overnight. I checked out the rearview mirror at intervals and, satisfied as I could be that I wasn't being tailed, I peeled off the circle to cross the Chain Bridge.

In the ten minutes it would take me to reach the hotel I had to figure out why Angela was here, how she found me, and what I was to do about her. A car ahead of me braked without warning and in my preoccupation I almost shunted into it. I cursed Hungarian drivers in general and Budapest drivers in particular.

The why and the how would be hers to provide. What to do with her was mine alone. I was here on a job. Not only would she get under my feet, she would be at risk by association. Same as Patricia.

A few minutes later I was handing the car over to a doorman for parking. I trailed my luggage into the circular lobby of the Corvinus

Hotel. Angela was already there, looking ill-at-ease in an armchair. After leaving instructions with the front desk to deliver my stuff to the room, I went to her side, bent to kiss her cheek, and sat in another armchair, facing her.

'Hello,' I said, making it warm to help her chill.

'Hello,' she said gravely. 'How are you?'

'Angie,' I said, 'wonderful as it is to see you so soon again, let's cut to the chase. What are you doing here?'

She hesitated, visibly discomfited. 'Do we have to talk about it now? Can't we just enjoy a drink together, like the friends I thought we were.'

'We *are* friends.' I stretched out a hand, took hers. 'But we're not lovers. We don't follow each other from one country to another.' I paused, let it register. 'Do we?'

'There's always a first time,' she said, essaying humour. The smile that accompanied it was nervous, tentative.

'I'm not in Budapest for the fun of it.'

'I gathered that.' She nibbled at her lip. She was pale and free of make-up, which made her even paler. It came to me that she wasn't in Budapest for the fun of it either.

'You need a drink.'

'At this hour?' But she didn't refuse.

I flagged a passing clerk and asked him to send a waiter. A family of three trudged past, their luggage heaped on an overladen porter. It was quiet and echoey in the Corvinus lobby, on account of the circular design and the high ceiling. I could hear people speaking out of sight beyond the curve as clearly as if they were next to me.

We ordered beer for me and medicinal brandy for her. She demurred, but without conviction. Pending their delivery, we sat holding hands. Nothing romantic about it, just me giving comfort, which I sensed she needed.

'Now tell me,' I said as a waiter set our drinks down.

She leaned forward to cup the brandy balloon in her palms.

'I've never drunk alcohol before lunch,' she admitted with a giggle, swirling the amber liquid around the glass.

'Live dangerously. Think of it as a pick-me-up. Now … cut out the

stalling. I want to know what brought you here.'

She tilted the glass and treated herself to a modest nip.

'My apartment was broken into,' she said, almost tripping over the words.

I weighed the import of this news.

'Naturally, I'm sorry to hear that, Angie. Still, I don't get the connection. I mean, why it led you to come looking for me. When did it happen?'

'The day before yesterday.' Another hasty gulp from the glass, as if to boost her courage. 'The thing is … they didn't steal anything.'

I frowned. Nothing stolen wasn't conclusive but it had implications for me.

'Was there anything worth stealing? I mean stuff of obvious value.'

'Some of my jewellery is quite valuable. And there was over five hundred euros in a drawer.'

Still inconclusive.

'They could have missed the money.'

She shook her head with emphasis. 'No. They emptied all the drawers onto my bed and scattered the notes all over.'

'Right, I see where you're coming from. Somebody's still after me and they were hoping to find some pointers to my whereabouts. Is that how you see it?'

She nodded.

'You may be right,' I conceded. 'But let's row back a minute – how did you know I was in Budapest, at the Clark Hotel? If you traced me so easily, they could too.'

She offered me a wan smile. 'No, they won't. You booked it while you were at my apartment, do you remember? Later in the day, while you were in the loo, I took a peek at your cell phone and the reservation details were there.' She glanced at me, lines of worry marring her forehead. 'I know I shouldn't have, but you're such a mystery man. I'm curious about you.'

'As I recall, the text stated only the name of the hotel, not its location.'

'True, but the record of your calls showed the code for Hungary and Budapest.'

Now I felt stupid, and naïve, and careless. I had two cell phones: the professional and the personal, the former requiring a password to unlock it. Without thinking, I had called the hotel on the personal cell. I hadn't deleted it, in case it was required to confirm the reservation when I checked in. It was the sort of oversight that one day could have a fatal outcome.

Angela was watching me, and my expression must have said something.

'Was it very bad of me?'

I gave a short laugh. 'No, honey, it was bad of *me*. It was rank carelessness. The kind my enemies would be quick enough to seize on.'

'Don't you think it's time you told me about your enemies, Jack?'

* * * * *

We lunched at the Spoon Restaurant, a tethered boat on the Pest bank of the Danube. From the top deck, screened from the sun by an awning, we had a close-up perspective of the river traffic and Castle Hill above Buda, topped by the Royal Palace with its great dome the resembled a rocket in a silo. It was Angela's first visit to the city and its aura of history and the juxtaposition of ancient and modern in its skyline entranced her.

'Will you have time to show me around?' she asked, as we finished our main courses of duck breast with endives (mine) and salmon with black couscous (hers), complemented by a bottle of 2017 Lellei Irsai Oliver, a dry, fruity white recommended by the sommelier.

'I ought to escort you to the airport and onto the next flight,' I grunted. 'You're in danger here.'

'I'm in danger back home.'

'Then go and stay with your family.'

'I'd much rather stay with you.' Her winsome smile almost won me over. We sipped our wines, exchanging eye contact over the rims of our glasses.

'Nothing I'd like better. It's just that I'm working, and I'm up against some nasty people, unconnected with the ones who tried to kill me while I was with you. Hopefully, I've thrown that lot off the scent by

coming here, but my job here means tangling with a bunch of mean bastards who'll have zero respect for your British passport.'

I was tempted to tell her about Patricia as an example of what could happen, but I didn't want to terrify her. She was already shaken over the sequence of events at her home. As I had owed it to Patricia to rescue her, so I owed it to Angela to protect her.

To change the subject I drew her attention to a boat hotel that was just passing under the bridge. Passengers lined its upper decks, gesticulating and pointing and filming as tourists do. Some were waving.

'They'll be mooring here overnight,' I said.

'Always wanted to do a river cruise.'

She watched the boat for a minute or two as it manoeuvred into its berth, then, 'Getting back on track, when you killed those two intruders it shook me badly, I don't mind admitting it, even though it was self-defence. Then the break-in coming on top of the killings was the last straw. But I'm no shrinking violet.' She knocked back the rest of her brandy. 'Maybe I should tell you more about my past, to help put your mind at ease about my ability to cope.'

'It wouldn't hurt.' I crossed my legs, and relaxed back in my seat, wine glass stem pinched between forefinger and thumb. 'Go ahead.'

She went ahead, and it was quite a past. Back in 2005 she had served as a medic in Iraq. Her husband, also a doctor, was there too but was killed when insurgent forces shelled the hospital where he worked. She hastened to explain that this was her first husband.

Feeling vengeful, she offered her services to the British army. She was competent with a rifle, had done competition shooting at Bisley. The Brits had to reject her offer as women were banned from serving in combat units back then. So she quit and signed up as a sniper with the nascent Iraqi security forces trained by the US. The conflict ended soon afterwards, so she had little opportunity to prove her worth; just a single killing, a high-ranking army officer whose name to this day she couldn't remember.

Aside from her expertise with a rifle, she learned unarmed combat skills when she returned to the UK.

'Quite the all-rounder,' I observed when she broke off. 'It seems

you're just as much of a mystery as I am.'

'We're a mystery couple,' she chirruped. 'Should make us compatible.'

If that was bait I didn't snap at it.

'Where does – did – your second husband fit in?'

'Nowhere that has any connection with my military past. We met about eight years ago, in Manchester, and got married. He contracted cancer and died, as you know.'

'I only know what you told me, Angie. And it seems there's a whole bundle you didn't tell me.'

'Does it matter?'

I shrugged. 'With all your combat skills I'm now wondering why you need me.'

Our waiter pitched up and cleared away the empty plates.

'Well,' Angela said, when he was done and gone, 'I don't have a gun, so that particular skill isn't much use to me. For seconds, if any more visitors are as well armed as those two in the basement, my unarmed combat abilities won't be much use either.' She levelled a long, searching look at me. 'Thirdly … I … missed you.'

The thirdly was unexpected. It was almost unknown for me to enjoy a platonic friendship with attractive women other than my sister, Julie. But with Angela it really was no more than that. The period of recovery from her husband's early demise had left her no spare emotional capital for other entanglements. She hadn't expressed by word or deed a wish for our association to be anything more than that of companions of opposite genders. That went for me too.

Now this English Rose was hinting that we might be, or could become, more than mere buddies. It made me vaguely uncomfortable. Although my real love was still beyond reach, I wasn't on the prowl for a substitute. I had toyed with a younger woman in Spain earlier in the year, but she dumped me for an even older guy, which took some swallowing.

Angela was the right age. She didn't look it, and she was in good shape, not to mention smart and clued up. If the timing had been better, I could do a lot worse. It was bad enough to have to worry about a

friend, without having to worry about a lover.

'No comment?' she said, maybe interpreting my silence as rejection.

'Not yet. I'm not sure how to react. I need to absorb it and examine my own feelings.'

She got miffed at that. 'If you need to *examine* your feelings, obviously you don't have any. Beyond our friendship, I mean.'

It was a fair summing up.

'What I mean is, I hadn't thought of you in that way before. We were buddies. We've been out together a few times. Our kisses are cheek to cheek, and we don't sleep together. What else can I say?'

'If that's the truth of it, there's nothing more to say. Thanks for the honesty. Do you want me to leave?'

I jerked upright. 'Hell, no, not at a personal level. I enjoy having you around. Let's see what develops if we spend a week or two together. My reservations are about security – *yours* not mine.'

'In that case, better not let me out of your sight. I could even be some use as your Woman Friday. When I know what it is you're doing here.'

'We'll see. For now, let's head back to my hotel and get you a room.'

I settled the check and we left, the contrast of bright sunlight after the awning-shaded deck of the Spoon darkening my vision for a few seconds.

While we sauntered along the river bank, watching for a gap in the traffic to allow us to cross the busy four-lane thoroughfare, a yellow and white two-car tram hummed past on the far side. Angela inserted her arm through mine. It felt natural enough. We drifted by a stall, standing in the shadow of a small turret not much larger than a phone kiosk. Budapest Info Point was inscribed on a placard at the front. The counter top supported a plethora of brochures in racks. Angela stopped and selected a handful, earning a wide smile from the red T-shirted male attendant.

'Thank you,' she said, very English with her good manners.

'Have a nice day, lady,' he returned, adding, with a nod at me, 'and you, gentleman.'

We scooted across to a grass median and waited again for a lull in the

stream of vehicles. When it came, it wasn't the kind of lull I expected. A blue SUV mounted the curb in front of us, both offside doors swinging open while it was still rolling. In a repeat of the incident at the Publin, when two hefty guys snatched Patricia, two more hefty guys – the second duo from the house on Balaton – scrambled out, each of them grabbing one of my arms, detaching Angela from me with a violent push. She stumbled and went sprawling, fortunately on grass.

I wasn't about to make it easy for them. A kick to the shin discouraged the bigger guy; his smaller companion would have been even easier meat except for the silenced automatic he was brandishing in his free hand.

To shoot me in sight of dozens of other road users was step further than he was prepared to take, but the gun plus silencer made an effective blunt instrument; he clubbed me with it, just above the ear, hard enough to hurt and send me staggering. The bigger goon now returned to the fray. In my dazed condition I was in a poor state to resist and between them they would have bundled me into the car had Angela not intervened and tackled the smaller guy. Still down on the grass, her dress up around her thighs, she lunged a pump-clad foot at his groin and was right on target. He doubled up and reeled away, retching. The big guy gave me a shove that would have stopped a locomotive and lost interest in me to tend to his sidekick. Back in the car they went, leaving the automatic behind. Rubber squealed and they were gone. The whole assault had lasted less than a minute.

Angela lay on her back, her dress still at thigh level, offering a tantalising hint of underwear. A car drew up alongside. The driver gave us the thumbs up along with his appreciative ogle. Nobody among the many car drivers and passengers using the same stretch of road had thought to hop out of their wheels during the fracas and come to our aid. For all I knew, abductions were an everyday occurrence in Budapest.

I kicked the abandoned automatic under a nearby bush and hauled Angela to her feet.

'You hurt?'

'Apart from a bruised bottom, no.' She brushed her dress down, glared at another rubbernecker who was grinning behind his window.

The middle digit she raised was not at all the Angela I knew; nor did it banish the grin from the guy's face.

She turned away from the passing traffic. Concern clouded her features as she reached out and touched the place on my head where the guy had clubbed me.

'You're bleeding, Jack.'

She whipped out a pocket pack of Kleenex, extracted a couple, and dabbed at the wound. It hurt, but I bore it in the best stiff upper lip tradition and kept the Kleenex pad pressed to my head as we set off for the hotel.

Another attempt, another escape. I was pushing my luck. Sara Wolff and her wolf pack seemed to have an efficient network of informants. How had they tracked me to this spot? On today's evidence, they were prepared to risk an abduction in broad daylight to remove me from circulation. Conclusion? They were worried. That was fine up to a point. Nervous people commit errors, make it easier to trip them up. The downside was that the Wolff mob had declared open war, and I was only a one-man army. I had opened up a can of vermin and the occupants were on the rampage.

Angela, understandably, had a few questions.

'Wait till we're back at the hotel,' I said, 'and I'll bring you up to speed as best I can.'

There was a small task I had to perform at the Corvinus. A suspicion was forming in my brain about how the Wolffs had tracked me down.

At the hotel front desk I asked for a meeting with the manager.

The clerk, female and frowsty, smiled her regret.

'He is away, sir. Perhaps you will speak to the assistant manager?'

'Whoever's in charge will do.'

She made a phone call, conveyed some mumbo-jumbo to the respondent, and received an affirmative reply.

'Does he speak English?' I asked the clerk as she marched me off to a distant line of doors, Angela tagging along.

'Of course. We all do.'

The assistant manager was young, dapper, and sporting a moustache from forties Hollywood B-movies. He was behind an ornate desk with

feet like a lion's claws. When we entered he jumped up and threw out a hand. Upright, he was hardly any taller.

'How do you do? My name is Mr Silvas.'

We clasped. His grip, if you could call it that, was slack and damp.

'How can I help you?' he enquired, gesturing an invitation for us to use the two seats in front of his desk.

I declined. This wasn't going to be a sitting interview. Angela took her cue from me and remained standing.

I waited until the clerk withdrew and said to Silvas, 'Has anyone asked you to report my presence here at the Cornivus?'

Instead of looking surprised, he looked shifty. He wasn't cut out for deception.

'You mean the police?' he ventured, after an overlong pause.

'No, I mean anyone but the police.'

Angela tugged at my arm. 'Jack, come away. We don't want trouble.'

'We've already gotten trouble. Now, Mr Silvas,' I said, resting my fisted hands on the desk and leaning over him, 'will you answer my question or do *I* have to call the police?'

He twitched and his eyes widened.

'No police, please. Bad for business.'

I reached across the desk, laid hold of the lapels of his cream suit and dragged him up close. Being on the weedy side, it didn't require much effort from me.

'Do I need to repeat the question?'

'No, no.' He managed to nod and wag his head simultaneously like a string puppet. 'Somebody come and give me photograph from you.'

A photograph! He meant 'of' not 'from', of course. I released his lapels. He smoothed himself down with as much dignity as his diminutive stature permitted.

'Show me,' I said, in a tone that threatened terrible retribution if he didn't comply.

The photo was in the top drawer of his desk. With evident reluctance he handed it over. It wasn't a good likeness, but good enough to pick me out in a crowd. The photographer had taken it without my knowledge at the Publin, where I met up with Patricia. At a guess the driver of the

SUV had been wielding the camera, shooting through the side window, which would account for the slight fuzziness.

'Who gave you this?' I said.

'But it is not you,' Silvas stammered. 'This man has a different name. Look on the back side.'

I flipped the photo over. Giles Devrese. The double mis-spelling was of no consequence. Thankfully, I hadn't registered at the Cornivus under my Belgian alias.

I tapped the edge of the photo on my thumbnail while I put my brain into gear.

'So you haven't reported my presence?'

He frowned. 'Presents?'

'You didn't tell anyone I am staying here.'

'Why should I? It is not you.'

'Correct. It is not me. It's somebody who looks like me.'

Angela put her mouth close to my ear. 'You can't trust this creep.'

'I know that.' I shoved the photo in my pocket. 'Now, before we leave you in peace, I want the name of the person who gave you this photo.'

Silvas shrugged his sloping shoulders. 'I not know him. Big man with head shaved and beard.'

I was willing to accept that as the truth. Short of creating a scene, I wouldn't be able to extract any more detail from Assistant Manager Silvas.

'All right,' I said, throwing in a menacing glower that I hoped would have him quaking in his suit. 'But if I hear you've been talking to anyone about me, I'll be back.'

His head jiggled frantically. It didn't make me trust him more. Even if it had, I was taking no chances.

'We're leaving,' I said to Angela, though she hadn't yet checked in. 'Get your luggage from the desk and meet me outside.'

'Where are you going?'

'To my room. I'll leave by the fire stairs, so they'll think I'm still here until it's too late.' I gave her a gentle push. 'Go on. Wait by the garage exit and watch for the Evoque.'

My secret departure went without a glitch. I collected Angela and programmed the GPS to guide us to the small suburb of Vecsés, near the international airport. We travelled south-west on Highway 4. As far as I could tell from the mirror, no other vehicle attached itself to us. I made a couple of detours and performed a U-turn just to make sure.

After returning to the highway from the second detour an exasperated Angela said, 'Do you always have to take these precautions when you go out in your car?'

I grinned. 'It keeps me alert.'

'It must also make your journeys twice as long.'

We left the highway and entered Vecsés via a long, dead straight road. The first hotel we came to was the Timon. A modest establishment with 3 stars, according to the sign over the entrance. We secured two double rooms easily enough. The proprietor, chubby with rosy cheeks, had limited English but passable French, so we would get by.

'Most people stay at the airport hotels,' he lamented in that language, to explain the availability of rooms.

'Is that a fact?' I said. 'Too bad.'

I signed in again as John Henley; Angela as herself.

For the present we were missing persons. How long we could keep that status was the big unknown. In the meantime, I still had a job to do.

II

ONE WOLFF DOWN

Chapter Nine

My only remaining lead was that provided by Patricia – Laszlo Farkas, who was name had featured on the envelope I had come across in the Balaton property. It would be harder to find him than the Wolffs, because at least I had photos of the Wolffs and would recognise Sara Wolff if I bumped into her in the street. Nor did I see how a meeting with Farkas would further my search for Vincent Wolff. Unless he could lead me to him.

'Why are you looking for these men, the Wolffs?' Angela asked, when I had explained that I was here to trace them. She speculated aloud whether I was some sort of debt collector.

'Do I look that disreputable?' I said, forcing a laugh.

'I don't know how debt collectors look.'

We were in the garden at the back of the hotel, sitting on a bench in the shade of a dilapidated beech tree, reviewing the state of play. We had the garden to ourselves but for an old guy with bare feet who was dozing in a sagging wicker chair.

When Angela came up with the question I had hoped but not expected to avoid, I was evasive, naturally.

'My clients don't have to explain why they want to trace someone, they just have to pay up when I succeed. If I succeed. Almost always money's involved.'

'I see.' Her eyebrows almost met while she tried to add it all up. 'Why are people looking for you then? And not just looking, but trying to *kill* you.'

'You think that attempt on my life at your place is linked to my job here?'

That hadn't occurred to me, because I hadn't accepted the Wolff contract until after the attack in Angela's basement garage. It also called

for creative reasoning to suspect Donovan and/or his principal of offering a contract that was nothing more than an elaborate baited trap. I did business in an environment where double and treble cross were almost a pre-condition. It was like a game of cards where all the players except you are cheating.

'They couldn't have been the police, I don't suppose?' she mused.

'The police?' That was a new angle.

'Well, most European police carry guns, don't they? Perhaps they came to arrest you and you … er, overreacted?'

'It's an interesting hypothesis.' I said, keeping my voice casual, and left it at that. If they had been there to arrest me, they had a funny approach. Unless my reputation was such that their orders were to shoot first and put the cuffs on the corpse.

But Angela, having launched the idea, wasn't ready to torpedo it.

'Have you ever been in trouble with the law anywhere?'

'Sure I have. Speeding tickets, parking fines, a murder or two –'

She reacted as if I had produced a gun there and then and stuck it in her ribs.

'*Murder*!' Immediately the word left her mouth, she followed it with an exasperated growl. 'I see. A joke. Sorry.' She stifled a titter, not at my joke but at her reaction to it. 'I'm a bit on edge. So much has happened to me these last few days, it's like being in a spy movie, pursued by enemy agents.'

If only it were just a movie, was my private sentiment.

* * * * *

In bed, staring into the dark, I put my brain to work. By some means or other, I had to bring matters to a head. Donovan wasn't putting pressure on me, but I was fast coming to realise that I could no longer work at my own pace. If the Wolffs were so paranoid they were prepared to drag me in off the streets in full public view, they might check out of Hungary altogether before I got my man.

The Balaton property was still the most promising lead, but I had left evidence of my break-in, so either they would relocate – the envelope

addressed to the mysterious Farkas could be confirmation that they were only tenants – or would be armed and ready for a repeat visit. Keeping the place under surveillance might produce results, if I could get close enough. Apart from the woods next door, most of the surrounding area was private real estate, large lots of land with a house in the middle, and the cover very sparse. Then it hit me, and it was so obvious I silently rebuked myself for not seeing it before. The lake! I could hire a boat and moor offshore from the Wolff villa, staying below decks and using binoculars to maintain a watch. Less dangerous too. They couldn't sneak up on me. I could even take Angela as crew, keep her under my protective wing.

It was coming up to four o'clock. Sleep was no longer on the agenda, so I showered, shaved, and the rest, and dressed in cargo pants and polo shirt, with a waterproof windbreaker – one with no dog damage – and prepared myself, not only for playing lookout, but for battle. The Boberg in the ankle holster as usual, and the SIG, presently in the Evoque, but soon to be in my carryall. Plus a pair of 10x42 image-stabilised Swarovski binoculars that accompanied me most places.

I roused Angela by cell phone at 7.30. She wasn't asleep and proved to be an untypical woman when it came to her morning ablutions. By eight, we were at breakfast, in the company of other residents eager to start their day; probably airline passengers or employees.

'Are you going to tell me why the hurry?' Angela enquired, as we polished off our coffees.

'Not here,' I said tersely, trusting no one and no place. 'Wait till we're in the car.'

Ten minutes later, we were bowling along the M7 highway, away from the city. I aimed to avoid the centre and skirt the south side via the ring road, with Balaton logged on the GPS as our destination. Not Szántód with its ferry port, which they might be watching, but a town on the north side, any of several with a marina and a boat for hire. Balatonfured was the biggest and boasted a marina of substance. This meant parting company with the M7 after about an hour's driving, and diverting on to a lesser road through the town of Balatonakarattya. From there it was all twists and turns and towns and villages. We entered

Balatonfured at 11.20-ish, with me fuming and fretting at the delay. Sara Wolff and helpers might already have moved out, now that the location was compromised.

'Chill,' Angela counselled as a red light halted us. 'You'll give yourself a stroke.'

'You chill for both of us,' I snapped back. 'I function better when I'm on edge.'

'Well, for heaven's sake, what's to be on edge for? We're going sailing, aren't we?' I sensed her quizzing gaze on me. 'Or are we?'

'We are.' I hesitated, having held off divulging the purpose behind our day on the lake. 'Only there's more to it than just messing about on the lake.'

She let me alone to concentrate on finding a route through the well-kept streets of Balatonfured, a town of mostly low-rise buildings and multitudes of obvious vacationers, to the lakefront. We cruised the length of an extensive beach, well-supplied with sun seekers even this early in the season, to the marina. We parked up in a supermarket lot and shopped for the makings of a picnic lunch, plus six-packs of Evian mineral water and beers sporting the brand-name Dreher, which I later discovered it was a local brew.

At the very end of the marina we found a boat rental outfit whose name began with an 'S' but was otherwise unpronounceable. I foresaw communication issues, but a young guy in the workshop had an English mother and was able to translate my requirements to the owner.

Before mid-day Angela and I were the proud crew of a thirty-foot Bavaria sloop with a black hull and a fin keel. The twenty-five hp auxiliary engine would provide enough grunt to get us out of trouble if the wind didn't cooperate. The boat was equipped for extended vacations with the usual bedding, pots and pans, and a TV. The name on the square stern was *Tengeri Nimfa*.

Angela turned out to have matelot blood in her veins. She cast off both mooring lines and jumped aboard, nimble-footed in her tennis shoes and dressed for the occasion in white shorts and a blue matelot sweatshirt. As we motored out of the port she was already inspecting the mainsail. I checked the condition of the standing rigging: it was stainless

steel, hence no rust traces and no fraying. All in all, it seemed to be a well-found craft, always a worry with a rental.

It was a blustery day. The masthead pennant confirmed the wind was blowing from the north-west, which would make leaving port easy. Later we would need to tack up the western side of the Tihany peninsula, where the Wolff's villa lay.

The sun went in as we left the shelter of the marina and the water was unusually choppy for a lake. I locked the helm and mounted the cabin roof to help Angela unfurl the mainsail, but she was ahead of me.

'You could see to the halyards,' she suggested as she shook the sail free of its securing straps, impressing me with her efficiency.

I pulled the lines out of their cleats, made sure they weren't binding. Angela was hanging onto the boom to prevent it from swinging and tipping us overboard. I yanked on the halyard until it hit its stop, making the sail flap around like a line full of washing. I felt the wind catch the canvas and push us over. Angela, freed from her role as boom restrainer, scrambled across the cabin roof back to the cockpit, and adjusted the helm to run before the wind, restoring calm momentarily. Now I was ready to put our craft through her paces, to see if she could really sail.

'Steer south-west,' I shouted.

The boat heeled as Angela spun the helm, and I grabbed the handrail that ran along the edge of the cabin roof. The mainsail was now extended to the full. I sheeted in and the canvas bellied outwards in the concave bulge that makes for maximum efficiency. The shore and the town receded, became just a clutter of buildings and little spots of colour representing vehicles.

Back at the helm, I cut the motor. All fell silent but for the creak of the mast and the burble of water rushing past the hull. As we weren't aiming for speed, I decided to leave the jib sail in its bag for now. We attached the safety lines we found hanging from a hook in a corner of the cockpit; once, a few years ago, I had cause to regret disregarding that vital rule. I altered course a few points to leeward, and the bow plunged as the wind slammed into the mainsail. The boat heeled to starboard, and I kept the sheets taut for maximum dramatics. We countered the

heeling, plunging hull by perching on the topsides. Angela, her face shiny with spray, slid her arm through mine and laughed with the fun of it. Sailing can get you like that if you're a true devotee.

'You're obviously experienced,' I said, as we sat side by side, hips in contact, for my part becoming aware of her sexually for the first time.

'Ralph and I used to own a boat. A bit smaller than this. Did a lot of sailing in the Severn estuary. We capsized in a storm once, lost the mast.'

'Wow. An incident to remember.'

We became so engrossed in chatting about sailing I passed the point where I should have gybed from downwind to wind abeam. Gybe-ing can be tricky but we carried it off with no crew members lost overboard and, with the mainsail sheeted well in, forward traction was barely reduced.

As we rounded the tip of the peninsula, I made a second change in direction. Once accomplished, we were tacking up its western shore, the Wolff villa not yet in sight.

'Now explain,' Angela chided, transferring to a seat on the opposite side of the cockpit.

I sighed. Explanations to people who knew little to zero of my real doings always involved half-truths and untruths.

'We're going to observe a house on the peninsula, by the water. It's being used by the gang I'm searching for. The same ones that tried to grab me yesterday.'

'I see.' She didn't look at all perturbed. Then I remembered her sniper and unarmed combat skills. She who had seemed so demure to me when I first met her. I also remembered other women in my past who had doted on boats and sailing. There was Gina, who led me in a new direction, away from the sordid pleasures of the flesh, but who died at my hands and in my arms. Then came Liza, for whom my love had been and still was ambivalent, a composite of paternal and amorous. Simone, my teenage standby, had never more than tolerated our jaunts at sea, claiming to be queasy about water. As she could swim like an otter, I took that claim with a pinch of salt. Sea salt, naturally.

Our idle chitchat had dried up and Angela returned to the purpose of the exercise.

'What do you expect to see?'

'I'm open. It would help to know they're in residence. Let's hope they haven't skipped. It's the only real lead I've got so I have to pursue it.'

'It all sounds very hit and miss. Will you confront them at some stage?'

'Not if I can avoid it.'

The boat was bucking a bit, and I considered shortening sail. In any case I would have to lower it completely when we came alongside the villa and dropped anchor. We were about half a mile offshore, which I figured was about right for spying out the territory without arousing suspicion.

My chief worry, that they might have bought a new boat or repaired the cruiser, proved groundless. The jetty was empty.

'We'll need to go below,' I said. 'I'll be using binoculars. If they notice us, they may use binoculars on *us*, and I can't afford to risk them seeing me in close-up.'

'They're bound to notice us anyway, I would've thought.'

'If they do, they don't own the lake so they can't come and shoo us away. They did have a couple of boats but I disabled them.'

She didn't ask how. 'Will we be here for long?'

I shrugged. 'Until nightfall at the earliest. Depends on what develops.'

'Okay. Well, I don't know about you but I'm ravenous, so I think I'll go below and see if I can put together a picnic snack. Fancy a beer?'

* * * * *

The sun was going down over Lake Balaton against a skyscape of lurid indigo ribbons, like paintbrush strokes by a mad artist. A heron, in silhouette against the sky, swooped towards the yacht, changed its mind without touching down, and flapped off to be absorbed into the greyness to the east.

The wind had dropped and the ensuing stillness magnified every sound from the shore. We even saw and heard signs of activity; a flicker of flames at a property a few doors down from chez Wolff hinted at a

barbecue in progress. Silhouettes moved back and forth in front of it and laughter drifted across the water.

'Somebody's having a good time,' Angela remarked.

'Wish you were there?'

Her smile was on the wistful side. She wasn't at ease with this adventure.

We were sitting in the cockpit, sharing a beer. The day had passed with no developments on shore, in fact no movements of any kind other than the patrolling dog, who seemed to have recovered from the crack on the skull. The driveway lighting had come on with the advent of dusk: six replica Victorian streetlights down each side. The windows remained dark.

'Sorry about this,' I said. 'If nobody shows by mid-day tomorrow, we'll head back.'

'So we'll be spending the night on board.'

'Looks like it. Don't worry, we have two cabins. I checked.'

She said something under her breath that might have been 'Pity', or more likely was my imagination in overdrive.

'I guess your toothbrush is back at the hotel,' I said.

'I'll manage.'

Despite the temptation, I didn't invite her to join me in bed. I wasn't in the mood, and as long as hopes of a reunion with Maura continued to glimmer, I had vowed to stay clear of casual sex.

I allocated Angela the more spacious bow cabin and took the stern cabin for myself. Sleep came only fitfully. Sometime before dawn I sat up and took a squint through my porthole. To my surprise light shone in two windows at the villa. No activity on the outside, but it was gratifying to know that the gang hadn't abandoned the house. Unless it was the landlord returning to reclaim his property. Only daylight would tell.

Feeling thirsty, I got out of bed and for the sake of minimal decency pulled on my undershorts. I opened the door and pulled up short. Angela was there ahead of me, sitting by the table with a glass of water at her elbow. She was dressed, but it was marginal. Her underwear, dark blue in the dim light, was the kind that reveals as much as it conceals.

'Sorry,' I said, going into reverse.

'Oh, don't be daft,' she said, grinning. 'We're grown up, aren't we?'

'Yeah. A bit *too* grown up in your case.'

I went forward, found a glass and trying not to eye her comely figure, turned on the tap.

'It tastes foul,' Angela warned me.

'Been in the tank too long, I expect. It's probably safe to drink.' I sat down on the other half of the seat, close but not touching. 'Couldn't you sleep?'

'Too much excitement.'

I sipped from my glass. It was heavy on chlorine but drinkable enough.

'Lights are on at the villa,' I said.

'Oh?' She eyed me, frown lines on her otherwise smooth forehead. 'Jack ...'

'Yes?'

She bit her lower lip. Whatever she had to say was not easy for her. If it was about her and me and our togetherness, I wished she would bite her tongue instead. Maybe my vibes reached out to her; she turned away from me, her bare shoulders drooping'.

'Nothing. It's nothing really.' Her voice was flat.

It wasn't nothing, but I was glad she held off, sitting there so demure in her silky underwear.

'I'll get back to bed then,' she announced, leaving her water untouched.

I watched her go. From the rear she was good looking too.

* * * * *

Dawn was still an hour away when I gave up trying to sleep. I surveyed the villa through a porthole. Two windows were still illuminated. A car stood in the driveway. Any occupants were keeping their heads down.

'So they're home,' Angela said, joining me at the porthole. 'Do we go visiting?'

'You don't,' I said. 'I may. What you can do is take over surveillance

duties now and again.'

'Consider it done. Fancy breakfast?'

'What have we got?'

'Nasty water and energy bars. Oh, and an apple between us. We didn't buy for a long siege, if you remember.'

'Bad planning on my part.'

We broke our fast by munching through our supplies. From her appearance, Angela could have just surfaced from a session with a beautician. The same couldn't be said for me: my hair looked as if I had slept in it, and my stubble was definitely not the designer kind.

After breakfast she took over from me and I used the break to shower. The boat's inventory included towels, albeit threadbare. I was squeezing through the doorway of the tiny bathroom, a towel around my waist but only just, when Angela gave an exclamation.

'A helicopter's coming down in their garden!'

I had heard the wop-wop of rotor blades overhead and thought nothing of it. I relieved Angela of the binoculars and focused on the villa. The chopper was just above roof height and descending. To the left of the house was a circular paved terrace that was made to measure as a helipad.

The murky dawn made it hard to read any markings on the chopper. Under international regulations all flying machines had to bear identification but this example appeared to be incognito. It settled on the terrace, gentle as a dragonfly touching down. Two people came out of the villa and went to greet it. Two more alighted from the chopper. They exchanged handshakes, two of them clasped shoulders. All very pally.

Two figures disappeared around the side of the building. In the murk they could have been anybody. A door in the side of the machine was opened from within. A delivery? If so, it was likely to be drugs. That would add up. Drugs were about the most lucrative form of illicit trade nowadays: portable, easy to conceal, high value-to-bulk ratio.

No unloading took place. The three guys went indoors. Minutes passed. I rubbed my eyes which were starting to blur over, thanks to the intense concentration.

'You want me to take over?' Angie asked.

'Not yet, thanks.' I was feeling the early morning chill too, in my damp towel and expanse of bare, also damp, flesh.

It was close on a half hour before activity resumed on shore. A yellow fork-lift truck came lurching round the corner of the house, several wooden crates on its prongs. It approached the chopper, lined up to face the open cargo hatch.

'They're loading some crates,' I said.

'What do you think is in them?' Angela's suppressed a yawn as she spoke.

I tweaked the focus of the glasses. Some stencilled hieroglyphics on the crate sharpened to become **РПГ-7**. It could have meant anything. Each crate measured about a metre long, by about a third of a metre high and wide.

'Take a look.'

She took the glasses and peered through the porthole.

'There's writing on the crates. It looks like Cyrillic script to me.'

'Cyrillic!' I knelt beside her on the seat and snatched the binoculars from her. She was right. What I had read as PNR7 was not that at all. 'You know what it is in our alphabet?'

She screwed up her eyes in concentration. 'I'm not exactly an expert but I think the P is an R, and the lower case n is a P. Not sure about the lower case r … it could be t. No, wait, t is like our t. I think … I think it's g. R-P-G.' She glanced at me. 'Does that make sense?'

I shook my head. 'RPG. It's just letters.' Then, in a flash of recall, it hit me. During my stint in Afghanistan with the Secret Service, the Russians had been supplying weaponry to the Taliban. We had seized a cache of grenade launchers in crates, just like those being loaded on to the chopper. And those crates had also been stencilled **РПГ-7**. NATO referred to them as RPG-7s.

The Wolffs were running guns.

I laid the binoculars beside me and dwelt on this new development. It had no obvious bearing on my contract to find and kill Vincent Wolff, unless an inexhaustible supply of weaponry was a factor. It did add a point or two to his villainy rating.

'What's up?' Angela asked.

'Nothing's up, love. It seems like the Wolffs are in the arms exporting business.'

'So? Does it make any difference what they do? All you have to do is find them – at least, that's what you said.'

The point she made was sound. It would make the twins vulnerable from a legal aspect, but since I was operating outside the law myself, the knowledge was of scant use to me.

'Can we go back now?' she said, her tone plaintive. 'I'm hungry and I need a change of underwear at least.'

'Your underwear looked just fine to me.'

She put on a mock grimace and opened her mouth to make a riposte when there came a soft bump on the starboard side of the hull. We both stiffened. A scuffling noise ensued, then a light footfall overhead. It became two footfalls.

All boaties know it's good manners to wait for an invitation before boarding a vessel. Our visitors were therefore not only non-respecters of etiquette, but were to be presumed unfriendly.

I had the SIG out of the bag and a round jacked into the breech while the boarding party was still up on the cabin roof, trying to be discreet. This far from the shore a sound suppressor wasn't needed, so I let it lie.

Angela, wide-eyed at the sight of the gun, obeyed with alacrity when I signalled her to go to the bow cabin.

'Stay quiet,' I whispered, and she nodded. In view of her sniper experience maybe I should have tossed her the Boberg, but my priority was to keep her from harm, not make her an accessory to my nefarious deeds. The door closed behind her with a click.

Somebody jumped down into the cockpit and the hatch slid upwards almost in the same instant. It was my old acquaintance Large, complete with shotgun. Maybe he had expected to find me still asleep or at any rate abed, but his unpreparedness was greater than mine and I shot first. I aimed for his shoulder and was right on target. He yelped. The gun went spinning away and he staggered backwards, clutching at his wound, his fingers dyeing red. A second figure replaced him,

similarly armed, and his gun boomed, demolishing part of the ceiling above my head. I shot him too, with less precision, three in the chest, knocking him off his feet. His gun clattered on the deck and everything went quiet, not counting a groan or two from Large.

No more boarders came to put me out of business. It didn't mean others weren't waiting in their boat for the call to arms, so I hurried up the cockpit steps and, keeping my head down, scoped out the starboard side. A grey inflatable similar to those used by the SBS bobbed there, tied to the rail. Nobody in it.

I lobbed both shotguns overboard. They could have been useful but they were too bulky to hide and might get me into more trouble than I was in already. The guy who had taken the three slugs was unknown to me. Large was on his back in the well, complaining to the world. I frisked him, found a compact automatic in his pocket, and gave it a Deep Six.

'Make a move and I'll finish you,' I said to him, in my best Hollywood tough guy voice.

He mewled but got no sympathy from me.

A quick scan around reassured me that the gunfire had gone unheard by the good lakeshore dwellers. It was too early in the morning for most folk to be up, and gunshots tend to be dispersed by open spaces.

I ducked my head back through the hatch opening.

'All clear. You can come out and no need to put your hands up.'

She came, not even hesitant. As she climbed the short stairway and caught sight the results of my handiwork, she paused. No shock registered on her face.

'Looks like you took good care of them.'

'You're a cool one,' I said, with a chuckle.

'In Afghanistan I saw much worse than this. Mutilation was standard procedure, before and after the killing.'

I was sickeningly familiar with the practices of the Taliban and other bands of outlaws.

'I should have killed them both. Now we've gotten a wounded man to deal with.'

She looked down at Large, stirred him with a sneakered foot.

'He doesn't have to be wounded, does he?'

It took several beats for her meaning to register with me. I exhaled with feeling.

'You volunteering?'

She made a motion of rejection with her hands. 'No thanks. Seeing it done isn't the same as doing it.'

'Especially in cold blood.' Which was an act of which I had only once been guilty, when justification and opportunity were too compelling to ignore. Oh, yes, and the temptation.

'We'll drop him off on their jetty,' I proposed. 'Somehow I don't think he'll tip off the police.'

She didn't comment, just sat down in the cockpit and watched me moodily as I cranked the engine and steered towards the shore. The real dawn was breaking and shafts of pale sunlight were lightening the eastern skyline, chasing away the earlier gloom. Nobody was about in the villa yard. The chopper was no longer there either, though in the heat of battle I hadn't heard it lift off. We chugged up to the jetty, staying outside the harbour formed by the L and taking it cautiously in case it was too shallow for our keel. Angela hopped out unbidden and secured the bow rope to a mooring ring affixed to the jetty. I unhitched the inflatable and towed it around the stern of our boat and handed her the rope.

'You need help with the garbage?' she enquired. There on the jetty, holding the rope, she made a becoming picture in her shorts and bare legs, which, while not long, were pleasing to behold, like the rest of her. She noticed the direction of my gaze and coloured up.

'You had your chance,' she said. 'Not only that, but aren't we supposed to be just good friends? To coin a phrase.'

'We could be better friends,' I said, the words popping out before I could consider how she might interpret them.

She tossed her head but didn't say 'No way'.

It was tempting to drop the corpse over the side and let nature take care of it. Lake Balaton is awash with pike, so I hear, and they're carnivorous and would appreciate the meal. Then I decided it would be more satisfying to leave the problem with the Wolff gang, while making

a point about the penalty for messing with me.

'Do you need my help?' Angela said, as I started tugging the dead guy over the cockpit seat. As I was working against gravity, I told her I could use another pair of hands.

She came back aboard, and with me at the head and her at the feet like in Italy, heaved the corpse onto the jetty in no time. Large needed no assistance. He got up, using the cockpit seat back to support himself, and climbed from the boat to the jetty unaided, albeit on wobbly legs.

'Better see a doctor about that shoulder,' I said, with a crooked grin.

He just glared at me, the message he didn't dare voice confined to his eyes.

As he lurched down the jetty towards the villa, a door opened and a woman stepped out. She was wearing a dark blue robe and glasses and went by the name of Sara Wolff.

She was also carrying a handgun. Too far away to be sure of scoring a hit, she waved it about, more I think as a warning to stay away than as a serious threat.

'Good morning,' I called out, and Angela giggled. 'Are we too early for breakfast?'

'What do you want?' she shouted back.

'An interview with Mr Wolff, either of them will do.'

'Mr Wolff is not here.'

Large had reached her by now. Hunched up and clutching his wounded shoulder, he stopped and she promptly dispensed some Florence Nightingale-style compassion by slapping his face and ordering him indoors. The Wolff organisation seemed to have a low tolerance of failure.

As Large entered the building, a man came out through the same doorway. He was of medium height, with fair hair, worn tousled as if he had this minute risen from his bed. His gun was bigger than Sara Wolff's.

'I'm Victor Wolff,' he announced loudly. 'You wanna talk to me, shithead? Well, now's your chance. Come ashore and keep your gun where I can see it.'

Chapter Ten

It was more of an inquisition than an interview, with Wolff playing inquisitor. At gunpoint naturally. He had swapped the shotgun for an automatic that looked too big for his hand. Sara Wolff toted a dinky pistol, and with such easy familiarity I assumed it was more than just window dressing. In addition, two more of their heavy brigade waited attendance, armed with the ubiquitous pump action shotguns, which may have come from their own stock.

It was history repeating itself, with one major difference: on the previous occasion I had been there to rescue Patricia, whereas now I had unwittingly presented them with Angela as a bargaining tool.

We gathered in their living room. They relieved me of the SIG but missed the Boberg. My other belongings were taken from me and spread across the table for the second time around. The two heavies frisked Angela too and they were proficient at it. She took the manhandling in her stride, no protests, only wincing in silence when one guy gave her backside a loving squeeze.

Sara Wolff directed us to a couch, while she and husband Wolff settled in matching armchairs. No refreshments were served. The heavies kept shooting glances at Angela, their approval unconcealed. One of them licked his lips at intervals, as if in anticipation of a repeat frisking, more thorough than before.

Wolff's opening line was about compensation for his boats.

'Well now, Mr Devreese, it seems you owe me for a destroyed speedboat and a badly damaged cruiser. Two hundred and fifty thousand US should cover it.'

'Isn't that what insurance is for?' I came back at him. 'Alternativel, we could all hoof it down to the local slammer and while you put in a complaint for grand theft marine and damage to said boat, I'll be

making a statement about kidnapping and gun running. That suit you?'

His sheepish grin was an answer on its own.

'Okay, let's say we set my claim for damage aside for now and talk business. I've heard a whale of a lot about you from Sara. Seems you wanna contact me, but nobody knows why. Gonna fill in the cracks?'

'Why not?' I said, easing back on the couch and lacing my fingers behind my neck, to appear cool and collected. 'You're running guns, we want some guns run. Make sense?'

He smiled. Extracted a pack of Pall Mall cigarettes from his shirt breast pocket, passed it over to Sara Wolff. She extracted two, lit them, and gave one to him. Very lovey-dovey.

'If I was a regular businessman, it would make plenty of sense.' He jetted smoke from his nostrils. 'Engaged as I am in an illegal activity, it makes for suspicion. People don't come looking for me at the 77 Bar and start questioning waitresses. As a way of making contact, it's kinda … er, indiscreet.'

'Everybody does business according to his own rules.'

'That's a fact. The trouble is, when you're doing illegal stuff you're just naturally suspicious of every jerkoff who sticks his nose in where he shouldn't.' His eyes speared me. 'Like you.'

'I told you why I wanted to contact you. If you want to turn it into a big mystery, be my guest.'

He chuckled. 'Right now, you're *my* guest. Sort of.' He examined the fingernails of his non-smoking hand, a rather effeminate gesture that might have made me speculate on his sexual orientation if his alleged wife weren't sitting a few feet away. It was at that point that I started wondering if this was really Vincent I was speaking to, not Victor. How would I know?

Through the window, part of my rental boat was visible. They had left a man on board. The body had been removed from the jetty, and Large driven off, no doubt for his shoulder to be tended by some quack specialising in patching up wounds, abortions, and other back-street surgery.

'I've survived in my business for twenty years because I take no one at face value,' Wolff preached. 'If somebody tells me yes, I assume they mean no.'

'That can be smart business practice,' I conceded, poker-faced. 'Taking the contrary view, it might mean you miss out on profitable opportunities.'

'The lesser of two evils,' he said with a smirk. 'You see, we made some enquiries about you, Mr Devreese from Belgium, when we found out your name. You appear to be a man with no history which is kinda unusual, wouldn't you say?'

I shrugged, as if my history or lack of it were not my responsibility. I noticed Angela staring at me, probably wondering who the hell was Devreese, and who the hell was the real me.

Wolff went on, 'To me it smells of a phoney ID. Not that that's a problem. When you operate outside the law, a phoney ID is almost goddam obligatory.'

'You said it.'

He drew on his Pall Mall. It was a long cigarette but it was already two-thirds consumed, the ash dotting his dark chinos.

'Anyhow, I need the truth. If you're who you say you are, just an ordinary joe with an unorthodox way of going about business, I can live with that. If not, we'll make you one sorry hombre. Now, I don't expect you to confess readily – if there's anything to confess – so we're going to take a scalpel to your girlfriend here.'

A cry of distress from Angela. I rearranged my legs to place the hidden Boberg where I could get at it.

'You wouldn't miss a nipple or two, would you, baby?' he asked Angela.

She cringed away from him.

It took all my self-restraint to keep me pinned to the couch. To go on the offensive, I needed an edge, and for that I needed a diversion. That meant letting them get all excited about slicing Angela up, assuming it wasn't just bluff and bluster, and focused on her instead of me. I just hoped she knew she could trust me not to let them hurt her. I touched her hand to convey reassurance.

'Tell you what,' I said, assuming a nonchalant air. 'Why don't we just forget about doing business? We'll get back on our boat and sail away into the sunrise.'

I would have stood up as if to leave, but to access the Boberg I needed to be sitting down with my left leg crossed over my right, bringing the holstered automatic close to my hand.

'And if you're an undercover cop?' Wolff said. 'Or from a rival operation trying to muscle in? What then?'

I had no answer to that. Wolff snapped his fingers at the heavies. They moved in on Angela; she leapt up, lashed out at the nearer of the two. Here, gift-wrapped, was my diversion. The heavies were otherwise occupied, their guns no longer covering me, while Angela's attack was distracting Wolff and his wife. If only for seconds it was long enough for me. I ripped the Boberg free of its holster. Unnoticed by Wolff, who was still watching Angela take on two guys twice her weight, I lined it up on his forehead

'Drop the guns – everybody!' I pitched it loud and authoritative. 'Or friend Wolff gets a third eye.'

Friend Wolff gaped. The automatic fell from his grasp and hit the floor. Mrs Wolff's toy gun did likewise. The heavies stepped away from Angela, tried half-heartedly to bring the shotguns to bear on me but Wolff rapped out an order. He knew where his best interests lay. The shotguns joined the other hardware at floor level. Angela retrieved one and pointed it at Wolff, her face so suffused with rage she was almost unrecognisable.

'You *bastard*,' she snarled, and her finger was up tight against the trigger. 'How about if I took a scalpel to your balls?'

Wolff blanched. For all he knew she was capable of it. She was pretty steamed up at what they had proposed to do to her, and I didn't blame her.

I tugged the sleeve of her sweatshirt. 'Come on, love. Leave the plastic surgery for another day. I need to ask a few questions of my own. You just keep them covered.'

She contented herself with a growl in her throat and backed up against the wall. Her hands cuddling the shotgun were steady. She who was so demure on the outside, was all steel at the core. And an ex-sniper, to boot.

'Now, let's start over,' I said to the Wolffs, stepping back to open up a buffer zone between them and me. 'Where's Vincent?'

'Vincent?' Wolff said, with a quick glance at his wife. 'What makes you think he has anything to do with the organisation?'

'Don't mess with me, Wolff. I've gotten photos of you and him together, in Budapest.'

'Jack, does it matter now?' Angela said. 'Can't we just get out of here while we're ahead?'

'In a minute.'

'It's all right for you,' she grumbled. 'It's not your boobs on the operating table.'

That she could joke about such a threat said much for her strength of character.

'Who's to say *you're* not Vincent,' I said to Wolff, 'not Victor.'

He folded his arms and looked smug. 'I'm saying it. You need to prove it, or not.'

'Can *you* prove you're Victor?'

'I'm his wife,' Sara Wolff cut in. 'I should know my own husband.'

'Unless you're both lying.'

But I was in a fix, and they knew it. Either I killed both Vincent and Victor – assuming I could locate the other twin – or I chanced it that the man I was looking for was here in this room. Neither option would sit well with my conscience or my code. The third option, to extract the truth whether by scalpel or blowtorch, didn't appeal and would only produce results if they were lying.

Just to test the theory I said, 'Suppose I turn Angela on you with that scalpel you were talking about.'

Wolff's colour had returned; now it departed again.

Angela wagged a no-no finger. 'Leave me out of this, Jack. I'm not your assistant torturer.'

I should have known she wasn't serious about giving his balls the decapitation treatment. My heart wasn't in the nasty stuff anyway. That apart, it behove me to uninvolve her in my mission ASAP, before she got hurt through me. I scooped up the other shotgun and the two handguns. So far on this jaunt I had collected enough of an armoury to start my own gun running business. Pity I had junked most of it in the lake.

'Let's go then, honey,' I said, adding for the Wolffs' benefit, 'But I may be back.'

'And we may be waiting,' Sara Wolff said, and her grin, appropriately, was wolfish.

* * * * *

'Who's Devreese?' Angela demanded to know, as we rounded the tip of the peninsula under full sail, the wind on our port quarter. The boat was heeling as it creamed through the restless waters, the sun pouring out heat from a cloud-free sky. Ideal sailors' weather.

'A name I use when I'm on a hazardous mission.'

'Like now?'

I nodded. 'Drop it, eh?'

'The less I know the safer I'll be, is that what you're saying?' When I didn't answer, she went on, 'But that's bullshit, Jack. Just now I was at risk of serious mutilation, but I know nothing. In a way that's even worse, because I couldn't answer their questions to stop them hurting me.'

It was an intelligent point. It put me on the spot. Either I told her all or most, or we split up, which, from the professional angle, was by far the smarter option. If only I were always smart.

* * * * *

From my hotel room I called Donovan. On hearing of my confrontation with an actual Wolff twin, he was full of praise.

'By God, it's a fecking miracle, so it is.'

'You're right about that, my friend, but keep in mind I've no means of telling whether it's Victor or Vincent I met. He and his wife claim he's Victor, but that could be just them throwing dust in my eyes. You've got to give me a physical feature to distinguish one from the other. A birthmark for instance, or a mole, or a tattoo.'

Silence was the only sound that came over the line.

'Well?' I snapped, when it had gone on for a good half minute.

'I'm checking.' Papers rustled, maybe just to placate me. 'No moles or birthmarks are recorded. You've seen the dossier, so you're as wise as I am. It's possible one or both of them had a tattoo or an operation done in the last eleven years, but unless we had absolute proof of which twin had what, we'd be no further forward.'

'Then it's fucking impossible,' I snarled into my cell phone. 'I'm wasting my time and you're wasting a thousand bucks a day.'

I got up from my hotel bed and paced with the cell to my ear, hoping the radio waves would generate inspiration. In vain.

'Well, whichever twin it is you met, can't you persuade him to tell you where the other half is? From what I heard about you, you're not shy of putting pressure on when necessary.'

He wasn't wrong, though I had just backed off doing that very thing. When you dispense violence on a regular basis, a day comes along when it starts to sicken you. I was in that place. The taking of life in self-defence, as I had done with the guys in the basement and with Extra-Large on the boat, were reflex actions. I could justify them to myself, and others, and live with the consequences. The deliberate dispensing of injury and death was turning me off to the point where I would soon be unable to do it. Even for a half million dollars.

'That won't happen,' I said decisively. 'Even if they were standing side by side I wouldn't know which of them I was being paid to waste.'

He admitted this was a problem without an obvious solution.

'If I could produce an unbiased witness who could tell them apart, would that do?'

'It would depend on who, and how.'

'Vincent has two sons. They would know their father, I imagine. We could interview them separately, in Vincent's presence. Would both of them lie?'

I laughed. 'If they knew their father was about to be killed, sure they'd lie. Put another way, if they knew he would be allowed to live if he was proven not to be Vincent, they'd also lie. That's not the whole story. First, I have to find both twins, then I have to get them to cooperate and meet up with Vincent's kids who may or may not be able to contribute. How the hell I'll manage that beats me.'

'A challenge, I agree,' he grunted, 'but not beyond your capabilities, surely?'

'Listen, Donovan. Suppose you suspend the expenses payments while you figure out how to solve the conundrum. I'll stick around here until I hear from you. Remember though, we don't know if Vincent is here; he could be in Kazakhstan or Tierra del Fuego or on Mars.'

He declined my generous offer. Worried, perhaps, that I might use it as an excuse to walk away, period.

'We'll keep the payments going for another ten days. I need you to be on call in case we get a break.'

'Your decision.'

We wrapped up our conversation, still on affable terms, still with nothing resolved.

* * * * *

That evening I escorted Angela to the theatre. At times a shot of culture was the drug I had to score to remind myself that I was a man with civilised tastes and an appreciation of the finer things in life. The theatre was the Operetta, a baroque pile in the heart of Pest, and the performance was Countess Maritza, an operetta by the Hungarian composer Kàlmàn.

As the show opened to a young gypsy girl flirting with a guy the programme told me was Count Tassilo posing as a bailiff, Angela leaned across and whispered, 'I once played the gypsy part.'

I turned my head to stare at her. 'You sing opera?'

'Yes. The gypsy's a soprano part but on the night the regular singer was ill and I had to stand in for her.'

'Talk about hidden talents. The singing sniper.'

She stifled a laugh. 'That's very funny. Anyway, it launched me into a part-time career on the stage. For several years I worked as a pro at places like Sadlers Wells and the Birmingham Alex.'

'Why did you stop?'

'When I joined the army.' She made a gesture that might have implied regret. 'I did a few shows after I was discharged but I'd lost the

buzz, so I gave up.' She squeezed my arm. 'Now, let's watch. It's the first time I've seen it since I was in it.'

In the row in front of us, a head pivoted and frowned disapproval at our whispering. I smiled an apology.

In companionable appreciation we watched the story of Countess Maritza evolve and let the music seduce us. The quality of the singing was unmemorable but the cast belted out the numbers with passion and panache, and earned a standing ovation.

It was an evening in which I put my other life on temporary hold. An evening of normality which served to remind me of what I was missing and, as always, made me think of Maura. Yet here I was with another woman, inching towards the beginnings of a relationship, that might or might not become meaningful. The sense of disloyalty, of betrayal, was strong.

Angela was quiet on the return drive to the hotel. I got the impression she was troubled, but didn't pry. If she too was comparing the events of the last few days, the violence, the killings, to which she had been an unprotesting party, I could empathise with that.

Our goodnight kiss was on the cheek.

'Tomorrow we'll talk,' I said, holding her arm.

'Agreed.'

And that was where we left it.

* * * * *

It was Sunday. As I was preparing to go down for breakfast, I received a call from a number I didn't recognise.

'Hello. Is it Mr Devreese?'

The accent gave her away.

'Patricia?'

'Yes, it is me. You say I must call you when I have buy a cell phone.'

I'd all but forgotten the girl's existence. 'That's right, I did. Are you okay? Are you in the apartment?'

She was and she was.

'It is very nice in Spain. Hot and sunny.'

'Good. Now listen, you just enjoy yourself. I'll wire you more money to CaixaBank in Sitges. Take your passport and collect it the day after tomorrow. Meet a nice boy, get married, go on a honeymoon.'

She chortled. 'You are so funny. When will you come?'

Good question.

'Soon maybe.'

We chatted for a few minutes more, mostly about her shopping expeditions and the motor scooter she'd bought for €500.

'Stay off the Internet,' was my closing advice.

'You bet.'

* * * * *

Angela wanted to go for a long walk. Alone.

'Suit yourself,' I said. 'I've got some exercises to do too, so I'll go downtown and look for a gym.'

After breakfasting on omelette, cheese, and toast, we parted company. I tracked down a gym walking distance away – the Toldi. The equipment was adequate, good enough anyway for an hour's running, ab crunches, and bench pressing. Some good looking women in scanty outfits were pounding away and pumping up their biceps. Distracting. It took the cold douche of the showers, delivered through a rainfall head, to calm my libido.

My bag over my shoulder, I walked back at a brisk pace. A modern building with ground-to-roof geometric windows along the front had a sign proclaiming it to be the Cream Café. I was getting used to the extensive use of English here for bars and pubs, even if the regular language was still impenetrable.

As I still had a kilometre to go, I decided to indulge in a break and an *espresso*.

I stepped through the door, which was standing open. After the brightness of the sunshine outside it took a few beats for my vision to adapt. The furnishings were a mixture of tables with canvas-backed chairs, and couches geometrically placed around coffee tables, the ambience too arid for my taste in bars. I opted for an upright seat at a

table by the window. A middle-aged waitress in regulation black and white approached, order pad at the ready.

'*Espresso*, double shot,' I said.

'Yes, sir. Anything else?'

I shook my head. She took off and I browsed over the other clientele as you do when you're on your own in a bar. On a couch with her back to me, was a woman who, viewed from a rear quarter angle, was a dead ringer for Angela. She was in deep discussion with a bald guy with wide shoulders, wearing a grey lightweight suit. He was at ninety degrees to Angela, so I could only see him from the rear quarter too. His baldness and broadness called to mind a dim figure from my past. The connection eluded me though.

The waitress deposited my *espresso* before me, accompanied by a smile, which I returned. The couple were talking in undertones and their words were inaudible. I risked another glance just as the woman's head swivelled sideways, exposing her full profile. It *was* Angela. She didn't notice me, being engrossed in her dialogue with Baldy. I rotated my chair to present my back to them. If they left before me, it was a certainty she would clock me, so I downed half my coffee, left a 500Ft bill under the saucer and slipped out.

A whole slew of questions arose out of that impromptu sighting. Who was the guy, what was his business with Angie, why hadn't she told me she was meeting him? The separate query of why the guy seemed familiar to me was also troubling.

Outside, I positioned myself across the road on a dilapidated bench seat. And waited. They were a while finishing their tête-à-tête. When at last they left, they lingered by the entrance while Baldy talked and Angela listened. They terminated the meeting with a handshake and separated, Angela to head back towards the hotel. She was wearing skinny jeans and a printed sleeveless top that was seductively clingy and emphasised her toned upper body. I watched, in mixed appreciation and disquiet, until she dwindled into an amorphous figure.

I hung about for a while before continuing my walk to the hotel. Back in my spartan quarters, I had barely closed the door behind me when knuckles rapped on it. I guessed it would be Angela and I was right.

'Enjoy your walk?' I asked, as she came in, brushing past me without an invitation.

'The walk was fine, thanks. Then I stopped for coffee and met a man.'

For her to admit it went some way to dispersing my bad vibes.

'Is this confession time? Have you fallen in love?'

She burst out laughing. 'Fallen in love?' Her expression sobered. 'I suppose you're joking.'

'Mostly. So what about this man? Did he hit on you?'

'Hit …? Oh, you think he was trying to pull me.' Her headshake was very emphatic. 'No, nothing like that. I popped into a café and we arrived at the door at the same time. He stood aside to let me enter first, and we sort of fell into conversation and finished up sitting together.'

I sat on the edge of the bed and, again uninvited, she joined me.

'Is there a moral to this story?' I said. 'Such as, attractive women shouldn't speak to strange men.'

Now she looked cross. 'Stop it, Jack. He claimed to be a marine biologist, here to attend a conference about pollution in Lake Balaton. From Linz, in Austria.'

'So far, so fascinating. Are you leading up to something?'

'In a manner of speaking, I may be doing just that. You see, although he talked authoritatively on the subject of freshwater pollution – it was rather worrying actually – I had a funny feeling about him.'

She paused, as if waiting for a prompt.

'Go on,' I said, to oblige.

'Yes … right. I'm hesitating because I don't want to sound paranoid.' She nibbled her sensually plump lower lip. 'It's just that it struck me he might have been following me.'

'Stalking, you mean?'

'No, not really. I mean, yes, it's possible, but I was thinking more of your enemies, whoever they may be. The threats those horrible people made …' She shuddered. 'Perhaps they'll try and get at you through me.'

She was thinking clever, albeit twenty-hours behind me.

'It already crossed my mind,' I said. 'And I've been contemplating sending you back to Italy, or the UK.'

She bridled at that. 'Sending me back? You can't treat me as if I were your personal property. You can't *send* me anywhere, and I wouldn't go even if you asked me nicely.'

I apologised with a sheepish grin. 'I wasn't implying I could order you around. Your safety's paramount, that's all. So far we've been lucky, but luck is fickle, and it doesn't last forever.'

'You don't want me here, I can tell, and … I can understand.' She clasped her hands in her lap, head bowed. 'To get back to the mystery man, suppose he *was* working for the opposition?'

'Did he ask any questions? And did you give him any answers?'

'No and no. Wait a minute though, he did ask my name. He said he'd guessed I was English.'

'Nothing else? Where you're staying, why you're here, who you're with.'

'Not a thing.' She was so emphatic, it wasn't hard to believe her. 'I even gave him a false name.'

'Did he give you his name?'

'Gerhard. I don't remember the last name. It was long and complicated.'

I stood up, stretched, and went to the window. Down in the street no bald guys were lurking; no guys at all, in fact.

'Whether or not he's a member of the Wolff pack makes no difference,' I said, turning. 'If you didn't tell him anything, he's no wiser than he was before he met you. If he's innocent, none of it matters a goddam.'

'I suppose so,' she said, though her tone hinted at doubt. 'It's worrying, just the same. They won't let up on us, will they?'

I bent my brain to the problem.

'Well?' she said, when I had still hadn't replied.

'Well, I'm sending for reinforcements.'

Two alternatives: Liza, who would jump at the opportunity, and Rocky, my Finnish stand-by. The decision was governed by the risk of harm to Liza. I would never again expose her to injury or worse, she'd suffered too much already. Rocky's involvement carried no such baggage. He was a mercenary. He would measure the dangers against his obligations and the financial gain.

I settled for Rocky.

Chapter Eleven

'It is good we work together again,' Vilho Granit, known to all as Rocky, said, resting his skateboard-sized feet on the coffee table.

I left off blowing on knuckles crushed by his handshake.

'I hope you'll think so when I give you the whole story.'

He chuckled. He had a chuckle that sounded like a can full of nuts and bolts being shaken.

'You try to frighten me?'

'Is such a thing even possible?' I countered.

From the size of him alone you would expect him to be hard to frighten. Well over six feet of solid meat, with biceps as fat as my thighs, and thighs as fat as my waist. Slight exaggeration maybe, but you get the image. His hair was almost platinum-blond and curly. The only wrong note was sounded by the piratical ear ring and the multiple rings on his fingers. I suspected the finger furniture was more an aid to pugilism than decoration.

We were drinking in what passes for a pub in Vecsés. It was called the Terrace, spelled just like that, in English. On the black oval sign a scroll bearing the words "Finest Beers". The resemblance to an English pub went no further. We were parked in a gloomy corner, and had the place to ourselves, the bartender apart.

Rocky had flown in from Helsinki, arriving late afternoon the day after I summoned him. Angela, for reasons best known to herself, was against bringing in an outsider, and was still sulking about it. She had taken a cab into the city to work off her annoyance among the downtown fashion boutiques, which include Burberry and Louis Vuitton.

'Tell me the story,' Rocky said, sampling his drink, a Hungarian liqueur the colour of black coffee, known as Unicum Zwack. You'd have

expected him to be swigging beer from the bottle but he was partial to liqueurs. Another of his many paradoxes. The tiny glass was lost in his ham-sized fist.

'Nice stuff,' he said, having almost emptied the glass. 'Now, tell me. Jack. What happen, why you want me here in this strange country?'

No stranger than Finland, was my private reaction. Language included. I shuffled my chair forward to reduce the gap between our two heads and ran it past him, more or less verbatim, avoiding long words that might confuse him. His English was workaday rather than fluent. Once or twice he asked for clarification. When I first mentioned Angela, it prompted a chuckle.

'You and women,' he said, and I detected a note of envy. 'They like you too much.'

'It's not like that this time,' I protested, asking myself, even as I uttered the denial, if it was exactly like that this time. I just wasn't ready to admit it.

'Finish your story,' he said, disbelief in every line of his square face.

I did just that. He absorbed it all and proved he had understood by his summing up, as I wound up my tale of woe.

'These guys totally same as each other, right?'

'That's what I'm told. The only difference I can visualise is fingerprints. I looked it up on Google and it says twins' fingerprints can be very similar but not identical. Seems they're not a genetic characteristic. Anyhow, that doesn't help unless I can get hold of a record of their fingerprints – for instance, if one or both of them have a police record.'

He made a grunting noise. 'No way to know that.'

'Unless you have contacts with Interpol or Europol.'

'I can try. But then you must make these twins give you their prints, no?'

I smiled grimly. 'There may be ways, if I can catch up with them.'

'But … say these twins have no record, and if no other difference between them, and all people around this Vincent tell lies to protect, you never sure you get the right guy.'

'That's my quandary.'

He snapped his fingers, making a noise like a branch breaking.

'DNA!'

'I already thought of that. From what I read on-line, the DNAs of twins can be identical. Not always, but often enough. Even if they have different DNAs, they would have to be on record. If neither of them has ever been arrested, they won't be.'

'Hmm. So you must kill them both.' He was a matter-of-fact sort of guy. For him, killing was just business.

'Or neither,' I parried.

'Or give up the job,' he said, logical as ever.

'That's on the cards, though I hate to fail.'

More grunting, accompanied by wriggling of his heavy brows. Suddenly he sat up, his face animated.

'I got it! Who pays you?'

Before I could answer, the waitress came to clear the table next to us. She asked us in broken English if we wanted refills. Rocky's glass had been empty from the first swallow and he said '*Ja*!' with emphasis. I shook my head.

'So?' Rocky said, when we were alone again.

'Who's paying me? Well, I'm not hundred percent sure, as I deal through an Irish guy called Donovan. But it's likely to be a woman I met in Spain a few days before her go-between approached me. A Frenchwoman with four kids, name of Sophie Morais – if it's kosher. I believe she's the wife or ex-wife of the hit, the guy I'm supposed to kill.'

'Good. She will know.'

I stared at him. 'You mean …'

'I mean she know if a man is her husband or not. So all you do is bring man to woman or woman to man, no matter which twin, and she tell you.'

The simplicity of it was too much for my over-racked brain. If the Marais woman was truly Vincent's wife, Victor wouldn't be able to fool her by pretending to be her husband. Aside from the prints, which were a long shot at best, it was the most foolproof method of getting an ID.

'Rocky, you might just be a genius.'

'Am I?' He grinned then frowned. 'What is genius?'

'A very smart guy.' I slapped him on the shoulder as the waitress put his Unicum Zwack on the table and removed the empty glass.

'Good. I will celibate.'

'Celebrate,' I corrected. 'Celibate and you definitely don't go together.'

'So, what you want I do and how much you pay?'

The job specification first.

'Follow Victor Wolff – if it is Victor – wherever he goes, and communicate any activities to me by cell phone. Make sure he doesn't spot you.'

'Where am I start?'

'I'll give you directions to his villa. Buy some glasses and keep it under surveillance until he shows up then don't let him out of your sight. You can take a break between midnight and eight, so you'll need some accommodation. Report to me twice a day and at other times if anything interesting develops, especially if he meets up with his brother. All clear?'

I had prepared a text description of Victor and Sara which I transmitted to him earlier on WhatsApp. I had also copied the studio portrait I had filched from the Wolff residence of what I presumed to be Victor, with Sara.

After a cursory glance he folded it and stuffed it in his inside pocket.

'You also have the descriptions I sent on WhatsApp,' I said. 'You'll recognise him when he arrives at the villa.'

'Okay. Anything else?'

'For now, no.'

'How much you pay?'

'Pay? Oh, say five thousand euros now, five when we're done. Plus expenses.'

He scratched his considerable chin while he weighed my offer.

'That okay for two weeks. If it take longer, it is two thousand every week more.'

'Fair enough.' We shook hands over his liqueur, which he then polished off in a single gulp.

To avoid his clashing with Angela, I had booked him in an hotel in

central Pest and hired him an SUV from Avis.

'All I need now is taxi for hotel,' he said, rising and towering over me.

'I'll change your diapers if you ask me politely,' I said, and made for the desk to enquire about a cab.

* * * * *

With Rocky launched on his mission I met up with Angela at the Timor. She had recovered from our spat and her pleasant, easy-going self was back in place.

'How did your meeting go with the Finn?'

'As expected. I hired him to keep a watching brief on the Wolffs. With any luck, Victor – if he really is Victor – will meet up with Vincent so that Rocky can track him to his hideout.'

Angela looked thoughtful. 'But how will he know which one is which?'

'Easy. I think. If he's gotten Victor in his sights, he'll know how he's dressed. When Vincent enters stage left, he's sure to be wearing a different outfit.'

'Sounds like a reasonably safe bet, unless they're so attached to each other they dress alike. Then what?'

'Then I report back to my paymaster,' I said. This much was true. It wasn't that I objected to lying to her, but when you tell lies, you need to remember them. My talents for lying and remembering were arguably no higher than average.

'Report back. Hmm. Then what?'

She was a persistent broad. Somehow she felt she had the right to pry and probe. Then again, the part she had played, albeit inadvertent, in various shootings and disposal of bodies did confer some degree of "right to know".

'Then, my dear Angie, he will issue instructions on the next step, or pay me off with a handsome bonus for wrapping it up in less than two weeks.'

'I wish he would. Pay you off, that is.'

We were in my room. She went to the window, gazed out at the

suburban landscape, her back to me. It was drizzling and the skies were an unrelieved grey. She was wearing jeans and a sweater, and still looked alluring. Irritating though her various persistences were, she did exercise a sexual pull that was growing harder to resist by the day.

'Jack …' she continued to gaze out through the window. Her voice was unsteady.

'Yes?' I prodded, when she didn't go on.

'Suppose … suppose I told you I … love you.'

My mind went momentarily blank.

'Suppose you did,' I said, to gain a breathing space, to cook up a snappy quip. My wit failed me. 'No … er, is that what you're saying, that you love me?'

She swung round, her eyes fierce. 'Yes, you idiot! Isn't that what I just said?'

'What you actually said was *suppose* you love me.'

'That means I do love you, you pedantic bastard!'

Then she was in my arms and her lips attached to mine. She was certainly a practised kisser. Lips, teeth, tongue, the whole works. It was a giant step up from cheek-to-cheek.

As we came up for oxygen, I said, 'Slow down, love, I'm still adjusting to your being in love with me.'

'What's the adjustment? Correct me if I'm wrong, but you're not in love with me, are you?'

I looked out over her shoulder at the dreary suburbia and assembled my feelings and how to express them to avoid causing upset.

'You're a sexy, good-looking woman, Angie, and I could jump into bed with you right now. My guess is you expect more than that. A bit of emotional reciprocity, for openers. Would I be right?'

'Emotional reciprocity?' she said, wide-eyed. 'Is that English?'

I withdrew behind a self-conscious grin. 'You know goddam well what I mean but I'll spell it out anyway: you're not just looking for a one-night stand.'

'Nor even a ten-night stand.' Her arms went around my waist and her loins ground into mine; as she was in heels, we were almost the same height at that level. My arousal was quick from then on.

'Careful,' I cautioned. 'You're testing my will power.'

She took a step backwards in haste. 'You're right that I wouldn't just want us to go to bed and … and screw the afternoon away. I'm the sort of woman who needs a commitment.' She hesitated. 'Not love necessarily, not right away, but more than just lust, if you get my meaning.'

'Sure I get it. Then again, part of falling in love could be making love in the old, traditional way.'

Because I still loved Maura, I doubted it would evolve along those lines. No reason though, conscience aside, why we couldn't have a stab at it.

"Listen, love,' I said, holding her at arm's length. 'I like you a hell of a lot, and I enjoy your company and your sense of humour. Plus, I lust after you plenty.' Her face creased into a grin at that admission. 'Look, we can work on it. Do like lovers do and see if it sparks –'

'Emotional reciprocity?' she cut in with a happy laugh.

She seemed content enough with my guarded avowal. It was a point of departure. As things turned out I should have used the opportunity to kiss her goodbye instead of hello. The heat in the kitchen was increasing. Angela's presence would be a constraint and a distraction; the more so if we became lovers rather than mere companions.

But as we kissed again, our bodies squirming against each other, my prick transmitting signals that were growing harder to ignore, I put my reservations on hold, to be exhumed another day, or week, or month, or, better still never.

* * * * *

To follow up on Rocky's idea, I needed the cooperation of Irish Donovan. When I phoned and requested a face-to-face, he flatly refused. When I cajoled, he softened his refusal, but it still amounted to a no. Only when I threatened to walk, did he give in. We would meet in Berlin at the weekend, where he was due to conclude a business deal.

It was now for me to play hard to get.

'No can do,' I said.

Although technically I was free to come and go in Germany, I remained at loggerheads with the German Security Police because of my contract killing of Frenchman Fabrice Tillou. The year before last I had risked a flying visit there, but I was loath to push my luck again.

My rejection understandably nettled Donovan.

'What do you suggest then?' he said truculently.

'How about you make a detour to Brussels or Paris?'

'You're asking a lot of feckin' favours, Henley.'

'It's in both our interests. I promise you, you won't be wasting your time.'

Sounds of disgruntlement.

'Can't you at least give me a hint what it's about?'

'When I see you,' I returned. 'Text me time and place where we can meet.'

I thumbed the button to cut him off before he had a change of heart.

* * * * *

Rocky came to dinner with Angela and me on Friday evening. He was not in jovial humour.

'I am standing in the rain for two days and nobody come to the house. Maybe they move out.'

'It's used as a weapons' store,' I said. 'They'll be back sooner or later.'

'It is the later I worry about,' he grumbled.

Angie and I laughed, and even he broke into a rueful grin.

We were dining at the Costed in downtown Pest, a Michelin-starred restaurant with a high curved ceiling bedecked with what could have been wisteria. Angela was bedecked in a little black dress, with strappy heels, and a stole. Very fetching. Rocky was less fetching in jeans with deep cuffs and a check shirt. Other diners kept shooting curious glances at him.

Angela had gotten over her original resistance to his involvement and was even flirting with him a bit. It was funny how, thanks to her declaration of love, I was seeing her in a new, even possessive light. I suspected that even the dress, short and tight, had been selected to

encourage guys to give her the twice over.

'Are you doing this for friendship or for money?' she asked Rocky, her true-blue eyes sparkling over the rim of her wine glass.

'For money, what else?,' he said in his big voice. 'We are friends but I must live, so I must work. As long as he pay me, I will be his friend.'

'They say money makes the world go round,' she said, going all coquettish. 'That and sex.'

She ran a tongue along her parted lips, her gaze on me. She was hot tonight and letting both of us know it.

'You are a lucky man, Jack,' Rocky said gruffly.

'Me?' I was about to add 'We're just good soul-mates,' when I realised that was the worst thing I could say to Rocky. Believing the field was clear, he'd be all over her, like a Doberman over a dachshund.

'Yeah,' I acknowledged. 'The luckiest.'

Angela pouted at me and swigged more wine. She was already three-parts loaded and still going strong. Our choice of grape was a Hungarian Bikavér – Bull's Blood – a potent red. After two glasses I had switched to water, reminding myself that I had to drive my soul-mate back to Vecsés.

She and I left Rocky on his ownsome around midnight. On the drive back to the hotel she sat with head lolling against the side window, hardly speaking. Her dress was much shorter when she was drunk I noticed.

'You feel okay?' I asked, as we left the highway for the final lap to the hotel.

'Feel … okay,' she mumbled. 'Love … you … don't love me.'

'Sure I do,' I said, knowing that whatever I said would be forgotten by the morning.

As I swung the Evoque into the hotel parking lot, she revived and circled both arms around my neck in an attempt to kiss me. I swerved, mounting the grass shoulder on the edge of the lot, and slammed on the brakes. She missed my mouth twice, but made it at the third attempt and entangled her body around mine like a boa-constrictor bent on crushing the life out of its prey.

Full blown sex in a car was yesterday's fashion. So was sex with

drunken women. It took physical force to deter her from tugging at my pants zip. I thrust her back into the passenger seat, and guided the car into a vacant bay in the parking lot.

The night clerk disapproved of her inability to walk in a straight line. He was well past retirement age and spoke zero English, useless therefore to apologise for her condition. We made it to her room, with her still requiring support to keep her upright. I helped her to her bed, removed her shoes, and left her to sort herself out.

The sex I put on hold until another day.

* * * * *

Although I avoided travelling within Europe by air to minimise traces of my movements, time constraints made flying necessary for my meeting with Donovan. I used my Devreese passport and it stood up to scrutiny, though I was baffled by my passport suppliers' ability to produce a document that passed all the computerised scans at airports. My best guess was that they paid for inside help. That my passports were essentially faked genuine articles.

Brussels Zaventem Airport, even at eight in the morning on Sunday, was all hustle and bustle, but as a Belgian citizen I went through passport control and customs as if they didn't exist, and my cab was dropping me off outside the soulless cube that is Brussels Sheraton Hotel a quarter hour ahead of my nine o'clock breakfast rendezvous.

When Donovan stepped out of the elevator, he was chatting with another guy – stocky, chubby-cheeked, suited up for a convention. They parted with a handshake.

'Well, hello there, Jack,' Donovan effused, all smiles and bonhomie.

'How are you?' I countered. I was still unsure how to take this guy.

He was fine, and pleased to meet up with me again, notwithstanding that I had disrupted his travel plans. He ushered me back into the elevator and we rose two floors. An open door faced us across a carpeted landing when we emerged. He led and I followed to find myself in a small conference room – oval table, six chairs, inspiring view of the airport under leaden skies.

'I assume you want to eat,' he said, inviting me to sit.

'You assume right.'

'Make yourself at home.'

As I made myself at home opposite Donovan, a waiter entered with menus under his arm. We chose our repasts from an unhealthy selection of breakfasts. The waiter departed.

Donovan interlaced his fingers, placed his large veined hands in front of him, and gave me an unsmiling stare.

'We have one hour, which is why we're doing this over breakfast, then I need to be on a flight to Berlin. What's it about?'

I had figured out my tactics while I was in the air. Now I was ready to sock them to him.

'I'm quitting.'

If the news took him aback, it wasn't reflected in his attitude by so much as a lifted eyebrow.

'You can't quit. We have a contract.'

That was the quirky thing about contracts to kill. Though they're unwritten, the contractee can't unilaterally revoke them. It's not a legal impediment, it's the law of the jungle, and you either respected it or you became a legitimate target for retribution. The flip-side of this clause was that the contractor *could* terminate and if the hit man agreed, the deal was cancelled.

'You could release me from it,' I pointed out.

He nodded his large head lugubriously. 'I could. Tell me what's your problem, boyo.'

'My problem is, as I figured from the start, it's impossible to get an infallible ID of Vincent. They're identical, apart from their prints, but neither twin has a record, so we have no means of using their prints. I met one of them, who claims to be Victor, but how do I know? His wife also says he's Victor, but she could be lying to protect both of them. She might not even be his wife, or anybody's.'

His chair creaked as he tilted back in it.

'We knew a lot of detective work was involved. That's the reason we're paying your expenses before we get to the job proper.'

'Taking your money and living high on the hog doesn't cause me

sleepless nights. But a year from now I could be no further forward and you'd be three hundred grand worse off.'

'Let her worry about the money.' He produced a handkerchief, blew his nose lustily into it. 'I sense you're not here just to hand in your notice. So, now that you've set me up to accept failure, would you care to tell me what you need to achieve success?'

Astute of him. He sat there like Buddha in his well-cut midnight blue suit and sober tie. Not super-rich attire, just middle class.

'I need to meet my employer,' I said, coming to the real purpose of this meeting.

This got me a reaction. Whatever he had expected, it wasn't that.

'Oh, do you now? To what end?'

'At some stage in the game, whoever she is, she'll have to positively ID her ex-husband to his and my face.'

'You're assuming that'll be necessary,' he said, and for the first time he acted uneasy. 'Not that I'm admitting there's a she involved, or, if there is, that she's Vincent's ex-wife.'

'Cut the bullshit, Donovan. It's his ex- all right, and using her is the only method of identification anywhere near reliable.'

'You mean by bringing them together and having her confirm it.'

I spread my hands. 'If you can think of a better way, I'll be happy to consider it.'

A tap came at the door and the waiter entered, pushing a cart. Our negotiations were deferred until the waiter served us. Donovan waved him away with a 10-euro tip.

'*Bon appétit*,' I said.

He speared some ham and deposited it on his plate, followed by a bread roll which he broke in half. I did likewise, but garnished it with a dab of Gorgonzola cheese.

'Even if I confirmed my employer was his ex-wife, and even if she were prepared to cooperate, suppose the twin we presented to her was Victor?'

'It could happen,' I admitted.

'Well, then. If it did happen, Victor goes home and we're still looking for Vincent, who might be anywhere according to the last message you sent. How the feck would you get round that?'

I popped a chunk of roll and cheese in my mouth. The bread was oven-warm and delicious.

'Two possibilities,' I said between chews, forking two Churchillian fingers at him. 'One – if turns out to be Victor, we keep him out of circulation until I track down Vincent.'

His head oscillated left and right like a metronome as he weighed the idea.

'The other possibility?'

'We mark him. Leave him with a permanent scar, ideally facial.'

He paused with bulging cheeks to whistle.

'That would do it, no feckin' mistake. Bejaysus, Jack, you're a mean bastard.'

'A professional bastard. Emotions don't come into what I do.'

'All right then.' He really had no choice but to accede to my request, but his resentment was palpable. 'Let me call his ex–'

'No!' I wiped my mouth with a linen napkin. 'I want to meet her in the flesh. I'm not accepting any more instructions by remote control. You're right about the contract – I can't break it unilaterally. But either she agrees to meeting me or she'll be spending her money for nothing. I mean, *I'll* be spending her money for nothing until she gets tired of supporting me.'

Rain pattered against the window. In the background an airliner was unsticking from the runway, the whine of its engines hushed by the room's soundproofing; it flew beyond the rectangle of glass and out of my line of vision.

He puffed through pouting lips. 'You have a point. Fair enough, I'll ask her.'

'When?'

'When I get back to Dublin at the weekend.'

I vetoed that with the flat of my hand on the table top.

'This won't wait. Talk to her now, while I'm here, and put it on speakerphone.'

Amid much muttering, he plucked an iPhone from his jacket pocket and made the call. He tripped speakerphone, and I listened with him to the rings.

A woman picked up. 'Residence la Marquise.'

'It's Donovan. Connect me with your mistress.' His French was good.

'*Toute de suite, monsieur.*'

A minute or so later a different female voice floated over the line.

'Don?'

'*C'est moi,*' he acknowledged. Still in French, he related an approximately verbatim version of our conversation. Of which I understood every word.

Her response was lengthy and not oozing joy. At intervals he nodded or plucked at his lips. I continued with my breakfast, poured coffee for us both.

Long before the negotiations were over and they were exchanging farewells, I had finished eating and was on my second coffee.

'It's agreed,' he said heavily, which I already knew. He was openly unhappy about this breach of the clause in the contract that specified I would deal through him, and the consequent dilution of his role as sole negotiator. Maybe he was worried about his pay being cut. 'I'll text you the arrangements.'

'Fine. And next time you call me an *espèce de conard* make sure I'm not around to hear it.'

His jaw sagged. 'Shit, I forgot you speak French. I … I'm sorry, Jack. You heard the bollocking she gave me. I needed to make it sound as though I wasn't just caving in to your demands.'

'Thanks for the breakfast. I'm heading back to Budapest this afternoon, so I'll say so long – for now.'

Chapter Twelve

Angela met me at the airport in the Evoque and drove us to the hotel.

'I hope it was worthwhile,' she said, as we sat down for drinks in the bar at the Timor. 'If all they have to do is get Victor or whichever to meet up with his ex-wife for vetting, why do they need you?'

If she had been aware that my assignment was not merely to find Vincent Wolff but to eliminate him, her question would have been superfluous.

'Victor would never cooperate. Even if they could find him without me.'

She decided that if I had to travel to meet Mme Marais, she was going to string along. I was against it.

'Listen, this is business, it's not a honeymoon.'

Regrettable choice of word. It had implications, wholly unintended, and Angela wasn't shy about exploiting them.

'Is that a proposal?' she said, with a coy sidelong glance.

'Be serious.'

Her hand was resting on my thigh, massaging it gently. I didn't object. We were fast coming to the stage in our cosy togetherness where sexual congress was inevitable, so why resist?

'You're not going without me,' she said, toying with her cup, 'and I'm not staying without you.'

'So if I leave without you, you'll leave without me.' I fixed my gaze on her. 'That's what you mean, right?'

She nodded without conviction. In truth, I didn't want her to leave. Whatever was going on between us deserved to be explored to see where it led. She wouldn't be safe, either.

'I may only be day or two,' I said, a last tottering protest. She had stormed the castle of my resistance – and it was a crumbling ruin to

begin with – and planted her standard on the battlements.

She left off fiddling with her cup and offered her lips for a different purpose from drinking coffee. I dragged her towards me and accepted the offering. Her lips were malleable and responsive. When we separated, her eyes were glowing.

'I love you … my sweet,' she said.

I hesitated. I didn't love her, and programmed love-talk wasn't my style. So I just reran the mouth to mouth stimulation and hoped she would settle for that.

* * * * *

That night we broke new ground and shared a bed. She undressed in front of me, without affectation or tease. Her late-thirties body was that of an athlete, and more boyish than curvy, with modest breasts. Very toned. Her body hair proved she was an authentic blonde. Just seeing her naked was on its own arousing enough. Then she crawled under the sheets and went to work on me with hands and mouth. My English Rose was no ingenue.

The foreplay was foreshortened by the mutual need to get to the main event. When at last I entered her she was moist and welcoming, and I penetrated my full length, provoking a breathy 'Oooh,' and a frantic rise and fall of her hips. The 'oohs' became more frequent, more prolonged.

From starting gate to finishing tape didn't take long. Maybe her famine was as great as mine. We climaxed within seconds of each other and afterwards clung together like limpets, sweaty and panting.

'It's been such a long time,' she confirmed in my ear. 'But it was worth saving myself for.'

'For me too.'

She slid away a few inches to get me in focus.

'I didn't do it just for that. I love you, Jack. I really have fallen for you.'

She spoke with reverence, as if falling in love with me was inconceivable. I struggled anew for a suitable declaration of my own.

'I sure feel something for you, sweetheart,' I improvised. 'Not love, not yet, but hitting it off in bed is a step in the right direction.'

She seemed content with that and snuggled into my arms, little sighs escaping her. Still embracing, we drifted off to sleep. I awoke in the small hours and her naked proximity roused me to a repeat performance. She needed no foreplay, and we went at it like two people demented. It was a session so intense that for a while it had me considering Angela as a woman with whom I could build the elusive new life that I craved. Then I reminded myself how Maura had refused to countenance living with a man who killed for money, let alone marry me, unless I gave it up.

For the present, Maura was out of reach. In the meantime, Angela was here, willing, and sexy as hell. Moreover, she had demonstrated that she wasn't bothered if the path of true love happened to be strewn with a corpse or two. You could call her the ideal consort for a hit man.

* * * * *

A conflict of priorities had arisen. At 7.18pm Rocky called with the news that a large van had stopped by the Wolff house, such as those used for moving furniture, and unloaded a great number of cartons and crates. More military hardware, most likely.

The second part of his communiqué pertained to a visit by a Wolff twin with two bruisers in tow. They had stayed for about thirty minutes. When they left, Rocky tailed their SUV. After losing them on the outskirts of Buda, he had a lucky break, catching up by happenstance when a police car flagged them down. Rocky pulled over to wait. Before long Wolff's SUV came along, keeping to the speed limit, and Rocky tucked in behind it.

'They come to place on the side of the river. Big house with wall and guard at the gate.'

'You have the address?' I asked.

'Moment. I need flashlight.' A click and a scuffling noise. 'Okay … the street is call Duna sor. No number on gate.'

'Stick around. I'm coming over.'

'Sure thing.'

No sooner had I cut the call when the phone burped to announce the reception of a text message. It was from Donovan.

SM not pleased but OK for meet
wednesday. Get a flight to Nice.
Hotel will be booked for you. Details
later. Don't screw it up.

The entreaty not to 'screw it up' I took as a sign he was still worrying about his fee.

This presented me with a dilemma. I needed to check out Rocky's discovery of a new location for the Wolffs, but if it called for follow-up action it might conflict with my Wednesday appointment to meet Sophie M. If I cried off, she might well withdraw her reluctant cooperation, leaving the identification issue unresolved. For now, I would have to trust Rock to keep tabs on the twin he had tailed, presumed to be Victor. If Mme Sophie fell in with my proposition, we could snatch Victor and haul him off to Nice as early as the coming weekend. A few logistical issues to overcome, but they could wait.

The roads were quiet and wet. I entered the street name of the Wolff's riverside property into the GPS and let it guide me. It took thirty-five minutes. The GPS was reliable, and didn't make a single wrong turn. Rocky's rental, a Kia Sportage SUV, black and anonymous, was parked at the start of Duma sor. I tucked in next to it and left the Evoque to climb in beside him.

'Which house?' I asked.

'We go a little more.'

He cranked the engine and edged the car forward. We passed two walled properties and came to a third. The gates were of wood and solid-looking. Because of the wall, only the two upper floors of the building were visible. It was a substantial property, the topmost level being smaller than the second floor with balconies on all sides. A chimney stack rose dead centre out of a shallow-pitched roof with extended eaves, a feature I had noticed on other Hungarian houses. The whole pile was finished in a pale crepi, colour uncertain in the poor light.

'Where's the guard?' I asked.

'Inside, in little cabin.'

'How do you know?'

'The gates are open when I drive past.'

'Any CCTV?'

He made a dismissive noise. 'Only one. It cover the gate. Nothing for the walls.'

He pulled over about fifty metres beyond the gates, leaving the engine running. Rain pattered on the windshield. Through a line of trees on our left the Danube trundled on, dark and turgid, the streetlights on the opposite bank casting reflections like a string of illuminated pearls. A brightly lit launch was plodding upstream. I lowered the window and rock music filtered into the car.

'Either we break in and snatch him, or we wait for him to come out.'

Rocky agreed these were the two alternatives.

'Break in is better because nobody can see us from street.'

We were thinking alike. Behind the walls were no witnesses, except a possible servant or two and the gate guard, none of them likely to go squealing to the law. On the downside, they represented opposition, potentially armed and protective. Could be bloody. Again.

'We'll need disguises,' I said, 'in case some public-spirited person complains to the police.'

Rocky shifted in his seat. 'What is public-spirited?'

'The kind of people our kind of people hate'.

'Ah.' He yawned and stretched, his elbow jabbing me in the rib cage. 'So we must decide how and when to get in without making troubles.'

'Come up with a plan. I'll be out of town for a while. Find out how many people occupy the house and what are their various statuses. How many are family, how many are friends, how many are domestic employees …' I noticed his perplexed look and elaborated: 'Servants, to you. Also, especially, how many bodyguards. Be ready to move when I get back, say by Friday. Keep an eye on Victor's movements and let me know if his twin joins the party.'

'You leave Angela for me?'

I laughed at his optimism, or was it opportunism? 'You wish. No, my friend, you'll have to find a playmate of your own.'

* * * * *

The morning we were due to depart, Angela developed a fierce migraine, a once a month event. The attack was so debilitating she could barely articulate. Travelling was ruled out. I didn't try to persuade her. Going alone was preferable and her illness therefore convenient.

It was a struggle for her to raise her upper body off the bed for a goodbye kiss. She managed the briefest of pecks, immediately flopping back down with a groan.

'I'll tell the hotel to send for a doctor,' I said as I shrugged into my windbreaker.

'No … don't. I've … taken … pills.' Even speaking was an effort. 'It'll be … gone by … tomorrow.'

Against my better judgment I called Rocky, asked him to drop in later to check up on her. His sigh was long and gut-deep and a hundred percent insincere. House calls would be no hardship for him. The only saving grace was that she was unlikely to be in any condition to entertain him in the manner his tongue was hanging out for.

* * * * *

The time factor again ruled out overland travel. Armed with the Devreese passport and credit card, I made the journey to Nice by Austrian Airlines with a brief stop in Venice. By mid-afternoon I was installed at Le Meridien Hotel on the Promenade des Anglais, with the inhale-exhale rhythm of the surf and the squeals of gulls infiltrating through the open window of my room, and the Mediterranean breeze stirring the lace drapes. This corner of France was as close as it comes to a second home for me, though it was years since I was last here. I left it as a wanted man. With my Devreese identity and hair darkened to nondescript brown with my colouring comb, I felt the risk was justified. It wasn't as if I would be sticking around for many hours and, having flown from an EU country, I wasn't even required to present a passport, real or phoney.

* * * * *

My first appointment was with Donovan on his own. We would see Sophie M later at her apartment in Monaco, another old stomping ground.

'This is getting to be a habit,' he said, his grin rueful, as we shook hands in the lobby. 'And what have you done with your hair?'

'Stress makes it go dark.'

He didn't press for a serious answer.

'At least you're making progress,' he said and went so far as to praise me for making faster progress than expected. 'It's the only reason Sophie agreed to meet you. She can see that you'll need her input to get over the final identification, and be sure you ...' His head did a quick left and right for eavesdroppers, 'don't zap the wrong fella.'

'Great. So what's the programme?'

'As soon as you're ready, we drive to Monaco. According to her instructions, I leave you there to discuss whatever it is you need to discuss.'

His tone dripped venom. He wasn't overjoyed at being excluded from the negotiations and/or being relegated to a subsidiary role. Or maybe, after my meeting with Sophie M, to a period of unemployment.

We walked through the automatic doors together, to a waiting white Mercedes limo, complete with driver.

'It's Sophie's,' Donovan explained. 'So's the chauffeur.'

His emphasis on the chauffeur, loaded with double entendre, made me glance sharply at him, but his expression was inscrutable.

* * * * *

Sophie's apartment was in the Carre d'Or district, on the avenue de la Costa. A spanking new, skyscraping monolith of concrete in a prime location.

'Penthouse, presumably,' I said as we drew up at the curb.

'Sadly not. Not that she couldn't afford it, but she wasn't first in line and lost out to two fecking Arabs.' He threw in a few more explicit

curses under his breath, from which I gathered that he was not in favour of Middle Eastern potentates snatching up prime real estate ahead of indigenous clients.

We rode in an ultra-silent, ultra-quick elevator to the eighteenth floor and waded through carpet as deep as a cornfield. A maid answered our ring. Middle-aged and sexless as a tombstone. She escorted us down a tiled corridor. On the walls, abstract murals, the dominant colours being shades of green and yellow.

The living area was vast. Fashionable open-plan with a separate kitchen. The maid offered refreshment. Donovan asked for a soda water. I declined, and the maid bustled off leaving us to inspect the decor. It was, unsurprisingly, furnished with no expense spared. Beige S-shaped couches with matching normal-shaped armchairs; glass-topped tables (one resembling a coffin), more tiled floors but with rugs in the seating areas. Walls bare of pictures or other adornment, which surprised me until Donovan mentioned that Sophie had been in residence for less than a month.

'The building's not finished yet, as ye'll have noticed from the scaffolding, but she's an impatient woman.'

Wall-to-wall French doors stood open, leading to a balcony big enough to accommodate three circular tables, each with six attendant club-style chairs. Plants were scattered about in square pots, their colours too vivid to be real. By tacit assent, we wandered over to the balcony wall. The view was a hundred and eighty degrees: the sky and the Mediterranean dominated, naturally; in the foreground the Port Hercule Marina, where I had docked *Seamist* more than once. Even more in the foreground was the Avenue d'Ostende, which forms part of the Formula One racecourse.

'Guess how much she paid?' Donovan said, envy in his voice.

'Twenty million bucks?' I said, a figure plucked out of the air.

He chuckled. 'And the rest. Thirty-five million it cost her, and she had to haggle for that. What I mean is *I* had to haggle on her behalf. And that's in euros, not dollars.'

'Jesus.' It brought home to me what a pauper I was by comparison. A few million in my various bank accounts, sure, but it wouldn't buy so

much as a studio in this building.

'*Bonjour, messieurs,*' came a voice, reminder of an evening at my former restaurant in Malaga. Sophie stepped through the French doors, the maid trailing in her wake with Donovan's soda water on a tray.

From that point forward we spoke only French.

Donovan did the puckered lips kiss on her cheeks, and I shook hands with her. Her clasp was cool and firm, and slow to release. I didn't fight her for possession.

She asked me if I was well, and I answered in the affirmative, and asked her the same, and she answered the same. At her invitation, we sat in individual armchairs, grouped equidistant from the coffin table which had solid sides instead of legs. She requested the maid to bring her a café latte. To me, a mark of good breeding is when the moneyed classes use 'please' and 'thank you' when asking a servant to perform a task. As Sophie did.

She was wearing billowing cream bellbottoms and a matching sleeveless top of some clingy material that made no secret of her lack of brassiere, nor her lack of need of support in that area. I also observed that she didn't shave her armpits. A free spirit then, our Madame Sophie. Her near-black glossy hair, shorter than Angela's, complemented her porcelain features, dominated by large, rather sad eyes. As for her lips, she came close to my idea of perfection.

I found myself speculating, uncharitably, which parts of her looks had been under the knife.

'It's very kind of you to come so far to talk to me,' she said, with an elegant crossing of her legs.

If the mountain won't come to Mohamed, was my thought, but I wasn't sure it would translate, so I stayed with plain French. 'It's important.'

'Indeed. From what Don tells me you are making excellent progress, even better than we had hoped, but now you have come up against a minor … impediment.'

'Correct.' I shot a glance at Donovan, to give him room to contribute. He chose not to, so I went on, 'If you're aware that I've made contact with one of the twins, but I don't know which, you'll also be

aware that I need your help to confirm identification.'

An art deco black enamel cigarette box reposed on the table. She opened it, selected from within, and inserted a pink cheroot with a gold filter tip between those luscious lips. Donovan was fast on the draw with a lighter. She smiled her thanks as he put a flame to the cheroot, and he basked, no, wallowed in it.

'Don, will you leave us now, please?' she said. She framed it as a request, but her tone implied refusal wasn't on the cards.

Donovan frowned, made as if to protest, then seemed to accept the futility of it.

'Very well. If you're sure.'

'I am sure.'

He used his hands on his knees to thrust himself up and out of the chair. He threw me a curt nod and left the balcony. That was the last I saw of him that day.

Sophie came to sit in the chair he had vacated, which was closer to mine. An intimation of her perfume teased my olfactories.

'It is my understanding that you wish me to help you ensure you kill Vincent and not Victor. From my point of view, I do not care if you kill them both. I understand your reluctance –'

'Refusal,' I corrected.

She regarded me neutrally. 'Refusal then. But as I was about to say, I had another reason for acceding to your request that has nothing to do with your employment.'

'Oh?' I leaned forward and waited for her to unveil the other reason. 'Something you want to keep from Donovan, I take it.'

'Sometimes it is best that we do not wash our dirty linen in public. Don is an old and trusted friend … in fact, once, when we were young, we were lovers. He, not Vincent, is the father of my second son.'

If this wasn't washing dirty linen in public, nothing was. Then again, she might not consider me as public.

'Are your kids not here?'

'No,' she said, shaking her head. 'They are at my house in Grenoble. They never come here.'

'Now look, Sophie, I don't know why you're confiding all this

personal stuff in me. None of it is relevant to what you hired me for and why I'm here.'

After a last elegant drag at her pink cheroot, she stubbed it out in an ash tray, art deco to match the case and the table lighter.

'You are right, Jack … you don't mind if I call you Jack?'

'Be my guest.'

'As I say, you are right, but I felt you should know about Don and why he acts for me in matters such as …' Her smile was bright, her teeth too white and even not to have been cosmetically enhanced, 'hiring a professional killer.'

The line of talk was making me uncomfortable. I didn't care to air my dirty linen either, in public or in private.

'Explain to me again,' she said, 'what you expect from me if you bring Vincent or Victor here to Monaco.'

Glad to get back to the purpose of my visit, I spelled out my plan to abduct the man I believed was Victor Wolff and bring him here for her to confirm that he was in fact Victor. Afterwards, he could be held someplace or marked, leaving me with the job of finding the other Wolff who, by this simple process of elimination, had to be Vincent. Once I established Vincent's identity beyond all doubt, I would complete the job and collect my wages. Game over.

'I see.' She lit another cheroot with no help from me, as I had no ignition. A trickle of smoke circled upwards, was caught in a breath of wind from off the sea and whisked away.

I waited. Let her come to terms with my request, which she did, staring out over the rooftops, blinking a little faster than usual.

'*Très bien,*' she announced at length. 'If there is no alternative, it shall be as you wish. How will you transport him with so many borders to cross?'

'By air. Only one border – when we land.'

'A private aircraft, I assume.'

'Correct.' Rocky and I had already settled the transportation issue. Rocky had a friend in Germany with an air taxi business. Not fussy about who or what he carried on his plane. Just expensive, as with all illegal enterprise.

'Very resourceful of you. But it may not be as straightforward as you suppose. What if it is Vincent you bring, what will you do then?'

My shrug was exaggerated.

'What you are paying me to do. When you've actually paid me, that is.'

She looked indignant. 'You will be paid, on that you may rely. Just make sure there is no connection with me. Give me time to place myself as far away as possible when you …' She was breathing fast, her face flushed. 'When you do it.'

'When I kill him, you mean.'

'Yes!' She clutched at my bare arm. 'Yes! When you *kill* him.'

She made an effort to bring herself back under control. Mashed her cheroot into the ash tray to keep the other stub company. Cleared her throat and went back to being businesslike.

'Now that I am clear what will happen,' she said, fiddling with the strand of hair that swooped around her left jawline, like a comma. 'I must tell you the second reason I agreed to see you. It is very simple – to explain, at any rate. Perhaps less simple to … ah, implement. Or understand. You see, Jack, I want very much to get to know you better.'

'Get to know me better?' I echoed, letting it percolate, trying to work out if I was pleased or appalled.

'That is right. Are you surprised?'

Was I? Yes and no. Some of the signals had been there from the start. I hadn't taken them seriously.

'I'm flattered,' I temporised. 'I would have thought here in Monaco men you would like to know better are as numerous as fleas in a dog house.'

Her forehead wrinkled. 'Dog house …?'

'It's a poor simile, and it translates badly. Forget it. What I'm trying to say is I can't see what makes me so special.'

'The experts call it chemistry, I believe. You set off a spark in me when I met you in Spain, and I want to see if a little stimulation will make it burst into flame.'

Some would say I was a lucky man. Here before me, mine for the plucking, was money and beauty in a single package. An irresistible combo to most males of my acquaintance.

'You're a very desirable woman, Sophie –'

'And a very choosy one,' she snapped, a hint of anger. 'I am not, as some of my contemporaries are, interested in a bit of rough.' The term she used was '*un paysan débraillé*'.

Then her graceful, composed side reasserted itself, and she treated me to a smile that had sin written all over it. On her own admission she had agreed to this meeting, not only to explore the prospect of my bringing Victor or Vincent for her to identify – she could have given her blessing over the phone – but as a *stud.*

It was so outrageous it wrenched a splutter of laughter from deep in my gut.

'What is it?' she demanded, eyes flashing. 'Am I amusing you?'

'Not at all. I just …' I groped for sentiments that wouldn't cause offence. 'I just find it hard to accept you would need to entice me into travelling to Monaco when you live in a town packed with good-looking guys who don't kill people for a living.'

'You think I am interested in you for your *looks*?' she flared, then returned almost at once to calm and controlled. Her mercurial temperament caused her to seesaw between extremes of behaviour, as if at the flick of a switch. 'It is true that if you had not been physically attractive, I would not have taken matters further. No, this is not about your handsome face, my friend. It is your special talents that fascinate me. I meet many attractive men, but until today I have not met one who earns his living doing as you do.'

Then it clicked. She had given me the clue to what made me stand out from the herd. It was the job that I did, the job she had hired me to do. Sophie Marais was gagging to get laid by a *killer.*

Chapter Thirteen

Sophie and I lunched together on the terrace of her favourite eating place, La Marée, renowned "Fish and Chic" restaurant on Avenue J F Kennedy. The waiting staff were all correctly attired in black and white, and soft music issued from a speaker over the entrance – Debussy, was my guess, but the name of the piece escaped me. The outlook was of the port and a billion dollars' worth of boatware.

Over our limoncello *aperitifs* I learned a bit about Sophie, notably that she was noble by birth, daughter of a Marquis.

'No, not de Sade,' she said sourly, when I made a crack about the progenitor of sadism. 'My father is the Marquis de la Tour Gondrin. Ninety-one years old and the acme of respectability.' A saucy grin transformed her rather doll-like features. 'Not at all like me.'

Her first husband had also been noble. 'An arranged marriage, to which, to my everlasting regret, I acceded. When he died in a road accident, I celebrated by getting drunk and going to the beach with another man.'

'You went to the beach?'

Her nod was accompanied by a wistful smile.

'To make love. I prefer lovemaking *al fresco*.' The smile vanished as she went on, 'Then I met Vincent. A charming man. He swept me off my feet. And so randy. At times he was almost too much for me.' She laid a cool hand on my forearm. 'I said almost. No man has ever been too much.'

That much I had already deduced on my own.

When she had used up most of her past, she insisted on delving into most of mine. In particular, as foreseen, she was desperate to hear what it was like to kill a stranger. Someone you didn't know, who had never done you harm.

It wasn't a subject I cared to air with her or anybody in a public place. We were on a terrace amid other diners and waiting staff, and she was asking me to go into detail about murders I had committed.

I lowered my voice. 'They have to be bad people, like Vincent. Guilty of major crimes against humanity or society. I don't kill a person because someone is willing to pay me a half million dollars.'

Her hand was still on my arm, only now she was squeezing it, her face flushed and animated.

'How do you do it? How will you kill Vincent?'

'Keep your voice down!' I warned.

'Oh!' Chastened, she drew back. 'I am sorry. I am not very discreet.'

Her earlier hit on me had already led me to that conclusion too.

'The answer to your last question is that I haven't decided. There are three stages to this job, and I'm still in the throes of stage one – finding him.' I picked at my salad, scoffed the last asparagus spear. 'The second stage is to confirm his ID, which is where you come in. Only then, when all doubt's been removed, will I finish the job.'

'*Le terminateur*,' she said, tittering into her cupped palm.

My sunglasses allowed me to contemplate her with discretion, especially the nipples that her flimsy top was designed to promote. Behind her dark lenses she might well have been observing me observing her; a knowing smile was tweaking the corners of her mouth.

'I'm curious to know how you will be sure it's the right twin or the wrong twin,' I said.

'By the tone his voice.'

'The tone of his *voice*?' That twins might enunciate differently would never have dawned on me. Plus, it would be easy to disguise.

'How else?'

'Mannerisms?' I hazarded.

'Yes, he has mannerisms that are peculiar to him, as do we all. But just think about that, Jack. If you bring me Victor, he will not try to impersonate Vincent, because he knows I wish to see Vincent dead. To fool me into thinking he is Vincent would be to sign his own death warrant.' An aristocratic eyebrow curved my way. 'Do you disagree with my reasoning?'

'Hard to fault it.'

'*D'autre part*, if you bring me Vincent himself, he will try to suppress any mannerism that proves he is Vincent. Such as his habit of tugging his ear lobe when he is thinking, or cracking his knuckles when he is angry. It may not be easy to hide these traits, but not impossible either. Therefore I cannot depend on the little quirks of Vincent to prove conclusively that he is my ex-husband.'

'So what was so special about Vincent's voice?'

'Nothing is special about it. But the timbre differs from that of Victor. It is only slight, but we were married for five years and we were lovers two years before we married, so I think I am qualified to judge. Also Vincent speaks French badly, despite living with me for these years. He was too lazy to learn it, and insisted we speak English together, whereas Victor was always interested in languages, and has fluent French, Spanish, and some Italian, I believe. I can think of ways to test his knowledge should it be necessary. Victor could pretend to speak French badly, but Vincent will be unable to pretend to speak or understand it well.'

It seemed to me a questionable method of ID-ing a prospective murder victim, but for the purpose of satisfying my code of conscience I had to assume she would get it right, otherwise her revenge would be meaningless.

'If you're confident, I guess I have to accept that.'

Or at least to reserve judgment.

Our conversation was put on hold while we placed our orders for food. The waiter recommended the *sole meunière*, and we both went for it – pan fried for me, grilled for Sophie, skipping the starter. As our waiter floated off, the wine waiter popped up, and greeted Sophie with oodles of deference.

'*Madame la marquise*,' accompanied by a stiff bow. I wasn't sure the daughter of a marquis was entitled to the title, but she didn't correct the waiter, so I guessed she wasn't averse to it.

'You choose,' she said to me, then added, 'If you know your wines, that is.'

'Some.'

From an extensive list of exclusively French wines, I settled for a 2015 Côtes du Rhône – Guigal Hermitage. Sophie endorsed my choice with a nod.

'*Avec une grande bouteille de Vittel*,' she stated.

The waiter bowed again. '*Avec plaisir, Madame la marquise.*'

I gazed down on the port, noting *Seamist's* old berth. A motor cruiser occupied it now, bigger and brasher and more polluting. It revived memories of four years ago, and Gina, and Jean-Pierre and his son, all dead now. I batted the images away.

'I used to keep my yacht here,' I said.

'You have a boat?' She wasn't impressed, just curious.

'Only a forty-footer. You too?'

She nodded. '*Effectivement.* I am not sure how much a forty-footer is in metres, but I believe mine is more like forty metres.'

'If you're so stinking rich, why break the law to take revenge on Vincent Wolff? Not to mention spending a million or more.'

She removed her sunglasses, nibbled at the curved end of an arm. Her eyes, deep and dark, scanned the seascape.

'It is not just a matter of money.'

A veil of sadness had descended over her face, like a dark cloud over a clear sky. Until now she had appeared and behaved as a hard-nosed, over-sexed, over-rich bitch. The kind of woman you avoid making an enemy of. Now glimmers of humanity were cracking the shell.

'You are entitled to know the answer, I suppose,' resignedly. 'If you are prepared to take risks to carry out my wishes, it is only right that you should know why.'

I didn't encourage her, just let her decide how and when to take me into her confidence at her own pace.

'Don is not in the picture,' she ventured at length. 'Good friend as he is, I have never been entirely confident in his ability to keep his mouth shut.'

'Keeping secrets is second nature to me.'

'So I imagine,' she said, her tone sardonic.

Inside her, conflict appeared to be raging. She was going to let me in on it, but the side of her that was not hard-nosed etc. was unsure.

'*Alors*, the reason Vincent must die, is not because he stole a great deal of money from me – which he did – but because …' She swallowed and looked away from me. She took a deep breath; her chin came up and the marquis's daughter that was in her upbringing and maybe her genes, if that were possible, blurted, 'He raped my daughter, Francine, when she was eleven years old.'

'Christ!' I felt for Sophie right away. My brush with the child porn trade a few years ago had roused in me a sensibility about all child abuse so profound that I would eliminate free of charge any person guilty of it. I laid a sympathetic hand on hers and murmured what I hoped were appropriate sentiments.

Leaving her hand under mine, she stared at me.

'You are a strange kind of assassin. Not that I am familiar with the breed, you understand, but you don't seem to fit the popular stereotype at all.'

'Forget about my strangeness. Where's your daughter now? She wasn't in Spain with you. Those two girls were too young.'

'He abducted her. Now she is dead.' Her voice was without emotion; the rest of her wasn't. 'When she grew older and was no more use to him, he killed her.'

'Do you know this for sure? Or is it hearsay?'

'Victor called me. He was sick about it and swore he had finished with Vincent for good.'

'When was this?'

'Not so long ago. It was because of this news that I instructed Donovan to find someone like you. Killing Vincent is a matter of family honour, apart from my personal desire to see him dead.'

Bad for her, not so bad for me. It provided grounds for the hit far more solid than money laundering and gun running. It satisfied my personal code.

'What about your daughter's … you know, remains?'

'Victor said they'd cremated her. He sent me the ashes.'

'So in your book, Victor's a stand-up guy.'

She snorted. 'No, not at all. Victor is a crook. But Vincent …' She shuddered, her eyes distant and narrowed as if she were re-living an

unpleasant incident. 'Vincent *est mal absolu.*'

Mal absolu. Pure evil.

* * * * *

In the afternoon we swam together for half an hour in the basement pool, then walked along the Promenade du Larvotto to her yacht. She presented me to the skipper, a husky, sunbrowned Englishman called Ronnie Drake.

'Like Sir Francis,' he cracked as we shook hands.

With no real justification, I wondered if skippering Sophie's yacht might not be his only duty.

He gave us a guided tour, though Sophie would have been acquainted with the boat's geography without his help, apart perhaps from the impressive engine room with its twin gas turbine engines. Drake boasted that they could propel the craft through the water at thirty knots.

At about six, Sophie and I took tea back in the apartment, very English.

'I thought the English half of you would appreciate it,' she said, as we sat side by side, knee by knee, on the inside curve of an S-shaped couch.

Then Angela called. I excused myself and transferred to the balcony to talk to her. She loved me, was her opening line. She missed me, the sequel.

I dispensed suitable hokum.

'How's your migraine?'

'Completely gone. It went last night. When are you coming back, darling?'

The 'darling' was new. Some women use the endearment lightly. I didn't know Angela well enough to say if it was window dressing or heartfelt.

'I'll be flying out of Nice at about ten tonight.'

'I'll meet you.'

'Great, thanks.'

More loving sentiments from her end of the line, more ambivalence

from mine. Back on the couch, Sophie had another surprise for me.

'I've decided not to insist you stay overnight,' she said. The decision appeared to have made her unhappy. It showed in the downturned mouth that drew unflattering lines from the corners to the jaw. Thin as a hair therefore scarcely noticeable and surely destined to receive attention from her plastic surgeon in the near future.

'That's too bad.' Relief eclipsed regret by a large measure. How would I have explained it to Angela?

'You want to know why?'

'I'm intrigued.'

She laid a hand on my arm, just below the elbow, massaging the pad of flesh there with her thumb.

'Because I am no longer prepared to settle for a one-night stand with you.' The hard-nosed Sophie was in limbo; she was studying my face with an intensity that was disturbing. 'A big part of me wishes to keep you here, yet you must finish the job you have started. You must kill Vincent. Only then can I put Francine to rest in my mind and concentrate on … other matters. You understand?'

'I guess so.'

'If you stayed tonight, I would not be able to let you go, I am sure of it. I know myself and already I feel I know you. My feelings for you are more than just the need to have sex with you.'

This foretold complications. I already had two women playing volcanic parts in my life – Maura (inactive) and Angela (all too active). A third, especially as exotic as this one, I could do without.

'So when you have completed your task, I wish you to come back here and stay.' Her eyes searched mine, hoping to find what I couldn't tell. The truth, most likely. 'At least for a while.'

Best to placate her, I felt, if I wanted to leave with my good conduct badge untarnished.

'It'll be no hardship.' I leaned towards her and brushed her lips with mine.

The door buzzer cut through our tender little interlude.

'That will be Don, I suppose,' she said, irritation in her voice. 'Come to drive you to Nice.'

It was Donovan all right. The maid brought him through to the living room. He wavered on the threshold, as if afraid his intrusion would incur Sophie's wrath.

'Hello, Don,' she said, without looking at him.

'Hello, Sophie, Jack.'

She retreated a step. Her hand came off my arm, and she extended it, fingers spread. I clasped it in mine.

'Goodbye, Jack. I will wait for your news.'

'Goodbye, Sophie. It's been an experience to remember.' *Une expérience mémorable* was how I expressed it in French. It might even have been an understatement.

* * * * *

As we entered the approach road to Nice Airport, my cell summoned me again. It was Rocky. Victor-Vincent was in residence at the walled house, he informed me. He advised moving fast as any delay might mean missing him. It was a valid point, but we were ill-armed for confronting this gang, and hadn't even thrashed out our tactics, which must include a back-up plan in case of failure. Also, we had yet to organise transportation of our captive.

'What about the plane?' I asked.

'Ah, yes. He cannot fly before tomorrow afternoon.'

'I want to meet him before we agree to use him. So that rules out snatching Victor tonight.'

Rocky grunted his agreement. 'Is better anyway. We need bigger guns.'

'You're right, but don't worry, I've got some.'

My hunch about hanging on to the shotguns was about to pay off.

* * * * *

The welcome home from Angela involved a surfeit of kissing, which led to the usual physical interaction. She insisted on being in charge, which translated as being on top. As I was suffering from travel fatigue it suited

me to be her plaything. She bumped up and down with great enthusiasm and brought us to a mutually happy ending.

'I hated spending a night without you,' she confessed in the aftermath. 'Did you miss me at all?'

'Like I'd miss my right hand if it fell off.'

She went up on her elbow and stared down at me.

'What a peculiar way of putting it.'

'All right then, honey, like I was all on my ownsome and wished you were there.'

She sighed and insinuated herself into my embrace.

'That's better.' Her hand was wandering, but I wasn't ready for it. 'I love you.'

I wished she'd cut down on the declarations of love. Whenever she said it, there was an unspoken invitation to return the compliment. Since all my love was reserved for Maura, falling in love with Angela was not on the horizon.

She dropped off to sleep, her hip and leg in contact with mine, and I was free to address the logistics of abducting Victor Wolff. Our equipment needs would include flashlights, a grapnel to scale the wall, tape to immobilise and gag Victor and others, and enough weaponry and ammunition in case we got into a shooting war. It was familiar territory. Pitfalls galore, sure, but wasn't that always the case? Surprise, speed, and firepower would see us through. Tomorrow I would fine tune the whole deal with Rocky.

I relaxed. Sleep came and held me in its embrace. I dreamed, as was so often the case, that Maura and I were together again, in Andorra, with her daughter Belinda clinging to my hand and demolishing my attempts at humour with her own childish logic. It was all so intense I woke up convinced I really was back with Maura. Reality set in soon enough and left me dispirited and wishing I were someplace else.

Then Angela woke up and brought me back to the present day. The emptiness of my life without Maura stayed with me though, the whole morning and beyond, until Rocky came to collect me for our rendezvous with the pilot. Angela expected to accompany us, but I fobbed her off.

'This is business. You and I are personal.'

'I'll remember that next time you want my help in a shootout.'

I winced, but just the same left her standing at the hotel entrance, hands on hips.

On the highway to the airfield Rocky and I talked over our forthcoming invasion of Victor Wolff's privacy.

'Have you gotten a plan for tonight?' I asked.

'Easy. We go over the wall, go in shooting.'

He was a simple soul.

'This isn't a Wild West movie we're making, my friend. We go in, but not shooting. We shoot only if we get shot at.'

'Chill, Jack. It will be fun.' He guffawed and smacked the steering wheel with the palm of his hand. The SUV swerved almost into the path of an oncoming tanker.

'Watch the road,' I barked as the tanker shot past, horn blaring, with half an arm's length to spare. 'If we have a pile-up, the police will be all over us.'

The airfield was about thirty kms to the west of Budapest. We parked before a row of buildings with hangars attached. It had a rundown air, though there were plenty of light aircraft scattered about the weed-infested apron. Rocky presented me to our pilot, who was German.

'This is Walter. Like the pistol.'

No last name provided, none requested. He was tall with cropped brown hair and a beard, and a trim physique. His English was more than passable.

'So you have merchandise for delivery to Nice,' he said, lighting a cigarette with a Zippo lighter.

'Live merchandise,' I emphasised.

'Yes, I know. Transporting people can be tricky.'

I glanced at Rocky, wondering how much he had told Walter.

'How tricky depends on the pay, right?' Rocky said.

'If the pay is good, the risks are lower,' Walter murmured.

I wasn't clear on how he made that calculation, I just figured it was all about hyping up the price.

'Ten thousand US dollars,' I proposed, to cut down on the haggling.

He accepted, as I expected.

'In cash.'

I nodded. 'I'll need a little time to get it from the bank. It'll be tomorrow or the day after.'

He ejected smoke down his nostrils. 'But Rocky says you must leave in tonight, before dawn.'

'Correct.'

'Normally it is cash on delivery. Even so, Rocky's word is good enough for me.'

A single-engine plane with high wings was taxi-ing towards us, seeking a space to park. We moved aside, the wind from its whirling prop rearranging our hair and clothing. Behind us was a racy-looking aircraft with a four-bladed airscrew, which proved to be Walter's. He introduced it to us.

'It's a Piper M500. Made in the USA. Seats for six, or four if there is some cargo – alive or dead.' He chuckled at his own brand of humour. 'Will the cargo sit in a seat or lie on the floor?'

'Does it matter?' Rocky asked.

'Yes. If on the floor, I need to remove the two rear seats.'

'Remove them anyway,' I suggested. 'For ten thousand you should be prepared to do a little manual work.'

He seemed amused by the idea.

'Okay by me.'

Rocky and I departed to prepare for our housebreaking operation.

* * * * *

I phoned Donovan and told him I needed ten grand by tomorrow afternoon. Not unreasonably, he asked why. I told him. He hummed and hawed then agreed, provided I deducted it from my final fee. He was assuming I would earn it. I was less sanguine.

The money would be forwarded to the K & H Bank on a street whose name he had to spell out for me.

'N-y-u-g-a-t-i. Then separate word t-e-r. It means street or

something. Number nine.'

'Make sure it's there the day after tomorrow.'

I cut off his retort.

* * * * *

It was after midnight and the house was in darkness. Street lights illuminated the gates and the asphalt area in front of them, and the guard was no doubt on duty in his gatehouse. It didn't matter to us; we weren't going in via the gateway. The street, being a cul-de-sac, was quiet and the windows of the houses across the road were like empty eye sockets except for a dim light in an attic.

We parked Rocky's SUV at the right-hand corner of the lot. We were both dressed in black: jeans, sweater, and leather windbreaker in my case. Both of us wore Beanie caps to hide our blond locks. The wall was about three hundred feet along the front and back, a bit shorter on the sides. An estimated eight feet high for its entire length.

We positioned ourselves at the right front corner. Rocky had padded the grapnel's flukes with rolls of foam. He slung it over the razor wire that straggled along the top of the wall, and it caught first throw – on a tree most likely. Google Earth had showed a grouping of trees in each of the four corners inside the walls, and along the driveway.

'After you,' Rocky said, with a grandiose gesture.

'You're so kind.'

I had been planning to go first anyway. The Mossberg shotguns I had brought from my conference with the Wolffs were not equipped with shoulder straps, but I had fashioned some from lengths of cord to keep our hands free. With my gun – cocked, safety set – slung diagonally over my shoulder, I shinned up the knotted rope to the top. Rocky threw me a rubber mat to spread over the razor wire. Straddling the mat, I paused to look and listen. A car buzzed past on the main road with a motor bike in its wake. Across the city a siren hee-hawed, too distant to cause worry.

'You okay?' Rocky called, his voice hushed. He was keeping the front and one side of the wall under observation.

'All good,' I replied.

The grapnel had attached itself to the nearest tree, about six feet above ground. I swung from it and let myself drop on the patchy grass below. The earth was hard, but I landed lightly enough. I tugged the rope and seconds later heard Rocky's grunts and gasps as he shinned up the rope. He was a bulky, heavy guy so it couldn't have been a cakewalk for him.

Over the mat he came. He dangled from the rope and let himself drop. He landed hard on his backside, expelled a belch of pain. But he was on his feet fast enough, to join me by the tree.

The quarter moon provided just enough light to guide us through the trees to a lawn, beyond which we could make out the driveway and the gatehouse, with its lit interior. A man was sitting at a table, facing away from us, and poring over a newspaper held up in front of him.

'He's bound to be armed,' I said.

'So we take him first,' Rocky said, slipping his shotgun off his shoulder.

We crept forward, placing our feet with care. The guy in the gatehouse remained oblivious of trespassers. He turned a page in the newspaper, scratched his head leaving a tuft standing up on his crown. I unslung my Mossberg, thumbed the safety to "Fire". I could feel Rocky's breath on the back of my neck.

The plan was for me to confront the guard, and for Rocky to stay out of sight and cover me in case some unknown third party intervened. He went into a crouch beside the brick lower half of the gatehouse, while I moved forward to the door.

When I opened it, the guard didn't even take his eyes off the Hungarian news. Total complacency.

'Hello,' I said softly.

The English greeting froze him. His head swung away from the newspaper and focused on me. Then on the gun whose muzzle he was staring down.

'Speak English?' I asked.

He just looked blank, continued to hold the paper in front of him. Maybe it was bulletproof. In a corner was a TV screen, depicting the gate from outside the walls. As surveillance devices go, it was basic kit.

I semaphored the guard to junk the paper and stand up. He obliged. I twirled a finger to turn him around. He obliged again. He was an obliging guy.

Rocky entered, a roll of duct tape in his hand. He trussed the guy up: mouth first, to silence him, then wrists, knees, and ankles in that order. Then he gave him an almighty shove. The gatehouse didn't measure above five feet square so the guy didn't have to travel far before hitting the wall. He expelled a grunt as he bounced backwards and hit the floor at our feet. He lay there groaning behind his gag, eyes open and glaring.

Rocky dealt him a kick in the ribs that extinguished the glare. We took our leave, headed up the short driveway to the house itself. The front entrance was a double door with stained glass side panels, accessed by a semicircle of three steps, at each extremity a lamp in late nineteenth century style. Although we had neither seen nor heard evidence of a canine patrol, I hadn't forgotten my experience at the house on Balaton. If we were attacked, I would take care of it with the silenced SIG, slung under my left armpit.

Rather than work our way around to the back of the building, increasing the chances of discovery, we would use the visitor's entrance. Noise was inevitable, whatever method we used to break in. Speed and surprise were the keys to success. Once inside, we would head upstairs without checking out the ground floor. The place was in darkness so it was reasonable to assume everyone was in bed.

My flashlight was a heavy-duty, rubber-sheathed job, built for smashing windows and heads. I used it on the glass panel to the left; the noise was less than I feared. Then we were in. So far so hitch-free it made me nervous. I began to suspect we'd been sucked into a trap, that we were expected, and Victor's mob had eased our path on purpose. But no, the hall was empty of life, unless you count still life. The paintings on the dark green-painted walls were mostly impressionist art. I spotted Monet's Water Lily Pond, bound to be a copy or a print.

We mounted the stairs, which were tiled, eliminating giveaway creaks. I made sure the Mossberg's safety was off. In situations like this, a fraction of a second gained can make the difference between firing first and taking a bullet.

At the head of the stairs a mezzanine with a scatter of armchairs and some bookshelves. Carpet underfoot, cream coloured and expensive. I counted seven doors leading off, three ajar, the rest closed. By tacit consent we each tried an ajar door first. My flashlight fell on an empty bed. Rocky backed out of his, shaking his head. The third ajar door led to a bathroom. I pointed Rocky towards a closed door and selected another for myself.

Door handle mechanisms are never soundless, so no use bothering to be discreet. Open the door fast and rush in was the approved method. I did just that, only to be find myself in another unoccupied bedroom, feeling foolish. It was Rocky who struck gold. I heard him yell 'Not move!' A pause then, 'Who the *fuck* are you?' from the startled occupant.

Rocky didn't need assistance from me. The commotion was sure to have awakened any other sleepers, so I tackled the next closed door. My flashlight picked out a man and a woman in separate beds, the man in the act of throwing off his bedclothes. He was naked, with all the attendant psychological disadvantages. With Rocky fully occupied, and another bedroom yet to inspect, I couldn't afford to be picky. I let him have it in the foot. The gun was loaded with birdshot so it barely slowed him; it took a second cartridge-load in the other foot, to bring him to his knees, cursing in Hungarian. By then the last of the closed doors was swinging open and my old adversary, Large, confronted me. He was also toting a shotgun, but awkwardly, his left arm being in a sling. He was a split second ahead of me and blasted off without taking aim even as I dived for the floor. The spreadshot gouged out a section of door jamb where I had been standing. As he clumsily worked the slide to shunt another cartridge into the breech, I gave it to him in the feet.

He dropped to his knees, hurt but not badly enough to prevent him from loosing off another round, and I felt the peripheral spread of shot tug at my windbreaker. My next round caught him in the groin. His howl was heart-warming. The gun slipped from his grasp and he crumpled to the floor, squirting blood over the expensive cream carpet. I hopped across the space between our two doors and scooped up his gun. He was writhing and whimpering and definitely *hors de combat.*

'Jack!' came Rocky's yell.

Before responding to his summons, I collected the shotguns from the disabled goons. The first guy was using a sheet to wrap his injured feet. I shut the door on him. Large was out of it for tonight and lots of other tonights.

I darted across to the other bedroom, now hauling three shotguns, all Mossbergs.

Rocky had hit the jackpot. On the right side of a king-size bed, his face a mixture of fear and fury, a white-faced Victor strove to sit up and hold onto his dignity. Not easy in pyjamas. If it was Vincent, not Victor, even better. Either twin would suit my purpose, so it was a happy outcome to the evening's work. On the left was Sara, her hair in fat rollers. Her face was a mask of rage; she looked ready to savage us.

'You'll be sorry for this,' she snarled, and Victor seconded her threat with an uncertain nod.

'You'll be sorrier if you don't shut up,' I said.

Her mouth clamped shut, and she retreated into to a silent simmer. While I kept the pair covered with my three guns, Rocky checked inside their night tables for smaller weaponry, striking lucky in Victor's. He pocketed the automatic he found there. Since taking on this contract, I had collected enough illicit hardware to cover my fee.

'What now?' Rocky asked me.

'See to the two I shot. There's a woman too, and if she's anything like this one, she'll be more dangerous than the guys. Tape up the guy with the sore feet and his girlfriend. The other guy won't need it.'

He went off, whistling. A good man to have around in a dust-up.

'Where do you get off busting in here?' Victor fumed. 'You're not here to do an arms deal, that's for sure.'

'You finally worked that out,' I said. 'Are you still Victor or have you become Vincent since I last saw you?'

'I'm Victor, goddammit! I told you, Vincent's not in Budapest.'

'What you tell me and what I believe are chalk and cheese.'

'Fuck you then.' Some of his colour had returned. He had reasoned that I wasn't here to kill him, or else I would have done it by now. I didn't toy with my victims the way a cat toys with a mouse. Deliver the message, do the deed, and depart the scene, had ever been my agenda.

'Get dressed,' I ordered, 'unless you want to go in your nightwear.'

Sara Wolff swung her legs over the edge of the bed. 'He's not going anywhere.'

She was wearing a red T-shirt and red night shorts, very chi-chi.

'He can go or stay, as he pleases. But if he stays, it'll be as a corpse.'

She was on her feet now, full of spirit, and looking for trouble.

'You daren't kill him. You need him alive, don't pretend different.'

I aimed the Mossberg at Victor. 'Alive, yes, but not necessarily intact. Would he mean as much to you castrated?'

'You talk tough,' Sara Wolff sneered. 'One of these days we'll catch you without your bodyguard.'

'You're at the wrong end of a gun to be making threats.'

Victor kept his peace. His wife was doing enough talking for both of them.

'You said yourself you're after Vincent,' Sara Wolff said, 'so why don't you just butt out and go after him?'

I treated her to a head-on view down the barrel of one of my shotguns.

'Sit down, Sara.'

She made an unladylike gesture but sat anyway, grabbing her glasses off the night table the better to focus on me. Defiant to the last.

'It doesn't matter to me whether this guy is Victor or Vincent. He's going on a little jaunt to meet someone. If he's Victor, he'll be back, eventually. Possibly in one piece. If he's Vincent …'

I left Vincent's fate up in the air, which is where it would remain until I found him.

'Well, he *is* Victor, so what's the point in taking him anywhere.'

At that stage in the talkfest Rocky strolled in, shotgun at slope arms.

'All fixed,' he announced beaming with self-congratulation. 'Hope we not need much more tape. That guy you shot in the bollocks need medical help.'

'He'll get it when we've gone.' I smiled at Sara Wolff. 'To answer your question, Mrs Wolff, it's a matter of identification. You say he's Victor, but then if he were Vincent, and on tonight's evidence sharing your bed, you'd say whatever it took to keep us from knowing he's Vincent, wouldn't you?'

Unable to dispute the logic, she folded her arms and looked surly.

'Which one do you *really* want? Do you want my Victor, but have to be sure he *is* Victor, or do you want Vincent, and have to be sure about him?'

'If this isn't Vincent, and you know his whereabouts, it might save time if you come clean.'

'But we don't know,' Victor protested.

'What you do know is, we mean business. That's why you've got two more wounded mutts out there. You can fuck with me all you like, but it's not going to change the end result.'

'We don't know where he is,' Victor repeated. He almost convinced me.

'Are there any physical differences between you?'

'No' from Victor, 'Yes' from his wife.

'Vincent snores,' Sara Wolff added, 'according to his latest girlfriend. Victor doesn't.'

Even if snoring or not snoring was a reliable means of figuring who was who, Sara Wolff might be lying. Maybe neither twin snored, or both. It was impossible to be sure they weren't just protecting Vincent, or protecting Victor, or just having a bloody big laugh at my expense.

Then Sara Wolff made an accusation that busted wide open my arms dealer subterfuge.

'Sophie Marais is behind all this, isn't she?'

'Who?' Even to my own ears it didn't sound convincing. They exchanged glances and fell quiet.

'Let's tape 'em up, Rocky,' I said. 'Leave his legs free, he needs to be mobile.'

Rocky moved into the centre of the room. 'Not much tape left.'

'Use it on him. We'll find some rope for her.'

Only 'her' wasn't about to submit meekly. She bounced off the bed, flung herself at me in a biting, spitting ball of red night attire. It's funny, but fending off a determined woman is often a tougher call than dealing with a guy. Their fighting technique is dirtier, and they have longer nails which they put to damaging use. Plus, the natural male tendency is to pull punches when hitting a female.

Her claws raked my cheek, just missing my eye, and her knee sought my groin but her aim was off. I pushed her away, hard enough to make her stumble. She recovered, came back at me as feisty as ever. Rocky, goddam him, was laughing when he should have been helping.

Knuckles landed on my jaw and I stumbled. I let go the shotgun and hauled off at her. I targeted her head but missed and connected with her shoulder. This time she went down, hitting the wooden floor with a crash that shook the house. Her glasses shot off her face. She proved she didn't need them for routine punch-ups by getting back on her feet, fast as a bouncing ball. Out of the corner of my eye I saw Victor on the move, coming to her aid; I heard Rocky's yelled, 'Stay put!' Then I was back in the toils with the human spitfire. Punch, gouge, kick. Enough was enough. I stiffened my hand even as I ducked her latest swing and chopped her in the throat with the edge. I put a lot of steam behind it and toppled her for good. She sprawled on the rug, choking, clawing at her throat, her legs flailing as she gasped for breath.

Victor left the bed and hurried to her side, doting husband to the core. He crouched beside her, making helpless motions, incapable of relieving her distress. I could have told him he couldn't help. She'd get over it in a few minutes and if we stuck around no doubt she'd soon be back on the offensive.

'Tie her up, for God's sake,' I snapped at Rocky. Blood was running down my cheek where she had used her nails. That, I could live with. What really bugged me, far more than my superficial hurts, was hitting a woman.

Rocky used what was left of the duct tape to secure Victor's wrists and gag him, then went off in search of materials to immobilise Sara Wolff, who was still spluttering and coughing on the rug.

He was back soon enough, with a ball of string and a pack of Band-Aid for me. Sara Wolff was recovering by now, but offered no resistance when Rocky tied her wrists and ankles, using most of the ball while I applied a patch to my scratched cheek. When he was done, he carried her to the bed and dumped her there.

'We go now,' he said to Victor, who glared but remained speechless, thanks to the tape over his mouth.

'Say goodbye to Victor, Sara,' I said.

Unless a mouthful of expletives counted as a fond farewell, she let the opportunity pass. We trooped out, me in the lead, Victor in the middle. I checked on Large, who was supine but conscious, breathing hard through his mouth. A puddle of blood had leaked from his lower body and spread tendrils over the tiles, already congealing.

Objective accomplished. It had been an untidy job. Could have been worse though if, for instance, the bodyguards had been in greater numbers and more competent.

Victor wasn't happy and made a lot of fuss behind his gag. He was also as obstructive as his bonds would permit, dragging his heels and generally being a nuisance. Rocky lost patience with him. He handed me his gun, and tucked Victor under an arm and transported him outside like a bundle of dirty washing.

The gatehouse keeper was much as we left him. A single green button operated the gate, on a control panel that included switches for the CCTV, lights, and other gadgetry. I thumbed the button for Rocky, and the gates slid open. He proceeded with caution, still hauling a squirming Victor, but the street was as dead as most suburban streets at one o'clock in the morning. After pressing the red button to close the gates I nipped through the diminishing gap.

From there to the car was less than fifty metres. More lightly laden than Rocky, I made it ahead of him and dumped my cargo of shotguns on the floor behind the front seats. Our reluctant travelling companion fitted into the trunk space with room to spare. Rocky used the roll of tape we had left in the car to secure his ankles and joined them to his wrists and his neck. When he was satisfied our captive was immobilised with no prospect of breaking loose, he extended the flap that screened the contents of the trunk, slammed the lid.

'Good job, eh?' he said, turning to me, chuckling, hand raised, fingers splayed.

We high-fived.

'Bloody good. Now, let's get the hell out of here.'

We got in, Rocky at the wheel, and started out for the airfield.

Chapter Fourteen

A pale band of light over the distant hills preceded the dawn. Above it grey furrowed clouds like a ploughed field, faintly luminous as if from lighting within.

'It's going to be hot,' Walter, our pilot, forecast.

Under cover of darkness Rocky and I had transferred Victor to the Piper while Walter saw no evil. We gave our captive a drink from a bottle of mineral water, which he glugged down like a man with a bottomless thirst. When he had drunk his fill, Rocky replaced the tape over his mouth.

'How you handle him in France?' he asked me.

'We'll be met.'

'It will be daytime,' he pointed out.

I patted him on his high, wide shoulder. 'We'll manage. Help will be available.'

'I can come, if you want me.'

'You're more valuable here. You might pick up Vincent's trail.'

'That is big might.'

Given that our only conduit to Vincent was the uncooperative wife of Victor, he was right about the size of the might.

'Do what you can.'

The only weapon I was carrying was the Boberg, nestling in its ankle holster. Even the SIG was too bulky to conceal and as I wasn't expecting a shoot-out, I had traded maximum hitting power for maximum discretion.

The tip of the sun's disc was just peeking over the hills to the east when Walter peeled us off the runway and set a course west-south-west, or, according to the instrument panel, two hundred and forty-eight degrees.

Our passenger was behaving, so I removed the tape from his mouth as a reward. He cursed both of us until his well of obscenities ran dry, then started over.

'Be silent, Victor,' I admonished, 'or the gag goes back on.'

The flow of bad language dried up, and from then on he confined himself to an occasional muttered curse.

The official forecast was for clear skies, random patches of turbulence, and showers over the Côte d'Azur. Our destination was about ten kms inland from Villefranche-sur-Mer. Walter had brought breakfast for three – bread rolls, croissants and boiled eggs, plus orange juice. Victor's status as kidnappee hadn't hurt his appetite. Living up to his name, he wolfed down his share.

At a few minutes after 11.00am we were coming in to land at what Walter referred to as 'a private airfield.' The touchdown was bumpy but Walter stayed cool and competent throughout.

We taxied up to a shack that looked abandoned.

'Is this the control tower?' I said.

My whimsy was wasted on Walter.

'It is just a hut.'

The engine stopped, the whirling disc of the four-bladed prop became four individual blades. Walter ran through his landing check, the way I had seen Maura do it. He may have been a people smuggler and therefore bent, but he was thorough.

The forecast showers hadn't materialised. Nobody was around so we transferred a grumbling Victor to the shack. We all needed a pee and used a very basic chemical toilet at the back. It meant removing the tape from Victor's wrists; either that or I gave him a guiding hand – literally. I opted for removal.

'Try anything and I'll put a bullet in you,' I said to him as he pissed without restraint into the can. I let him feel the Boberg between his shoulder blades.

'Who owns this field?' I asked Walter as we reassembled inside the cabin.

'A friend,' he said shortly, and I let it go at that. When dealing with lawbreakers, the less you know the safer you are.

I called Donovan and handed my cell to Walter to give directions for the pick up. For the next half hour we mooched around, shutting Victor in the cabin in case he was tempted to make a daring escape. He fretted vocally about his confinement, but there was no one to hear except Walter and me.

The car that showed up was a black limousine with darkened windows. The driver stayed behind the wheel. He was black too, and bald and wearing wrap-around darkened windows. No other distinguishing features, which I guess was what made him useful.

We bundled Victor into the back seat, his arms still bound.

'You'll be sorry about his,' he said to me.

'If you're still alive to make me sorry when it's all over.'

'Don't forget my money,' Walter said, as I hopped in beside Victor.

'You'll get it. I never welsh.'

He stepped away from the limo, raised a laconic hand, and was lost from sight as we took off on a narrow twisty lane with woods to the left and a long incline of dilapidated vineyard on the right.

Almost home and dry. And if Victor was shown to be Vincent, I would have successfully completed the first phase of my contract. All that would remain was for me to kill him.

* * * * *

We drove to Monaco by a circuitous route that left me confused as to the location of the airstrip, which was surely the intention. Before long we were entering the principality, filtering into its principal artery, the Boulevard d'Italie. It evolved presently to become the Boulevard des Moulins, then the Boulevard de Suisse, which bordered the southerly aspect of Sophie's apartment block. We swung into the entrance to the building's basement parking garage, coming to a halt beside an elevator. The place was empty but for parked cars, mostly luxury brands. Our driver unlocked the rear doors by remote control, got out and opened the door on my side. I dragged Victor out with me.

'You're expected,' the driver said in American English, the first words he had uttered in my presence. 'Just walk in, don't buzz.'

'Thanks,' I said.

A goodbye nod from the driver. A very discreet hombre, no wasted dialogue. Big bastard, too.

I stuck the Boberg in Victor's spine and urged him towards the elevator. We rode up to the seventeenth floor, with Victor casting aspersions on my ancestry until I again threatened to restore the gag.

The door of Sophie's apartment stood ajar. Music drifted through the gap. I pushed the door open and pushed Victor after it. He stumbled and glared over his shoulder at me. Without speaking, I reminded him I was still holding a gun.

'Anybody home?' I called out.

A door opened to the side, and a man stepped out: medium build with an air of taste and distinction, enhanced by the excellent cut of his suit and his pompadoured hair.

'Monsieur Devreese?' he said, 'or is it Mynheer?'

'I'm Walloon,' I said.

'*Alors, monsieur*. You are very prompt.'

'Where's Mme Marais?' I said.

'The *marquise* will be here presently. In the meantime …' He extended a manicured hand towards the interior. 'Let us make ourselves comfortable.' He looked sharply at Victor. 'You are Mr Wolff, I presume,' he said in English.

'*Victor* Wolff,' my captive snarled. 'And just who the fuck are you?'

'We will establish in due course whether you are Victor or Vincent. In the meantime, if you must know, I am a lawyer. Or if you prefer the *lingua franca* of your world, a mouthpiece.'

His familiarity with underworld jargon made me smile inwardly.

We moved in a group into the living room with its curved couches and some jade statuettes that hadn't been there on my previous visit. Sophie was getting settled in.

'What do we do with him if Sophie … the *marquise* decides he's Victor?' I asked the lawyer.

'Oh-oh. Straight to business, eh, like a true North American.'

I jumped. Why did he think I was American?'

'I'm not American,' I said, inserting a warning edge into the rebuttal.

'I told you, I'm Belgian Walloon.'

'Of course. No doubt many Walloons speak with a *Quebecois* accent. Please be seated.'

We all sat. The lawyer in an armchair, Victor and I on a couch facing him.

'If you are really Victor, you have nothing to worry about,' the lawyer said in fluent but French-accented English. 'If you try to make problems, we have to assume you are Vincent.'

Victor seemed to get it. If he behaved himself, he was home free. If he didn't, Sophie would infer he was Vincent. He relaxed a shade, leaning back into the cushions and looking pensive.

'Smart boy,' I said. I still kept the gun on my lap.

From where we were sitting, the sea and sky were both blue, with just a scattering of clouds along the horizon. The sliding doors were open, enhancing our enjoyment of the music of the construction industry.

'Do you practice law in Monaco?' I said to the lawyer, to break the tension.

'No,' he said.

'I didn't catch your name.'

He smiled vaguely. 'Call me Pierre.'

Cautious then. If Pierre was his real given name, mine was Vladimir Putin.

He crossed his legs, interlocked his fingers, tapping his thumbs together.

A door opened someplace in the apartment, and I heard footsteps on high heels. *La belle marquise* made her entrance, luscious in a patterned off-the-shoulder top and black flared pants, her near-black hair in a new asymmetric pixie cut.

'Hello, Pierre,' she greeted, 'and hello, Jack.'

Too late to warn her that Victor knew me as Gilles Devreese.

Pierre was treated to a platonic brush of her lips on both cheeks, I full on lips-to-lips. The lawyer didn't seem surprised, unlike Victor who said 'Jesus Christ' under his breath.

In English, Sophie said, 'And last and very much least, hello to you, Vincent.'

I jumped. *Vincent*?

Victor said, 'Fuck you, Sophie. You know I'm not Vincent.'

'Do I?' She smiled archly and seated herself next to Pierre, facing Victor-Vincent. 'How do I know, Vincent?'

'Stop calling me Vincent, you cow! I'm Victor.'

I looked at Sophie, half-expecting a signal to indicate which twin he was. Her attention was all on Victor.

'Is he Vincent?' Pierre asked in his cultured Parisian tones.

Sophie nibbled her lip. 'He could be,' she said at length.

On our previous meeting she had boasted that she could tell them apart. Now she was stonewalling.

'I'm not fucking Vincent, I told you!' Victor, getting rattled, raved.

'Maybe you need to prove it,' I suggested. 'In fact, I would say you definitely need to prove it.'

He slumped back on the couch. 'How can I prove it? We're identical, no birthmarks, no moles, nothing. I do my hair different, but she wouldn't accept that as proof.' He scowled at her. 'Would you, bitch?'

'Not at all.' Then, addressing me, 'The problem is proving he's not Victor. I can't ask him things only Victor would know, because I don't know what they are.'

I could see the difficulty

'You could ask him things only Vincent would know. Like the location of any moles or birthmarks on you.'

'I don't have any such marks. In any case, Victor has often seen me in a bikini, even topless.'

'I thought you said –'

'Never mind what I said,' she cut in, reproving me with her eyebrows. Then it clicked. She was waiting for Victor (or Vincent) to give himself away in his speech. How had she put it? The timbre of his voice, little nuances, his fluency or lack of it in French. She didn't want to alert him that he was being secretly tested with every word he uttered.

'Suppose you are telling the truth, that you are Victor, and that you are here because of confusion over your identity.' She said it in rapid French. If he was Victor as he claimed, able to converse in the language, he would understand well enough. If he was Vincent, whose French was

more rudimentary, he might not grasp it.

He replied in French, as fluent and idiomatic as mine, without the Quebec accent.

'No need to assume, Sophie. I have on me a current Hungarian driver's permit. If there's any confusion, it's in your own mixed-up head.' He used the word *déboussolé* to mean mixed-up. It's an obscure word, and I expected its use would go some way to convincing Sophie that this was Victor. His non-linguist brother Vincent was unlikely to have been familiar with such a word.

She sighed. 'If you are Vincent, your French has improved in leaps and bounds.'

'Is that conclusive?' Pierre asked.

'I believe so. That and his voice, which is a slightly higher octave than Vincent's.'

'But is it enough?' I said. For my part, it wasn't quite. After all, she expected me to murder his twin brother on her say-so. However, they could hold Victor here while I chased Vincent. If I was successful, I would bring Vincent here by the same route as Victor, put the two of them next to each other, and let Sophie interrogate them.

'It will do,' she hedged. 'For now.'

'For now!' Victor yapped. 'What does that mean?'

'It means you will stay in France until my friend here has located my ex-husband and made me a present of his head.'

When Victor's gaze transferred from her to me, I said, 'It'll still be attached to his body,' just in case she was serious.

He leapt to his feet. 'You can't keep me here, for fuck's sake!'

'Yes, she can,' I said.

'Yes, she can,' Pierre seconded, in French.

Victor blustered in a concoction of English and French, part threatening, part pleading.

It was left to me to put a stop to it. 'Sit down, Victor,' I said, twirling the little Boberg on my forefinger like a Hollywood version of a gunfighter.

He subsided onto the couch, his fury contained for the present.

'You have someplace secure to keep him?' I asked Sophie.

She nodded. '*Certes.*'

'It may take a while, even months, to find Vincent and bring him to you.'

'You need not worry, Jack.' Behind her eyes a hidden message, unrelated to the matter of Victor and his incarceration. 'I will be waiting.'

I reminded myself that I was expected to show up for stud duty when all this was over. Would I oblige? I wasn't sure. If payment of my fee depended on it, I might just have to suppress my puritanical side and bear it.

I glanced across at Pierre. His expression was as imperturbable as a Tibetan monk's. If he had been Sophie's legal representative for many years he would have grown accustomed to her peccadilloes.

Sophie turned her lovely head towards him.

'You know what to do, Pierre. I don't wish for any details, or to see the men who will come for Victor. Is that understood?'

'*Madame la marquise*,' he murmured, her obedient servant.

'Very well.' Back to Victor, now metaphorically gnashing his teeth. 'Do not worry, Victor. They will not harm you unless you misbehave. The conditions of your imprisonment will not be disagreeable. If you need a girl, they will provide one. On the other hand, if you attempt to escape, you will be kept underground, in chains, with no TV, no books, just your memories to help you pass the time.' She smiled, but it wasn't the kind of smile that reassures. 'Do I make myself clear?'

'Bitch.'

'Good.' To Pierre, 'Make your call, then rid me of this vermin.'

To me, 'You stay, Jack. We'll dine together this evening and get to know each other better.'

Maybe my moment of truth was coming earlier than predicted.

* * * * *

Having no flight booked for my return to Budapest and Angela's waiting arms (the exact words she used in her WhatsApp missive), I was a free agent. Sophie had offered me a room for the night. She hadn't offered

herself to go with it, but if I fancied that particular fringe benefit I was sure it would be on the menu.

After the collection of Victor Wolff by two guys who looked more like FBI agents than goons, and Pierre's departure with them, Sophie apologised for abandoning me but she had an engagement, and would I mind amusing myself for the rest of the afternoon.

That left just the maid, who stayed invisible, though I heard her moving about the kitchen. As the apartment fell quiet, I mooched out onto the balcony and viewed the expanse of concrete that only ever grows upwards, like saplings in a dense forest thrusting upwards, desperate for light. Over the rooftops a drill was making a racket, and there were various clanks and rumbles and thudding noises to all points of the compass, to keep one from falling asleep. The royal palace was about the only point of serenity in the whole over-developed shambles.

Freed of Sophie's distracting presence, I could now to reflect on her invitation to a night as her guest. The prospect of sharing her bed drew me back to the period in the long grieving fallout of the killing of my wife, Marion, when I screwed – and that's exactly the right term – just about every attractive female who was up for it, including the paid variety.

Until, about four years ago, I fell in love. Being in love was a state I had by then written off as unattainable. I still loved Marion, or her memory, or her spirit, when Gina popped up on my radar. She made me rediscover the true me and regain my self-respect. Alas, she wasn't around long enough to guide me along that straighter, narrower track. She died in violence at my own inadvertent hand.

Post-Gina, once the immediate mourning was behind me, I reverted to the old morally barren routine. Then Clair, American, classy, and chic, crossed my landscape. She lifted me out of my directionless rut, though we never quite made it romantically speaking. My bond with her daughter, Lizzy, who renamed herself Liza, came to be much stronger. When Clair was abducted, I was elevated to *de facto* guardian. Liza was sixteen, far older in experience, and though she tried it on with me more than once, I proved to myself and to her that I was no longer in the market for sex for sex's sake. Liza was still a part of my life, albeit passive.

All it would take to make it active was a phone call or a Skype. But I was resolved not to go down that route, no matter how irresistible her blandishments.

After Clair and Lizzy, I met Maura. If Marion was my great love when alive and continued to be in death, Maura came to share her role. Maura was very much alive and the only reason we weren't together was my work. She was unwilling to commit herself and above all commit her daughter to me for as long as I killed people for profit. In fact she was adamant that she wouldn't.

I had tried to renounce my lethal trade but was caught up with an organisation from which escape was forbidden. You did their bidding, picked up your pay check, and went on to the next contract. My contract with Marquise Sophie had not come to me through *Il Sindicato*, but until I could break the bonds of my enslavement to the organisation, I had to remain at their disposal. Nowadays, when I worked for outsiders, it was for no other motive than to amass enough wealth to make me financially independent.

Which is where I was today. Financially independent, but unfree. Fettered to *Il Sindicato* and at pains to remain on good terms with them; to convince them to let me go, with no intent to do me harm.

The vaguest notion of how to sever this unwanted connection was forming in my head. It meant confrontation. It meant offering them a deal they couldn't refuse, in language they understood – and I don't mean Italian.

There and then, I swore to myself and to Maura, that this, the impossible contract to kill Vincent Wolff, would be my swansong, my crowning hurrah before the end of the end.

* * * * *

We dined at her home, at a mahogany oval table designed to seat a round dozen on mahogany chairs, with padded seats, oval backs, the exposed woodwork gilded. Regency style, or the French equivalent – Louis XVI? My knowledge of antique furniture was sketchy.

Donovan and a female companion joined us. Her name was Suzette,

and she was young, voluptuous, and spoke excellent English. So we conversed in that language – about Monaco, Ireland, and sailing, Brexit, China, and Donald Trump. Nobody mentioned business, legal or the other kind. Nobody mentioned the Wolff twins either. It was typical dinner party causerie and apart from Sophie's pressing her leg against mine at frequent intervals, just to remind me of her proximity, it could have been a gathering of ordinary middle-class people who weren't plotting the death of a man who raped a child.

A high-profile chef had been hired for the evening, and Sourface the maid served us. The main course of *entrecote de boeuf grillé* was the best I had tasted since many meals ago. We called the chef out of the kitchen to heap praises on him. He took it in his stride; I suspected he was used to it.

After the dessert – a heavy-on-chocolate concoction that Sophie called *caprese cioccolato*, that was equally delicious – Donovan and Suzette didn't stick around for digestifs. As the door closed behind them Sophie's hand crabbed across the table linen to seize mine.

'You will stay tonight, yes?'

I nodded. I couldn't think of a reason not to, real or invented.

'Are you married?' she asked.

Did she care?

'No. Used to be, many years ago.'

She pursed her lips to perfection.

'Divorced, eh?'

'No. She died.'

'Ah.' She didn't say she was sorry. Not a hypocrite then.

I never enjoyed talking about Marion's death. It still hurt, the more so as her death came about because of my job as an officer in the British Secret Intelligence Service.

'So, you will stay but you will sleep in the guest room.'

She expected me to be disappointed. To console her, I fabricated a sigh.

'I am sorry,' she added.

'You're the boss.'

'You see, Jack, I know myself all too well. You remember, I explained

when you were here before. If I allow you to make love to me, I will try to keep you here. Then Vincent would escape my revenge. It will make it easier for me if we keep our association on a professional footing for the time being.' Her sly glance spoke volumes galore. 'But only for a while.'

It suited me. It would delay the day when I had to confront my conscience.

'If Vincent is such a scumbag, how come you married him?'

'It is a fair question. I am impulsive, he was attractive, and he awoke the sensual side of me in a way that my first husband never did. He was very virile then, and we made love every day, often more than once. He gave me an appetite for sex that I have never been able to satisfy since. So …' She gestured with her hands, as if to wash them of the consequences, 'I went looking elsewhere. I did not realise that he also was looking elsewhere, with ever younger girls, culminating in his rape of Francine. All this came to light after he left and took her with him as his plaything.'

I sipped my wine, a red Côtes du Rhône. The label told me it was a Laurent Dublanc 1980 vintage. Most wines from the region are vinified for consumption within five years, but I could find no fault with this sampling. Marquise Sophie knew her wines.

'He stole from you too, you said.'

'Yes. A great deal of money. Millions, in fact. Fortunately …' A harsh, humourless laugh, 'I have plenty more, inherited from my father, and every year the investments he made while he was alive add to my fortune.' She gazed at me unblinking. 'You would do well to remember it.'

'I will remember it,' I promised.

Perhaps she was hinting that I could be a kept man as well as a kept stud. I kept a straight face. Her come-on was all a bit too overblown to be taken seriously. I'd had a hard night's day and I needed a good night's sleep.

'May I borrow a toothbrush?'

'You will find all you need in the bathroom of your bedroom.'

She waggled a goodnight with her fingers.

* * * * *

'Why did you have to stay the night?' Angela enquired, as we lay side by side, watching the sunlight peek through the gap at the top of the drapes.

'To settle Victor Wolff in his new temporary home. He wasn't cooperative.' The lie tripped off my tongue. It was white enough, and I'd had plenty of practice over the years. So far, lies apart, I'd done nothing to feel guilty about.

'Not because of this *marquise* person then? Is she attractive?'

'A crone,' I said with a straight face.

She moved closer and pecked me on the cheek.

'And she's positive he's Victor, not Vincent.'

'That's what she said.'

She made an impatient sound. 'You're not very communicative this morning. Will you go after Vincent, now that you know Victor's safely behind bars in France?'

I kicked free of the duvet and swung my legs off the bed.

'You know, love, it might be best if I was less open with you in future. I've kept you in the loop because you saved my life once, and helped me out since. You deserved to know what I'm embroiled in, because it puts you at risk too.'

As I pulled on my shorts and stood up, she got up on her knees on the bed, and stuck her fists on her hips. Naked and tousled and cross, and sexy-sexy. Almost enough to tempt me back to bed. But no, I had a major mission ahead of me – find Vincent. It wasn't as if I knew where to start.

'Deserve be damned!' Angela snapped, 'Whatever you're mixed up in, I want to be part of it. Physically, I mean. First hand. Shooting and all.'

I groaned. 'Look, you'll just make it more difficult and more dangerous. If I have to watch out for you, I won't be doing my job.'

'Well then, you'll just have to suck it up, won't you?'

Why was I so attracted to feisty women? Why couldn't a sweet, petite, domestic house-wifey type fall for me? One who's prepared to

stay at home and cook and iron and generally be obedient. Apologies to the #MeToo gang for such blasphemous thoughts.

I crossed the room and pulled the drapes. Sunlight burst in, a silent explosion, followed by a second explosion, not silent, as the glass in the left-hand window pane shattered and sprayed into the room in a volley of lethal shards that missed me only by the thickness of the hairs on my chest.

My reflexes sent me diving to the floor.

'Get down!' I yelled at Angela, and her reflexes were a match for mine, as she tumbled over the side of the bed, my last view of her being her bare behind.

I hadn't heard the shot, suggesting that the gun was fitted with a sound suppressor.

'What happened?' Angela squeaked, peeping over the bed.

'Somebody's using me for target practice.'

'Oh! Is it the same people as came after you in Como?'

In the street an engine fired, then sounds of driving away in a hurry. I risked a squint over the window sill in time to scope a silver-coloured sedan, make unknown, as it rounded a corner. The rear licence plate could have been German.

I stood and Angela, taking her cue from me, crawled over on her knees to join me.

'It's okay,' I said, patting her shoulder. 'He's gone.'

'Do you think it's same people?' she asked again.

'Who knows? If it is, how the hell did they trace me?' I moved from the window, stepping gingerly around the broken glass. 'It might be unconnected. It might be Victor's gang.'

But if it were Victor's gang, what would be the point of killing me? More fruitful to snatch me off the street and take me away for a quiet chat.

Angela had wrapped herself in her robe and was picking up bits of broken window. I stooped to help her and we disposed of the glass in the bathroom bin.

'It'll take some explaining to the manager,' she mused.

'It doesn't matter. We'd better find another place to stay anyhow.'

Which we did, right after breakfast. We packed, paid up, and headed out of town, with me, still jumpy, scanning the rearview mirror for any vehicle that stuck with us for more than a few blocks. Once on the open road, through countryside that consisted of fields full of cereals and pasture, traffic thinned out and I could relax.

'Where are we going?' Angela wanted to know, as we entered a town called Cegléd.

'Search me. I'm just driving and making sure nobody is tailing us.'

She looked back down the empty road. 'Is anyone?'

'Not so's you'd notice.'

'We'll have to stop sometime,' she pointed out. 'Can't keep driving forever.'

I agreed. 'But I don't want to go too far from Budapest. My only lead to Vincent is Victor's wife and the two houses.'

'You don't even know if he's in the country.'

'They're paying me to find him, so I've got to make an effort.'

A dark cloud extinguished the sun, and seconds later rain speckled the windshield. Cegléd was a rundown little town, with few commercial enterprises at its centre. People out walking stared at the Evoque as we passed, respecting the 50kph limit. Most of the residential properties were single-story and in need of a coat of paint or more.

At a major intersection I turned right. The sign read KECSKEMET, which could have been anytown, anyplace. We cruised on, and after an uneventful thirty minutes of many meadows and few people, we came to Kecskemet, a sizeable city packed with baroque architecture. Another right turn led us onto Highway 5 to Budapest, and I was finally satisfied that no undesirables were keeping us company. By now it was raining hard and, just as the Bates Motel of "Psycho" fame loomed up in a downpour, I espied a billboard for the Mizse Motel. Tired, like Janet Leigh, of driving, I steered the Evoque off the highway and into the forecourt, parking in echelon between other cars. The building was two floors only and shaped like an E with the middle stroke missing. The entire ground level frontage was floor-to-ceiling glass, behind which was a dining room, to judge by the tables with white linen cloths and the usual eating tools.

Angela remarked on it. 'Better not eat there, you'll be a sitting duck.'

She had a point. From here on, I needed start evaluating locations from a sniper's perspective.

'There are seats towards the back of the room. It wouldn't be possible to get a clean shot.'

'You mean they might hit another diner instead of you,' Angela said tartly.

'No,' I growled. 'I mean they won't try for a shot if there's somebody in the way.' Well, I thought that's what I had meant.

'You bloody hope.'

Each of us piqued with the other, we didn't speak again until we'd ascertained that the motel had vacant rooms, signed ourselves in, and dragged our luggage up one floor to the bedroom we would be sharing. It was clean and spacious, with a skylight window and pine floor. The bed was sized for strenuous activity. As soon as I closed the door behind us, Angela flung herself into my arms.

'I'm sorry, darling. I didn't mean to imply you'd let an innocent person get killed in your place. What you said makes perfect sense.'

'Unfortunately, so did what *you* said.'

We kissed and made up, no holding back from her. Angela's kisses were supplemented by some thrusting of hips and general squirming. Before either of us could say 'Let's go to bed' we were in bed and unclothed and going at it as if a worldwide ban on sex outside marriage was about to come into force.

* * * * *

A message was waiting on my cell phone when I arose next morning.

Hello. when will you come to spain. I meet
some nice boys but not as nice like you.
big kiss.
patricia
X

After a moment's reflection I texted back that she should be patient, enjoy herself, and let me know when she ran out of money.

While Angela was in the shower, I considered where to go from here. Sara Wolff was my obvious and almost only conduit. To make her talk, if she had anything to say, violence might be called for. I couldn't see myself applying thumbscrews to a woman, even as a last resort. The next-to-last resort was the enigmatic Mr Laszlo Farkas, whose name Patricia had obligingly provided – and almost paid dearly for. She might still yet.

A new line of enquiry would at least be a change of scenery. I still didn't know where Farkas fitted in the overall picture. Was he a friend or an enemy of the Wolffs; a business associate or a business rival? Would he betray Vincent Wolff for a price?

When I called Rocky to let him know about my new accommodation, I held back the coordinates.

'Nothing personal,' I assured him. 'Just taking precautions.'

He accepted my explanation with good grace.

'We have to find a man called Laszlo Farkas,' I said next. 'He's an associate or contact of some kind, of the Wolffs.'

'Have you look in the telephone book?'

'In Budapest there are about two hundred called Farkas, and six Laszlo Farkases. It seems both names are quite common.'

'Maybe he not in Budapest.'

'Maybe he not. But think about it, Rocky. If there are six Laszlo Farkases in Budapest, there'll be at least fifty in the whole of Hungary.'

'You want I check them out.'

I chuckled into the cell. 'Unlikely they'll all be at home when you call. Also, our man will know by now I'm after him. He's not going to just answer the door when you press the buzzer.'

A brief hiatus while Rocky pondered. I imagined I could hear the meshing of cogs.

'Suppose I stake him out.'

'How long do you think it would take to stake out fifty locations spread across Hungary?'

'We could do half each.'

'Yes, and when we're done, none of them could be our man. I can't even be sure it's his real name.'

Rocky uttered what I assumed was a Finnish expletive.

'Exactly,' I agreed. 'He may not live in Hungary, or even in Europe. Same goes for Vincent.'

'It is fucking impossible, Jack.' More pondering, punctuated by the odd grunt, then, 'You have to ask the Wolff woman.'

Bringing me full circle.

To keep him employed, I told him to check out all the Farkases in Budapest. He didn't sound overjoyed about the assignment. I chopped off his protest with a reminder that I was paying for his services whether he worked or not.

'We'll talk again in a day or two,' I said, and killed the connection.

* * * * *

Then I got a lucky break. Or rather, Angela did.

We had driven into downtown Pest to allow her a day's shopping, while as a change from manhunting I had a date with the K & H Bank, to collect €10,000 for Walter, our obliging people smuggler.

Angela and I parted in St Stephen's square, as coincidence would have it in front of the 77 Bar, with an arrangement to meet on the steps of the St Stephen's basilica at one o'clock. As my appointment at the bank was not until noon, I felt a little cultural induction wouldn't come amiss, and mounted the steps to the basilica. I passed under the massive arch with its Doric columns into the interior, its coolness welcome after the heat in the square. After a tour of the vestibule, admiring its famous relief and mosaics, I penetrated into the sanctuary, with its glass paintings, towering pulpit, various statues, and the gigantic pipe organ dominating it all. The heavily gilded interior decoration created the illusion of being in a cavern with walls of gold.

Although not religious, I could be impressed by the works of art that many cathedrals and churches represented, even those of twentieth-century vintage like St Stephens. The numbers of tourists of all hues rather spoiled the ecumenical aura with their flashing cameras, but who was I to cavil, being myself a nominal member of the clan?

From the basilica I walked to the K & H Bank in Nyugati tér, an

asymmetrical plaza with a handful of mature trees and an expanse of asphalt dedicated to parking spaces for the Great God automobile. Not Budapest's most attractive spot. Collection of the money transferred online by Donovan, was straightforward enough. My John Henley passport passed the bank's security checks, and I left the stern, stone-faced building with an envelope containing a hundred €100 bills, later to be rendered to Rocky, who in turn would pay off Walter at his convenience.

It was past the appointed hour, and I hustled back to St Stephen's Square, where an agitated Angela awaited me at the foot of the basilica steps. She was wearing sunglasses but removed them as I showed up.

I started to apologise for my lateness, but she cut me short.

'Never mind that. I've made a discovery.' Her eyes were shining. 'I would have called you but my mobile battery's dead. In fact that's why it happened.'

'What happened?' I asked, mystified, tugging her aside to avoid the passing people flow.

'Well, I was in the old town and I wanted to take some pictures with my mobile. I managed a couple then the battery died on me. Across the street was a camera shop, so I thought I would get a cheap camera so I could take the photos without having to come back.'

'Makes sense,' I said, curbing my impatience.

She frowned at me. 'Stop being patronising. I need to explain what went on. You see, I went into the shop and it was the kind that has a studio where they take photos, including ones for passports. While I was waiting to be served, I was glancing around, as one does, and I spotted a selection of passport-size photos in a frame on the wall.'

'Did you buy the camera?'

She made a frustrated growl in her throat.

'No, I didn't. Because I saw the bloody photo of *him*.'

'Him?'

'Strictly speaking, it could have been either of them, but in the photo his hair was different. No, I mean, it was the same colour and everything, but the style was different. No parting, and longer.'

Though she hadn't finished her tale, I was suddenly ahead of her.

'You think you saw a picture of Vincent, is that it?'

She nodded excitedly. 'I couldn't swear it was Vincent. It could have been Victor, but the different hairstyle makes it possible, wouldn't you say?'

Now I was sharing her excitement. I grabbed her arms.

'I do say. Did you speak to anyone in the store about it?'

'No … no. Best if you do it.'

It was reasonable to suppose that the photo would carry a reference number, which would enable the store to track the name of the subject from their files. If it was Vincent, they might have contact details. Then again, they might not. These days photo studios could process passport photos in a half hour. If paid for in cash, the store would have no need of an address or phone number.

Whichever, it was worth asking the question. Money would buy the answer; it almost never fails.

Chapter Fifteen

FotoFit was the name over the window, and it was in a shopping mall on the edge of the Inner Town, next door to a Vision Express franchise. Angela took my hand and towed me across the store to view the photo. Behind the counter, a bespectacled young guy in a FotoFit T-shirt was serving a middle aged woman of a certain weight. He spared us a glance, then turned back to his customer.

'There!' Angela pronounced, tapping her finger on a standard passport-size portrait among a montage of about fifty similar mug shots.

I peered at it. It was a Wolff twin, all right. The hair was swept back from his forehead and worn long in the nape of the neck; the Victor I knew wore his closer cropped with the sides buzz cut.

'It could be Victor when he wore his hair differently. It might be years old.'

'Don't be so negative! It'll be easy enough to find out.'

It would too. I hugged her to show I was grateful to her for coming up with this valuable lead.

We hung about, pretending to look at cameras, until the customer departed, her purchases in a bag bearing the FotoFit logo.

The salesman came over to us and said '*Szia.*' Pronounced 'seeya' it's Hungarian for 'hello.' Also, quirkily, for 'goodbye'. I had looked it up on my first day.

'Do you speak English?' I queried. '*Ou francais, o Espanol*?'

He grinned with genuine pleasure. 'I can speak English. How can I give you help?'

I led him to the montage and pointed to the photo of the Wolff twin.

'We are trying to find this man. He is my wife's cousin. She has not seen him for twelve years and would like to find him.'

Angela affected a wistful, searching-for-a-missing-person air.

'Please help me,' she said, using her feminine wiles to drum up his sympathy.

'Of course, if I can.' He lifted the montage off the wall and carried it to the counter. He checked off the number of photos to the left and above, reversed the montage, and checked off the backs of the photos, all of which had a five-digit reference printed on them.

Two girls entered, dressed in mini-minis and giggling to each other, and wandered over to the other side of the store to view some studio portraits. Our salesman rose above this distraction and jotted down the number, which I read upside down as 031219.

'One moment,' he said, going through an open door behind the counter.

'Fingers crossed,' Angela whispered, though I don't know why she was whispering.

The salesman returned with a piece of paper that appeared to be a handwritten receipt. Promising.

'It was in the winter. I remember him because he was not very nice man. He came back to collect the photos.'

If he picked them up in person, no address would have been required.

'But,' the salesman went on. 'because we were busy, they were not ready. He needed them for early the next day, so we arranged to deliver to his house in the evening by courier.'

If he had been female I would have kissed him.

'That's good news, isn't it, Angie?' I said, maintaining the missing cousin facade.

She nodded and bestowed a ravishing smile on the salesman. He beamed.

'What name do you have there?' I asked.

He squinted at the receipt.

'It is Farkas. The first name is not there.'

Farkas! First name Laszlo, for sure. So Patricia had given me a direct link to my quarry all along. Angela, who wasn't in on the Farkas connection, opened her mouth to query it, but when I nudged her arm she held her tongue, glaring at me.

'It's Laszlo,' I told the salesman. 'There can't be two guys with the same face and a different name.'

'So you can tell me where he lives,' Angela said, breathless with girly gratitude.

He hesitated. 'Normally we are not suppose to give customer information to other peoples.'

The 50,000 Ft bill I dealt him took care of his scruples. He made sure the giggling girls weren't watching, but they were too engrossed in the portraits to notice our act of bribery. The bill vanished into his pocket.

'I will write the house for you,' he said to Angela. Her face, and indeed her whole image, were too wholesome to belong to someone with evil intentions. I could almost read his mind.

He wrote it on a pink post-it note: 111 Tragor, Sashegy.

'Where's Sashegy?'

'In Buda, south on Gellert hill. Nice place.'

It wasn't one of the two addresses we already had for Victor, so this was a hot tip, maybe the hottest yet. Thanks to Angela, I had at last picked up the scent of Vincent Wolff. I just hoped he wasn't away on a world cruise.

* * * * *

The suburb of Sashegy contained a high proportion of individual properties on oversized lots. For the most part old, grand buildings with sweeping driveways and well-tended yards. Double garages abounded, trebles not uncommon, and some of the wheels parked in the driveways wouldn't have shamed Hollywood's Beverly Hills.

Number 111 lay behind a high chain-wire fence. No gatehouse. Perhaps Vincent alias Laszlo was less paranoid than his twin brother. A guy on a tractor mower was cutting the lawn; he paid no attention to us. I drove on beyond the next lot, to number 115, and stopped at the roadside. There was no sidewalk, just a grass shoulder.

'What's the plan?' Angela said, stroking my forearm.

'Ring the buzzer?' I hazarded.

'Hmm. Sounds rather unimaginative. Won't you need Rocky?'

'Depends. How about *you* ring the buzzer?'

She shrank back. 'Me? Why?'

'Think about it. They don't know you. We come up with some perfectly innocent reason for calling on him –'

'Like selling encyclopaedias, for instance,' she said scathingly.

'Seriously, you won't be able to pose as a Hungarian, so there has to be a very plausible reason for an English person to come visiting. Let's say you're an old flame or a distant relative, looking him up. Look, love, you don't have to get cosy with him, or go inside the yard even. All you need to do is establish if he's home or away. And if he's away, when he's expected back. Then walk away.'

'And if he's home and invites me in? Do I accept and take afternoon tea and crumpets with him?'

I chuckled. 'No, you get in your car and get the hell out of there. You'll have established what we need to know.'

She wasn't mollified. Her tone was acerbic as she said, 'This is a side of you I haven't seen. Until now, you've been keen to keep me out of harm's way. What's changed?'

A green Bentley convertible swished past, a blonde woman at the wheel, cigarette dangling from trout-pout lips. If I needed confirmation we were in the moneyed zone, women driving Bentleys provided it.

'You're always insisting on being involved. Now I want to involve you, and you're sore about it. It's a practical issue, love. There's a CCTV camera at the gate. If I go ringing the buzzer, I'll be recognised by the description Sara Wolff is sure to have given Vincent. Same goes for Rocky. You can see that, can't you?'

Some of the light of battle faded from her eyes.

'Should I dress tarty? Skimpy outfit, short skirt, make-up laid on with a trowel, all that jazz.'

I sighed. 'No need for any of that. All you'll be doing is talking to a hole in the wall.'

'All right.' She lapsed into a sulk. 'Shall I ask for Mr Wolff or Mr Farkas?'

It was a good question. Wolff or Farkas. I mulled it over.

'Wolff,' I decided. 'If he answers in person, cut and run. We'll know enough for our purpose. If a third party answers, say you're his niece, here on vacation. If he's out, pump them for as much detail as you can. Where he's gone, when he's coming back, stuff like that. Natural questions.'

It was feeble. Inventing a more plausible cover was beyond me, short of setting up an elaborate scam.

'Got it,' Angie said. 'Just one last request: I want that little gun you're always flashing. Just in case your low-risk plan becomes high-risk.'

* * * * *

It worked out even better than I had dared hope. She drove up to the wrought-iron gate in Rocky's Kia SUV rental. Dressed in a dark blue business suit – skirt at a demure knee length, no cleavage on display – she exited the car in front of the gate, positioned herself under the CCTV camera, and pressed the circular red buzzer.

Rocky and I watched from the Evoque, parked out of sight of 111.

'I find something,' Rocky said, his mouth twitching to suppress a grin.

'What's that?'

I wasn't particularly interested in his findings, preoccupied as I was with Angela's role play. Through the binoculars I watched her speak into a grill set in the gate pillar.

'I find what Farkas mean,' Rocky said.

'What Farkas mean? Who cares what it means? It's a name, that's all.'

He exploded into a guffaw. 'You don't know? It mean wolf.'

I removed my eyes from the glasses to stare at him.

'Farkas means *wolf*?'

He nodded, still chortling, his shoulders quivering.

When Patricia had presented me with the Farkas lead the day Wolff's goons snatched her, she had been sending me directly to Vincent Wolff. There was irony for you. There was also confirmation that this was my man.

Back to the binoculars. Angela's was still speaking into the grill. I saw

her mouth form a final 'Thank you very much.' She climbed in the Kia and, as instructed, U-turned back down the road.

By prior arrangement we reconvened in the parking lot of a Spar supermarket.

'He's out of town,' Angela said snappishly, clearly still steamed up over my thrusting her into in the line of fire.

'Who did you speak to?' I asked.

'Some kind of underling, I imagine. He spoke English with an American or Canadian accent – I can't tell the difference. I asked for Vincent, but he referred to him as Mr Wolff. He asked who I was. As instructed, I told him I was his niece, in Budapest on holiday.'

'So the sum total of our knowledge is that he's not in Budapest.'

'Not quite. He's in Germany.'

'Oh, so you did manage to wangle a bit more information.'

Her expression was deadpan, but her eyes were smiling. I realised then she was just punishing me.

'Go on,' I said, keeping my impatience in check. 'What else?'

'He's in Passau. He'll be there for five days, then flying directly from Germany to the States for three weeks.'

Rocky gave his bellowing laugh.

'You should see your face, Jack.'

'Okay, okay, very funny. You didn't happen to get the name of the hotel, and what he'll be having for breakfast, did you? How did you cajole them into being so cooperative?'

'By putting on my sultry, come-hither voice.' She leaned towards me and planted a kiss on my cheek. 'Didn't I do well?' she murmured in a sultry, come-hither voice.

I had to admit she had extracted as much as was extractable without arousing suspicion.

'Passau not a big city, is it?' Rocky said.

'Big enough. And we've only got five days, according to Angie. And it's in Germany.'

Germany, home of a vindictive cop called Schmidt who was eager to renew our acquaintance and lock me up until I was old enough to qualify for a pension.

Although I had ventured over the German border a year ago, my stay had been brief and uncontroversial, not to mention unavoidable. No abductions, shootings, gang warfare, etc. If I were to re-enter it, bent on removing Laszlo Farkas alias Vincent Wolff, to deliver him to his vengeful ex-wife, it would be as a lawbreaker, with potential for gunplay, mayhem, and arrest. If it all went bad on me, my ID as Gilles Devreese wouldn't save me, nor even Jack Henley. The law had my picture and my prints and my real name.

'Is there a problem for Germany?' Rocky rumbled.

'Yes, *is* there?' Angela chimed in, studying my face with a little frown.

'Could be.'

I wasn't about to confess all to either of them. But they deserved some explanation.

'They want me for questioning over a … a misunderstanding a few years ago.'

Angela seemed amused.

'Compared with your trail of transgression here in Hungary, I wouldn't have thought a teeny misunderstanding would even make a blip on the radar.'

'They have my fingerprints. Hungary doesn't.'

A young couple with two toddlers came down the line of cars and stopped by the one parked next to the Evoque, a battered Beetle with rust infesting the wheel arches. We suspended our debate and watched as the guy unlocked the doors and they strapped the kids into baby seats in the back. The woman gave us a nervous smile and audibly locked her door as soon as she was inside the car.

'See how you frighten people,' I said to Rocky.

He gave a who-cares kind of snort.

The Beetle chugged off, and Angela squeezed my hand.

'You can do it, darling. You're Superman. Rocky can go on ahead to search for him and let you know when he's successful. Then you go gettim. Right, Rocky?'

'Sure. So long as I get expenses.'

* * * * *

As I was still leery of revealing the identity of our latest hotel to Rocky, we went to his, the Szonyi, in Pest, on the street of the same name. We assembled in his room to Google the town of Passau. In particular its closeness to the border, and accessibility from Hungary.

'Seventy-one hotels,' Rocky said, looking gloomy. 'Maybe more if you count *gasthofs*.'

'Seventy-one phone calls isn't so many,' Angela demurred.

To me, well versed in the creativity of the criminal fraternity in laying smokescreens, things were never as straightforward as they seem to the law-abiding.

'If we can depend on getting honest answers.'

'Why shouldn't we?'

'Because, my love, Vincent Wolff is a criminal, could even be a fugitive under his true identity. Criminals avoid being caught by taking precautions.'

'Such as?'

'Using a phoney name. Using a proxy. Bribing the management not to reveal he's staying at his hotel. Staying in a different town. Renting an apartment.'

Her mouth turned down.

'I didn't think of that.'

'Still, we have to try, and hotels are the logical place to start, but phoning won't cut it for the all reasons I've just mentioned. We have to question the front desk, not the manager, and we have to pay for answers. If he's using another name, we'll need to show them a photo.'

'I see,' she intoned, looking pensive. Understanding was dawning on her. Knowing that Vincent was doing business in Passau was only a small part of a big equation.

Rocky scratched his head, worry lines on his brow.

'It will be tough call.'

'Don't sweat it, Rocky. You've gotten nearly a week before he takes off. Make a list of all three-star and upwards, and start with the five-stars. This guy has money. If he's in an hotel at all, he won't be slumming in a back street dive.'

'That's right,' Angela agreed. 'You can visit, oh … twenty hotels in a day, surely.'

Rocky brightened. 'Two times more if you come to help, Angela.'

Much as I distrusted my Finnish friend's motives, it was sure to speed up the process if Angela shared the burden.

'I don't mind going,' Angela said. 'It makes sense. And the sooner you can get your job done, the sooner we can kick-start a life together.'

'If you're sure …'

She shrugged. 'You decide. I'll do whatever you say.'

As for me, I was torn between the need to remove her from the dangerous orbit of my presence, and the desire to keep her close by, where I could protect her. And she would have Rocky to ward off the bad guys.

'Go with Rocky,' I said with a resigned sigh. 'Just don't be seen together.'

'Except after dark,' Rocky chuckled.

I didn't react to his needling. Though I was sure he'd come on to Angela if she gave him the smallest encouragement, I wasn't jealous of him. It came as a surprise to me that I cared that much. Just my ego, most likely.

* * * * *

They left in Rocky's rental early in the morning, with instructions to report back twice daily and in between if they had news. They had a good six hours driving ahead of them. By road was tedious but would involve no paper trail, no flashing of passports. Safer all round. Essential for me when I joined them, because of my status in Germany.

This left me a yawning void of a few days with only myself for company, unless I paid a social call on Sara Wolff and her band of toughs. Before they came calling on me again, armed with a sniper rifle.

After breakfast, I headed into the city. No specific aim, just keeping on the move to thwart my enemies. A moving target is harder to track, harder to hit. Over coffee, at the Divino Bar, round the corner from the 77, I asked myself if I couldn't be better employed, couldn't make some contribution to the manhunt, instead of cruising Budapest's tourist attractions. Nothing obvious came to mind. Victor was under lock and

key in France and therefore to be discounted. Vincent was in Passau until the weekend, and with a bit of luck and a lot of sidewalk pounding we would determine his whereabouts before then. The rest of the gang, be it singularly or jointly run by the twins, was of no professional interest to me, apart from the potential threat they posed to my back under the provisional leadership of Sara Wolff.

That being so, it only remained for me to watch my back, stay out of trouble, and be ready to link up with my fellow conspirators.

A better course might have been to await Vincent's return, now that I had his address. But if Angela's feedback was reliable, he would be away for almost a month. Too much can go wrong in a month.

As if he'd heard I was at a loose end, Donavan texted me to meet him at the airport. His Lufthansa flight was scheduled to land at 3.40pm but was already ten minutes late, so be prepared to wait.

It was well after four when he showed up in Arrivals. For security's sake we went outside and sat in the Evoque.

'Sophie wanted news first hand. She's suddenly become very impatient for progress. I'm due at a conference in Moscow tomorrow, and I agreed to stopover here for a friendly chat.'

'I'm a friendly guy most of the time, so you've come to the right place.' I twisted sideways to face him. 'Let me fill you in on the latest developments.'

'I'd be very happy if you would.'

So I filled him in. At the end of my resume, he was silent for a few beats, then said, 'Let's see if I've got this straight. In summation, you're staying in Budapest while your colleague and your girlfriend go to Passau to make enquiries. That it?'

'That's a simplified version. There are reasons why Germany is not a healthy place for me to be. When we know where Vincent is staying, I'll go get him, and hopefully it can be done in a single day. But for me to stay there any length of time is to put myself in jeopardy. I could be arrested.'

He grunted.

'It's a pity you didn't tell me at the start that some places are effectively out of bounds to you. Suppose Vincent had been permanently based in Germany?'

The criticism was merited, and I acknowledged it.

'That's easy to answer. I would have declined your generous offer of employment and our paths need never have crossed again. But he isn't based in Germany, so up until now it hasn't been a constraint.'

More grunts. Still not happy then.

'Well, thanks for the heads up. It looks promising, I have to say. But if he slips through your fingers on account of this German … problem, I won't be pleased. Sophie will be even less pleased.'

'You want to terminate the contract?'

It would be no hardship to me, even at a loss of a half million dollars.

'You keep trying, don't you? No, just get on with it. You've done well so far' grudgingly '– though I'd have preferred you hadn't dragged the *marquise* into it. In fact …'

'In fact?' I nudged.

'You must know she's got the fecking hots for you. She wants Victor delivered and done with, and you at her beck and call.'

'Like you.'

A turboprop airliner took off behind the tower, engines shrill as it climbed away into the blue. Donovan watched it go as intently as the handful of onlookers must have watched Orville Wright doing the world's first heavier-than-air hop at Kill Devil Hills. Something was bothering him.

'For your guidance, Jack, I not only look after Sophie's business dealings, I also try to influence who she does business with, and keep her from growing too fond of the wrong type.'

'Like me.'

'You're saying it.'

He seemed to be trying to decide how much he dared reveal. His breath was coming down his nose in little snorts, his eyes darting from side to side. Ill-at-ease with the role I was pressuring him to play.

'Let me give you a comradely warning. I've only seen her like this twice before. Once was with me, all of twenty years ago. It was a rough ride, I can tell you. She's an all-or-nothing woman. When she's in 'all' mode, there's no satisfying her. I was young then, so I could keep up. The guy who replaced me was forty. She screwed him to death.'

'Way to go.'

'Fine, be flippant. My advice to you is do the job, collect your million, and jump back into whatever feckin' hole you crawled out of.'

This was male rivalry blustering, and I bore him no malice. He was still in love with her, and couldn't bear that younger, better maintained specimens had replaced him. Potentially that included me, though it was none of my doing.

So instead of ejecting him from the car for being rude to me, I said, 'Out of curiosity – when she's in "nothing" mode, how does she get by?'

For a second I thought he was about to take a swing at me. Big but flabby and overweight, he was in no shape to trade punches, but his emotions threatened to overrule his common sense. After an internal struggle, he shrugged and slid lower in his seat.

'Keep it to yourself, will you, for Christ's sake, but she hires guys; gigolos, I suppose you'd call them. She likes to play the dominatrix, so she pays these fecking idjits to let her chain them up while she goes to work on them.'

It didn't surprise me, or shock me. Just as long as she didn't try it on me. With or without wages, she could keep her peccadilloes.

It was getting close to the departure time for his Moscow flight. He offered his hand to shake. No sense in rejecting him and incurring his ire. I didn't intend to give him grounds to challenge me to a duel. No, when this was all over, which I fervently prayed would be soon, I would take the money and run. As the saying goes.

When he took his leave there was less of an air of self-importance about him than on previous occasions. Another instalment of my expenses was due, but I hadn't reminded him of it. The first had shown up in my account without prompting, so I had no reason to suppose the second wouldn't. If it didn't, well, no pay – no cure, as they say in reverse in the salvage trade.

III

TWO WOLFF'S FOR THE PRICE OF ONE

Chapter Sixteen

The call was from Rocky.

'What's up?' I said, setting aside the newspaper I was browsing in the hotel lounge. It was a Sunday and it felt like a Sunday, with the lounge deserted and only the whine of a vacuum cleaner to disturb the peace.

'It's Angela. She's gone.'

'Gone?' It didn't impact on me straight off. 'How do you mean?'

'Fuck, man, she is gone. She is not here anymore.'

I sat bolt upright. 'She left without telling you?'

'Right. I think because it is not possible she can tell me.'

He went on to relate that she had not joined him at breakfast. After eating, he went to her room. She didn't answer the door, so he prevailed on the cleaner to open it with her passkey. The bed had been slept in, and her clothes and luggage were there. Plus her toothbrush, make-up, and all the other bits and pieces that accompany people on their travels.

'Fuck!' The answer was obvious. 'They've taken her, goddammit! Where were you – asleep?'

'Probably. It happen in night is my guess. So, yes, I am asleep. It is safer if I am sleeping with her, but from respect of you, I am not.'

'Okay, okay,' I soothed. 'Wind your neck in, Rocky. I'm not blaming you.'

'So … you come today?'

'Yeah,' I said, cursing inwardly. 'I'll aim to be there by this evening. Text me your hotel coordinates.'

'Copy that.'

Next stop my room, to pack. Some of Angela's gear was still lying around and so was her carryall. I dumped it all in the bag with little finesse and checked out. Less than thirty minutes after ending my

conversation with Rocky, I was on the M1 six-lane *autópályán*, heading west towards Vienna.

Two borders to cross. In theory, no passport control to worry about. Nevertheless, it was always with a degree of trepidation that I left one country and entered another.

The Austro-Hungarian border came up after an hour and a bit. A red-white-red panel denoting the Austrian flag announced Republik Österreich. Below it, a blue panel with the twelve EU stars. The next sign proclaimed Raststation Nickelsdorf with the usual gas, restaurant, etc symbols. Finally, an overhead gantry with more info I didn't need. Then it was just the open road, now become the A4 *Autobahn*. I fed gas to the engine, eating up the Austrian kilometres. Here I was, on another mission to rescue a missing maiden. When I wasn't concentrating on my driving, I tormented myself about Angela and my culpability in sending her into tiger country.

Vienna edged into view on the GPS screen. I passed Schwechat airport where a jumbo was touching down on the runway. It had begun to rain, a fine drizzle from sullen skies. I peeled off the freeway into a Jet *tankstelle,* refilled the tank, and went in search of some lunch.

A text from Rocky buzzed. It contained nothing new. He was checking the hotels she had visited yesterday and so far had gotten nowhere. I told him I had reached Vienna and would be in Passau before nightfall.

They had snatched her for bartering purposes, that was a cert. Either we restored Victor to their bosom, or if Victor was expendable, they would want to swap her for me. That would serve to get me off their backs.

With the car and me both refuelled, I resumed my journey. The drizzle behind me absorbed Vienna, and I motored through the flat valley of the Danube with its endless geometric cultivated fields arrayed on either side. Up ahead, the forested hills of the Böhmerwald were invisible in the mist and low cloud. I had trekked there in my youth.

Linz, birthplace of Hitler, was the only town of any significance on my route. I by-passed it on the A3 then, with less than a hundred kms to go, quit the *Autobahn* system in favour of a standard two-lane

highway running alongside the Danube.

To avoid entering Germany sooner than necessary, I stuck to the south side of the Danube, and stayed with it until I came to a bridge, where I had no choice but to cross into Passau. I drew up at the curbside to prime the GPS to guide me to the Hotel König in the old town on the north bank of the promontory, a short drive away. Minutes later I was parking up in front of it.

From the outside it was unimposing, just a fat cube with apricot-hued stucco finish and an entrance surmounted by a half-round sunburst window. I had alerted Rocky of my ETA and sure enough he was in the lobby waiting for me. Old reliable.

'Let's talk,' I said, with the greetings done.

'Over here.'

He escorted me to a discreet corner of the lobby, and we sat in armchairs at a round table.

'It may be a bad idea to meet at your hotel,' I said.

'This is not my hotel. In any case, I have move my things and Angela's to other hotel.'

'Smart thinking.' I grinned at him. 'You're a helluva guy, Rocky.'

He couldn't help a self-congratulatory smirk. 'I always do my best.'

'No contact from the enemy?' I asked.

'So far, no. What you think they want?'

I tugged at my lower lip to stimulate inspiration. It didn't work.

'Me or Victor – or even both of us.'

'We can make nothing until they contact us. Angela has my cell number, and your number. So we expect call or message.'

'They'll probably make us sweat for a while.'

I was wrong. Even as I uttered the words, my cell trilled. The number on the screen was Angela's.

'Angela?' I said, before my caller could speak.

It wasn't her. It was a man with a German accent.

'Hello, Mr Henley, or whoever you call yourself these days. We have a friend of yours here. Would you like to speak to her?'

I mouthed 'Angela' at Rocky. His jaw jutted, a frightening sight if you didn't know what a big softy he could be.

'Jack, darling.' A breathless-sounding Angela. 'Where are you?'

'Not far away. Are you okay? Have they hurt you at all?'

'Not really. A bruise or two, but that's only because I put up a fight.'

I found I was gripping my cell hard enough to hurt.

'Don't put up any more fights, love. You can't win, so just avoid getting hurt. Tell me, who's holding you – Vincent?'

'Yes, he –'

'That's enough conversation between the lovebirds.' The German-accented guy was back. 'All you have to do for her safe return is surrender to us.'

It didn't sound like much. I could almost see myself doing it. Or at least making a show of cooperating. Unlike heroes in movies, I was not about to hand over my guns and hope that Vincent's mob would treat us right. If I parted with my only means of defence, I could kiss the future goodbye.

'You don't want Victor released as well?'

'Victor?' He seemed bemused by the question. 'Ah, I see. Yes, yes, of course, we must have him back.'

It was as if it hadn't occurred to him he could get two for the price of one.

'Who are you?' I said. 'Is Vincent there?'

'Of course he is here. I am his associate here in Germany.'

'Ex-SS no doubt.' He didn't like that. Many Germans are sensitive about their barbaric past. 'Let me speak to Angela again.'

'Sorry, no. But I will have her send you a message.'

A pause, a scuffling noise and a crash of something heavy. Then a shriek – female, and whatever was being done to her wasn't just a game of BDSM. The shriek died away to be replaced by sobbing. I heard a faint 'Oh, you bastards, you bastards.'

I was shaking with suppressed rage, going from hot to cold and back again.

'Jack …' Rocky stretched out a hand, his face lined with concern.

'That enough speaking for you, Mr Henley?' the German asked with amusement in his voice.

'Don't touch her again, you piece of shit. There's no need. I'll cooperate.'

At that very moment, I meant it – I would cooperate. Later, as rationality returned, I would plot and scheme to (a) restore Angela to me, and (b) make sure Vincent and Co. paid in pain of their own for any harm they had done her.

'We will meet tomorrow morning. Instructions will be texted.'

'No, we meet now! No waiting.'

'Tomorrow,' he repeated. 'Tonight we will have a little fun with your sweetheart. Or maybe a *lot* of fun …'

He hung up. When I tried to call him back, I couldn't get through. A message droned at me in German, but was beyond my language skills to unravel.

I relayed the gist of the conversation to Rocky. He bunched a fist and smacked it several times in quick succession into the open palm of his other hand.

'They better not hurt her. I like her. She is nice woman.'

'Agreed. But now we need to be practical, not emotional. Figure out what's our next move when we hear from them.'

Our first next move was to find accommodation. The front desk clerk recommended a certain Hotel Dreiflüssehoff and phoned through to book rooms for us.

We went out into the drizzle and the fading light, got into our respective transportation. With me leading, we weaved through the streets of Old Passau, to the Dreiflüssehoff, four stars-worth of clean, white, attractive building surrounded by landscaped gardens ablaze with blooms.

My night was restless. Although Angela wasn't much more than a passing fancy, I had become fond of her and, more importantly, it was my fault she was in Passau. It was almost a repeat of the Patricia scenario, with Angela suffering for trying to help me.

As Rocky and I breakfasted in the rather sterile dining room, we speculated on how we might rescue Angela without my having to exchange myself for her.

'If only we know where they stay,' Rocky said, taking a Rocky-sized bite out of his toast. 'We could surprise them.'

'If only.'

My sardonic tone didn't go unnoticed.

'Hey, Jack, we already checked more than thirty hotels.'

'Leaving forty still to do,' I reminded him. I tasted my coffee. Usual hotel quality. 'You already checked this one, I suppose.'

He stopped in mid-bite and stared at me.

'This one?'

'Sure. In case you didn't notice, it's an hotel.'

He completed his bite, munched reflectively, all the while frowning.

'We didn't come to this part of town yet.'

'As we're here, don't you think we should ask?'

'I'll do it.' He got up and strode off to the front desk, still chewing.

I finished my coffee, scoped the room for suspicious characters. Families, couples, solos, the usual eclectic mix. None of them resembled the Wolff twins. The morning sun was slanting through the windows, highlighting the dust motes and raising morale, mine excluded. If I was just up against Vincent and a couple of goons, I was confident I could take them. If they were mob-handed, it might be more problematic. The overriding priority was to make Angela safe, and myself safe second. To free her, I had to stay alive and in working order.

Rocky reappeared clutching a post-it note. His face was flushed.

'He is *here*!' he said, keeping his voice low. He passed me the post-it note. 'He staying here.'

'Jesus!' I read the note. 'Laszlo Farkas, sixteen.'

'That his room number. Second floor.'

I mopped my mouth and got up from the table. '|Is he in his room?'

'They not sure. Customers always keep keys these days, so not possible to say if in or out.'

I recovered the SIG and the Boberg from their hiding place in the Evoque and teamed up with Rocky by the elevator. The hotel had only two floors above the ground floor.

'Are you carrying?' I asked.

He patted the small of his back. I didn't ask what it was, where it had come from, and how he was managing to smuggle it around Europe. Ignorance really is bliss sometimes.

'Those shotguns would be nice for us,' he said.

I nodded. We had unloaded them in a garbage dumpster on the return drive from our abduction of Victor. Though they would have contributed usefully to our armoury, transporting them from Hungary to Germany would have been pushing our luck beyond the pale.

'Why we not use the stairs?' Rocky queried.

'Because people on the second floor of hotels often use the stairs. That means there would be a high chance of bumping into Vincent.'

'That is good, no?'

'Do we want a fight with Vincent in public?'

'Ah.'

The elevator was descending. It stopped and the door retracted. Two elderly women stepped over the threshold and went on into the dining room, nattering away to each other.

In the cage we were joined by a woman on her own. She punched floor 2 and presented her back to us. She had a shape that was more convex than concave, swathed in a print dress that was a size or several too small.

The elevator came to rest. We went around the woman and it was quite a journey. We stepped onto the familiar territory of the second floor: pale walls, pale carpet. Room 16 was to the left. Incredible that I had spent the night three doors away from my prey.

A cleaning cart was positioned by an open door at the far end of the corridor, and someone was la-la-ing "Hey, Jude" in the room beyond. Rocky moved ahead until he was just past no. 16. I took up position on this side and rapped on the door.

Movement within. A murmur of voices.

'*Wer ist das*?'

My German was not of the best. I had assumed Vincent, being American, would reply in English. If it was Vincent.

'*Der manager*,' Rocky responded. '*Es gibt ein problem mit dem Sanitär.*'

A problem with the plumbing? I gave him full marks for initiative, not to mention fluency in German.

Rumble, rumble. Footsteps. A door flung open. A very surprised black guy looked down the tube of my SIG's sound suppressor

'Who the fuck are you?' the black guy demanded. The gun hadn't shocked him, which pointed to his being of the lawless fraternity.

We advanced and he retreated, expression wary, but not at all intimidated. Rocky kicked the door shut, and freed his gun from the back of his pants. Unfortunately it wasn't silenced and therefore of limited value.

Vincent was standing by the open door of a closet, a jacket on a hangar in his hand. He shared the black guy's surprise and lack of fear. His brow darkened. He would be unaccustomed to looking down the business end of a gun, unless it was for demonstration of his stock to a prospective buyer.

'What d'you ...?' He broke off, glared at me. 'You're Devreese. You're the punk who's been giving Victor grief.'

'Mr Farkas, I presume. Nice to make your acquaintance. It's been a long time coming.'

He whistled. 'Hey, Samson, meet Mr Gilles Devreese, though I doubt that's his real name. He's the shithead Victor told us about.'

Samson glowered and didn't seem inclined to shake hands.

'Frisk 'em,' I ordered Rocky, careful not to use his name. So far, his ID wasn't compromised; I owed it to him to preserve his incognito.

Vincent Wolff was in a silk robe, making it hard to hide anything bigger than a toothbrush. Rocky ran his hands over him just the same. Samson, who was in jeans, a black T-shirt, and loafers, didn't have much hiding space either. Rocky extended his search and came across a Glock automatic in the top drawer of a bureau.

'You're making a big mistake,' Vincent said at last.

'You've already made more than one. Where's the woman?'

He gave me a puzzled look.

'What woman, schmuck?'

'Cut out the games, Vincent. I'm talking about Angela Renwick. The woman you kidnapped yesterday.'

He gaped at me. He was almost convincing.

'I *did*?'

'Don't make me get rough, Vincent. You're in a bind, and if you don't play ball, you'll be in an even bigger bind.'

Silence fell on our little group. Vincent seemed lost for words; I had said all I was prepared to say. The answers were Vincent's to provide. It was Samson who broke the impasse.

'Listen, mister,' he said, 'You gotta be confusin' us with some other honkies. We is here to do business deals, we ain't mixed up in no kidnappin'.'

I expelled a theatrical sigh. 'Why do people like you always have to make it difficult? Is it bravado or just plain stupidity? You phoned us last night, I spoke to one of your flunkeys and I spoke to the woman. Now – where are you holding her?'

'Fuck you, asshole,' Vincent snarled. 'We don't have your bitch. We don't even know what the fuck you're after!'

An automatic fitted with a sound suppressor adds up to over a foot of steel. I whopped Samson across the cheek, breaking skin. Blood flowed, and he clasped his hand to the injury, calling me bad names and spitting fire.

Vincent made a half-move as if to counter attack, but thought the better of it when Rocky rapped 'Hold it there!'

'That was just a demo,' I said to Vincent, touching his cheek with the tip of the SIG's silencer. 'You're next.'

He flinched and took a step backwards. Samson had found a Kleenex in his pocket and was dabbing at his cheek and looking murderous.

Out in the corridor, the cleaning cart rattled past our door; it had a squeaky wheel. The cleaner was still la-la-ing: now it was "Yesterday". A Beatles fan, then.

'You wouldn't dare use those things in here,' Vincent sneered.

'You want to put that to the test? Mine is silenced, in case you hadn't noticed.'

He had no answer to that.

'So,' I said pleasantly. 'Do you want a taste of what I gave your friend? Where's the girl?'

'Fuck you,' Vincent said. His use of expletives was becoming monotonous. He and his twin brother had much in common.

'We don't know what you talkin' about, man,' Samson blurted. 'We ain't got no woman of yours. Hell, we ain't got no women at all here.

Wish we had.'

'Who was the guy who phoned me?' I persisted. 'Sounded like a German.'

Vincent shrugged; Samson spread his hands as a sign of ignorance.

'Let me make them talk,' Rocky said.

'Not so fast,' I said. I brought out my cell phone, consulted the texts and WhatsApps. A text was waiting. I read the few anonymous lines that would send me to the town of Mamming, to wait in the parking lot at the junction of Schwaigener Strasse and AmSportplatz. I was to be there before 1.00pm, and to come alone and unarmed.

I let Rocky see it.

'Well, I received your message,' I told Vincent. 'So you want me to go to some town called Mamming and wait for your playmates to bring Angela to me.'

'That's not from anybody connected with me.'

I was beginning to half believe him. Something was out of kilter about this scene.

'We'll see. You can come along with me and we'll make an exchange for you instead of for me. That sound like a smart move to you?'

'Very smart!' Rocky enthused through a broad grin.

Vincent had a different take on it.

'It won't get you anywhere. This broad you're looking for is none of my business.'

'Let's find out, shall we?'

We needed to immobilise Vincent and Samson. The drapes were operated by cords, of which there proved to be enough to bind wrists, leaving some in reserve for ankles if necessary. The next hurdle was sneaking them out to the car unseen.

Rocky went to hunt for the emergency exit. He was gone less than a minute and came back to give a thumbs up. The corridor was clear of cleaner carts, so we hustled the ungodly pair out and down the stairs to a service road alongside the hotel building. Nobody was about. While I kept our prisoners covered, Rocky slipped out and retrieved his car. We dumped Samson in the trunk and Vincent in the floor space between the front and rear seats. I trussed his ankles with the remaining drapes

cord. A gag would have been useful, but I settled for threatening him with a KO instead.

'Motherfucker.' Vincent's vocabulary was expanding.

'I'll lead, you follow,' I told Rocky. 'But wait until I'm out of sight before you start off. When you get to the place where we're supposed to meet, don't park too close to me. Just stay in your car and be ready to move in if I signal.'

'What signal you make?'

'If I get the chance, I'll zip up my jacket. If not, if you see me in trouble, use your initiative.'

'Huh? What is inish-tative.'

I patted him on the back that was as wide as a door. 'Just come and help.'

'Okay, Jack. You got it, you got it.'

The promise of action was giving him an adrenalin rush: the challenge would be to keep him from going too far and breaking things.

I returned the SIG to its usual compartment in the Evoque, made sure the Boberg was accessible. After inputting Mamming into the GPS, I drove out of the hotel parking lot into a stream of Passau traffic. It was just after eleven-forty. The GPS informed me I would reach my destination at 12.38.

Deeper penetration into Germany would make the thin ice I was already treading even thinner. It might even melt.

* * * * *

The meeting place was in the suburbs on the west side of Mamming, beside a river. A handful of other cars were parked there, none of them occupied. I selected a vacant bay in a distant corner. A few minutes later Rocky's Kia made its entry, filtering into a gap between two cars, where it would be less noticeable. Smart thinking, Rocky. As I watched, his head sank beneath the level of the windshield until only the top half was showing. To a casual observer, his SUV would appear unoccupied.

One o'clock came and moved on. I yawned, amused myself by consulting Google on my cell phone for the fastest route to get me from

Mamming to the border. If I crossed into Austria at Braunau am Inn using *Bundestrasse* 20 it would take me at least forty minutes. No use chafing over an emergency that might never arise.

By two o'clock I was wondering if I had fouled up the venue. I left the Evoque and walked across the lot to a street that served as a bridge over the river to check the name. Schwaigener Strasse. I strolled along it to where the bridge began; a road led off to the right, paralleling the river. Am Sportplatz. This was the place, no mistake.

Passing Rocky's car, I kept my eyes straight ahead. For all I knew, he might have been asleep. A banging on the inside of the trunk lid was accompanied by a faint yelling of 'Help!' If the rendezvous was being staked out by Angela's abductors, speaking to Rocky would be a giveaway. So I pretended to stop and admire my surroundings – not that there was much to admire – and issued a warning to Samson to shut the fuck up or I would put a bullet through the trunk lid.

He took the hint. I resumed my saunter back to the Evoque.

At four and still no contact, it looked as if I had been screwed by the guy who called me. If Angela really was being held by Vincent's proxy, why would the guy fail to show? It made no sense.

If the exchange with Angela was a bust for now, I needed to go to work on Vincent and extract the truth. We would head out into the country and find a remote spot where he could scream his heart out. A burp from my cell phone held me back.

It was another text from the supposed proxy.

I told you to come alone. Your woman will pay.
Come tomorrow same time different place.
I will text location.

What was going on here?

If the texter had somehow discovered I wasn't alone, he would also guess Vincent and his black buddy were prisoners in Rocky's rental. With Vincent in my hands, Angela no longer had value as a bargaining chip. A straight swap for Vincent was the only logical outcome, so delaying our meet would serve no purpose. *Your woman will pay.* Pay how? It wouldn't be with the small change in her purse, that was for sure.

And at a practical level, what was I supposed to do with my captives

for the next twenty-four hours?

I tried texting back some threats of my own. The message 'not delivered' flashed at me. It wasn't often I felt like hurling my cell phone across a parking lot. Necessity overruled emotion. I knew better than to abuse that indispensible piece of gadgetry.

In Rocky's car we travelled out into the countryside, finding a wooded area a few kms down a country lane. A rough track ran through the trees. We bounced onto it and halted in a clearing, the sunlight filtered by the foliage dappling the sparse grass underfoot. A great location for lovers. Rocky hauled Vincent out and I ripped off the gag and untied the cord around his ankles so he could stand. His nerve was cracking. As soon as he could speak, he was pleading.

'Look, man, I know you've been looking for me, but I'm not to blame for your woman going missing. If I was, don't you think I'd've been trying to do a deal by now?'

It was a reasonable premise, though not wholly convincing. I decided on a last go at getting his cooperation.

'Your German sidekick texted me, but I can't get back to him because he keeps shutting down his cell. You must have a way to communicate with him, so use your cell to either call or leave a text. Tell him if he doesn't deliver the woman to me within the next hour, I'm going to make a nine millimetre hole in your kneecap.'

He went white. 'You can't do that!' he yammered. 'It's none of my business, I tell you!'

'So you won't do it?'

'I can't! Fuck!'

I drew the SIG from my belt. 'Hold him, Rocky.'

'Sure.'

Vincent squirmed away from Rocky's reaching hands and made a run for it. Rocky, who despite his bulk could move fast when speed was of the essence, caught up with him and brought him down in the wet grass.

'Your last chance, Vincent,' I said, moving up and standing over him. Rocky used his weight and muscle power, both considerable, to keep him still. Kneecapping was my favourite threat. It never failed to

incentivise, hence I had never needed to honour it.

'No! You can't …'

He was right about that. I couldn't. Not because it would turn my stomach to inflict injury on the guy, but because I didn't believe he would allow me to cripple him rather than release Angela.

I knelt beside him. 'Chill, Vincent. I've decided not to bust your kneecap after all, provided you cooperate in another way.'

His head bobbed like a demented puppet's.

'Sure, sure … anything you say.'

'We're going back to Budapest,' I said to Rocky. 'Get the pilot on the phone. Tell him we've got another package to deliver, but we need a place to store the goods for a day or two.'

Rocky cottoned on right away. He grinned as he plucked his cell phone from his jeans pocket.

'What about the darkie?' he said.

'Not sure. We'll leave him behind, I guess. He can't do us any harm.' To Vincent, I said, 'You – back in the car.'

While Rocky wandered off to make his call, I settled Vincent behind the front seats in the Kia, re-tied his ankles. I took a peek at Samson, who had somehow untied himself and tried to leap out of the trunk. He was easily discouraged by a chop to the neck, and fell back, choking and gurgling. Not a pretty sight, so I shut the trunk lid.

I returned to Vincent.

'Sure you wouldn't like to confess before we lock you in the trunk too?'

'The hell with you!' he snarled. 'I'm here on business. I got meetings with important people.'

'They'll understand,' I soothed. 'And if they don't, at least you'll still have two good legs.'

Rocky's call to Walter proved fruitful. Fifteen thousand euros' worth of fruitful. I wasn't taking for granted Donovan's generosity in subsidising the additional expense, but if he didn't, I would gladly use my own funds just to see the whole exercise wrapped up.

'How we get him back in Hungary?' Rocky was voicing my own thoughts.

'We unload Samson here and now and replace him with Vincent, well-gagged. Then you drive him back to Budapest and meet Walter. That okay with you?'

Rocky massaged his chin between thumb and forefinger. 'It a long way for him, shut in there.'

'You're too soft-hearted. You don't know his history. Stop en route and buy some water. Whatever you do though, don't take any chances with him, like letting him out to stretch his legs.'

His nod was dubious. 'What about you? You not need help for find Angela?'

'I'll manage. Look, Rocky, I've been looking for Vincent for two weeks. Now that I've found him, I can't just turn him loose. Besides, we'd be spending all our time watching our backs.'

'Yes. No half million dollars for you either.' He said it unsmilingly, so I figured he was trying to send me a message.

'Are you suggesting the money's more important to me than saving Angela?'

His shrug was eloquent.

'Bastard,' I said without heat.

He was wrong about me, but only by a slender margin. My options regarding Angela were non-existent. I could only wait for the bad guys to contact me. The moment I received their instructions I would go in to action, and God help them if they had seriously hurt her.

Rocky had still succeeded in making me feel lower than a whore's morals.

'Your point's taken,' I said. 'But the one has nothing to do with the other. I'll do whatever's necessary to bring Angela back. Period.'

'Okay, Jack. I believe you.'

We released Samson, relieved him of his wallet, credit cards, ID documents, and cell phone, and bade him goodbye by giving him five minutes to make himself scarce. He was so glad to be out of the trunk I guess he didn't think about the consequences of being stuck in Germany without papers and funds.

'You won't get away with this!' Vincent raged from his resting place on the floor of the Kia.

'You're supposed to cooperate, remember? In exchange for your kneecap.'

That quieted him. Even when we replaced his gag and loaded him into the trunk, he didn't struggle. His eyes glared death and destruction one minute and pleaded to be freed the next. I almost felt sorry for him. Then I remembered Sophie's eleven-year-old daughter.

Rocky reversed down the track. As far as we could tell, our little drama, screened by the wood, had passed unobserved. We returned to the parking lot by the river. Rocky dropped me off to collect the Evoque and we set off for Passau in convoy with the rush hour traffic. If any disturbances came from the trunk, they weren't serious enough to cause Rocky to pull off the road. Maybe Vincent was cooperating, or maybe he was saving his ructions until we parked. But no, we pulled into the hotel forecourt and the contents of the trunk remained passive. While I mounted guard over the rental and its unholy passenger, Rocky went up to pack. He was back with his baggage in less time than it would have taken me to smoke a cigarette, had I still indulged in the habit.

'Call Donovan before Walter takes off,' I said. 'You need to make sure they'll be ready with a welcoming committee in Monaco.' I passed him the slip of paper on which I had written Donovan's cell number. 'See you in Budapest as quick as I can make it.'

'If you need me back here after I give him to Walter, you call me.'

'You bet.'

We shook hands and parted, still pals.

With Vincent out of my hair, I was now free and unencumbered to sort the much larger problem of saving Angela from person or persons unknown, without having a clue where to start. In the meantime, she was at the mercy of her abductors. And who the hell *were* they working for, if not for Vincent?

Chapter Seventeen

Another bad night. Angela was the cause, my own guilt complex the catalyst. It was rare for me to feel so powerless to deal with a problem. It was screwing me up inside.

Breakfast consisted of black coffee. While I was drinking it, the expected message was delivered to my cell phone. It consisted of an address in the town of Regensburg, a time – noon – and the usual injunction to come alone and unarmed. Coming alone was obligatory now that Rocky was back in Hungary. Coming unarmed was not going to happen. My trusty Boberg would nestle in its ankle holster and hope to remain undiscovered until I needed it.

The sun was in and out of a sky stocked with stratocumulus. I put on sunglasses to complement my grey chinos and a short-sleeved shirt of many stripes. My windbreaker I tossed onto the passenger seat. My appearance was smooth, suave, and debonair.

Regensburg, where once the Messerschmitt company produced its WWII fighters, lies about a hundred and fifty kms north west of Passau. Further still behind enemy lines, but that couldn't be helped. With Passau behind me I pulled into a turnout on a lonely stretch of road and used my colouring comb to darken my hair, and applied my dark, go-everywhere stick-on moustache. It was amazing how much these two touches altered my appearance. The colouring could be rinsed out, so switching back to the real me only required access to a faucet and a towel.

It was still well short of noon when I guided the Evoque into a multi-storey parking garage in the centre of Regensburg, a medium-sized city straddling a river, with lots of red roofed buildings. All very neat and tidy. The directions had specified top deck, which was open to the elements. The blue sky was shrinking, taken over by angry grey clouds.

Only a handful of other cars were parked on the top deck and all were empty. I got out and rested my backside against the Evoque's front end, heart thumping.

On the stroke of noon – literally, a nearby church bonged out the hour like the knell of doom – a nondescript Audi emerged from the up ramp and advanced at walking pace down the avenue between the parking spaces. Its tinted windows made it impossible to discern the occupants. It came to a halt in front of the Evoque, effectively blocking it.

I remained in position, propped up by the Evoque, arms folded, sunglasses giving me that air of mystery. Not mysterious enough as it transpired. My assumption was that they would frisk me, and if they missed the Boberg, we would all go off together to be reunited with Angela. It was taking an awful lot on trust, notably by me who trusted no one, but up to this point I had no choice.

The man in the passenger seat of the Audi stepped out and in an instant my worst fears about returning to Germany came home to roost. The man was no stranger to me. He was bald, tall, and slim. He was dressed immaculately in a dark grey suit of finely-woven wool, with lighter grey pin-striping. It hung on him to perfection. Not what you'd expect in a cop – at least not a Brit or American cop.

But this was a German cop. The name I knew him by, which may have been false, was Schmidt. He was a senior officer in the *Bundeskriminalamt* state security division.

Back in the day when I figured retirement would be a walkover, he and I had locked antlers over what I intended to be my final contract. With the regrettable complicity of the Swiss police, he illegally removed me from Switzerland, where I was then resident, transported me to Germany and held me incommunicado for the best part of two weeks. In the end he couldn't make the murder charge stick, and I was released. Not before he swore to catch up with me 'one day' and make me pay for the crime he knew about and the other crimes he suspected.

What was his farewell sentiment?

'One day, I think we shall meet again, you and I. You are scum, and scum always rises to the surface. Next time you rise to the surface, I shall be there to scrape you off.' Original line in threats. Delivered in English too.

The driver came around the car. He was armed and pointing it at me. His name came back to me too – Vogel. Schmidt's helpmate. My age or thereabouts, wrinkle-free narrow face, thinning hair. Sartorially speaking, not quite up to Schmidt's standard.

'Well, hello, Herr Schmidt, Herr Vogel,' I said, maintaining my outward cool. 'Are you just passing through or is this a welcoming committee?'

'The latter,' he replied, flaunting his near-perfect English. 'You are most welcome, Mr Warner. I have been waiting for you for four years.' He snapped fingers and an order at Vogel.

As Vogel approached me, Schmidt produced his a gun of his own, identical to Vogel's.

I was front-handcuffed before being frisked one-handedly by Vogel. It was as diligent a going-over as I had ever experienced, and the Boberg didn't escape his attentions.

'A-ha!' he exclaimed as his fingers brushed over the holster. 'You seem to carry excess baggage, Mr Warner.'

His English wasn't quite up to Schmidt's standard, but it was streets ahead of my German. I didn't respond. For a start, I couldn't think of a suitable quip.

The Boberg disappeared into his hip pocket, and he retreated out of arm's reach, as cops are trained to do. Hit men, too.

'So, we now have you on toast, as you Britishers say.' Schmidt was fairly gloating. I was making his day and how. 'Now we must go for a little ride to my office.'

My mind was working on the implications behind this encounter. How did Smith and Vogel come to be in a place where I was supposed to meet up with Angela's abductors? Samson was the obvious suspect. For him to bring in the police didn't make a lot of sense, but it was the best I could do to explain the puzzle at such short notice.

We all piled into the Audi, them in the front, me in the back behind a mesh screen. I accepted my lot without resistance. A chance of escape was likeliest to occur when I was being transferred from one location to another. They hadn't yet confiscated my cell phone so, keeping my cuffed hands down low out of sight, I texted basic details of my

predicament to Rocky: circumstances and name of town. My message also contained a caveat not to respond because my cell would soon be in possession of the police. Not that I expected him to be able to spring me, though if anybody could, he was that anybody. When I was done, I deleted all text and WhatsApp messages. Fortunately, it was the personal cell, not the pro, which was in the hotel room safe.

In downtown Regensburg, south of the river, we made a series of turns that brought us to journey's end in a cul-de-sac, dominated by a five-storey oblong building whose only claim to architectural excellence was a lack of it. Both men covered me with their weapons as we transferred from car to building. We crossed a lobby furnished only with a wall-to-wall counter manned by a woman police officer in the regular pale blue shirt, with short sleeves and epaulettes.

'*Grüss Gott*,' she said as we drew near.

Schmidt and Vogel acknowledged her greeting from God. We swept past, no booking, no questions, and no protest from the policewoman.

We rode an elevator to the top floor and ended up in an office that looked as if it were designed to be vandal-proof: everything in steel, on bare floors covered by vinyl. Standard interview desk, two chairs for the cops, a single chair for the poor sap under interrogation. My pockets were cleared out: Devreese passport, cell phone, wallet, loose change, plus the car key fob clipped to my belt loop. I was invited to sit in the interviewee's seat. Well, not exactly invited; Vogel pushed me into it.

I didn't get mad. I stayed cool and respectful. Getting beaten would only weaken and possibly disable me, when I would need to be at optimum physical efficiency if an opportunity arose to make a break.

'You want coffee?' Vogel asked.

'Sure,' I said. 'Thanks.'

'Black okay?'

'Sure.'

He went off through a side door. Schmidt kept me company, gun still at the ready, backside on a desk, the top of which was bare but for a grey telephone.

'Nice hair,' he commented, smiling in a smug, triumphant way, as if catching me was the highlight of his career. 'I seem to remember you

were blond. Is the moustache real?'

'Yes.' I peeled it off to prove it.

'Very funny. You English and your strange humour.'

'Yeah. You Germans and your square heads.'

His grin slipped. It wasn't smart, trying to score points off him when I was already at his mercy, but some people bring out the reckless in me. When they do, I feel a compulsion to strike back, as if they had struck me physically.

'Have your jokes, Warner, or do you prefer to be called Devreese?' A small chuckle, as if he had cracked a joke.

If he was hoping to get under my skin with his sneers, he failed.

'Yes,' he continued, undeterred, 'you must enjoy your pathetic attempts at humour while you can.' A pause before adding, 'Which won't be for very long.'

Vogel returned with a plastic tray bearing three plastic cups, all steaming. He set it down on the bare desk.

'How about getting rid of these?' I said, clinking the cuffs at them.

Schmidt considered my request then shrugged. Vogel took this as an OK and removed them. They had been overtightened and my hands began to tingle as the blood flowed back into them.

'Thanks,' I said, massaging my wrists and flexing my fingers. Everything worked. I tasted the coffee. It was the usual scuzzy stuff as provided by law enforcement offices the world over. Schmidt and Vogel were downing it without grimacing though; they say you can get used to anything if there's no choice.

A rap came at the door to the corridor. Schmidt nodded to Vogel, and Vogel went to answer it, opening the door a few inches and peering through the gap. I heard a female voice but the words were inaudible.

'*Ja, warum nicht.*' Vogel said.

He backpedalled a few paces, still gripping the door knob, to admit our visitor. In she strolled, reeking confidence, self-satisfaction and good looks. Almost the very last person I had expected to encounter in a police HQ in Regensburg, Germany.

Angela.

* * * * *

Stunned, I could only gape at her. I could make no immediate sense of her presence here. Questions jostled for asking space. How did she come to be here? Had she after all been a prisoner of Vincent's crew and managed to escape? If she had, and was in fear of being recaptured, was that why she had run to the police?

Then I noticed that she was dressed differently from usual. A dogtooth check suit with a knee-length skirt, a white rollneck sweater, sensible shoes. Very businesslike-chic.

As she planted her feet before me, a vestige of a smile escaped her lips – those lips that I had often been in intimate contact with in the past two weeks.

'Hello, André.'

The impact of that 'André' was delayed. I'd never told her my real name, so how come she was using it now?

'Angie?' The questions were still there, awaiting answers, but in my dazed state I found them impossible to articulate.

'Yes, it's me. I'm not a mirage.' Her gaze shifted from me to Schmidt. 'Did he cooperate? You found his little gun, I suppose.'

'Yes, though we might have missed it if you hadn't warned us.'

'Good.' She studied me, frowning slightly as if she was disappointed that I had made it so easy.

It clicked at long last. Like a coin dropping into a slot, the explanation dropped into the brain cell that unscrambled the inexplicable.

'You're helping the *police*?' My voice was hoarse with the shock of it.

'One of them, actually. I'm from Europol.'

Adapting to the notion of this woman as a police officer, and myself the victim of a skilfully constructed entrapment, was a lengthy process. It was still beyond credible. I struggled to convince myself it was true, that I wasn't dreaming all this, I really had been set up.

'You mean you've been working with them all along? You and Schmidt …' My voice broke. I couldn't bring myself to accuse her of being in cahoots with him. I cleared my throat, tried to cling on to my

composure. ‘How did they come to select you for the job?’

She laughed then; a jeering laugh, the kind of laugh that’s at the expense of the person on the receiving end.

‘They showed me your photo. I thought you looked yummy, so I volunteered.’

A hint of the inner rage fuelled by that comment must have shown through. She took a backward step, and Vogel made a warning movement with his automatic.

I bit my tongue, held off the name-calling that the sense of terrible betrayal almost dragged from me.

‘Well, aren’t you the sneaky broad,’ I said at length. ‘That stuff about your husband, your kids …’

‘A fiction, I’m afraid. I’ve never been married, never had kids. The part about my career in the army, the sniper work, etcetera, that was all true.’

‘You certainly gave a star performance at a personal level.’

‘Details are not required,’ Schmidt cut in. ‘We have it all on tape.’

Second shock, though more anti-climactic. Once the extent of Angela’s betrayal had sunk in, any additional perfidy was just part of the proceedings. The blindness of my trust in her, and my failings in watching my back, were making me re-evaluate my professionalism.

Schmidt wasn’t about to allow me to dwell on recent history.

‘Soon you will attend a line-up, and Frau Thomashoff will identify you as the man who killed Fabrice Tillou. Then we will finally have you where we want you, and put you out of business until you are an old, old man.’

The Thomashoff woman was the mistress of Fabrice Tillou, who had sought to avenge his death by killing me. She failed. Now she would succeed, using the forces of law and order to exact her revenge. Less satisfying at a personal level perhaps, but at least it would be legal.

‘Just in case she has another change of heart, we can always hand you over to the Italian police. They are anxious to solve a double murder in Como, and we can provide them with a very reliable witness –’ he tipped his head towards Angela, ‘– should they need it.’

‘You’ve got it all figured out, haven’t you?’ I said, addressing Schmidt

but with my focus on Angela. She reddened slightly, as if her dirty work was not something she had relished, that she was even abashed by it. Not that it mattered a hoot. She was a cop, and cops enforce the law, even if the methods are not always to their taste.

'It was self-defence,' I stated. 'Didn't you find their guns?'

'Oh, yes. We know they were under orders from the Syndicate. As for the guns … we dropped them in a deeper part of the lake. The *carabinieri* don't even know they existed.'

They were screwing me royally. Either I got my comeuppance here in Germany, or I would be handed over to the Italians for trial and sentence and an extended stretch in an Italian penitentiary.

'You've certainly done your homework,' I said, trying to make light of it. 'With especial thanks to the lady from Europol. Maybe she'll get promotion or a medal. An Oscar too, I shouldn't wonder.'

Again she flushed. Inside that perfect rib cage a heart was still beating then.

'Enough talk,' Schmidt decided, smacking the palms of his hands together as if about to applaud his achievement. 'The line-up will be in ten minutes.'

'Could I have him for those ten minutes, Werner,' Angela said. 'I want to talk to him on his own.'

Schmidt made a face. 'That's not –'

'*Please*. If it weren't for my willingness to use my body to get a result, you wouldn't have caught him. It's not a lot to ask.'

He huffed and puffed, then said, 'Ah, *scheiss drauf*.' To Vogel, '*Komm. Ich kaufe dich ein Kaffee*.'

They handcuffed me to a bracket fixed to the desk and went out together. Angela and I were left alone, facing each other across the interrogation desk.

'Something you want to say to me?' I asked.

She sat down in one of the chairs opposite.

'You may find this hard to believe, but our initial meeting in Gib really was by chance. I was on vacation, hoping to meet a nice guy. Fed up of being on my own, I suppose.'

'So you met me and I wasn't nice enough.'

'That's the trouble. You were nice enough all right. How was I to know you were a bloody hit man, for goodness sake?' She was genuinely angry. She had deceived me, yes, but my deception of her was just as big.

'When I went back to work after Spain,' she went on, 'I was seconded to the investigation into the Wolff's gun running activities, which was ongoing at the time. We had found out the twins were operating out of Budapest and I was sent to shadow them.'

'Are you telling me it was a coincidence, your showing up in Budapest?'

'In a manner of speaking. The coincidence is that you were hired to dispose of Vincent, and I was part of the Interpol-Europol effort to close the twins' operation down. I knew you were there of course, but I had no idea why, or that it might be of interest to Interpol. Not until you told me what you were doing.

'When I reported to my boss that your and our interests coincided, he did some digging about Jack Henley. It didn't lead anywhere, so he fixed me up with a miniature camera to take a photo of you. I also got your prints on a spoon. That was enough to identify you as André Warner. Schmidt got to hear about it on the internal grapevine, and that was that. He horned in on my department's enquiries with the object of nabbing you and the Wolffs as part of the same sting. Vincent only came to Passau because my boss posed as a big weapons buyer for an Arab state to lure him there, in the expectation that you would be lured too, enabling Schmidt to arrest you legally inside Germany.'

'Shame you let Vincent slip through your fingers.'

Her nod was rueful. 'You were a step ahead of us there. When I had to abandon Rocky and be "kidnapped" to make sure you walked into our trap, it meant giving up the hotel search for Vincent, so I was replaced. They tracked him down at the Dreiflüssehoff later in the day you hijacked him.'

'Yeah, too bad. Aside from that though, the entrapment side of the operation was very slick and I fell for it. You can congratulate yourself on a job well done.'

'I can understand your feeling aggrieved. I'm sorry, I was only doing my job.'

'Pity you couldn't do it without pretending to be somebody you're not, feeling things you don't feel.'

'That's what undercover policing entails. It's how we catch criminals.'

'Like me.'

She shrugged. 'You said it, André.'

* * * * *

Schmidt and Vogel marched me to the elevator and from there to the basement. I stood in line with five other guys. It was just a formality. They didn't resemble me at all. We faced a wide mirror that was clear glass on the other side, where witnesses made their identifications in anonymity. In my case there would be but a single witness and, if Schmidt was to be believed, the outcome was not in doubt.

So it proved. We returned to the top floor, a smirking Schmidt, Vogel, and me.

'You have been formally identified as the man who shot and killed Fabrice Tillou,' he announced, 'and now we must formally charge you.'

The process was tedious, and involved two uniformed officers, male and female. Name, parents' names, date of birth, address, measurements, weight, photographs, eye prints, fingerprints. When it was done we returned to the fifth-floor interview room.

'We need a statement,' Schmidt informed me.

'You're not getting one,' I snapped back. Whereupon he lashed out with the back of his hand. The blow had enough force behind it to send me reeling. I recovered, seeing red, and went for him. My fist crunched into his cheek with all my resentment behind it and he tumbled backwards over the desk. As I followed through with murderous intent, I was vaguely aware of Vogel closing in.

'Stop or I shoot!' he yelled.

Almost I didn't obey him. The red mist that had obscured my vision was suddenly wiped away, as if blown by a gust of wind. My fist remained suspended over Schmidt's head, the blow undelivered.

'Get away from him,' Vogel ordered. The muzzle of his gun was

targeted on my upper body.

I drew back, breathing hard, self-control restored but only by a slim margin.

'Don't touch me again,' I snarled at Schmidt, now heaving himself off the desk. His cheekbone was weeping blood and his eyes were unfocused. It had been one of my better punches. I might yet come to regret it.

'Statement,' he said, staggering a little as he walked around the desk and dragged open a drawer. A large notepad appeared, then a dinky recording machine. He sat behind the desk and extracted a ball pen from the inside pocket of his jacket.

He pointed at the interviewee chair. 'Sit.'

Loath to allow him even minor victories over me, I still hesitated. Finally though, I sat and faced him.

'I want a lawyer.'

'Later. Statement before lawyer.'

'The other way round.' I was fairly sure German law worked like English and US law. I was less sure how long they could hold me now that I had been charged. Maybe indefinitely.

Outside was fine and sunny again, the clouds beginning to scatter. No sounds intruded on the eyrie of Schmidt and Vogel. Apart from the uniformed officers and Angela I hadn't seen any evidence of life. The BKA, of which Schmidt was a senior officer, was disconnected from the regular police force, having jurisdiction over crimes committed with a political element. Frau Thomashoff had been the wife of a government minister of the day, hence my unorthodox arrest and removal to Germany without the lengthy protocol of extradition. This time around I had made it easier for them. I was already here, the Thomashoff woman was more cooperative, and the case was open and shut.

They didn't push the statement issue. I was denying it all anyway, so it would have been very short. A return ride to the basement resulted in my being allocated a cell. The usual layout: bed, upright chair, table. No TV, no luxuries. A lawyer would be summoned. When? *Zu gegebener Zeit.*

I also made the acquaintance of Sergeant Koch, officer in charge of

the cells. He spoke only German, so cosy chats were out.

To be fair, I was not badly treated. Later in the day they fed me – goulash with a slice of carrot cake for dessert – left me a bottle of Bitburger beer, provided some magazines (in German) and a paperback crime novel in English. I'd fared worse in some hotels. To pass the hours and keep me in shape I performed a hundred press ups, sit ups, and did some running on the spot.

Lights out was at 10.30pm. Sleep came so instantly that when I awoke at dawn I suspected them of drugging me.

Breakfast was served by Sergeant Koch, along with a message.

'*Die Frau kommt später.*'

My pidgin German translated this as 'the woman is coming later'. The only Frau I could think of likely to pay me a visit was a lawyer. I prowled about my cage, used the john, read a couple of chapters. Mid-morning my visitor arrived. Not a lawyer after all, but my fifth columnist lover, Angela Renwick, undercover police officer.

'Hello, André,' she said, after Koch had left her on the other side of the bars. Still dressed severely, though the skirt and the heels were both a few inches higher today, a reminder of her shapely legs.

'Hi. Come to gloat, commiserate, lecture, or what?'

'It was my job. I'm sorry it had to be you.' She bit her lip. 'Sincerely sorry, I mean.'

I shoved my hands in my pockets and stared at her.

'Sorry it had to be *me*? What does that mean? What difference did it make whether it was me or some other sucker? I'm nothing to you, just another criminal to arrest.'

She moved closer, gripped a bar in each hand, her knuckles showing white.

'That's just it. What I didn't tell you yesterday is that you're … you're not nothing to me.'

I wasn't sure I'd heard aright. 'You must be kidding. You're telling me you deceived me from the get-go, just to entice me to Germany so that Schmidt could put me behind bars, but all along I *meant* something to you?' I shook my head. 'Even if I believed you, I don't get it.'

Now she was reaching through the bars, touching my arm. Her face

was a map of regret, her lips trembling.

'Yes, I started out as a cop, just doing my job. Then … I got to like you, despite all the violence you attracted. Then, I got to more than like you –'

'Shut up!' I growled, smacking her hand away. 'Why've you come to tell me this? Is it supposed to make me feel better about us? Don't come to me to expunge your guilt.'

My raised voice brought Koch back into the ante-room.

'*Gibt es ein Problem*?' he enquired of Angela.

'*Macht nichts*,' she muttered, not looking at him. '*Alles gut.*'

'Okay,' he said, and with a stern backward glance, left us.

'André … I didn't come for any of the reasons you said. I came to give you something.' She had a purse slung from her shoulder on a long strap. She snapped the catch and fumbled inside it. Her hand reappeared with a paper bag containing an object; she passed it across to me. I only had to feel it to recognise it as a handgun.

I didn't question her motives or what she intended me to do with this lifeline. I stuffed if under the mattress of my bed, and returned to the bars.

'It's not a gun that fires bullets,' she said, her voice lowered.

'You mean it's a toy?'

'No, no, it's a gas firing gun. It fires CS gas and blanks. It's modelled on the Walther PPK. You can buy them from gun shops here.'

She reached for my hand and this time I clasped it.

'You must be crazy to do this. They'll suspect you right away.'

'Maybe they will. They can't prove anything, and why would I help them arrest you if I was going to help you escape?'

Now my arms were through the bars and I was holding her.

'Maybe they won't be able to prove it, but they'll know.'

She tossed her head. 'Let them know. You risked entering Germany to rescue me. I didn't need rescuing, which somehow makes it an even greater debt I owe you.' Her fingers touched my cheek, fleetingly. 'Oh, André, if only it could have been different. Me not a cop, you not a … a whatever you are.'

'You'd better go,' I said gruffly. 'Don't make them wonder what's going on in here.'

'Yes, of course. Another thing. They collected your car. It's in the parking area behind the building. You won't be able to use it though, I couldn't get the keys and your other stuff. I'll get it back to you somehow.'

'Getting away without transport, papers, and money is going to tax my ingenuity,' I said, with a rueful grin.

'No, it won't. I called Rocky. He's going to meet you. He'll be on station from –' she consulted her wrist watch '– just about now. You go left at the front of the building, then first left again. That's where he'll be, at the corner.'

'You're a star.'

'Never mind the flattery. You've got a gun, now use it. You can't kill with it, but they won't know that. With your reputation they'll assume you'll stop at nothing to get out of here.' She gave a small shudder. 'The downside of that is that they won't hesitate to shoot *you* – and shoot to kill!'

Between the bars our lips came together in a last, lingering kiss. It brought back good memories, bitter-sweet now that memories were all that would remain. The moment our lips parted company she left, visibly upset, without so much as a goodbye. The door slammed behind her and I listened to her footsteps down the corridor until they faded from earshot.

Useless to speculate on her change of heart. I needed a plan. Pointing a gun at Koch was only the opening gambit, as was removing the pistol strapped to his waist. Escaping from a building crawling with police, that was the challenge. If I could get my Henley passport and stash of cash from my hotel, I could manage the rest.

The Walther lookalike was a nicely crafted piece of work. The magazine was empty but the bag contained a circular plastic box of fifty rounds. They resembled blanks, but the label on the box stated CS gas. The brass casings had black plastic tips, otherwise they felt and loaded like live rounds. Seven in all, plus an eighth in the breech. The Walther PPK had been good enough for James Bond, so I guessed it would do for me.

It was a while before Koch returned to collect my breakfast debris. I almost felt sorry for him when I produced the Walther. He'd had a soft

job, taking care of remand prisoners, probably never looked down the muzzle of a gun before.

If he'd been smart he would've stayed out of reach. But he was aged about fifty and hadn't risen above sergeant, so he wasn't smart enough. He came to my beckon and raised his arms when I made 'stick-'em-up' motions with the Walther.

His gun was much meatier than mine and could be presumed to be loaded with genuine bullets. It was an H & K. Made in the Fatherland, and packing a big punch. The Walther went in my pocket where, being compact, it made scarcely a bulge. Now for the door to my cell. The lock was a combo type and without Koch's cooperation I was stuck. Instead of walking out, he meekly entered the numbers and the door swung open. To him, of course, I was a killer and therefore unpredictable. Why take chances for a lousy sergeant's salary?

'Inside,' I ordered, as I stepped outside. Gesturing to make sure he understood.

'*Ja … ja*,' he said, his expression hangdog. He was going to be in trouble with Schmidt later.

As he knew the combination of the door I couldn't simply lock him in. Even if I could, he would be able to yell for help. By more sign-talk I got him to kneel. I removed his holster belt and pants belt using them to secure his wrists and strap him to a bar in a far corner of the cell, out of reach of the door. My pillow slip served as a gag. I worked fast, conscious that at any moment another police officer might come calling.

My luck held. I went to the door used by Koch for his comings and goings. I opened it a crack on an empty corridor. Good. Several doors off. Bad. My objective was the stairwell up to the ground floor. It was part way along the corridor, beneath an illuminated NOTAUSGANG sign. Delay would only increase the prospect of discovery so, with a friendly '*Auf wiedersehen*' to Koch, I scuttled along the corridor. On reaching the stairs, I paused to listen. No sounds of life, just a faint hum of machinery. I went up in leaps of three steps, hit the half-landing, then three more steps of three and I was peering around the corner into another corridor. And another NOTAUSGANG sign, over a door with a locking bar. Beyond lay freedom.

The wall opposite the stairwell had opaque glass panels along the upper half. Vague shapes moved behind them, accompanied by muted voices. A door to my left opened and I ducked back into the stairwell, the H & K ready to frighten, though not to shoot. Killing or even wounding a cop was not on the agenda today, or any day in the future.

Again I lucked out. Footsteps receded away from me. Now I was out in the corridor and walking at a normal pace, hoping not to be noticed through the opaque glass. I depressed the locking bar, the door swung open and I emerged into a parking lot. The Evoque caught my eye at once. What Angela didn't know because I hadn't told her, was that I kept a spare key fob in a magnetic box attached to the underside.

A man in coveralls was just getting out of a police car near the entrance, which was guarded by a barrier. I shoved the gun down the back of my pants waistband. I waited until he entered the building then advanced onto the lot, using the parked vehicles as a screen wherever possible. My brain was assessing the advantages of recovering the Evoque without compromising my break-out. The barrier was the stumbling block. I decided to stick with the plan organised by Angela.

As I crossed the parking lot, I quit trying to be invisible and instead tried to be casual. The guy who had entered the building now exited it, right in front of me.

'*Grüss Gott*,' he called out cheerily, and I responded with a cordial grin and a hand wave, not trusting my ability to sound Germanic.

Then I was strolling past the barrier and into the street. A left turn, as specified by Angela, would take me along a tree-lined road, with parking spaces on both sides. *Alemannen-strasse*. Now I was walking briskly, just a guy out exercising, swinging my arms as recommended by experts to send the red corpuscles coursing through arteries and veins. The adrenaline was certainly rushing around at top speed.

Rocky, bless him, was there, where Angela said he would be, at the next corner on the left. The Kia, the sun glinting off its black bodywork, the muffler emitting a thin streamer of smoke. I cruised up alongside, tapped on his window. He didn't look, just nodded. The door unlocked audibly. Seconds later I was sitting beside him. We grinned at each other.

'You're a mad bastard,' I said, and punched his arm; it was like

punching a concrete pillar. 'You should have left me to rot.'

'I know. But Angie told me she not love me any more if I don't come to fetch you.'

We chuckled companionably. He engaged drive and we set off down *Alemannen-strasse*, away from the police HQ. No sirens wailed in our slipstream, nor during our drive through Regensburg, past the Neo-Gothic cathedral with its twin openwork spires, nor through the suburbs, and out into the countryside, where cows chewed cuds and sheep grazed and the world was at peace.

As we drove he brought me up to speed on the Vincent scenario. He had delivered our man to Walter and contacted Donovan to arrange for him to be met. To ensure Vincent's good conduct during the flight, Rocky drugged him. With what and where it came from, he wasn't saying. I was puzzled why Donovan hadn't reported back to me, to confirm safe receipt of the goods, then remembered that my cell phone was back in Regensburg. Fortunately, I still had my spare, back at the hotel.

After two hours on the road, as we neared the outskirts of Passau, Rocky slowed then suddenly swung the car left, off the highway.

'What's going on?' I asked.

'We cannot cross the border here. It is river border and they will have road blocks on bridges by now. We must go east, into Czech Republic.'

Up until now, the border hadn't crossed my mind. In the euphoria at having gotten clean away I had been happy to leave it all to Rocky. It came back with a jolt that I was far from home free, and even if we made it to Budapest I was still a fugitive from Europol. I even considered excluding Budapest from my journey plan, and heading west for France or Switzerland. Travelling overland without a passport was do-able within the EU, though random checks still take place. More importantly, my Henley passport was too valuable to abandon. Faked genuine passports are hellishly hard and expensive to acquire, and equally hard to renew. The several thousand euros that were sitting with it in my hotel room safe would also be useful.

So we went east, entering the Czech Republic via a logging track in the Bayerische Wald national park, a heavily forested area that straddles

the border. I could have borne to know how Rocky, a Finn, was familiar with such an obscure route. He didn't offer to enlighten me, so I let it go.

We avoided Austria, staying in Czechia and not encountering a solitary police car. From Czechia we crossed into Slovakia. By then it was well past midday and Rocky needed sustenance. We found a roadside café in a village called Trnava that offered "best food" in English. A jolly waitress in Slovak folk dress of flouncy printed skirt and blouse with puffy sleeves served us cabbage soup (*kapustnica*) followed by dumplings (*knedle*) with *espresso* coffee that was the best I'd tasted since Spain.

Hungary was less than an hour's drive distant, even using country roads. We came to it and crossed the border without reducing speed. Budapest being less than another fifty kms, we were drawing up outside our hotel while the sun was still high in the sky.

'Good going,' I said. 'I owe you big time.'

'You owe me a pay rise,' was his rejoinder, teeth flashing to show he wasn't expecting one.

'You'll get it. You deserve it.'

'Fucking right!'

From my room, I phoned Donovan for an update. He didn't answer. Sulking maybe. I sent a short text instead.

'Anyway,' Rocky said, money-fixated as ever. 'We must pay Walter, then we can leave Budapest. Our work is finished, no?'

'Yours, yes. Mine, in a manner of speaking, is just beginning. My real work, anyhow.'

Chapter Eighteen

We checked out of our respective hotels and out of Budapest that same afternoon, in favour of a pension hotel in the village of Erd, just outside the capital. Rocky had a few grumbles about the move, but I reminded him that Angela knew where we were holed up and might yet have a reversal of loyalties.

It was intended as an overnighter, for me at any rate. In case Schmidt had issued a description of me as dark-haired, I used the opportunity to wash the colouring out and became a natural blond once more. Come the dawn, I would head west, retracing my route through Slovenia, Italy, and into a corner of France, for Monaco. There to complete the job Donovan had hired me for weeks ago.

Two texts reached me on the morning of my departure. Angela, to whom I had entrusted both my cell numbers, congratulating me on my escape. She also vowed to do her best to return the Evoque to me at a time and place to be agreed.

The second text was from Donovan, confirming all was well with our "guests" and when did I expect to arrive in Monaco to fulfil the contract.

In three days, I texted back, requesting him to book me a room as before, at the Meridien, in Nice.

Before leaving I organised a rental car – a Kia SUV, the twin of Rocky's apart from the colour, which was grey. It took time as, in order to use it elsewhere in the EU, I needed a special document, and green card insurance. Afterwards a visit to the bank to arrange payment of Rocky's wages to his account in Helsinki, plus a bonus, plus an extra €15,000 for Walter, which I was banking on Donovan to cover. I donated the H & K automatic to Rocky's private collection, to dispose of as he saw fit.

He and I said our final farewells with a high five.

'Until you are in shit again,' was his parting crack.

'Keep your bag packed. It could be as early as tomorrow.'

We did a man hug, then he was a diminishing figure in my rearview mirror, his arm raised in valediction until I rounded a bend and he was no more. I would miss him.

The journey was tedious but uneventful, which is always good. Events are to be avoided when you're carrying illicit weaponry and have the police on your back. Even though I had travelled through three countries since my escape, there was no telling how far and wide the tentacles of the German police might extend. Border inspections are obsolete, but the police retain the facility to erect barriers at short notice.

For that reason I took to a dirt road when crossing from Hungary to Slovenia. The tactic didn't eliminate the risks, only reduced them.

Next came Italy. After much contemplation of maps and GPS, I settled for the mountain route, through the small town of Zaga to the Italian hamlet of Uccea. Six kms of winding road with a poor surface. No traffic worth mentioning, just a single truck coming in the other direction. A dilapidated ITALIA sign marked the border, with the usual depiction of the EU twelve-star flag beside it. No barrier, no police vehicles. I breathed in my relief and parked at the roadside, where I took a public pee, French-style.

The road divided, the right fork leading to Uccea, the left to the city of Udine. If they were expecting me, they would have been waiting before the fork, not after, so I felt safe enough taking the faster route, to Udine.

Inside Italy I felt relaxed about using the major highways, and, leaving Udine on Sunday morning after an early breakfast, I made fast progress to France, where I faced new choices. At the Mediterranean end of the Franco-Italian border are three points of entry, all of them busy, then nothing for about twenty kms, where two minor roads cross over. To use either of these meant swinging north at Ventimiglia. The road was narrow but well-paved and traffic was sparse. I came up to the border at about ten after six, the sun on its downward trajectory, dazzling me as the road veered west.

It would have been a pity to get so far only to fall at the last hurdle,

so I dismounted out of sight of the border crossing and scrambled up a rocky hillside, armed with my binoculars.

My heart lurched when I focused on the little wooden cabin at the roadside, and the black and white Gendarmerie sedan behind it. A *gendarme* was leaning against the car, smoking, and looked bored. Was he here as a matter of routine, or on the lookout for me? Surely if they were manning the borders to catch me, they'd use more than a solitary country cop.

I convinced myself he wasn't there to arrest me and retraced my steps down the hill to the SUV. The Hungarian plates were unusual enough to attract more than a passing interest and resigned me to being questioned.

So it proved. He flagged me down, flipped his cigarette into the road, and adjusted his *casquette.* Thumbs in belt, he approached me as I drew to a standstill, my innocent tourist grin in place.

'*Bonjour, monsieur,*' he said, affably enough it seemed. '*Vous venez d'où?*'

'From Hungary,' I said in French, seeing no point in pretending otherwise as the plates were a giveaway.

No eyebrows were raised. He requested my *papiers.* I handed over my Henley passport, hoping it hadn't been compromised by Angela, together with the car rental contract, and the green card. He studied the passport, lingering over the stamped pages. The latest entry was two years old.

'What is your destination?'

'Grenoble.' An ex-paramour of mine lived there, and I was well-acquainted with the city if he tested me on it.

'*Ouvrez le coffre, s'il vous plaît.*'

I switched off the engine, got out, and went around the back to open the door to the cargo space. Inside was my luggage, contents all innocent. Nevertheless he insisted I open it for a good rummage. He was thorough. If the absence of weapons or drugs disappointed him, he didn't let it show.

'What were you doing in Hungary?' he asked.

'Meeting a friend,' I said, adding, with a wink, 'A woman.'

He didn't return my wink or make a passing joke about women. He tapped my passport against the palm of his hand then, presumably accepting that I was a harmless Brit, restored it and the car documents to me.

'Very well,' he said. 'You may continue. *Allez-y.*'

'Thanks.'

As I moved off, down a steep hill, I caught sight of him in the mirror: he was standing in the middle of the road, writing in a notebook.

* * * * *

From the balcony of my top floor room at Le Meridien Hotel, I looked out over the curve of the shoreline, with its rim of white surf segregating the silver sands from the milky blue of the sea. Behind the sands, the Promenade des Anglais, and behind the promenade the bulwark of Nice's front line buildings, of which Le Meridien was prominent. The fronds of the queen palms on the seafront were brown and drooping, owing to the infestation of a species of weevil from Africa, which was turning them into husks. But the grass strips that bordered both sides of the road were a lush emerald green, and clearly not starved of water.

Phase one of the contract was as good as over. It was too soon to celebrate, but at least the impossible part was wrapped up, and had proved to be possible after all. The second phase, the kill, was still to come and might take place as early as tomorrow. I wasn't looking forward to it, only to putting it behind me and steering my private life back onto a straighter path.

As for the downsides, my arrest had served as a reminder that I was ever more vulnerable in Western Europe. The deception that Angela had practised on me was a shock, only part-redeemed by her subsequent *volte-face*. The loss of the Evoque was a minor nuisance I could live with.

I connected my cell phone to its charger. I showered. I sat out on the balcony and watched the people traffic down at street level and the boats scudding about the Bay of Angels. When I grew blasé over the view, which was after all merely an array of mundane elements – sky, water, sand, vegetation – grouped in an aesthetically pleasing setting, I went

inside. I used the hotel phone to call Donovan and ask him to send word to Marquise Sophie of my presence in Nice.

He agreed to do it, then wrong-footed me by announcing that he himself was in Nice, staying at the same hotel as me.

'We must stop meeting like this,' I joked. 'People will talk.'

'Let's dine together and really give them something to gossip about,' he proposed, joining in the gag. 'We need to discuss the next step.'

We arranged to meet in the hotel's rooftop restaurant at eight.

* * * * *

At his request, I chose the wine – a Sangiovese red to complement the tomato-based sauce of my ravioli starter. He was indifferent. He shared the bottle with me, but I guessed he was hankering for a Guinness.

'I hope you're taking good care of the twins,' I said as we clinked glasses.

'Not my department. I spoke with Pierre yesterday. They're being held in the same place, in a basement with no windows, a steel door, and three armed guards working four-hour shifts.'

A prickle of unease ran down my spine.

'The same place? You mean in the same *room*?'

'Why not? It's secure. Two rooms means double the chances of one of them breaking out.'

I tried to rationalise my concerns, to express them in a form he would understand.

'The object in leaving Victor in Sophie's care, once she'd identified him, was to ensure the twin still at large was Vincent. You remember Vincent? The twin we're really interested in.'

'What are you talking about?' Nettled now. 'I'm not a feckin' idjit.' His Irish brogue was always more pronounced when he was miffed.

'What I'm talking about is keeping them segregated, so we know Victor is Victor and Vincent is Vincent. If I've understood you correctly, Vincent and Victor are locked up together, which cancels out the advantage of keeping Victor out of circulation.'

For a beat or two he didn't speak.

'Agh, you're worrying over nothing. Sophia identified Victor, didn't she?'

I just stared at him.

'Well, for feck's sake, she can identify him again.'

'You make it sound so easy. Just remember, if the ID isn't guaranteed – and I mean guaranteed – reliable, I won't be snuffing anybody.'

'Your food's going cold,' he pointed out.

Silently fuming, though it wasn't his doing, I set about my ravioli. We ate without speaking for a few minutes. The food was too good to spoil with acrimonious debate.

He finished his crab tempura ahead of me, dabbed his lips, and said, 'Sophie's expecting us for lunch tomorrow at her place. That convenient for you?'

'She's the reason I'm here.'

He grunted. 'If I were you I'd be careful to stay within the bounds of professionalism.'

'The bounds of professionalism?' I echoed, my tone mocking. 'You mean I shouldn't do anything that's not connected with the contract.'

He looked sour. 'I mean .... feck it, you know what I mean.'

I swallowed my last ravioli, took a sip of wine, and leaned back.

'You needn't worry about Mme Sophie and me. She may have ideas, I don't. Once the job's done, and the fee paid, you've seen the last of me, and that's a promise.'

We set the sensitive stuff aside and moved on to chat about Ireland, which would be my favourite country it weren't for the weather. He discoursed on its history inside out and I learned much that was virgin territory to me. We ended the evening on amiable terms and, as he was without transport, I offered him a ride to Monaco for tomorrow's lunch date with *la marquise.*

* * * * *

On my bed in my undershorts, I made a call to Angela. Her cell phone was off. I hoped that wasn't an ominous sign. Next I tried Patricia and listened to a message in her imperfect English: she was 'no available' and

I was to leave a number. I didn't bother. While I was in the mood for telecommunicating, I contemplated trying Maura. I took a rain check on that too. Even if she would speak to me, it would only be a souvenir of how much I missed her, and the futility of clinging to a wish that would never achieve fulfilment.

I switched on the TV and tuned in to a Netflix movie. It sent me to sleep in minutes.

* * * * *

As with most of the other borders I had crossed over the past few days, entering Monaco was a non-event. The only confirmation that you are technically leaving France and arriving in another country is a roadside sign, edged in red, inscribed MONACO, indistinguishable from the town perimeter signs all over France.

As a precaution against being separated from my luggage, I had checked out and shifted it to the car. Donovan was spending an extra night at the Meridien.

'Business,' he explained laconically, though I didn't enquire.

Nobody intercepted us as we descended to the port. We passed a parked police car with two officers inside, and the officer next to the road gave us The Stare. In my experience the French police subject everyone to this treatment, so I didn't get paranoid about it. As we halted for the lights at the Princesse Charlotte intersection, I glanced in the rearview mirror. Behind us was a black sedan, make unknown, the driver a woman with glasses and platinum hair. She was wielding a lipstick. She had been sitting on our tail since we entered Monaco. The lights went green, and we traversed Avenue Princesse Charlotte. The black sedan dropped back but stayed in contact.

Donovan noticed my preoccupation with the rear view. 'Problem?'

'Can't tell. Car behind us, been there for three blocks.'

He twisted round in his seat, made a dismissive sound.

'Even so,' I said.

I skipped the Avenue de la Costa, the logical route to Sophie's parking garage, and remained on the Boulevard de Suisse. At the lights

I made a right turn. The peroxide blonde carried straight on.

'You see,' Donovan said.

'Yeah. It never hurts though.'

It wasn't possible to double back, as the streets were all one-way in this section of Monaco, so I made another right followed by a left then, with the outraged GPS exhorting me to do U-turns no matter their illegality, I eventually came back onto the Boulevard de Suisse and thence to our objective, the entrance to the basement garage of Sophie's apartment block. Donovan had a pass for the barrier. As before, the garage contained only a scattering of vehicles.

'Some apartments aren't occupied yet,' Donovan observed, 'and others have absentee owners.'

Up on the eighteenth floor we were greeted, if that's the right word, by Sophie's sour-faced maid, whose name I learned today was Lucette.

'She's the ultimate in efficiency,' Donovan whispered aside to me as she led us through to the living room.

'Looking like that, she'd have to be,' I said in an undertone, and he tittered discreetly.

Lucette offered no refreshment. I mooched around the room, was drawn to one of the two antique bureaux: its entire surface was home to a collection of photographs in identical silver frames, like an array of solar panels. Sophie featured in several of them, with her kids. Five kids, not the four I had met at my restaurant in Spain. Then I remembered the girl, Francine, raped and abducted by Vincent, her step-father. I picked her out in some of the family shots, the eldest of the three girls by about eight or nine years. Dark, near-black hair, same as her brothers. Very pretty – same as her half-sisters. An adjacent head-and-shoulders studio portrait emphasised cobalt blue eyes and a generous smile. Sophie and her offspring were a handsome bunch all round.

'You are looking at the photograph of Francine?' Sophie's voice behind me.

I turned. Donovan was on his feet.

'Yes, and the others.'

'Francine was very special to me. She was my first, then the boys, then I had no more until the other two girls, ten years later.' Her mouth

twisted in distaste. 'By Vincent. I love them too, but not the same. Because they have fair hair, they are a constant reminder of him.' She looked at me, a trace of appeal in her eyes. 'You can understand this.'

'I'm not sure I can, if only because I have no children, never had a family.'

She nodded in understanding. 'Yours is not the kind of profession that would allow it, I think.'

Never a truer word was spoken. So far, my efforts to normalise my life had all crumbled to dust.

We had been conversing as though we were alone. Donovan issued a reminder of his presence with a discreet cough into his furled hand.

'Hello, Don,' Sophie said, upping the charm and offering her cheek. 'So nice to see you. Are you well?'

'And yourself,' he said, seeming grateful for any crumbs from the *marquise's* table. I almost felt sorry for him.

'It is another beautiful day,' Sophie proclaimed. 'Let us sit outside.'

We all moved towards the French doors, but Sophie restrained Don with a raised hand, like a cop stopping the traffic.

'Not you, Don. You and I will meet here for lunch. Until then you are, how is it said in English, a free agent?'

He thanked her through his teeth and probably cursed me under his breath. A nod to both of us and he withdrew to another part of the apartment. It had plenty of parts, so I assumed Sophie was confident he wouldn't be able to overhear.

On the terrace, she summoned Lucette without using her powers of speech. The maid just materialised like a ghost.

'A drink?' Sophie suggested.

'Too early for alcohol,' I said. 'How about a tonic water?'

'I will join you,' Sophie said and, taking my arm, guided me to a chaise longue-type seat in basket weave. I sat and she sat beside me, not quite in bodily contact.

'I try to protect him,' she lamented, 'but he doesn't appreciate it.'

'Donavan? Protect him from what?'

'Anything illegal.' Her gaze travelled over my face. I reciprocated in kind and it was a pleasure. She was an exceptionally good-looking

woman. 'Such as abduction, such as … murder.'

'Why? I mean why should you specially want to protect Don. You let him hire me and act as my controller. It makes him an accessory to murder.'

'I had not thought of it in that way.' She took a break while Lucette served our tonics. When she resumed, it was with a wistful air, her eyes on a distant point, out in the Med. 'He and I were close once but when I married Vincent I was faithful, for a while.' Again the facial scrutiny. 'But I remained fond of Don until a few years ago, when quite suddenly he became an old man, while I … I considered myself still a young woman.'

'And you still are.'

'You are so gallant for an Englishman.' She sipped tonic water, her eyes never leaving me.

'Only half English, don't forget. The rest of me is closer to France.'

A siren whooped in the street below. As if the sound were the trigger for a change of subject, she said abruptly, 'We must decide about Vincent.'

'Decide? Does that mean you're uncertain that you still want to get rid of him?'

'No, not that.' A laugh, harsh, jarring. 'Never that. He is filth of the worst kind. He must die.'

Based on what she had told me about him, I seconded that death sentence.

'So what's the decision?'

'How and when he must die?' She placed a languid hand on my thigh, stroked back and forth. It was distracting, but no hardship to endure. It made me think of Angela.

'At present, I don't have a gun, so shooting is out.'

She stared at me, a frown creasing the bridge of her perfect nose.

'You have no gun? But you must.'

'There are other ways to kill, Sophie. I can even do it with my bare hands. If you don't go for that, I could borrow a chef's knife from your kitchen. You know the kind – long blade, triangular shape.'

Her shrug was dismissive. 'I am not familiar with cooking tools. You

would not have a problem with that, sticking a knife into him?'

Knifing was not my style. I would sooner keep my victims at arm's length or further, and the bloodletting at a minimum. The bare hands method was preferable. I could use a choke-hold to block off his carotid arteries, or collapse his trachea with a blow to the throat with the edge of my hand. Clean but very close and personal and therefore also not my first choice.

'Tomorrow we will go to the place where he – they – are being kept. We will identify Vincent and you will kill him. If necessary you can borrow a gun from the guards.'

'Simple as that,' I said, and it really was that simple in the physical sense. No gain in delaying or making a big performance out of it. The guy had it coming, and more. Rape and murder of his wife's eleven-year old daughter. Crimes don't come much nastier, or punishment more deserving.

'So we are agreed.' She was still squeezing my thigh. I was still enjoying it, and my enjoyment was all too noticeable.

'Yes. Tomorrow.'

'Don will make the arrangements.' She drained her glass of tonic water. 'Now, let us have lunch.'

* * * * *

That evening, we dined out at the Café de Paris, next door to the Casino in Monte Carlo. Sophie got mildly tipsy drinking limoncello instead of wine, and back in the apartment she got more than mildly wanton. She took the lead right from the start, stripping down to her underwear which was white, tight, and minimal. To complement it she wore white stockings, the type that stay up with no visible accompaniment. Her figure was an amalgam of runway slender and Monroe curves.

It was sex for its own sake. She was an exciting woman and only a eunuch could have failed to be aroused by her techniques that owed more to the hooker sorority than the aristocracy. My mind remained on a different plane, mostly silently apologising to Maura for enjoying it so much. As for Sophie, it was hard to satisfy her at any level. 'More' and

'faster' were her favourite injunctions. I did my utmost.

Her expectations exceeded my potency. It might have gone on until daybreak if I hadn't slipped away when she fell into a doze pre-dawn. I bedded down on a couch to slide within minutes into an exhausted slumber, enhanced with lurid dreams in which I was at the mercy of a horde of Sophie clones, all naked, all hell bent on killing me by debauchery.

Chapter Nineteen

The house was more of a small chateau, imposing from the outside, in a state of disrepair within.

'Only the west wing is habitable,' Sophie informed me as we stood by her car, a 7-series BMW in two-tone black and maroon.

'Is that where they are?'

Her smile went nowhere near her eyes.

'No, they are in the basement. I didn't want them to be too pampered.'

We were on the high ground behind the perfume town of Grasse. It was blustery, and the wind was hot, as you would expect on the French Riviera in early August. It was building up to a *mistral*, when it would turn cold. Two birds of prey were circling in a sky marred with wisps of high cloud, the sun pale and hazy.

On a bench beside the entrance door, a man was sitting, smoking and watching us. Beside him on the tiled terrace, a tabby cat dozed in a patch of sunlight.

'Who are you?' Sophie said, with all the icy hauteur that members of the aristocracy affect when addressing lesser beings.

'Raoul.' He remained seated, drawing on his cigarette. He was of stocky build, a full head of smarmed brown hair, clad in blue jeans and a matching denim jacket.

'Are you one of the guards?' Sophie asked.

'Who wants to know?'

'Your employer.'

'Pierre is my employer.'

'And I am Pierre's employer.'

The message penetrated – he was in the presence of nobility, the source of his daily bread. He went from surly to servile in a flash. He tossed away the cigarette and jumped up, an ingratiating grin displaying

teeth of any colour but white.

'You're the *marquise* then?'

'I am she, and I would like you to take us to the prisoners.'

'*D'accord, madame la marquise. Toute de suite.*'

Sophie didn't need an escort to find the basement. She sent Raoul on ahead, and she and I strolled leisurely behind, her arm linked with mine.

'You are sure you can do it,' she said.

It wasn't framed as a question, so I figured she was sure too.

'If you confirm beyond all doubt it's Vincent I'll be killing, it'll be no hardship. He merits it.'

'Very much so. It is a pity Pierre locked them in the same room. It would have been so much easier not to have to go through that tiresome identification process again.'

We trailed after Raoul, through an open door with flaking paintwork. Inside, it smelled musty, and cobwebs abounded in ceiling corners and crevices. Furniture in the hallway comprised only a hulking dresser with a mirror that reached almost to the ceiling. The glass was smeary and cracked along one corner. Underfoot, flagstones, polished smooth by centuries of feet.

'How old is this place?' I asked.

'It was built in 1744, but part of it was torn down during the Revolution. My father's great-great, oh, I don't know how many greats, grandfather rebuilt it in the 1850s. It is not much used now.'

'Except as a prison?'

She fashioned a pout. 'Only this once. I don't make a habit of imprisoning people. In any case, it was your idea. Afterwards, I think I will close the place for good.'

A closed door led to a descending stairway. It was lit but gloomy. She went in front, holding onto the steel rail, which wasn't all that firmly attached. The stairs were stone or concrete and in poor condition.

'Watch your step,' I cautioned.

'Thanks,' she said testily. Not a woman who cared much for Walter Raleigh-style chivalry in a man.

She had been withdrawn and monosyllabic over breakfast. Donovan ate with us, though God knows where he spent the night. Chances were

he'd taken my place in her bed. I'd formed the impression that any prick would serve.

This morning we were back to business. We would go to the chateau, which was near Grasse, and I would do to Vincent what I was being paid to do. For my sake, we would have to remove Victor from the immediate area, as a potential witness to murder. Sophie had already warned me she intended to be present, if only to see Vincent squirm and beg. Which, she assured me, he would do.

'So might all of us,' I remarked, 'if our lives depended on it.'

After breakfast she had set in motion an internet transfer of fifty percent of my fee, standard practice in my contracts. When she pressed the key to debit her account in Luxembourg a quarter of a million US and beamed it to my account in Switzerland, she displayed no emotion at all. She might have been settling her grocery bill.

'The rest when he is dead, *n'est-ce pas*?'

'Those are the terms of the contract.'

Her acknowledgement sounded grudging. I didn't care. She had signed up for the package and I expected her to honour it in full. We said goodbye to Don, who on Sophie's instructions was to stay uninvolved. I sensed his relief.

Now, as we reached the foot of the stairs and encountered another guard, her insouciance was of the past. She was becoming increasingly animated, as if the prospect of seeing her ex-husband murdered before her eyes was a thrill on the level of riding a roller coaster.

The downstairs guard, sitting in a rocking chair, was as unprepared for our arrival as Raoul. Sophie trotted out the same spiel and asked him his name.

'Gérard,' he said. He was chewing gum, his jaw moving sideways like a goat's. Sophie looked on him with distaste and ordered him to open the door to the twins' prison. It was the only door in sight and was locked with a massive key that hung on a hook screwed into the door jamb.

Gérard left his chair and produced a gun from inside his blouson: a Colt Python magnum revolver, an old friend of mine. Noisy, but it wouldn't matter if he let it off down here. Except to our ear drums.

'Usually I unlock and stand back,' he said, addressing me. 'Then I tell them to open up. That way I make sure they don't jump me.'

His procedures couldn't be faulted. I would have done the same.

When the key turned in the lock, I heard movement inside. Gérard backed away, his gun levelled. He was pint-sized, so it was hard for him to look threatening, even behind a gun.

'*Sortir de là*!' he called.

The door creaked inwards. A figure filled the gap – Victor? The hair was done as I remembered Victor's, buzz cut sides and back, longer on top.

'Not you again,' he growled at me.

I smiled pleasantly. My quarrel was not with Victor. In my book, he was free to go. If it was Victor.

Then Vincent surfaced, stood beside his twin. If it was Vincent. His hair style, previously worn longer and rumpled, was now indistinguishable from Victor's. They had even switched either shirts or pants, so I could no longer rely on their clothing to identify them. They were a cunning pair.

'Somebody give one of them a haircut?' I asked Gérard.

'They asked for scissors. I lent them a trimmer.'

'Obliging of you. So now, we can't be sure who's who.'

'I will know,' Sophie scoffed. 'You cannot fool me with a haircut, either of you.'

I decided that the twin wearing the pants Victor had been wearing when I took him prisoner probably was Victor; they were more likely to have swapped shirts than pants. Then again, they might have anticipated my drawing that very conclusion. While I was distracted by the identity question, the twin I took to be Vincent suddenly bulldozed his brother into Sophie and the two of them went sprawling on the floor. I moved to intercept Vincent; the guard bellowed '*Ne bougez pas*!' but he wouldn't dare shoot, not to kill at any rate. That was my job.

Vincent barged into me, and we went down in a snarl of limbs. Sophie screamed, the guard fired a bullet into the ceiling. While I was trying to heave Vincent off, another shot resounded through the basement, followed by a sound as of a body falling.

'*Arretez!*' came the command. Vincent dragged himself clear of me and struggled to his feet. I did likewise. Somehow Gérard had transferred the Colt to Victor. How this could have happened I couldn't figure, but I guessed the scuffle had been staged, that the twins had bribed Gérard with promises of vast wealth, and that he in return had demanded that he appear to be an innocent party.

Sophie was with her back against the wall, hands splayed, eyes blazing.

'You fool!' she spat at Gérard.

'He's no fool,' I said. 'This is a set up. He's working with them.'

At least I could make sure he never received his Judas money from the Wolffs.

'What!' She went for Gérard, claws unsheathed.

'That's enough!' Victor rasped, and Vincent grabbed her wrist and swung her round, slamming her into the wall, chest first. She gave a squawk of pain, and subsided to the flagstones, her breath coming in sobs.

Three of them against little old me. Not good odds, even with a gun.

Victor waved Gérard's Colt and pointed to the open door. 'Inside, both of you.'

I hesitated. Resistance was probably hopeless, but capitulation could mean a worse fate. I was about to try for my gun when a voice hailed us from the top of the stairs.

'Hey, what's going on?'

Raoul, the outside guard, was there, with a gun of his own. Victor loosed off a shot at him but missed, the bullet chipping a piece out of the wall, and ricocheting away through the doorway. Raoul fired back and hit Gérard, who went down backwards, arms outflung. Victor's next two shots, blending as one, were on target. I didn't see where they struck, but Raoul clutched at his chest and toppled forward, head first down the steps. His gun was knocked from his grip and came down with him, bounced once, twice, on the steps and the third time into my waiting hand.

It was an automatic of unknown genre, and Raoul's two shots meant there was a round already jacked into the firing chamber. It happened so

fast my reactions felt almost sluggish. But I recovered in a hurry, and even as Victor swung his pistol to cover me, I fired once, twice. Blood sprayed from his arm, splattering Sophie, who was standing beside him. It wasn't his gun arm and didn't prevent him from taking a pot shot at me, the bullet zinging past my ear like a rampaging mosquito. I returned his fire; several hasty shots, targeting his body mass. He went down.

I hadn't shot to kill. In the heat of such moments, the survival instinct kicks in. Sophie, blood spatters and all, grabbed the Colt from Victor's slack fingers and brought it up to cover Vincent, who was about to challenge her right to ownership of the gun.

A shot that came close to parting his hair made him think again

'You're still alive,' I warned. 'Don't push your luck.'

The two guards were down. Gérard was groaning and writhing, Raoul, our saviour, was still. Victor too. Vincent was unhurt.

'Which one are you?' I asked him, not expecting the truth.

'Victor,' he replied promptly.

'*Is* he Victor?' I said to Sophie.

If he was Victor, that meant Vincent was dead, and my task was done, the contract fulfilled. I could pocket my second quarter of a million and be homeward bound within the hour.

'I … I'm not sure. There's something wrong with his voice … it's croaky, it doesn't sound like either of them.'

'He may be putting it on, now that he knows that's how you ID him.'

'If he is Victor, he will be fluent in French.' She addressed Victor in rapid fire French, ending in a question.

'*Foutez le camp*,' he said, proving he could use bad language in French, at any rate.

'Tell me the time of day in French,' Sophie said, her confiscated gun zeroed in on his gut.

He obliged.

'That was too easy,' Sophie sighed. 'He *must* be Vincent. I can sense it!'

A precarious inference, leaving plenty of room for doubt. But it satisfied Sophie even without the voice recognition.

'It's Vincent, I'm certain of it,' she said, her words punctuated by a

groan from the floorbound Gérard.

'You're wrong!' Victor-Vincent yelled.

'Shut your mouth!' I turned to Sophie. 'Are you sure enough to want him dead?'

'You need to ask?' She shot me a fierce look. 'Go on, kill him! It's what you're being paid for.'

The gun – it was a French Manurhin PP, modelled on the Walther – was ready to do its business. A .32 round was awaiting the striker pin. At this range, a head shot was preferable, and it would take but a single bullet to achieve a result. Sophie had asserted that this was Vincent who stood before me, still alive, and that he deserved to die. The other twin, whichever he was, I had killed in self-defence. It was my fervent wish that the body down there in the dirt was Vincent, allowing me to walk away with the twisted satisfaction I gained from killing a deserving case. But wishing it wouldn't make it a fact.

'Kill him!' Sophie shrilled, her lips drawn back over her teeth, her expression fierce; her recent impact with the wall had started a nose bleed, and the rill of drying blood from nostril to chin added to her wild demeanour.

To reduce the temptation, I set the safety and slung the gun away from me. It slid across the flagstones, coming to rest by the stairs.

Sophie glared, her disbelief patent. 'I have paid you to kill Vincent. We have a contract, you must honour it, damn you!'

Victor-Vincent chuckled. In effortless French, he told Sophie she was a perverted, murderous bitch, and if he had a gun in his hand, he would put her down on the spot. This evidence of his command of the language should have made him Victor. I wanted him to be Victor, to let me off the hook, and justify my refusal to kill him.

'That good enough for you, Sophie?' I said and made for the stairs. She didn't respond and when I reached the top stair, I swung round and contemplated the tableau below: Victor-Vincent smirking, arms folded; Sophie, holding a gun on him, but it was only window dressing; the other twin lifeless on the floor, like a cast-off doll; Raoul too, whose intervention had saved us, and Gérard, on his back, making a lot of fuss about a bleeding arm.

If wishing made it so, Vincent was no more, and the surviving twin was Victor. The odds that I had killed Vincent were 50-50. Sophie had paid fifty per cent of the fee. The way I saw it, we were quits. It suited me to leave it like that, to draw a line beneath the impossible contract.

I had a new lodestar, a new plan, formulated as I slept after my debauched session in her vast bed. If I could make it happen, contracts to kill and people like Sophie, with money to burn on burning their enemies, would become of the past.

* * * * *

Lacking transport, I travelled on foot to Cabris, the nearest village. At an auberge called the Chevre d'Or I prevailed on the proprietor to summon a cab. By 3.00pm I was re-entering Monaco to collect my rental car. I discovered I had left the keys on the night table in Sophie's bedroom. I ascended to the eighteenth and thumbed the buzzer, hoping she hadn't returned ahead of me,

Lucette was alone, and reluctant to let me in without her mistress. Maybe worried I might ravish her. When I explained I was only there to collect my keys, she stood aside and stayed by the door while I went through to the bedroom. As I was clipping the keys to my belt loop, I heard an exclamation.

'*Que voulez-vous, monsieur*?' It was Lucette's voice. The answer was indistinct, but I had other matters on my mind and gave it no attention until I was back in the entrance hall, where I was confronted by the visitor who was proof that the long arm of the law really is long – Herr Schmidt. Plus the faithful Vogel, plus two uniformed Monegasque policemen to make it official.

They were still out on the landing but on catching sight of me Schmidt charged through the doorway, hand diving behind his back where I knew was stashed his police-issue H & K.

Heedless of his shouted, 'Wait, Warner!' I was across the living room, hurdling an armchair, and out on the balcony. If I was to avoid being cornered, the only route was over the rail. Up or down was the choice, though up was not a choice at all as there nothing within reach to hang

onto. Down meant dangling from the rail and swinging my legs and body back and forth, pendulum-fashion, then letting go when my feet were above the floor of the lower balcony. It would be a hard landing, but a lot less hard than if I missed it altogether.

All this ran through my mind in seconds. I could hear the voices of Schmidt and Vogel as they charged through the living room. I didn't have the luxury of time to calculate angles, power-to-weight ratios, and wind speed. It was go now or surrender. The apartment below had an awning, fortunately retracted, otherwise the balcony would have been inaccessible. As Schmidt burst out through the open French door, I straddled the steel rail and went over it in a controlled fall, sliding my hands down the upright bars until they made contact with the balcony floor. I dangled there, my weight now supported by the strength of my grip, my feet just brushing the rail below. I tried not to think of the seventeen floors between me and the unforgiving asphalt of the street. At the next apartment to my right, one floor down, a guy was leaning out over his rail, goggling at my antics.

'Don't do it!' he shouted in bad French, taking me for a prospective suicide. 'I am coming for you.'

Then Schmidt's head popped up above me; he reached over the rail to grab me and prevent me from dropping onto the balcony below. Even as his fingers curled around my wrists, I swung my legs forward and let go of the bars. My weight wrenched me from Schmidt's grasp and I heard him swearing as I landed on tiles, rolling over as parachutists are trained to do, and still cracking my elbow and crunching my shoulder.

I was confident Schmidt wouldn't shoot me. For a start, he very much wanted me alive, if only to boast what a clever cop he was. Second, a German cop letting off guns in Monaco was sure to get him into hot water. Among the cop fraternity there are rules about such behaviour.

The apartment where I now found myself was occupied; the French door was open and a grey-haired woman was in the kitchen, her back to me. I couldn't afford to be discreet. The layout of her apartment would be similar to Sophie's so I had no need of directions to find the front door. The woman heard me passing through and spun round with a

stifled scream, wielding a large wooden spoon. I threw her a wave and plunged into the hallway and out through the entrance door, almost bowling over the guy from the next apartment.

'Ah, thank God!' he cried, clutching at me. 'There is always another solution.'

At the head of the stairwell on the floor above, commotion, shouting, running feet. I dragged the startled Good Samaritan across the landing with me and darted behind a pillar where the stairs fed into the passage. It was just wide enough to screen the pair of us. I placed a finger over my lips in a plea for silence; he nodded in sympathy. People were trying to save me from ending it all, was how he saw it.

From my meagre cover I watched as Schmidt and the rest hurried across the landing to the door of the apartment I had just vacated. If any of them had glanced back, it would have been all over for me. My Good Samaritan neighbour just stood in silence beside me. Any moment I expected him to yell for help.

None of the four police officers glanced back. Schmidt pressed the buzzer and, without waiting for an invitation, barged in. As the last of the quartet passed through the doorway, I shook hands with the bemused Good Samaritan and made for the down stairs. I didn't get much of a start. I was on the last step when I heard their voices, instructions being issued, then more of the running feet. As they couldn't be sure whether I had gone up or down, they would have to split their forces, which would at least reduce the odds.

Instead of continuing my descent, I darted behind another pillar, a continuation of the one on the floor above. The pounding of feet lessened as they reached my landing and rounded the corner to the next stairway. Schmidt was leading by several stairs, with a burly uniformed cop struggling to keep up. As the cop passed within inches of me, I grabbed his belt from behind, jerked him backwards. He fell with a yell. Schmidt, unaware, hurtled down to the next level. While the cop was still sprawled on the stairs, groaning, I had the flap of his holster unbuttoned and his sidearm was in my hand. He made a feeble attempt to fight me off, but I planted my foot in his chest to propel him down the stairs to the bottom. The thudding and wailing alerted Schmidt and

he went into reverse, drawing his gun as he remounted the stairs.

I pumped a single shot over his head from the cop's automatic, which sent him ducking for cover. He bounced back up in a crouch and returned my fire. I didn't hang about to exchange bullets in case he got lucky.

Upstairs was not an option because I would meet Vogel and the other uniform coming down. Down was now out too, without going through Schmidt. The dilemma was resolved for me when a door opened across the corridor and a man came out, dressed in shorts and T-shirt, hauling a sports bag from which the handle of two tennis racquets protruded. He saw me and came to an abrupt halt.

A few rapid shots down the stairwell to keep Schmidt's head down, then I hurried over to the guy in shorts who was rooted to the spot.

'Back inside,' I said in English, then in French, making a motion with the gun.

He stayed cool, keeping his arms down by his sides, as he retreated into his apartment. I kept the flat of my hand on his back to encourage him, kicking the door shut behind me.

If Schmidt had resumed his ascent and spotted me going into the apartment, I could expect a hammering at the door within the next minute. None came. As I stood there, panting a little, my hostage watchful but not intimidated, I was already considering my next step. Once the police realised I was no longer on the stairs up or down, they would search all the apartments on this floor. I had bought a half hour at most.

'Are you going to stay long?' the guy said in passable English. He was about fifty, pepper-and-salt hair, and a modest paunch.

'Anyone else in here?' I asked.

He shook his head. 'My wife is out.'

'Okay. I've no quarrel with you. The best thing you can do, for your own safety, is to not interfere. Don't try and be a hero. I won't kill you, but I can and will disable you if you don't behave.'

'I'll behave.'

'Good. Now shut yourself in one of the back bedrooms. You can lock it if you like. Whatever you do though, don't come out. If you come out,

I shoot.' I pointed the gun and said, 'Bang. Like that. Clear?'

He managed a weak smile. 'Clear.'

Then I was on my own. I stayed away from the balcony where I might be spotted. The living room was fitted with a bar in a grey-blond wood, with a set of well-stocked shelves behind the counter. As a rule I avoided alcohol when I needed to keep my wits sharp; on this occasion I was seduced into breaking my rule by a three-quarters full bottle of Laphroag single malt whisky that occupied pride of place on the top shelf, its green bottle making the spirit look anaemic. I located a chunky glass under the counter and poured in moderation – a finger, if that. It went down like a luge on the Cresta Run.

Up here on the sixteenth floor all was quiet. My host was behaving himself. At some point Schmidt, either in person or by proxy, would come calling. When they realised I hadn't left the building they would go through it, apartment by apartment, logically starting at this floor. With only six apartments to search Schmidt would be here before long.

* * * * *

Twenty-five minutes elapsed between my entering the apartment and the zzz of the door buzzer. It could have been an innocent caller, but I had to assume it was Schmidt and his party.

The door was fitted with a spyhole. A peep through it confirmed my fears: Schmidt and a uniformed cop were standing there.

I opened the door. My borrowed gun was a SIG, same model as mine, and I made sure it was very visible. They showed no surprise at having finally run me to ground.

'Hello, Warner,' Schmidt said. My gun wasn't scaring him, though the uniformed cop was more nervous, keeping Schmidt between him and me in case I resisted arrest.

'Come in, Schmidt. Bring your buddy with you.'

We all traipsed through to the living room, me to the rear.

'Now,' I said as we assembled between two long white couches, 'Put your gun on the floor, slow and easy.'

He obliged, his actions very precise. He was nothing if not respectful.

I ordered him to sit down.

'*Maintenant, vous,*' I said to the cop, assuming he was Monegasque and spoke French.

He lifted his automatic from his holster and made like Schmidt. I sent him to join the German.

'Now we have what's known as a situation,' I said, kicking both guns under the couches. 'I've always avoided killing policemen. In fact, I've always avoided killing any innocent person. But you may leave me no choice. If I don't kill you, I don't get away.' I smiled warmly at them. 'You see my dilemma, Schmidt.'

'You could tie us up,' he suggested.

'Then Vogel shows up and unties you. Not only that, Schmidt, I'm getting a little tired of your vendetta against me.'

'So what do you propose?'

'It's simple, really. I need you dead, so you're going to kill yourself.'

He wasn't impressed. The corner of his mouth lifted in a sneer.

'Interesting. How would you like me to do it? Cut my wrists?'

For a kraut he had quite a sense of humour.

'Nothing so messy. I'm going to demonstrate with your friend here.'

'You could use us as hostages.' Schmidt suggested, a note of desperation in his voice.

'To tell the truth, Schmidt, I want you off my back. I didn't realise, when you threatened to catch up with me one day, that you really meant it. It needs to end, here and now.'

In French, I rattled off an instruction to the uniformed cop to go onto the balcony.

'You too,' I said to Schmidt, adding, in case he didn't know French. 'Follow your pal.'

They complied on dragging feet, sliding the French door back and walking up to the rail, turning as they did so to face me.

To the cop, I said, '*Et maintenant, sautez.*'

His eyes bulged. '*Sautez?*'

'Over the rail. Now – or I shoot you in the gut.'

Any cop would know what a gut shot did to you. It was lethal, it would lead to a long-drawn-out, agonising death.

'Are you crazy?' Schmidt said, his brow darkening. 'You think you can make us jump from sixteen floors up?'

'Either that, or I break my rule about shooting cops. You remember nine-eleven and the twin towers? They called them the Jumpers. They jumped from way up high rather than burn to death. You won't burn if you don't jump, but a bullet in the gut is worse they tell me.'

Schmidt, his face contorting, his cool finally heating up, took a step towards me.

'Watch it!' I rapped, my finger tightening on the trigger.

He pulled up, mouth forming a snarl, as I repeated my instruction and threat to the cop. His face white, the cop twisted round and peered over the balcony. He would see that some apartments had extended awnings and they might break his fall.

'Now!' I ordered. 'Or you get a bullet in the gut.'

And just like that, he went. Over the rail, letting himself fall sideways, a wail ripped from his mouth. I heard the thud as he landed on an awning, then a splintering noise, accompanied by more wailing. Then … nothing.

The outcome was of no interest to me. I was focused only on persuading Schmidt to do the same.

I said, 'In the movies they usually count to three, or five, or more. This isn't a movie, Schmidt, so no count for you. Go now or you're a dead man.'

So help me, moral code or no moral code, in my desperation to be rid of him, I believe I would have made good my threat if he refused. I must have convinced him too, because he cocked a leg over the rail, then his other leg. With both hands gripping the rail, he looked down, gulped visibly, then back at me over his shoulder. He was afraid, but not cowed.

'You had better hope I don't survive, you scum,' he said through clamped teeth. 'If I do, I will get you wherever you hide.'

I fired, aiming so that the bullet just missed putting a notch in his ear. I didn't want him found with holes in him. Like the uniformed cop, he just let himself go, straight down. No wailing for him though. In control to the last – if it was the last. The same kind of thud followed, a little longer coming, maybe because the first awning had been ripped

away. A faint scream arose from the street, then a squeal of brakes. I didn't linger to check the cause. I was out of that apartment and pounding down the stairs. If Vogel was searching the top floors and had heard the shot and the commotion, he would likewise be on his way down.

On the twelfth floor an elevator had just arrived, the doors already sliding shut. I forced them apart, startling a middle age couple who had boarded ahead of me. We acknowledged each other, and continued on the ground floor, where they exited. Less than a minute later, I reeled, dry-throated and sweating, into the underground parking garage.

In case the police had staked out the place, I moved with caution. All was clear. I reversed out of my bay and drove up the ramp, sunlight flooding the interior of the car, dazzling me and forcing me to reduce speed and lower the sun visor before entering the busy street. I was emerging at the side of the building, therefore it wasn't possible to check the fates of Schmidt and the cop. He or they were clinging to awnings or lying on the sidewalk, deceased at their own hands, leaving mine clean. Technically, that is.

A horn blasted me as I edged into the stream of traffic. I trudged with the rest to the intersection with Avenue de la Costa, to make a left into Avenue de l'Hermitage, for the A8 *autoroute* to Nice.

The siren behind me was so unexpected I didn't connect it with me. Only when the black-and-white police car bobbed up alongside me, did I wake up to the threat. The police officer in the passenger seat signalled me to pull off the road. The alternative was to elbow them aside, using the superior weight of my SUV. I swung the wheel hard left and put my foot down. Metal crunched. I pushed the police car onto the sidewalk, creating a gap that I exploited by accelerating down the centre of the road where there was just enough space between the lines of traffic for me to shoehorn through.

The ululating siren pursued me along l'Hermitage. They clung to me like a sticky bud, but with both lanes full they had no room to pass. I clipped a white van, earning a blast of outrage from its horn. The lights at the Avenue de la Costa junction favoured me, and I made the turn on complaining tyres, the police car right up my rear end.

Now I could give it the gun. I whipped past slower vehicles, leaning on the horn, bullying a path along the centre line, cars moving to the left and right out of my path. Some didn't and suffered as a consequence. The hairpin bend by the Dutch Consulate brought my speed down to a crawl, but my pursuers were likewise slowed. The traffic was thinner here, and I roared past the multi-level parking garage to the junction with the Avenue d'Ostende, which forms part of the F1 racing course. I was forced to brake before cutting in on the stream of vehicles just ahead of a bus. The police didn't make it. In the mirror I saw them edge out behind the bus. I took advantage of my gain to blast past the other road users, dodging in and out between vehicles, making metal to metal contact now and again. The air became full of blaring horns. There was a bus lane on the next stretch and cars obstructing my path nipped into it to avoid being side-swiped.

The police driver knew his stuff and made up the ground he had lost, until once again he was tailgating me. At the point where Ostende splits, a small car was creeping out from a side road. I struck it a glancing blow, spraying sparks and ripping off its door mirror. It spun off while I hammered on up the gentle incline of Rue Grimaldi. Traffic was much sparser here, and I cranked up my speed to over a hundred. Pedestrians were the biggest danger now but, luckily for me and for them, they had the sense to scuttle for the safety of the sidewalk while I was still some distance from running them down.

The police again attempted to come alongside but were prevented by the occasional vehicle coming towards us. I burst out of the shadows of Grimaldi, braking hard into the traffic circle and going round to the final exit, Avenue Prince Pierre.

Climbing all the time now, the roads narrower and the police unable to do more than stick with me. It became apparent that they were already radioing for assistance when another police car drove into the circle on boulevard de Belgique. It didn't block the whole road, just my side of it, as if I wouldn't dare break the law by crossing over to the wrong side. Another sideswipe rendered it *hors de combat,* but a truck leaving the circle was coming at me head-on, and as I swerved back into the right lane we clashed fenders, and more damage was done to Avis's property.

Beyond the circle, Belgique was almost open road, and I gunned the Kia for all it was worth. Siren still howling, the police car that I couldn't shake, was right there with me the whole stretch up to the tunnel under the Jardin Exotique. After the tunnel the vast cemetary to the left ended in yet another circle.

As we crossed the Monaco border a second police car joined the chase, also exercising its siren. Down a slope, running parallel to the sea, several bends in succession tested the Kia's roadholding. At an acute angle I charged into a wider road with houses on the left and trees on the right. Pedestrians slowed to gawk at this scene from a Dirty Harry movie. By now I was sweating at the effort of staying ahead and staying on the road. An SUV is not an ideal form of transport for a high-speed chase, unless it's cross country, and there was no countryside around here. Cap d'Ail, which I was now passing through, is among the most built-over stretches of the Côte d'Azur.

I never heard the shot. Just felt it go past, and the windshield gained a hole with radiating cracks, like a spider web. They must have been desperate. The code of conduct for French police allowed them to shoot only in self-defence.

We thundered past a church with a white spire, traffic thickening up again. Something had to give. Not my gas anyhow; I still had half a tankful. I decided to try a high-risk tactic I had used once before, in Milan. It involved braking harshly for a split second, then speeding up again without coming to a standstill. The pursuer's natural reaction is to stand on his brakes to avert a collision, and the sudden deceleration can cause a loss of control. Well, that's what happened in Milan.

For the tactic to be effective I needed to build up speed. I shot past a lumbering truck. Both police cars followed through, the second narrowly missing an oncoming bus. The road ahead was now straight and clear for several hundred yards. I booted the gas pedal to the floor, keeping an eye on the rearview mirror, the other on the road. The speedo needle hit the 120 mark. Now! I jammed my foot on the brake. The Kia shuddered and swerved as the tyres gripped, rubber squealing. I heard the scrunch of metal and, as I accelerated again I risked another glance in the mirror. The first police car had tipped over onto its side

and sliced through the low wall of a private garden, while the second had fared even worse, cartwheeling and becoming airborne. I returned my attention to what lay ahead, slowing again as I came up behind a short line of dawdling cars led by a motor scooter.

For now I was in the clear. Police reinforcements were sure to be en route, preparing road blocks with stingers or tyre-deflation strips. It was time to take to the hills and exchange my battered SUV for a less conspicuous set of wheels.

Though I didn't know it yet, the worst of my woes were behind me. At Costa Plana I left the highway and wended up the hillside towards the village of Les Serriers at a more sedate pace. Just short of the village I ran the Kia into a wooded area where it would be screened from the road. It was now dusk and, like most French villages, Les Serriers was almost asleep. Outside a closed *boulangerie* on a deserted side street, I stumbled on a Renault 21 of a certain vintage, too old for electronic ignition. How to start a car without a key was a skill they taught me during my qualifying period for MI6. The engine roared into healthy life. A last furtive scope up and down the street, and I was away.

The steering was sloppy and the brakes in need of attention. Aside from these minor deficiencies, the car was perfect for my purpose – decrepit and nondescript. I stuck with the rural route and after a couple kilometres more I entered the village of Carpre. I chugged by a twenty-four-hour gas station, was overtaken by an impatient Porsche, who pipped his horn at my crawling speed. No offence taken. The A8 autoroute La Provençale was just ahead. I hit the on-ramp, nursed my wheels to a resentful eighty, and keeping to the slow lane on the *autoroute* with its frequent toll stops, I was in among the outskirts of Nice with the onset of dusk.

A replacement rental car was my next need. Near the central station I came across a rental business that was still open, though it was only a few minutes short of 8.00pm. I dropped the Renault off on an abandoned building site. I could now pose as an arriving train passenger and therefore excite no comment.

After the day's drama, what followed was anti-climactic. I hired a Jeep Cherokee to take me to Perpignan. I would drive through the night,

drop the Jeep off in Perpignan and switch to a Renfe-SNCF train, bound for Barcelona. Having hopefully erased my trail, I aimed to be back in Spain for breakfast the next day, and in Sitges by the afternoon.

It was a demanding itinerary but it panned out all right. Dawn was still over the eastern skyline when, bleary-eyed and hungry, I blew into Perpignan. I grabbed some machine-coffee in the rental company's waiting room. They drummed up a taxi to the station, where, feeling like a limp rag, I entrained on the ten o'clock TGV for Barcelona.

By 10.25 France was behind me, and I was safe inside Spain where I was a non-person to the forces of law and order. For how long, that was the question. Now that Europol had me on their hit list, the whole continent would soon be a no-go area.

Chapter Twenty

For the first time since breakfast I checked my cell phone. I had three missed calls: Donovan, Patricia (returning my call, most likely), Donovan again, and a text from Angela.

Hello, André. I'm not in trouble with the police over your escape. I also rescued your car. It's with me in The Hague. I'm at the Europol head office for a while then I'll drive it to my house in UK. When you're ready, contact me and we'll make arrangements. Either you come here or I'll go to you or whichever. Hope you got away all right. Love you. I think.

It was generous of her to rescue my car, though I only lost it because she was a party to my entrapment. In the cold light of my regained freedom, I could forgive her that. She had only been doing her job, but if she was harbouring ambitions to resume our embryonic fling, I would have to disappoint her. Betrayal at a personal level engenders strong negative emotions in me. Twice before in my life, I had been betrayed by a woman and the incidences were still painful to recall.

From Barcelona by cab to Sitges. The third floor apartment where I had installed Patricia was overlooking the marina; you could see *Seamist* from the balcony and the master bedroom. When I stepped out of the elevator and up to my front door, I buzzed before inserting my key to give Patricia a chance to make herself decent. But

She wasn't home. In the bedroom I found vestiges of her presence: clothes in the closet, the usual feminine bits and pieces in the bathroom. On the whole it was clean and tidy, table cleared, dishes washed and stacked, and no dust. In better shape, I had to admit, than when I was in residence.

My personal and sensitive belongings, including a laptop computer, were locked in a closet with a reinforced door and a combination lock, in my study, a cubicle of a room where I conducted my bank and investment business and all matters confidential.

I had lunched on the train, so the next priority was a shower and a siesta. While I was in the shower I heard movement in the apartment. The bathroom door opened and Patricia's head poked around it.

'Gilles!' she squealed and came at me in a flurry of shopping bags.

The door of my shower was clear glass, so I was exposed in all my naked glory. She didn't mind. Nor did I, except that I had new plans for changing my lifestyle and they involved not getting involved. Especially not with a girl half my age. Been there, done that all too often. So I shooed her off, shopping bags and all.

'Wait outside,' I said curtly, and she obeyed at once, tail between her legs, making me feel like a louse.

When I entered the living room, she was just pouring fresh perked coffee and seemed to have recovered her spirits.

'Want some?' she asked.

'Sure. Thanks.' I sat at the breakfast bar, still towelling my hair. 'And don't call me Gilles. It's not my real name.'

'Oh. I quite like it. What is your name?'

I wavered between André and Jack. Settled for Jack.

'I like Gilles better,' she said, then leaned over the counter and deposited a kiss on my lips. 'There. You not deserve it, but I give it anyway.'

She had a forgiving nature.

'Tell me what you've been doing.'

'Let me see …' She assumed a thoughtful air. 'I keep your house nice. Meet boys, play tennis, swim. Oh, and I try to learn Spanish.'

'You've kept busy. I'm impressed.'

The look she gave me was inscrutable. The picture of wide-eyed innocence. Lovely eyes too, cobalt blue. Her best feature. They were familiar, I had seen them on another face. Recently. I poked around in my memory bank. I didn't have to poke far. The equally lovely features of Sophie Marais, *marquise*, swam before me. The face differed from

Patricia's except for the eyes, which were identical in shape, size and colour.

My heart lurched as I recalled the story of Sophie's youngest daughter, raped and abducted by Vincent Wolff, at the age of eleven. Eleven years ago. Reported dead, but no proof beyond hearsay. If she were alive today, she would be about twenty-two.

Patricia was twenty-two.

That wasn't the only coincidence. Her hair was near-black, the same as in the picture in Sophie's apartment. In Budapest, she had been employed by a business connected to, or owned by either or both of the Wolff twins. Many questions remained which only Patricia herself could answer. What cans of psychological worms might I open if I started interrogating her?

'What are you thinking, Gilles … er, I mean Jack?' she asked. 'Your face is very … what is the right word … fierce?'

'Yeah.' She was facing me over the breakfast bar. I reached over and took both her hands. My mind was made up. 'I was thinking about you, actually.'

'Oh?' Her eyes acquired that mischievous sparkle I had noticed before at any hint that something might be cooking between us. 'You want me to go to bed with you?'

I laughed. She was so transparent, not to mention blatant.

'It's a nice idea, but no, love, it's more complicated than that. I … I want to ask about your past.'

Her face closed up. It was like a shutter descending, darkness blanking out the light.

I ploughed ahead anyhow. 'It's important to you, and to … someone else close to you.'

She tugged her hands free of mine. 'Ask your questions.'

'Is Patricia your real name?'

'Yes.' Sullenly.

'I don't believe you. But we'll let that pass for now. Where are your parents?'

'Dead.'

'Sorry, I don't believe that either.'

It was her hostility that was fuelling my conviction that Patricia and Sophie's daughter Francine were the same person. If she had no history to hide, why be so evasive? If she was being honest, if Patricia was her real name, and her parents really were dead, she would have no reason to resent my asking.

'Let me try and make it easy for you. I'm convinced you're Francine Marais, you're French, and your mother is Sophie Marais. Your natural father is dead, but your step-father is Vincent Wolff, who may be very much alive.'

If only I could be sure he wasn't.

She stared at me with a dead expression. I was resurrecting past demons that she had succeeded in exorcising, and she wasn't grateful for it.

'Suppose you are right. What difference it makes to anything?'

'A big, big difference. It means you don't have to go back to Hungary, you don't have to work for your step-father, you don't have to do porn on the Internet.' I grabbed her hands again, squeezed them. 'Is that enough for a start?'

She stared back at me, unblinking. Inside her, a reserve of defiance.

'Maybe I like what I do.'

'You can learn to like other things. Go and live with your mother in Monaco. You'll have a great life, meet some nice guys, get married one day. Be normal.'

'What you know about normal?' But the aggression was gone; her question was sad, not bitter.

'Not a lot,' I admitted. 'But I made my choices freely, nobody imposed them on me. You're young enough to take a different path. All it takes is to want to do it.'

She said nothing. Her lip was trembling; tears were only just below the surface. She had a tough outer shell, constructed over the years when she was Vincent Wolff's plaything. But I was cracking it.

'You *are* Francine, aren't you?'

She nodded, hung her head. A tear splashed on the back of my hand.

'Did Vincent take you away, and refuse to let you go?'

Another nod, another tear.

'He rape me when I was eleven. After he take me away from *mama,* he rape me often. When I was thirteen I become … with baby. He force me to have abortion. After that he not touch me.'

Rape, pregnancy, abortion, it was some kind of miracle she wasn't totally screwed up.

'Why did you stay, when you were older?'

She wiped tears from her cheek. Still she wouldn't look at me. The shame went deep.

'He tell me he will kill me if I try to escape. And kill my mother. I hated him. Once, I bit him, make him bleed.'

She bared her teeth and made a pretence of biting. She had large, strong teeth that would make formidable weapons.

'He punished me for that,' she went on. 'Give me beating with a riding crop.'

In the street a horn sounded impatiently. A raised voice responded. Driving in Spain involved a lot of hooting and swearing.

'Would you like to go home?' I asked. 'Back to your mother and your brothers and sisters.'

She gulped, nodded, eyes wet with tears but now maybe touched with happiness.

'Yes. Yes, I would.' Now she was clasping my hands in hers. 'Will you come with me, Gi … I sorry … Jack? Will you take me? I trust you.'

'Sure I will.'

Even as I uttered the promise, I was wondering how. I couldn't return to Monaco for a while, and even France was tempting providence anew. I would figure it out. For sure, Sophie would have to meet me outside France. Italy was the nearest alternative for her, if not for me. Better still, Sardinia, where I had other business to conduct.

'Here's an idea to cheer you up. Tomorrow we'll take *Seamist* out. That's my boat.'

'That sounds fun,' Francine said, with a shaky smile.

'It's a date then.'

We dined out that night, slept in separate rooms – me in the shakedown in my office – and next morning rose early. The sun was shining, and a breeze was blowing. Perfect conditions.

'Will I be okay like this?' she asked over breakfast. She was in denim shorts with a tank top.

'Sure. Just take a sweater in case it gets cold later.'

By 9.00am we were heading for the marina, Francine hanging onto my arm, her usual cheeriness restored. She made attractive arm candy. Good for my ego.

I gave her a lesson in how to cast off, and we left the port under steam power, Francine excited as a fashionista on a shopping spree. Clear of the port, I steered *Seamist* into the wind and let Francine take charge of the helm with instructions to stay on course, while I crabbed forwards over the cabin roof to raise the mainsail. I released the retaining straps. The halyard was already attached to the head of the sail. I hauled away and up it went, flapping and crackling as the wind caught it. I pushed the boom to starboard and wound the halyard around the drum, then used the winch to crank the sail up to the masthead. *Voila*! We were sailing.

Back in the cockpit with a shining-eyed Francine, I relieved her at the helm and watched the sail fill out as I veered to starboard. The boat began to heel, the wind fairly shoving us along on a parallel course to the shoreline. The beaches were packed with sun worshippers and the sea dotted with boats like ours, smaller and larger, sail and motor powered, a typical August day on the Spanish Costas.

'I love Spain,' Francine confessed, then looked up at the masthead with its streaming pennant. 'And I love this.'

'Sailing? Yes, it's great fun, but there's a lot to learn.'

'Will you teach me? Today, I mean.'

'I can teach you a few basic procedures, but if you really want to learn sailing, it's best to go with a sailing school.' To lessen the impact of the wind I made some adjustments to our course, from close reach to close hauled, skirting the dead area. 'Meanwhile, I need to tell you something about Vincent, if you're good with that.'

She chugged a big breath, let it out slowly as if she were blowing into a breathalyser.

'I can handle it.'

'First of all I should tell you … he might be dead –'

'Good!' The emphasis was stark.

'Agreed, if it's really him that's dead. The trouble is, the one I shot could be Victor. Even your mother couldn't guarantee it was him.'

'You shot him?' More curious than shocked.

'Self-defence. It wasn't planned. The thing is, your mother paid me to find Vincent, then to kill him. Now I'm not sure if he's dead.'

A strong gust pushed at *Seamist* and she canted over, causing Francine to grab at the wheel. I let the boat go where the wind took her and didn't fight it.

'I hope he is dead.' The venom in her voice impressed me.

'No way to be sure.'

A motorsailer crossed our bow, a guy and a girl perched on the topsides, waving to us. We waved back and swept on over their wake.

'Listen, Francine, I can't go to Monaco for the time being, or even to France. I might get arrested. So we will have to meet your mother outside of France. Most likely, Italy. You okay with that?'

'Yes, it's okay. Could we sail there in your lovely boat?'

It was not a silly suggestion. From Sitges to Porto Torres, on the north-west coast of Sardinia is about five hundred nautical miles, say three days sailing in average conditions. Not entirely to be recommended single-handed, but with Francine as crew, gaining experience with every sea mile, it was viable.

So I said, 'Would you like that?'

'Ooh, yes. It will be magical.'

'Then all we need is your mother's agreement to meet us there.' I produced my cell phone. This close inshore, reception was still good.

I was missing Sophie's number, so I called Donovan. He answered, but was dubious about releasing her number.

'Okay, call her and ask her to call me back.'

He hummed and hawed but could raise no real objection. It was more than a half hour before I heard from her. By then we had gybed round to face east, with the wind astern and all calm and restful as we ran before it. The most relaxing form of sailing known to man. The sky was blue, but clouds were stacking up over the mountains north of Barcelona, like white cauliflowers. Not threatening yet, but I would keep

a nautical eye on them.

Then the call came.

'This is Sophie. Am I speaking to Jack?'

'Yes, it's me.' I handed over the helm to Francine and indicated we should keep to a straight course. 'I need to meet up with you.'

'Really? You gave me the impression you couldn't wait to get away. Not only that, but you owe me a quarter of a million dollars or completion of the contract.'

'It may already be complete,' I hedged.

'Don't bullshit me, Jack. You're a good-looking fellow but looks will only take you so far with me.'

'If I were to suggest we meet outside Monaco and France, are you willing to come?'

She started to object, then thought the better of it.

'Is that a yes?' I said, winking at Francine to reassure her that the conversation was going as planned.

'To what purpose?'

I answered her question with a question of my own. 'You would need to bring Victor or Vincent, whichever he is. I may be able make the ID rock solid.'

'How?' So much suspicion in such a short word.

'Just trust me. I also have a surprise for you. A very pleasant one.'

'You intrigue me, Jack, though I'm not sure I should trust you in view of recent events. Where do you want to meet?'

'Sardinia.'

She took that in her stride, no queries, no objections.

'State place and time.'

I gave approximations and promised to text her more precise data.

'On Friday, you say. It's inconvenient, but I'll make it.'

'And be sure to bring Victor-Vincent.'

'He'll come. Especially if he thinks it might lead to our getting back together. He wants access to my money.'

'Before you go, have you any idea what happened to the two cops who fell off a balcony in your building?'

'Two cops? Ah, yes, I heard something about that. Was that you?

They are not dead, if that is what you mean.'

'That's what I meant.' I was glad for the Monegasque cop, ambivalent about Schmidt.

Seamist heeled to port as a sudden gust from the other direction caught us. The boom swung over with a thump, and Francine used the helm to brace herself and counter the slope of the deck.

'What can I do?' she yelped.

'Nothing, just hold on to the helm … the wheel.'

'Are you with someone?' Sophie said, a new note of suspicion in her voice. 'I thought I heard a woman speaking.'

I could have told her it was her long-lost, believed-dead daughter, but it would have sounded like a joke in bad taste. Plus, I didn't want to spoil the surprise.

'Just a friend. We're on my yacht.'

'I see. Anyway, we are agreed to meet and I will expect your text.'

I signed off with '*A bientôt.*'

'That was my mother, yes?' Francine said, blinking fast, emotions taking over again.

'It was. She'll be in for a huge surprise when she meets you,' I said, adding, 'In a good way.'

That earned me a wide smile. I relieved her at the helm and guided us back onto a starboard tack, the wind now driving us along on a broad reach, the bows delving into the wavelets and tossing up bursts of spray that splattered us back in the cockpit.

'I'm going home.' Francine said it with a kind of awe. 'I'm really going home.'

* * * * *

The weather had been kind to us. A steady westerly, blue skies, occasional swell. When we docked in Puerto Torres, on the north coast of Sardinia, Francine had not only become adept at boat handling, she had fallen in love with sailing. Just like Liza before her.

We entered the port in the backwash of a Grimaldi Lines ferry. The turbulence tossed us about a bit, but I let Francine stay at the helm until

it subsided and we reached the calm of the marina, when I took over and manoeuvred *Seamist* to a vacant short-stay berth behind a fishing launch.

'You know this place?' Francine asked as she tumbled a fender over the side.

'I was here a few years ago. With a friend.' A friend now deceased, I didn't mention. 'It's Italian, remember, so we may have communication problems.'

'You not think they speak Hungarian here?'

For a moment I took the question seriously. I was about to answer when she gave the game away by laughing.

'I make an English joke,' she said, giggling, and planted an impulsive kiss on my cheek. 'I learn from you. What is that word you call it?'

'Irony,' I said, with a touch of irony.

I arranged with the harbourmaster to berth for a night or two. We changed from our sailing attire – Francine from shorts to a print dress, a staid knee-length for her mother's benefit – and went to explore the town.

We had several hours to kill before Sophie's expected arrival. In the town centre was a Lidl superstore. As a dedicated female, Francine was compelled to go for a walkaround inside. Otherwise there wasn't much in the form of tourist attractions. We happened on a ristorante pizzeria a little after mid-day and dallied there for an aperitif and an early lunch. We were on our drinks when the Sophie's call came through.

She was brief and to the point: she informed me she was at the Hotel Libyssonis, room 202, and that Victor-Vincent was with her. She would expect us at three.

Not that it mattered now, but I wondered what subterfuge she had used to persuade Victor-Vincent to come along for the ride. It was a certainty she hadn't told him she was meeting me. If she was still more than half-convinced the surviving twin was Vincent, she would insist that I honour the contract, probably there and then. After hearing about Francine's ordeal from her own lips, I would be more than willing to oblige.

Provided Sophie could remove all doubt from my mind that he *was* Vincent.

* * * * *

If a killing there must be, I would need the means. The Boberg was of the past. There were two guns on the boat, one equipped with a silencer. The downside was that carrying a bulky pistol through the streets of Porto Torres didn't feel like a smart move. The only alternative was to kill him with my bare hands. It was feasible, and I had the required expertise. But I couldn't guarantee the outcome. It was not unknown for people to come back to life after receiving the supposed *coup de grâce* by shutting off the carotid arteries.

Let be Victor be the surviving twin then. If it were Victor, nobody would have to be killed.

* * * * *

The Libyssonis was a modest place, though purported to be the best hotel in town. I had stayed there during my only previous layover. Pink stucco walls, with a pillared front porch flanked by palms. The hotel name was surmounted by a clock that seemed to be working. I recalled a vast swimming pool at the back, but that was all.

Francine was a mass of nerves.

'Do you think she will recognise me?' she fretted as we mounted the stairs. 'Maybe she not like me.'

'Just don't mention the Internet,' I advised.

Then we were outside room 202. It had a buzzer, but I ignored it and knocked. The door opened, framing Donovan in the aperture.

'Hello there,' he greeted, affably enough. His gaze shifted from me to Francine. 'And who might this be?'

'Let's save the introductions until we see Sophie,' I said.

He backed into the vestibule. To the right was a bathroom, to the left a closet, straight ahead the bedroom proper. We moved forward, Francine clutching my arm.

'Relax,' I murmured out of the corner of my mouth.

'I cannot.'

Sophie was sitting on the edge of a single bed, a glass of colourless

liquid in her hand; by the French door that served a balcony, was Victor-Vincent, also with a glass. Behind him an outlook over the rooftops to the Mediterranean.

'Hello,' Sophie said, her gaze on Francine, not me.

'Recognise her?' I said, pasting a fatuous grin on my face. This reunification of mother and daughter was giving me enormous pleasure.

Sophie stopped in mid-headshake. Vincent was coming forward, suppressed fury spread across his features. His reaction made him Vincent, not Victor. Vincent's was the guilt.

'*Maman*?' Francine ventured as she and her mother drew near to each other.

'Francine? *Francine? C'est bien toi*?'

'*Oui … oui*.'

No more words were exchanged. They were in each other's arms, hugging, kissing, incoherent. Don and I kept our distance; I felt like an intruder. Not so, Vincent. He came at me with a fistful of switchblade.

Donovan was behind me. As I leapt backwards out of knife range, I ran into him and we went down together, me on top, which made for a soft landing. Sophie and Francine squealed and stumbled towards the nearest corner, where they clung to each other. Some family reunion I had engineered. Vincent rushed forward and, from my spread-eagled posture on the floor, I raised my foot to catch him in the solar plexus and vaulted him over my head. Briefly airborne, he came in to land with a crash that shook the room. Donavan lay complaining in Irish expletives as I struggled upright and bore down on the stunned Vincent. The knife lay by the door. I kicked it away. He didn't need it anymore, and neither did I.

'Patricia … Francine, come over here,' I said.

She came, looking anxious. Sophie came with her, clutching her daughter's hand with both of hers.

I stirred the comatose form with my toe. 'Is this Vincent? You said you could identify him.'

She shrank back. Sophie, closing in behind her, said, 'What are you trying to do, Jack?'

'I'm trying to get confirmation this is Vincent.'

'Can she tell?' Donavan said, back on his feet and standing over the man I hoped was Vincent.

'She told me she can.'

'How?'

Francine knelt beside Vincent, shivering. He stirred, still only semi-conscious.

'Well?' I said, my tone harsher than I intended.

She turned towards me, the beautiful cobalt blue eyes that had betrayed her parentage, moist.

'I will see.' Now she bent over his head, examined his left ear. 'It is him. It is Vincent.' She beat her fists on his chest, sobbing and mouthing in what I assumed to be Hungarian, her first language this past decade.

'How can you tell?' Sophie asked, her voice hushed. 'Even I was no longer a hundred percent sure.'

'When I bite him on the ear, it leave scar. It is still there.' Rising to her haunches, she pointed. I bent to look: on the lobe were two faint indentations, corresponding I guessed to Francine's incisors. At last I had the proof, the confirmation that this was the man I sought and that he truly deserved to die for his abuse of Sophie's oldest daughter when she was only a child.

Francine threw herself into her mother's embrace and they stood there, both of them now in tears.

'What are you going to do?' Donavan asked me.

'Do?' I gave him a bleak look. 'Kill him, of course. That's what you hired me for, isn't it? Much more than that, it's what he deserves.'

Vincent was regaining consciousness. His gaze met mine and locked there. I straddled his chest to keep him still. I made a W of my hands and placed them around his neck. His eyes widened. He moved beneath me, but I was too heavy and he was too light. His hands came up to break my grip, but he was still stunned and too feeble to do more than pluck at the sleeves of my windbreaker. I squeezed, my thumbs depressing his carotid arteries. From his mouth, choking sounds issued. He struck at me, but I didn't even notice. I was intent on destroying this man and felt neither compassion nor compunction as his struggles abated, and his blows became ever weaker until they ceased altogether.

It takes four minutes for cerebral hypoxia to set in, and for the brain to die. I gave it a full five and nobody tried to dissuade me. The room fell quiet apart from the weeping of the two women and the cry of gulls swooping low over the harbour.

It was over. I got to my feet.

'What shall we do with the body?' Sophie asked, her practical side quick to reassert itself.

'Your closet has a key. We'll stuff it in there and lock it. Reserve the room for another night and put a DO NOT DISTURB sign on the door. Then catch a flight back to Nice. It'll be at least twenty-four hours before he's found.'

'What about you?'

'Me? I'll be on the high seas, destination unknown.'

She promised to transfer the second half of my fee as soon as she returned to Monaco.

'Forget it,' I said. 'When it comes to ridding the world of vermin, I'm happy to accept part of my reward in a sense of achievement.'

'I will never forget what you have done for me,' she said, and ran the backs of her fingers down my cheek. 'Shall we meet again?'

I shook my head. 'Except by happenstance, no. My life is about to change forever.'

'Ah. I see. There is a special person waiting for you?'

I just inclined my head to let her down gently. She was philosophical about it, as I had expected her to be. Marquise Sophie would never be short of studs.

Donavan helped with wedging Vincent's corpse in the closet. A jacket was hanging there. I emptied the pockets of passport, wallet, even coins, and chucked them all in his overnight bag which I would carry on board *Seamist*, and later dump in the Med.

We left shortly afterwards. Sophie hadn't brought much luggage, and she abandoned what there was, to bolster the pretence that she was staying another night.

Outside, the four of us gathered by her rental car. Francine with her arm looped through her mother's, hugging her. Happiness was written large on her face.

'Thank you for everything, Jack,' she said, and detached herself from her mother to hug me around the waist. It was a long hug, the kind that says a great deal without the need for speech. She smelled faintly of lavender.

'Remember what I said,' I whispered in her ear, the loop of her earring brushing my lips. 'No internet. Be a good girl from now on.'

That giggle again. 'I promise.'

Sophie's turn: she and I exchanged kisses, the real mouth-to-mouth kind. A reminder of what could have been but would never be. When we eventually uncoupled she was flushed, her breath sawing through parted lips. She was the most sensual woman I had ever known.

'If ever you change your mind, *chérie*, you know where I live.'

That left only Donovan. I had never warmed to him, but we weren't enemies either. When I needed action, he had been there. He thrust out his hand, and I crunched knuckles with him. He would be overjoyed to see me exit stage left and leave the field clear for him to revive his love-in with Sophie. I privately wished him success.

Doors slammed. The engine turned and fired. Sophie and Francine waved smiling goodbyes. Then the car was in motion, picking up speed, and I was standing alone in front of the hotel, the breeze flicking at my hair, the afternoon sun burning the back of my neck. I watched the car as it descended the hill until it was lost in the melee of traffic.

I felt bereft of purpose, like a becalmed sailing ship. The feeling wouldn't last. A new purpose beckoned. Not a contract, impossible or otherwise, in fact not a contract at all. Just an obstruction blocking the path to the new life I had hankered for since I met Maura. I was about to remove it, even if I had to pay the ultimate price, because if I failed the future was as empty as a black hole in space.

Chapter Twenty-One

Sardinia was the headquarters of *Il Sindicato*, my erstwhile employers, lately become adversaries. The ambush in Paris and at Angela's apartment in Como may or may not have been their doing, but I had two objectives: to find out, and to put an end to it. Their double failure to take me out was not likely to deter them. Au contraire. Once a contract had been issued, it was essential to carry it out to a successful conclusion. If not, their reputation would be tarnished, and their ability to carry on their dirty business degraded. *Il Sindicato*, like the Mafia based to the south in Sicily, and the Unione Corse to the north in Corsica, ruled by fear. Failure diminished the fear.

My contact at the Syndicate, Giorgio du Poletti, aka Giorgy, had denied implication in the attempted killings. But then I had never expected him to admit it, only hoped for a pointer in the midst of his denials. In the absence of other enemies seeking my downfall, the Syndicate was number one suspect.

Either the threat had to go, or I did. No middle road. No compromise. I was intent on confronting them and their *Capo di Tutti Capi*, or boss of all bosses, Giulio Troisi. I was going to do a deal, if possible without violence or bloodletting, and set myself free of their shackles for once and for all.

* * * * *

Although no forensic evidence had been left in Sophie's hotel room to connect me with Vincent Wolff, I aimed to be away from Porto Torres in the small hours, before the body came to light. I would continue in *Seamist* for the first stage of my journey down the island, as far as the town of Bosa, on the west coast. The boat was a handful to manage solo,

but it wouldn't be a new experience. Other people had sailed around the world in similar-size vessels.

That night, I slept on board, anchored a few miles along the coast, round the next headland and screened from Porto Torres. Just in case. The sea stayed tranquil and *Seamist's* gentle motion lulled me to sleep. In the morning I darkened my hair and pasted the fake moustache on my upper lip, before setting off under diesel power for Bosa, about eighty kms down the coast. The sea had become choppy with occasional gusts. Nothing *Seamist* and I couldn't handle. By early afternoon I was entering the estuary where the Bosa marina was situated. It was easy enough to bribe a berth out of the harbourmaster, who also phoned a local car rental firm and booked transportation for me.

The function of the rental – an Alfa Romeo that had led a hard life – was to convey me on the final lap of my journey to the lair of *Il Sindicato*, on the south side of the island. It would be my third visit. On the previous occasion I had shot dead the man who ran the show. The heir apparent, Giulio Troisi, had set me up to do it, and I had obliged, in full ignorance of the stratagem used. In theory, that killing made Troisi beholden to me. In underworld parlance, he owed me. Tomorrow was to be collection day.

For an equaliser I had called on the services of my current supplier, Keith Jupp, a resident of northern Spain. Jupp would deliver anywhere in Europe and North America, in this instance at a fabulous price, as it involved a boat and a floatplane. The modified gun would cost a relatively modest $6000. The rest of the cost, some $27,000, was split between the plane and the boat. The plane would land beside the boat some distance offshore for the transfer of the package.

As for the gun itself, it was no ordinary firearm. Keith made them to order, but always kept one in stock for emergencies. It was colloquially known as a whippet, christened by Clyde Barrow of Bonnie and Clyde infamy, who sawed a few inches off the barrel of a Remington pump-action shotgun so that he could 'whip it out' when needed.

You rarely came across whippets, even among the outlaw fraternity. They could be double-barrelled or pump-action. Mine was pump-action. This type of gun presents challenges in cut-down form because

the magazine has to be shortened as well as the barrel, which involves some minor re-engineering and reduces the number of cartridges it can handle – down to three 65mm for the Ithaca Model 37 Stakeout, plus a fourth in the breech. This particular gun has a folding pistol grip but no stock.

The barrel length of the Jupp-modified variant was eight inches, the overall length just over a foot, not much more than some big revolvers. The loading and ejection ports are the same. This enables you to reload as you go – during breaks in the action – and keep the magazine topped up. It's deadly at close quarters, doubly so when loaded with 00-SG cartridges, which contain eight .33 calibre lead balls. Enough to rip a hole in a brick wall. The modifications to mine included a front hand-grip to prevent the muzzle from riding up when fired. The downside to the reduction in length is a vicious, wrist-spraining recoil.

My package as ordered would include a case of twenty shells. I wouldn't need more. Before I got to the twentieth, either my enemies would all be dead or I would.

* * * * *

It was mid-morning, the sun was history, having retreated behind some stormy clouds. Rain was falling intermittently. Setting off from Bosa in the beat-up Alfa, I joined the SS131 to the south. Two hundred and forty kms lay ahead. It was high season, and the tourists were out in numbers, so I didn't expect to make it to my next stopover before late afternoon.

I took a break for lunch at a busy bar I had used before, in a town where the highway meets the sea, with the odd name of S'Archittu. It was just as downscale in the reality as in my recall, but they served a decent pizza, which I supplemented with a bottled Moretti beer. I would also overnight in the town, at a B & B called the Torre del Pozzo, a place where the facilities were modest and the management asked no questions.

A young guy who bore a close enough resemblance to Antonio Banderas to make me do a double-take, dropped off my delivery from Keith Jupp after dark. He had a wide, white grin and spoke crude

French. The package changed hands in the lobby. It was shoe-box shape, but longer, and wrapped in bubble-pack with so much duct tape holding it together I had to borrow a knife from the kitchen to cut it off.

I completed the inspection ceremony in the car, with Antonio beside me. If it wasn't as ordered, he would be on the receiving end of my displeasure as there was no one else around to shoulder the blame.

When I revealed the gun in all its gunmetal glory, he drew in an awed breath.

'*Quel flingue!*'

'The hunting season starts soon,' I joked, and he chuckled.

'What kind of game you after?'

He didn't expect an answer, and I didn't disappoint him. He accepted a €100 tip as his right. The fee itself was already paid, by Internet transfer.

With a '*Bonne chance*' and a friendly salute he jogged off towards the beach, where an inflatable would be waiting to transport him back to his boat.

In the privacy of my poky €60-a-night room, I conducted a more thorough examination. Keith had done a fine job on the conversion, even welding a new sight on the muzzle. The whole was a handy size, though still too bulky to conceal about your person. I would wear a windbreaker with loose sleeves, and slide the barrel down inside the left sleeve with the pistol grip hooked over the armpit, for easy access with my right hand. It would be noticeable, but not at first glance, and not at a distance. The shells I would distribute about my pockets, apart from the four already loaded in the gun.

My inspection involved loading and ejecting a few shells to test the smoothness of the action, then a complete strip-down and reassemble. I was familiar with the Ithaca Stakeout and could dismantle it and put it back together in minutes.

Tomorrow was destined to be an important staging post in my life as a professional killer. In more precise terms, I intended it to be the finishing post, no matter what the result. If anybody died, I would regret it. I was on an errand of reconciliation. I would talk softly and wield a big gun.

* * * * *

The weather was back to its regular sunny and hot and windless, and the sea was as calm as a lake; down in the bay a small yacht was trying to coax some traction from the inert air, but its sails hung lifeless and no wake was visible.

On the road again, with swarms of tourists in their overloaded cars and camper vans. No use trying to hustle. I didn't have an appointment and nobody was expecting me, so apart from an urge to see the last of Troisi and *Il Sindicato*, I was content to go with the trend.

Riola Sardo, Nurachi, Donigala, Oristano. The towns, all congealed with traffic, came and went at uneventful intervals. When I came to Cagliari, the capital, I took a lunch break and mingled with Sardinian peasants and German tourists. The babble of languages was something to hear.

With Cagliari and the sun behind me, I arrived at the house that spelled journey's end. It sat atop a hillside, on the edge of the town of Simius, and bore the name La Cima della Scogliera. The lettering was in gold leaf, set into a stucco archway that surmounted the entrance to the walled grounds. The sliding gate was of steel and would resist any attempt to break through short of a tank. It was open, but its open-ness was not meant as an invitation. This was one house where gatecrashers were not welcome.

By the entrance was a gatehouse, not unlike that at the Wolff's Budapest mansion. As I got out of the Alfa, leaving the engine ticking over, a guy stepped forward to greet me in Italian. I understood little of it, but it didn't have a cordial ring.

'You speak English?' I enquired.

He glowered and went back into his cabin. A phone call and a few minutes later a golf buggy came trundling down the driveway, depositing a guy in a polo shirt and shorts by the cabin. He was about my age, and I recognised him from my previous stay as a guest of *Il Sindicato*.

'Hi,' he said, his tone neither friendly nor hostile. 'What can I do for you?'

His English was American, with no regional bias.

'My name's Warner. I do jobs for the Syndicate. I know Mr Troisi, and Giorgio du Poletti personally.' I omitted to add that Troisi was only his boss because I had rubbed out his predecessor, Luigi Santorino.

'Uh-huh. I remember you. I'm Jimmy Fontana. Nobody told me you were expected.'

'That's because I wasn't. I need to see Mr Troisi on an urgent matter.'

'Urgent? In what way urgent?'

'A matter of life and death.'

He was chewing gum and he masticated on it for a beat or two, his brow creased.

'Sounds serious. Suppose I check with the boss.'

'Suppose you do.'

He entered the cabin. The gatekeeper stayed outside to watch over me. As a concession to the heat he was in shirtsleeves, though with a dazzling tie, and his pants were black, with red suspenders. Black suits were *de rigueur* for the guys who worked here.

Local flies had discovered my presence and commenced strafing runs on me when Fontana came off the phone.

'You're good to come ahead,' he said, a fraction more welcoming.

The next step was a frisk. He was expert at it. Then he went over the car, interior first, before going down on his knees to shine a flashlight on the underside. I had taped the Ithaca to the inside of the sill, making it invisible unless the inspection was carried out from directly underneath the vehicle. The shells were under the front seats, tucked in places that were too small for a handgun and therefore unlikely to be of interest.

'Follow me,' he said, brushing driveway grit from his pants.

He U-turned the buggy, and we started up the driveway in convoy. The land on which the vast property sat was elevated, and added to its already commanding presence, though the design of the building itself was unexciting, considering what it must have cost. White stucco finish, like most houses on the island, with a row of Doric columns at the front. The windows were tall, English Regency style, subdivided into small oblong panes, all behind bars. To keep people in, or keep them out; probably a bit of both. The gable roof was terracotta tiled, with chimneys

at intervals. The final touch was a flagpole; bare the last time I saw it, today sporting the Sardinian flag, which is white with a red cross, like the English cross of St George. Unlike the English flag, a silhouetted head is portrayed in each quarter, representing the Four Moors, who in turn symbolise the four victories by the Kingdom of Aragon over the invading Moors. Quirky, if you ask me, glorifying your enemies' profiles.

The courtyard behind the house, with its Olympic-length pool, served as a parking lot. Fontana directed me to an empty bay, and I lined up and parked, nose outwards for a fast exit. I got out, stretched, and did a swift audit of my surroundings. Several people of both sexes sprawled around the pool on sunbeds. The girls were the usual plastic bimbos you get wherever the mob congregates. Paid by the hour to keep the troops entertained. I looked for Giorgy, but it wouldn't be his scene. He was on the management side, not given to mixing with the lower life and being too much in love with his wife to be induced to stray.

A girl beckoned me over; about eighteen, maybe less, well-endowed and almost-clad in a red bikini the size of three small handkerchiefs. The guy she was with didn't appreciate her invitation. It earned her a loud smack on the buttocks. She didn't seem to mind much, just let out an exaggerated squawk and poked her tongue at him.

Fontana peeled me away from the flesh display and towards the grand entrance. Now was the moment to arm myself.

'I left my wallet in the car,' I said and, without waiting for his permission, made for the Alfa. The gun was stashed on the right side; Fontana was on my left, and wasn't even paying me any attention, being absorbed by the vision of a slender, athletic girl climbing the steps up to the diving board. She was naked and not shy about it.

I crouched beside the Alfa and groped under the sill. The Ithaca came to my hand, and I ripped it free of its nook. From inside the car, working fast, I retrieved as many of the cartridges as I could find. All the while I kept Fontana under scrutiny in case he tired of watching the naked girl who was now striding along the diving board, gesticulating to her audience and swivelling her hips. Exhibitionist to the core.

She dived like a swooping swallow, at which point Fontana lost interest.

'Hey, you done?' he called to me.

I backed out of the Jeep, a dozen cartridges in my pockets, the gun down my sleeve, my windbreaker zipped. It was as discreet as I could make it. If they frisked me again, inside the house, I would be in trouble.

'It fell down the side of the seat,' I said as an explanation.

He made an uninterested sound through his nose and motioned me up the steps to the grand entrance.

As expected, two more friskers guarded the entrance hall. The defining moment was imminent. Their unpreparedness was my only advantage, which meant bringing the gun into play before they frisked me.

I had practised drawing it from my sleeve the previous night. It was awkward on account of its length, and for sure I wouldn't win any awards for Fast Draw of the Week. To survive beyond the next few seconds, I would have to shoot first. Both the guards were armed with full-size pumpers. To use them on me, they would have to create space between us. I reckoned I could just about beat them to it. Fontana was conceivably the most dangerous of the three: the vague outline of a handgun was noticeable under the polo shirt he wore loose over his pants, and if he was any good at his job, he would be able to access it in a heartbeat.

The taller of the guards crouched to pat down my legs. The shorter guard was standing a few feet away, yawning, his gun dangling from his hand. I could guess his state of mind: this guy is one of us, who needs this security bullshit? Fontana's back was towards me, so when I made my move he wasn't even aware of it. The Ithaca slid from my sleeve without snagging on the material, and with the safety already off was ready for instant action. The shorter guard reacted sluggishly, brought his gun up to blast me a millisecond too late. I gave it to him in the right arm, almost dislocating my wrist, so savage was the recoil. The impact of the cartridge's eight .33 calibre balls at point blank range sent him reeling away in a haze of blood and tatters of flesh and shirt. As Fontana twisted round, going for his handgun, I was pumping the second shell into the firing chamber and squeezing the trigger as I did so. Aiming to disable rather than kill, I got him in the shoulder. His automatic went

left and he went right, and that was the extent of his contribution.

The frisking guard, who had been on his haunches, fell backwards in surprise, dropping his gun. I kicked him in the chest and he lost his balance and toppled over. As he floundered on the floor, I let him have it in his right arm too.

A brief lull in the activity allowed me to reload three cartridges and I was thumbing the last through the loading port when a bunch of goons burst into the lobby, flourishing handguns. That was the trouble with low-grade muscle, they were about as subtle as a fighting bull in a bullring.

'Hold it!' I yelled, the reloaded Ithaca covering them. Even if they didn't understand the words, they understood the language of spreadshot. Guns clattered to the floor. Despite their numerical superiority, none of them was willing to offer himself up as a sacrifice.

'Hold it!' I yelled again, reinforcing the warning, though all were now unarmed.

There were five of them, all shapes and sizes. They looked around, taking in the three groaning figures leaking blood on the tiled floor. So far nobody had died. In that respect my plan was holding firm. It was bound not to last.

'Get Troisi!' I snapped at the group. Movement outside warned me that reinforcements would be coming to investigate the gunfire. With the group covered, I took a few steps back and slammed the door shut. It had solid bolts at the top and bottom. The top was too high to reach without taking my eyes off the goons, but I managed to ram the lower bolt home just as someone hammered against the door and began leaning on it. It was built to be leaned on, so they didn't make much impression.

The group of five were still frozen in place. I fired a single demonstration round, aiming high. Plaster spattered on their heads.

'Troisi – pronto!' As I bawled at them, I fed another cartridge into the magazine while keeping them covered.

A pair of goons took off, hopefully in search of the *Capo di tutti capi*. And then there were three, which was a small improvement in the odds. I advanced on Fontana, who was sitting up now, nursing his shattered

shoulder and cursing with great fluency. His automatic had skidded on the tiles and was lying near my feet. I confiscated it; it would come in handy as a back-up weapon. It was a Glock, the compact model.

Minutes ticked by. A hammering came at the entrance door. I turned and fired into it, low down, making a hole as big as a side plate, and was rewarded with a scream. Super-fast, I was back facing the remaining three goons while thumbing a replacement cartridge into the mag. Their stances hadn't altered. Theirs was the kind of respect I liked.

Then Troisi put in an appearance, in the company of the two goons and another guy, well-dressed enough to be a cut above the muscle. Troisi had a large black cat in tow.

'Warner!' Not intimidated by my weaponry, Troisi crossed the lobby, tugging at the leash, the cat digging its claws into the tiles to no avail. The well-dressed guy tucked in behind him, out of the line of fire.

'What the fuck is this? What are you doing here?' Troisi's English was excellent right down to the expletives. The cat rubbed itself against his leg, tail vertical and straight but for a little kink at the tip.

'Just a social call, Giulio.'

'Is all this really necessary?' he said, gesturing from left to right over his wounded warriors. 'We allowed you in, in good faith.'

'Find someplace we can sit and talk,' I said, 'and all your questions will be answered. First though, call off the gorillas inside and out or I'll use this on you.'

Giulio Troisi. The Syndicate chief they said was a man of his word, a man you could trust to honour his promises. I was about to put that reputation to the test.

He distributed orders to the crestfallen goon squad who had capitulated so readily. They shuffled off, leaving their weaponry where it lay. Nobody paid heed to Fontana and the other wounded still sprawled on the floor, in varying degrees of distress.

'Don't forget the guys outside,' I said to Troisi. They were still putting pressure on the door, which was creaking and shuddering. Even doors designed to resist police raids can only stand so much.

Troisi's companion produced a cell phone, and as he spoke into it, the pressure on the door ceased.

'If any of your chimps steps out of line, just remember, you go first.' I warned Troisi, then shifted my stare to his buddy. 'And you next.'

The guy's complexion went from sallow to a fetching shade of green. Not much of the right stuff there then.

Troisi, more composed, inclined his head down the corridor.

'This way,' he said curtly.

The room was much as I remembered it. The décor and furnishings were unchanged in the past two years. Couches and lounge chairs in apricot leather in three groups, each surrounding lozenge-shaped coffee tables. Tiled floor, rugs of many shapes and shades, laid at forty-five degrees to the walls. The external wall was all window and French doors, offering an uninterrupted panorama of sea and sky in matching blues.

Troisi introduced his associate to me as Rinaldo. I figured he was Troisi's number two, occupying the position Troisi himself had occupied until I advanced his promotion by removing the top man. Physically unimpressive, a beak of a nose below beady eyes and a forehead with more lines than a subway map. Maybe his assets were all cerebral.

We sat in a three-way arrangement. Troisi in a lounge chair with the black cat curled up on his lap, Rinaldo and me on separate couches, at right angles to him. I kept a firm grip on the Ithaca, resting it on my knee, pointing at Troisi.

Troisi opened the proceedings.

'Do you like cats, André?'

'On the whole. What's this one's name?'

'Satan.' He chuckled; the cat yawned, displaying impressive fangs. 'Apt, don't you think?'

I didn't answer. Satan regarded me with a hungry glint in his yellow eyes. His tongue, very pink in contrast to his black fur, flicked at the corner of his mouth as if he were salivating over the prospect of a prime cut of Warner steak for supper.

'Now, my friend,' Troisi said, the balm of his words belying the tumult that was sure to be brewing within, 'tell me to what we owe the unexpected pleasure of your company on this beautiful summer morning, and the reason for the violence that, as I understand, was not initiated by us.'

'You're right. Not this time. But in Paris, and again on Lake Como, it *was* initiated by you.'

It was a stab in the dark, as I had no proof that the ambushes were at the instigation of *Il Sindicato*. Anyhow, it was a stab that pierced. He didn't even pretend to deny it.

'Let's assume you are right. Where does that leave us?'

'Us? It leaves me justified in snuffing you out, and any of your goons who are too dumb to stay neutral. The cat too, if he gets protective. If you're gunning for me, you'll get me sooner or later, so it might as well be now when at least I can take you with me.'

My logic was inarguable.

His face was pale, but his voice was level as he said, 'You know why we want you out of the way. If you can resolve our concerns, I will listen.'

Whether this willingness was real or fake was not for me to judge, not being clairvoyant. This was not a man susceptible to panic, and he could be plotting to bring about my demise even as we negotiated.

'All right, Giulio. Here's the deal. I want out – period, and I don't want you coming after me, and in particular I want you to stay away from Maura Beck and her daughter. That's it.'

'I see.'

He bent his head to Satan and murmured to him. The cat mewed back, twitching his tail.

'You always consult the cat?' I said.

My weak essay at humour didn't register with him.

'If we agree to this,' he said, smooth as a politician deflecting an embarrassing question, 'what are you proposing as *quid pro quo*?'

Quid pro quo. A mobster who knew his Latin. But then he was Italian, which is almost the same.

'Firstly, I'm offering peace. If you leave me alone, I'll leave you alone. You may think you can send your clowns after me and eventually one of them will succeed. That may be true. But you had better make sure the first one succeeds, because if he doesn't I'll be back here. And next time it won't be with this –' I patted the Ithaca '– it'll be with a sniper rifle of a particular kind and you won't even see me when I zap you. You won't

dare leave the building, or even show your face at a window. No more sunning yourself on the terrace with your bimbos, no more trips to the … what's it called … that restaurant you're so fond of in Cagliari? No more voyages on your yacht. You'll be a prisoner here until finally I convert you into a corpse.'

If the prospect daunted him, it didn't show on his features. He was as impassive as his feline companion.

'Is that it? Your proposition.'

'Not all of it. That's what's called negative reinforcement.' I edged forward on the couch. 'Here's the positive. I'll transfer a million US dollars to your private account the day after I leave here – provided I don't leave in a coffin.'

At last the stone facade cracked. Troisi was arguably more impressed by the profit than the avoidance of loss. Or maybe he found it more convincing than my threats, deadly serious though they were.

'It's a proposition worth considering,' he admitted, stroking Satan's neck with a bent forefinger. The cat purred. 'Your threat I have to take at face value, and I will admit it would not be pleasant to live under sentence of death, even if you failed to carry it out. The second part, the million dollars, is of course a much more attractive proposition.' He cleared his throat, shifted his position, folded one elegantly-trousered leg over the other. All delaying tactics, buying a respite to marshal his response.

'Here is my counter proposal,' he said at last, smoothing the wrinkles from his cream short-sleeved shirt, with its red GT monogram over the breast pocket. He was very sartorial. 'Two million, not one. A million to me, a million to *Il Sindicato*.'

I didn't hesitate for long. It was worth it to me, and I could afford it. So I didn't haggle or procrastinate.

'Okay.'

'We have a deal?' he insisted.

'We have a deal.'

Rinaldo looked relieved. In English, he said, 'As *consigliare*, I appreciate your million contribution to the treasure chest of the organisation.'

'Spend it wisely, Mr Rinaldo. In case your boss breaks his word and I have to come back and kill you too.'

'I won't break my word,' Troisi said.

Did I believe him? On balance, yes. Did I trust him? Emphatically, no. But above all he was a businessman, a pragmatist. At the very least, I represented aggravation. At the worst, elimination and potential harm to the business interests and repute of *Il Sindicato*.

Our handshake to seal the deal was mutually wary. I risked a pat on Satan's velvety head with equal wariness. He hissed at me and his jaws came together like a sprung trap, a cat's whisker short of my fingers; only my quick reactions saved me from a savaging.

Troisi tutted and admonished the cat with a tap on the nose. 'He is not fond of strangers.'

'I believe you,' I said. 'I'm leaving now before he starts to really dislike me. You two gentlemen will accompany me as far as Cagiliari.'

Troisi frowned. 'André, André,' he said in a chiding tone. 'This is not necessary. We have made a deal. There must be trust on both sides.'

If it was overkill on my part, it was better than being killed.

'You're coming with me, Giulio. It's nothing personal, just me taking precautions at the cost of a small inconvenience to you. Instruct your people not to tail us. You can take a cab back here.'

His overdone sigh was for effect only.

'Oh, very well, I suppose I must humour you.'

He would humour me only as long as I had him at gunpoint.

He summoned a maid and entrusted Satan to her. She made sure to keep her distance as she led it from the scene.

We left together – Troisi, Rinaldo and me – and ran the gauntlet of the five goons inside, and the dozen or so outside. I used Troisi and Rinaldo as a shield, keeping the Ithaca trained on Troisi. He issued orders, incomprehensible to me, but the guys stood aside and let us pass, resentful, truculent, but disciplined. They all watched us as we walked to my rental car. Somebody catcalled, and Troisi shouted '*Silenzio*!'

In order to control my hostages after we climbed into the Alfa, I directed Rinaldi to drive, with Troisi in the front passenger seat. I banned them both from wearing seat belts. Myself, I buckled up in the

rear seat and pressed the muzzle of the gun against the back of Troisi's seat.

Down the driveway to the gate, the gatekeeper lounging beside his cabin. No gun in evidence. Troisi leaned out of the window on his side and barked Italian at the guy, who raised a hand in acknowledgement.

Through the gateway, onto the road to Cagliari, the sea winking on our left in the late afternoon sunlight. I realised I was holding my breath. I released it, relaxed into my seat, and dared to believe I really had gotten away with it.

'It's called Dal Corsaro,' Troisi said, half-turning his head towards me.

'What is?'

'The restaurant I am so fond of.'

Chapter Twenty-Two

The digital photos Maura had transmitted to me on WhatsApp were of a chalet-style house, with a wooded backdrop and a yard that was lawn, flowerbeds, and bushes, including hydrangeas and rhododendrons. Close by the house was a kidney-shaped swimming pool, and on the edge of the belt of trees a pond carpeted with lilies. It was on high ground just outside Bar Harbour, Maine, overlooking the town where her parents lived and Frenchman Bay. A million dollar outlook.

Other photos she had sent over the months of separateness were of her with daughter Belinda, of her parents, and of the family group of four.

It was over two years since Maura and I parted. We had been reunited for a few too-short weeks in Finland, the winter before last, and that, apart from a brief encounter in New York City, was the sum total of our recent togetherness.

She had relocated to Bar Harbour a year or so ago after it seemed she might be at risk from *Il Sindicato*. I had her land line number, her two cell phone numbers, a Facetime connection, and her two email addresses. The means of communication were all there; we just seldom used them. In her case, because she didn't trust her resolve to cut me out of her life unless I quit my profession. In my case, because I didn't want to pressurise her to resume our relationship against her moral instincts and determination to protect Belinda from bad stuff.

Before setting off, I had agonized over whether to give her advance notification or drop in on a wing and a wish. I opted for impromptu. It would be too easy for her to reject me on the phone, and if she said no, I wouldn't feel right in overriding her wishes. Whereas if I just appeared on her doorstep she was unlikely to slam the door on me.

So on a day in late August I drove the Aston Martin to Santander,

ferried to Portsmouth, and drove some more to Heathrow on highways bumper to bumper with traffic. The flight was smooth enough, and I rehearsed over and over my speech to Maura, when I would swear I had given up the killing business, and would henceforth be a law-abiding citizen, and, if she would have me and wanted to legalise the knot, never again touch a gun or any other instrument of death.

Promises are easy to make. The tough part is keeping them.

From JKF airport by rental car – a Beamer sedan for a change – up through Connecticut, Mass. and New Hampshire to Maine, a day's driving good as. Interstate highways to Bangor, then state highways for the last lap. When I crossed the bridge from the mainland to Mt Desert Island, I had the odd feeling I was coming home, though I had never set foot there. It was after six in the evening, vacationers were out in force and it was no use trying to hurry, impatient as I was to see the second and third loves of my life again.

The GPS guided me past the town of Bar Harbour and up an incline by the name of Eagle Lake Road. A right turn onto Arata Drive, and I was within walking distance of Maura's house.

Trees were dominant on her lot. They lined the cobbled-stone driveway, and the lot was ringed in by them. At the end of the driveway, attached to the house, a double garage with separate doors. The right-hand door was raised and an Audi e-tron electric SUV stood inside.

I drove up to the garage at a crawl and parked so as to block the Audi in case she attempted to escape in it. In dread of a negative reaction, I sat there for a minute or two, guts churning. This woman was not merely important to me, she was my whole life. If she spurned me, if my renouncing the killing wasn't enough, I was all out of options.

'Hi.' The voice was female but higher-pitched than Maura's. I lowered the window, removed my sunglasses. Recognition instantly bloomed in the face of the young girl who stood there, holding the handlebars of a scooter.

'André!' The squeal was pure delight. Half of the team at least was pleased to see me.

I got out. She let the scooter fall and launched herself at me. We held each other tight, my arms around her shoulders, hers tight around my waist.

'You're back!' she burbled into my chest. 'You're back, you're back, you're back!'

'I'm back,' I agreed, hoping it would be more than a flying visit. 'Have you missed me as much as I've missed you?'

'Oh, lots more! Mommy's missed you too.'

Belinda, answered to Lindy, was now ten. Her blonde hair was darkening, her face was as pretty as ever, if not more so, and she had gained some height. She was wearing shorts and a green T-shirt sporting the message "Let's go GREEN".

'Your Mommy's in, I suppose,' I said.

She finally released me and stood there, grinning her delight, and clutching my hands in hers.

'Yes, she's making a cake.'

'She doesn't know I'm coming. Shall we go and surprise her?'

Lindy agreed that would be a super idea.

But we never got as far as the front door. It opened and Maura, perhaps drawn by the commotion, came out onto the veranda, hands gloved in flour. She came to an abrupt stop, gaping, perfect cupid's-bow lips parted in surprise. Take-your-breath-away gorgeous: lissom figure, shapely legs, face to kill for. All the clichés applied to her. Her chestnut hair, with its subtle kink, was caught in an untidy ponytail, and had grown a year's worth since I last ran my fingers through it.

She didn't just walk towards me, she jumped down from the veranda without using the two steps and cannoned into my embrace. I was still attached to Lindy, so we made up a hugging threesome. Maura and I kissed hard and for so long that Lindy separated us by pushing, squirming, and wriggling her body between us. Then we were all laughing and talking nonsense over each other.

The kissing resumed, with Lindy getting cross, and forcing herself between us again. It all calmed down in time, and with our arms around each other, and Lindy riding my shoulders, we went indoors.

'Duck,' I warned her as we crossed the threshold.

With the door closed, we continued our reunion embrace. Maura's cat, Oswald known as Ozzy, even horned in, mewing for attention, and twirling around our legs. He was a black Persian and the double of

Giulio Troisi's cat, which was an unfortunate memento. There was a second cat in the family, called Griswold, pet name Grizzly, but he was forever absent.

'How long are you staying?' Maura asked, those fabulous, hypnotic, lapis-lazuli eyes quizzing mine for clues. 'Or are you staying?'

'I'm staying. If you'll have me.'

'Oh, I'll have you all right.' She brushed flour off my shoulders and arms.

'For good?'

She went very still. Now her gaze was troubled, and I knew why.

Now was the time to tell her. Nothing to gain in deferring it.

'I've quit.'

'You've … quit?' She sounded as if she didn't quite believe it. 'You're not in the … the whatsit business anymore?'

'I've quit,' I repeated. 'I've retired, permanently. I want to be with you and to marry you and to be a father to Lindy.'

'Yes, yes!' Lindy squeaked, jumping up and down.

Maura's response was more measured. 'You're serious? You really mean it?'

'I'm serious and I really mean it.'

She released me and stood back. Lindy frowned at her.

'Mommy, what'sa matter? I want André to come and live with us.'

Maura shushed her. 'I know you do, sweetheart, and so do I. But there are some little matters we have to discuss first. Okay?'

'Ohh-kaay.' A sigh of resigned acceptance of parental authority.

'That's fine,' I said. 'I didn't expect you to take my word for it and lay down the welcome mat. We have a mountain of baggage to unload.'

She nodded. 'Don't get me wrong, darling. I love you and want you just as much as ever. It's just that we've had so many false starts, I hesitate to rejoice. I'll need convincing that you really have turned your back on the you-know-what trade. That you won't be tempted or intimidated back into it, like, oh, you know, a junkey giving up on drugs then finding the pain and the sacrifice too much and returning to his old ways.'

'What's a junkey, Mommy?' Lindy asked, always quick to pounce on new words.

'I'll tell you later, sweetheart,' Maura said.

I took her in my arms, under observation from a not-entirely mollified Lindy and a purring Ozzy.

'It won't be like that. It's over. Period. I made a deal with the Syndicate. It was expensive, but it was worth it many times over to have you back.'

She puckered her lips at me in a contactless kiss, like she used to do so often it became a trademark.

'We'll talk over supper, when Lindy's gone to bed.'

'I want to talk as well,' Lindy protested.

'Tomorrow, sweetheart. Tonight, Drew and I must talk grown-up stuff. In the morning we'll talk to you about what we've agreed.'

Lindy, fists on hips, wasn't having any.

'If you send André away, I'll *never ever* speak to you again!'

Maura crouched before her, trying to suppress a smile and failing. 'In that case I'd better not send him away then, had I?'

'You better not!'

Maura fixed drinks – whisky sour for me, a Chardonnay white wine for her – and we sat on a couch, our bodies in contact, and yarned, keeping off sensitive issues. Lindy refused to be sidelined, chipping in at the smallest hint of a pause in the palaver. The living room, with its beamed ceiling and stone fireplace, was furnished cottage-style with chintz and dark oak and a round oriental-pattern rug between the two couches. In a dim corner, a grandfather clock. Nothing that I could see had come from her Las Vegas house, aside from some pictures by her favourite artist, Thomas Moran, and various ornaments including the three statuettes of nude female figures in bronze, adorning the bureau. A Swiss Atmos clock that was new to me reposed on a built-in shelf above the fireplace. Even Ozzie seemed to be glad I was back, climbing onto my lap, purring non-stop.

Later, Maura cooked for us – cheese filo tart starters, locally landed lobster and mussel moqueca main course, all delicious – and we made small-talk during the candlelit repast, Lindy easily holding her own and refusing to let the grown-ups relegate her to junior status. When the grandfather clock chimed the hour of nine, Maura ordered her off to

bed, no arguments.

I hugged her goodnight, punctuated with a kiss on the tip of her nose, which made her giggle.

'I'll be up in five minutes,' Maura said to her retreating back.

'Shall I come?' I said.

'No!' Maura said sharply. 'Not yet.'

My initial assumption was that she meant me to come up after her. Then it sank in that she actually wasn't ready to let me play surrogate daddy to her daughter. Not until decisions had been made about the future, and if we were to spend it together or apart.

'Do you read her a story?' I asked, to cover up my confusion and disappointment.

'Not any more. She reads her own stories.' She smiled to herself. 'Avidly.'

She was away upstairs for about ten minutes. When she returned, she was brisk and businesslike, as if she were preparing for a conference. I topped up our wine glasses and clinked hers, although she wasn't holding it.

'To Lindy,' I proposed, and she drank to that in gulps. Fortifying herself, I guessed.

'So let's talk,' she said. She wasn't smiling, and the usual lovelight was absent from her eyes. The message was – I refuse to be emotional about us. This is going to be serious stuff, truth or consequences. The game show, not the Mexican city.

It was fine by me. I intended to be as honest with her as she could stomach.

So we talked. Or rather I did the talking, she did the listening. I opened by relating how the UK Government recruited me because of my MI6 experience, to infiltrate an organisation that was intent on securing independence for Gibraltar. I told her about Linda and our brief fling, and how it ended. Also about Elena. No fling there, unless you counted the way she flung herself at me, but I didn't deny that I'd been tempted often enough. My shooting of the renegade Spanish General Irazola and his high-ranking subordinates was among the omissions. Instead I told her about the British Government's offer of a

million pounds to kill the leader of the independence movement – an offer I declined in favour of doing what was right.

When she heard that she stretched an arm across the table and squeezed my hand.

From Gibraltar to Hungary and the contract impossible. My task was to find a certain Vincent Wolff, I explained, leaving out the second clause in the contract. I freely disclosed Vincent's crime against his wife's daughter, feeling it would add justification to my cause, as Maura, being the mother of a girl child, was bound to empathise with it. I kept shtoom about the collateral killings, focused instead on the challenge of identifying the twin. Patricia alias Francine featured in my tale, but at least I could claim to have saved the girl from the Internet flesh market. I admitted to my liaison with Angela, making light of it. The wild night with Marquise Sophie I edited out. It only degraded me and sure as hell wouldn't advance my cause with Maura. Likewise, in my version of events, I succeeded in tracing Vincent but implied that I had left it to others to carry out the ultimate sanction.

Other omissions included the one-night stands that interspersed the last two years, and the paid sex that filled the bill when my libido demanded sustenance. There hadn't been many of these cats in the night, but again it was a case of too much honesty being bad for the digestion.

It was a self-serving hash, and I wasn't proud of the deceptions and omissions. I justified it to myself by my conviction that I could only win Maura over if I kept the bad truths from her. It was the wrong foundation on which to re-start our relationship, potentially for life, but I knew my Maura, what she would and wouldn't stand for. If winning her over meant forfeiting my integrity, I would make that sacrifice without a qualm.

The clock was striking eleven when I dried up. I emptied my glass, avoiding her eyes, expecting to see only censure there. Then her hand returned to mine.

'Darling' she said, and there was no censure after all, only the look of love that I had grown to expect in the days when we were lovers through and through. 'Thank you for telling me. I won't ask you point-

blank if you left anything out. If you … if you … killed anyone. I'll accept that you …' A deep inhalation here, 'you may have done, but I'm turning a deaf ear. Let it be enough that you're here, you're safe, and you've renounced the killing for good.'

'Can you do that?' I said, slightly choked.

'I think so. Let me sleep on it and give you my decision at breakfast.' She smiled her smile of old. 'Can you live with that?'

I nodded. 'I can live with it. Not so sure I can sleep with it, but what's a sleepless night in such a worthy cause.'

'Now it's my turn. You've come clean with me, I need to do the same with you.'

My immediate conclusion was that I had a rival.

'There's someone else,' I blurted. 'Is that it?'

'Not exactly. Wrong tense. There was someone, sort of. A guy called Ken, about your age, not quite as good-looking but presentable enough. A widower with no baggage. A bank manager, if you can believe it.'

'Okay … okay.' I wasn't sure how I felt or how to react. It would be unreasonable to object, considering my own infidelities.

'It didn't last long. It ended on the night we made love.'

To hear her talk about making love to another man sickened me. I couldn't help it. She had been unattainable to me these past two years for reasons sacrosanct to her, but I had still thought of her as my woman. Not for sharing.

'You made love,' I said dully.

Her hand moved to my cheek, her fingertips stroking, light as a butterfly.

'Yes, darling. We'd been dating for … oh, about two months. In fairness to him, he'd shown masses of restraint, but I let him persuade me the time was right. It was one of those periods when you and I hadn't communicated for a while, so you could say I was ripe for the plucking.' She paused, her gaze holding mine as if entranced. 'I agreed to go to bed with him, but insisted on the lights being out.' She chuckled. 'Not my style, if you recall.'

I recalled too much, that was my problem. My return grin was sickly.

'Anyway, when it came to … doing it, I could only go through with

it by imagining he was you. So there we were, in the dark, me with my eyes shut tight, being made love to by your stand-in.' Her fingertips strayed over my lips; I kissed them. She had succeeded in making me feel bad and good, resentful and grateful.

'Go on.'

'There's no going on. That's all I have to confess.'

'Thanks for sharing that with me, love,' I said. As if at a signal we leaned towards each other across the dishes and condiments and kissed ourselves breathless.

As we sat back, beaming inanely at each other, I said, 'What happened next? Between you and my … er, stand-in.'

'Nothing happened. It made me realise that a substitute wouldn't satisfy me. It had to be the real McCoy or nobody. Ken and I became an ex-item the next day.'

'I'm relieved to hear it.'

'One final thing I have to say. Or rather, it's a request.'

I shrugged. 'Request it.'

'Would you mind sleeping in the guest room tonight?'

Disappointment bloomed, but I kept it off my face. I even dug up a smile of sorts.

'Sure, I'd mind. Who'd want to pass up the opportunity of a night in the sack with a hot broad like you?' She knew how my humour worked, and laughed. 'But I get it. I can wait until tomorrow and hope for a favourable decision.'

'Thank you for understanding. There's one thing I want you to know. Whatever I decide, I love you more than I can find words to express, and I can't imagine ever not loving you.'

On that note we dropped the heavy talk and set about clearing the table, accompanied by the banter that had always peppered our dialogue. It was late when we retired to our respective sleeping quarters. A single goodnight kiss, admittedly steamy, was my quota.

'I love you,' she breathed in my ear.

'I love you,' I breathed back.

And for that I had to settle.

* * * * *

'Darling ...'

'Mmm?'

'Make it last.'

She spread her legs and I accepted the invitation like a starving man accepting a crust of bread. The meeting of our bodies was akin to a returning home from a great trek over a barren waste. The sexual fit was as perfect as ever. Maura wasn't inventive – she left that to me – but she was energetic and vocal with it. We left the lights on. She preferred to see and be seen, and I knew I would never grow tired of that sinuous body with the supple breasts that undulated with the rhythm of our lovemaking.

Making it last, after the extended drought, proved beyond my means. It was all over in minutes – for both of us. We stayed attached, our faces inches away, our mouths melding.

'Sorry,' I said. 'I'll take longer next time.'

'Me too.'

Maura's big decision had been in my favour. Somehow I had sensed it would, though I worried throughout the night that it wouldn't. As a celebration we went on a picnic with Lindy on Eagle Lake, with a half a million vacationers for company. We swam and played beach tennis and ate ice cream and made like families make. Afterwards, as the afternoon drew to a close, we drove into Bar Harbour to meet Maura's parents.

They were in their sixties; him very Germanic with cropped grey hair and the bluest eyes I had ever seen; his wife very American, with hair that should have been grey but was blonde. Both very communicative. They had heard about me, albeit with few details. To them I was an investor and businessman, and they didn't burrow any deeper. It was enough to convince them that my intentions in the matter of their only daughter were honourable. Maura laughed off her father's traditional attitude towards a prospective suitor; I didn't. I gave him the assurances he sought, and my sincerity must have gotten through to him, because he seemed to warm towards me as the evening progressed. Her mother too, though being American to my Anglo-Canadian, maybe it was just

easier for her to relate.

We stayed for supper, Lindy dominating the cross-table talk with her reminiscences of our life together in Andorra. Nobody asked why our togetherness had been interrupted. I sensed that Maura had already given her parents the rundown on that episode, amending the reasons somewhat. They would have been less welcoming had they known the truth about my profession. In some respects I felt like a fraud.

When we left, a sleepy Lindy stretched out on the rear seat of my rented Beamer, I felt we had turned another corner, that we were approaching the home straight to that state of contentment that I had aspired to recapture ever since the death of my first wife, Marion, all those years ago.

* * * * *

From the day of my introduction to Maura's parents the path ahead was as smooth as a speed skating track. If you exclude a bump one morning in late August when a text message came through on my cell phone, while I was in the shower.

When I entered the living room, my hair still damp, my skin tingling from the cold shower, Maura was at the breakfast table, Lindy opposite her, and my cell phone between them. Not its usual place of repose.

'Hi, André,' Lindy chirped, ever full of goodwill to all people.

'Hi, precious. How was your night?'

'I had a lot of dreams, all about you.'

'Wow. Was I being a good boy?'

Her head bobbed. 'We were sailing in your boat.'

She had never seen my boat, but I had described it to her.

'There was a big storm,' she went on, bouncing in her seat. 'We nearly sunk but you saved us.'

I sat down across from Maura, who seemed not to be her sunny self. She wouldn't even meet my eyes.

'Well, I'm glad I saved you. Was Mommy there too?'

Lindy nodded as she crunched into her toast.

Maura said, 'You had a text message.'

I reached for the Kelloggs Corn Flakes packet. 'You read it?'

'You mind?'

'No, just curious.' I dumped cornflakes in my bowl, noted the patter of rain on the French doors.

'Good. It did that buzzing thing, and being nosey, I looked.'

Maura never tried to belie her frailties. The 'being nosey' was typical of her honesty in airing them.

'Do you want to read it to me?'

'Better read it yourself. It's very personal'

My grin was awry, mirthless. 'A little late to worry about that, isn't it?'

The text, as I half-expected, was from Angela.

Darling Andre
Why havent I heard from you??? Even if
you arent interested in me you must be
keen to recover your Range Rover!
Its sitting in my basement garage pining
for its owner as I am.
Just answer my calls dammit!
When all's said and done seems I love you
too much for my own good.
Angie XXX

I cast my mind back to my confessions to Maura. Had I intimated that Angela was more than just a flavour of the moment?

'Why haven't you spoken to her? She's obviously upset.'

'I'll text her. Explain about us.' I made to reach for Maura. She avoided me, standing up. 'Look, angel, I came clean about her. It was short-lived. I liked her a lot, that's all. It didn't mean anything.'

'It seems to have meant something to her, wouldn't you say? Did you, do you, love her?'

Now it was my place to take umbrage.

'You can ask me *that*? No, you dumb broad, I didn't love her. I love *you*.'

'So kill it off then. It's not fair to her to leave her hanging like that.' The curves of her lips mutated into a gash of displeasure. 'Or were you

keeping her in reserve?'

'Come off it, honey. I don't like to hurt people, so I was putting off the evil day. It's no more sinister than that.'

But she still wasn't convinced.

'You don't like to *hurt* people? You didn't mind kill –'

'Quit that!' I yelled. 'Shut up before you say something we might both regret.'

Lindy decided to participate in the yelling match. 'Stop arguing, Mommy!'

You could always rely on her to side with me, as if she were worried that I would disappear from her life again if Maura and I had a falling out.

'It's not your mommy's fault, sweetheart,' I said. 'It's my fault.'

Then Maura was burrowing into me, damp-eyed and contrite, her lips seeking mine. Very little seeking was required. We kissed and made up there and then.

Lindy, true to form, barged in on the hugging circle, and we stood there clinging to each other and laughing and generally being silly.

Later, during a stroll on the Bar Harbour waterfront, Maura said soberly, 'That was our first real row since you came.'

'That wasn't a row. It was insensitivity on my part and over-sensitivity on yours.'

Later still, in the evening, I texted Angela an apology. I also gave her the full story about Maura and Lindy, and promised to have the Evoque collected. Before transmitting the message, I let Maura take a peek. She feigned uninterest, but read it just the same.

Angela replied within the hour, weepy but understanding, and hoping to remain friends. We were listening to Brahms' German Requiem. Maura had become an aficionado of classical music, thanks, she claimed, to my own love of it. She had proved too, it by reserving front row seats at a forthcoming Dvoràk & Stravinsky concert by the Bangor Symphony Orchestra, at Bangor's Waterfront Pavilion. It would be our first concert together.

That night, as if she were making up for her part in our disagreement, Maura was a tigress in bed. We ran the sexual gamut, and

she gave it both barrels. When it was all over, sometime before dawn, we lapsed into exhausted slumbers from which we didn't wake until mid-morning, when an outraged Lindy came stomping into our room to roust us out.

'Dirty stop-in-beds,' she scolded, and would have dragged the sheets off us if we hadn't hung on to them.

'Out!' Maura reinforced the command with a pointing finger.

That earned her a stuck-out tongue followed by a slammed door.

We were back to being a family and for me it was like paradise regained.

* * * * *

It was the week before Christmas. A thin coating of snow lay on the ground and the sky presaged more. Lindy accompanied me shopping in Bar Harbour for Maura's present, which was to be a surprise. Tourism is the town's *raison d'être*, therefore most of what's on sale is out-and-out junk. But after trawling the centre I did come across a proper jeweller, tucked away just off Main Street. The salesman, thin and cadaverous but with a pleasant disposition, proved to be a partner in the business. When I told him I was looking for something unusual, he snapped his fingers.

'I've gotten just the thing,' he declared, a smile cracking his lined features. 'My brother was over in England last month and he came across a stone called Blue John. It's a semi-precious, a form of fluorite.'

I didn't ask what fluorite was, but exchanged frowns with Lindy, who didn't seem over-impressed. Until he brought out from under the counter a circular piece of purple polished stone with yellow streaks. He handed it over to me and I ran my thumb over the unctuous surface.

'It's not valuable like a diamond or an emerald,' the salesman explained, 'but there's only two mines over there in England, in the same location. Far as I know, nobody else imports it into the US, so your lady will be out there on her own when she's wearing it.'

'Are you going to buy it, André?' Lindy asked.

'Do you like it?' I hedged.

'Yes, I think it's cool. 'Specially if nobody else will be wearing it.'

'What can you set it in?' I said to the salesman.

'You want gold?'

'Sure, I want gold. Twenty-two carat.'

He delved back under the counter and came up with a variety of pendant necklaces mounted on a board. To include Lindy in the process I let her choose. She settled on a design that resembled tiny leaves linked up to form a circle.

'How long to mount it?' I said.

'Come back tomorrow. You want an inscription on the back of the pendant?'

I sought Lindy's input.

'Do I, sweetheart?'

'You mean like words?'

'Uh-huh.'

'Yes,' she said, nodding. 'Definitely.'

I kept it simple. "Maura, all my love always, André" and the year.

From the jewellers, my date and I strolled next door to the Coffee Hound coffee bar, and sat at a little round table. I ordered a cappuccino, and for Lindy a strawberry milk shake. Maura, a bit of a martinet about her daughter's dietary regimen, rarely sanctioned what she termed 'junk drinks', so it was left to me to do the spoiling.

Out of the corner of my eye, I watched Lindy as she vacuumed up the milk shake through a biodegradable paper straw. In looks, she didn't favour Maura that much, but she was a little beauty in her own right. If it was my destiny to be her surrogate father, I would be forever worrying about the company she kept, the boys she was meeting and, later on, dating. Good-looking girls were magnets for all males, not all of them with honourable intentions. Who knew better than I?

It would be a huge responsibility. If I had believed in God, I would've prayed that I was worthy of it and, moreover, capable of it. As it was, being an unbeliever, I just hoped.

'I like it when we go out without Mommy,' Lindy said, breaking into my musings.

'That's not a very nice thing to say.'

She looked crestfallen. 'No, I don't mean I don't like going out with

Mommy, but she stops me having stuff like milk shakes and burgers, and you're cool with it. That's what I mean.'

'I get it. Mommy's tough on you, and I'm the soft touch. That right?'

She nodded and flashed a grin at me that was at once captivating and seductive, in the sense that she was able to bend me to her will without apparent effort. It was her very innocence that seduced me. In the hands of Belinda Beck I was putty.

We sauntered back to the car, gloved hand in gloved hand, window shopping for more Christmas presents. André Warner, contract killer (retired), playing daddy and revelling in it.

Chapter Twenty-Three

Maura was out when we returned to the house. A note on the kitchen island read "Gone to town, back before twelve. Love to both. M. xxx."

Instinctively, I consulted my watch. It was several minutes after the hour, but even before I had a chance to start worrying at her lateness, the door opened behind me, and there she was, a shopping bag in each hand.

'Hello, darling,' she said, and came up close for the ritual kiss.

'Hello darling yourself.'

Lindy, who had shot off to her bedroom, reappeared still in her parka. A casual 'Hi, Mommy,' and she returned to whatever vital task required the privacy of her room.

'Where've you been?' I asked Maura, not because I needed to keep track of her movements, but because I was interested in everything she did. Maybe I worried a little too, in case Troisi's promises were a sham.

'As you see, shopping.'

'Christmas gifts?'

'Yep. And I had to see my doctor.'

'Doctor?' Alarm flared, as it always would if ever her health became an issue. As a rule she was free of ailments, apart from her asthma, and very fit owing to a daily exercise programme we shared.

'Before you start presuming the worst, I'm fine. Everything's normal according to the scan.'

'Scan?' I grabbed her by the upper arms, probing her wonderful eyes. 'Why did you need a scan, goddammit? What aren't you telling me?'

'Leave off coming the heavy, will you? A scan's no big deal, and the baby's perfectly normal.'

I released her, feeling foolish. 'Okay. Good, fine.'

Then, as her revelation kicked in, I froze, vocal chords included. I

stared at her for so long she exploded into laughter.

'Can't take it, buster? Prospect of being a dad frighten you?'

I found my voice, though it emerged as a croak. 'You really mean it? You're pregnant?'

'I believe that's the term generally used to describe my condition'.

Then we were in each other's arms, Maura gasping as I crushed her to me.

'Steady on, caveman! It's not just me you're squeezing.'

'Sorry.' I reduced the pressure, held her at arm's length. 'Is it a boy or a girl?'

'It's too soon to tell, dope. I'm only two-and-a-half months down the road.'

'We've got to celebrate. Where's the champagne?'

'What d'you mean, where's the champagne? Is this a wine bar?'

Linda re-entered the living room to enquire what all the commotion was about.

Maura told her in straight language, then we were all laughing and talking at the same time.

For a heartbeat in time, I might have been the happiest man alive.

* * * * *

After the Wolff job was over and done, I had retired the cell phone I used for professional calls. I dumped it in the top drawer of the night table on my side of the bed and left it to discharge in peace. As the days and weeks passed, in my state of conjugal bliss I forgot its existence.

Until one afternoon in late January, I was in the master bedroom, returning my wallet to the same drawer where I kept the cell and noticed, in passing, that it was now on top of the table, attached to its charging cable. Puzzled, I went through to the living room where Maura was vacuuming.

'Honey,' I said, raising my voice over the howl of the vac. 'Did you put my other cell phone on charge?'

'Yes.' She carried on vacuuming away. 'I saw it in your drawer. Its battery was flat, so I thought I would charge it up for you.'

'Were you looking for something? In my drawer, I mean.'

'I guess so.' She switched off the vac. 'Actually, I was looking for a gun.'

'A *gun*? You need a gun?'

'No, it wasn't that. I already have a gun, as you know. It's locked in the safe. No, I was wondering if you had one, because if you had, I wanted to put it with mine so they wouldn't be lonely.'

'I haven't touched a gun since I left Europe.'

'Fine. It's funny, but I only thought about it this morning, don't ask me why. The thing is, darling, I don't want guns lying around the house.' She made an apologetic shrug. 'Sorry about trespassing on your private space.'

'You're joking. You trespass on my private space every bloody night!'

The double entendre predictably triggered a giggle.

'Now,' she said, 'if you'll move your big feet I'll get on with the hoovering.'

'Time we had a housekeeper or a maid for jobs like this.'

'I don't mind doing it. And I value my – our – privacy.'

'You should think about it though. With your condition, that is.'

More giggles. 'I'm pregnant, not suffering from muscular dystrophy. You want me to retire to bed and stay there until I give birth?'

She flapped me away and restarted the vac.

Back in the bedroom, I unplugged the cell. It was a just another reminder of too much that was bad about my previous existence, events that I wished to erase from my past, like a computer erasing a redundant file.

As I was about to shut the drawer on it, it warbled.

Maybe it was habit, or curiosity, or my attention was elsewhere – on babies and fatherhood, for instance – but I committed the irrevocable error of answering it.

The voice was of the past. All too familiar, though I hadn't heard it for months.

'André?'

'Giorgy?'

His sigh sounded like relief. 'Yes, it is I. I have been trying to reach you.'

Giorgio du Poletti, my former *Sindicato* go-between, was part of the bad. Consigned to the forgettable past.

Before I could respond, or even kill the call, he went on, 'We have a rather special contract to fill. It could have been custom-made for you. The only –'

'Giorgy, stop right there,' I broke in. 'We made a deal. No more contracts and no more vendetta.' Growing angry now at this intrusion on my newly constructed paradise. 'Where the hell are you?'

'Where am I?' His tone mystified. 'If it matters, I am in Sardinia, at La Cima della Scogliera.'

'Good. Put me through to Troisi. I made a deal personally with him, you bastard.'

The line went quiet. In the background I heard a woman's voice singing "Mi Chiamano Mini" from La Bohème; Maria Callas, if I wasn't mistaken, as pure and distinct as if she were on the line herself. Through the window I saw Lindy and her girl sidekick from across the street trying to scrape up enough snow from last night's meagre dusting to make snowballs. Two unrelated acts linked only by the symbolic yet different purities they represented. They would forever lodge in my memory because of what Giorgio du Poletti said next.

'I regret I cannot oblige you, my friend. Troisi is dead.'

END
of story
but turn the page to see what's in store for André Warner

COME BACK, ADOLF HITLER

André Warner, Manhunter – Vol VII

by Lex Lander

Toby's office at the Ministry for Foreign Affairs had not altered in the two years since I was last privileged to be his guest, except for a garish painting that I was sure hadn't been there then. It hung, slightly askew, behind his chair, where he could only look at it by turning through a full hundred and eighty degrees. Deliberate positioning? What little I knew of his tastes in art was more orientated towards the likes of Gainsborough, Constable, and Turner.

Tea and biscuits had already been served and, once the handshaking and exchange of cordialities were behind us, Toby played mother as to the manner born.

'One lump or two?' he enquired, tweezers poised over the sugar bowl.

'None, thanks.'

'Sweet enough already, eh?' he cracked.

I groaned. 'Toby, don't you know when a joke is past its use-by date?'

He wasn't crushed by my put-down. He moved seamlessly on to the topic for today as I settled into the familiar over-stuffed visitor chair.

'What do you know about biological engineering, André?'

'Biological engineering? About as much as you could engrave on the head of a pin.'

'As much as that? I'm impressed. I never took you for an intellectual.' He picked up a dog-eared paperback book that was lying on his blotter and skimmed it across to me. 'Ever come across this book?'

It reached me upside down. I reversed it. The jacket was dominated by a white swastika and little else on a dark background.

'The Boys from Brazil,' I read aloud. I was about to shake my head when I had second thoughts. 'Wa-a-ait a minute. Wasn't there a movie

with that title? Didn't Gregory Peck play Dr Mengele, that scumbag SS doctor who absconded to Argentina at the end of the war?'

'To Brazil,' Toby corrected drily. 'Hence the title. The film wasn't a patch on the book. But if you remember the story, it will do for now.'

'Something about cloning Hitler, wasn't it?' I chuckled. 'Crazy hypothesis.'

His eyes lost their usual twinkle. 'Maybe not so crazy.'

I stopped in mid-chuckle. He was regarding me with the sort of expression I associated with his being the bearer of doom-laden tidings. Such as an offer of employment.

'What?' I said. 'Are you telling me …?'

He stood. He was tall and imposing, a man who exuded authority without effort. He walked to the window and stood there, hands clasped behind his back. On the window ledge a brace of pigeons were cooing at each other and bussing beaks. Toby had gained their allegiance by feeding them biscuit crumbs from his elevenses snack.

'I'm telling you this much. If you read the newspapers, off or on line, you'll know the far right is on the rise in Germany. It's already risen in Austria and Hungary – the other two members of the wartime axis, as coincidence would have it. Or perhaps not such a coincidence. Now we've had some intel from our people in Berlin about a secret society with a charismatic leader who has yet to show his face in public. It's not much higher up the intelligence scale than gossip, but the story is that this fellow bears some resemblance to dear Adolf, not only physically, but in his ranting speeches and they way he dazzles his audiences. The gossip also goes that this society is intent on infiltrating the *Alternativ für Deutschland* party and converting them into a new Nazi party.'

I was ahead of him. 'With a cloned Adolf as its *Führer*?'

'That seems to be the general idea.' He shuffled some papers on his desk, wrinkled his forehead. 'Frightening thought, what?'

I was unsuccessful in suppressing a splutter of mirth. 'You aren't serious, are you? You really believe Adolf could be cloned, presumably to resemble the Fuehrer physically, but also to possess his charisma, his ability to bend millions of Germans to his will, and his propensity to wage war. Even if it were feasible, do you think the country would be so

barmy as to rally behind him again?'

'Do you think they wouldn't?'

I stared at him. Christ. He really *was* serious. Him and the powers-that-be actually believed a new Adolf Hitler was on the rise. It was corny. It would make a great story.

'Come back, Adolf Hitler,' I said, my tongue lodged firmly in my cheek. 'All is forgiven.'

* * * * *

But Germany's old enemies have not forgiven. Rumours of the rise of a Hitler clone start a panic in the UK, France, and the USA. The order goes out: he must be taken out before he takes over.

* * * * *

'Infiltrate and eliminate' is how the British express it. André Warner is their chosen tool. France surprisingly concurs, perhaps afraid of repercussions if it gets out that they've despatched a hit man to take out a German citizen. The Americans refuse point blank to sign up for the British initiative. They have their own ideas how to achieve a final solution for the Hitler wannabee and avert World War III, and in their usual secretive style aren't about to confide in their allies.

COME BACK, ADOLF HITLER will be published in 2021

Also by

Lex Lander

and available from Amazon

Check out Kaybec or write to us at
www.kaybecpublishing.com / kaybec.publishing@mail.com

Check out Lex or write to him at
www.lexlanderauthor.com / authorline@gmail.com

Printed in Great Britain
by Amazon

52716565R00201

Printed in Dunstable, United Kingdom

76738937R00180